Hagia Sophia and the Byzantine Aesthetic Experience

Nadine Schibille
University of Sussex, UK

Routledge
Taylor & Francis Group
LONDON AND NEW YORK

First published 2014 by Ashgate Publishing

2 Park Square, Milton Park, Abingdon, Oxfordshire OX14 4RN
52 Vanderbilt Avenue, New York, NY 10017

Routledge is an imprint of the Taylor & Francis Group, an informa business

First issued in paperback 2019

British Library Cataloguing in Publication Data
A catalogue record for this book is available from the British Library

The Library of Congress has cataloged the printed edition as follows:
Schibille, Nadine.
Hagia Sophia and the Byzantine aesthetic experience / by Nadine Schibille.
pages cm
Includes bibliographical references and index.
ISBN 978-1-4724-3758-7 (hbk)
1. Ayasofya Müzesi. 2. Architecture--
Aesthetics. 3. Aesthetics, Byzantine. I. Title.
NA5870.A9S34 2014
726.6094961'8--dc23

2014016691

ISBN 978-1-4724-3758-7 (hbk)
ISBN 978-0-367-60035-8 (pbk)

HAGIA SOPHIA AND THE BYZANTINE AESTHETIC EXPERIENCE

Paramount in the shaping of early Byzantine identity was the construction of the church of Hagia Sophia in Constantinople (532–537 CE). This book examines the edifice from the perspective of aesthetics to define the concept of beauty and the meaning of art in early Byzantium. Byzantine aesthetic thought is re-evaluated against late antique Neoplatonism and the writings of Pseudo-Dionysius that offer fundamental paradigms for the late antique attitude towards art and beauty. These metaphysical concepts of aesthetics are ultimately grounded in experiences of sensation and perception, and reflect the ways in which the world and reality were perceived and grasped, signifying the cultural identity of early Byzantium.

There are different types of aesthetic data, those present in the aesthetic object and those found in aesthetic responses to the object. This study looks at the aesthetic data embodied in the sixth-century architectural structure and interior decoration of Hagia Sophia as well as in literary responses (ekphrasis) to the building. The purpose of the Byzantine ekphrasis was to convey by verbal means the same effects that the artefact itself would have caused. A literary analysis of these rhetorical descriptions recaptures the Byzantine perception and expectations, and at the same time reveals the cognitive processes triggered by the Great Church.

The central aesthetic feature that emerges from sixth-century ekphraseis of Hagia Sophia is that of light. Light is described as the decisive element in the experience of the sacred space and light is simultaneously associated with the notion of wisdom. It is argued that the concepts of light and wisdom are interwoven programmatic elements that underlie the unique architecture and non-figurative decoration of Hagia Sophia. A similar concern for the phenomenon of light and its epistemological dimension is reflected in other contemporary monuments, testifying to the pervasiveness of these aesthetic values in early Byzantium.

Dr Nadine Schibille is a Lecturer in Art History at the University of Sussex, UK.

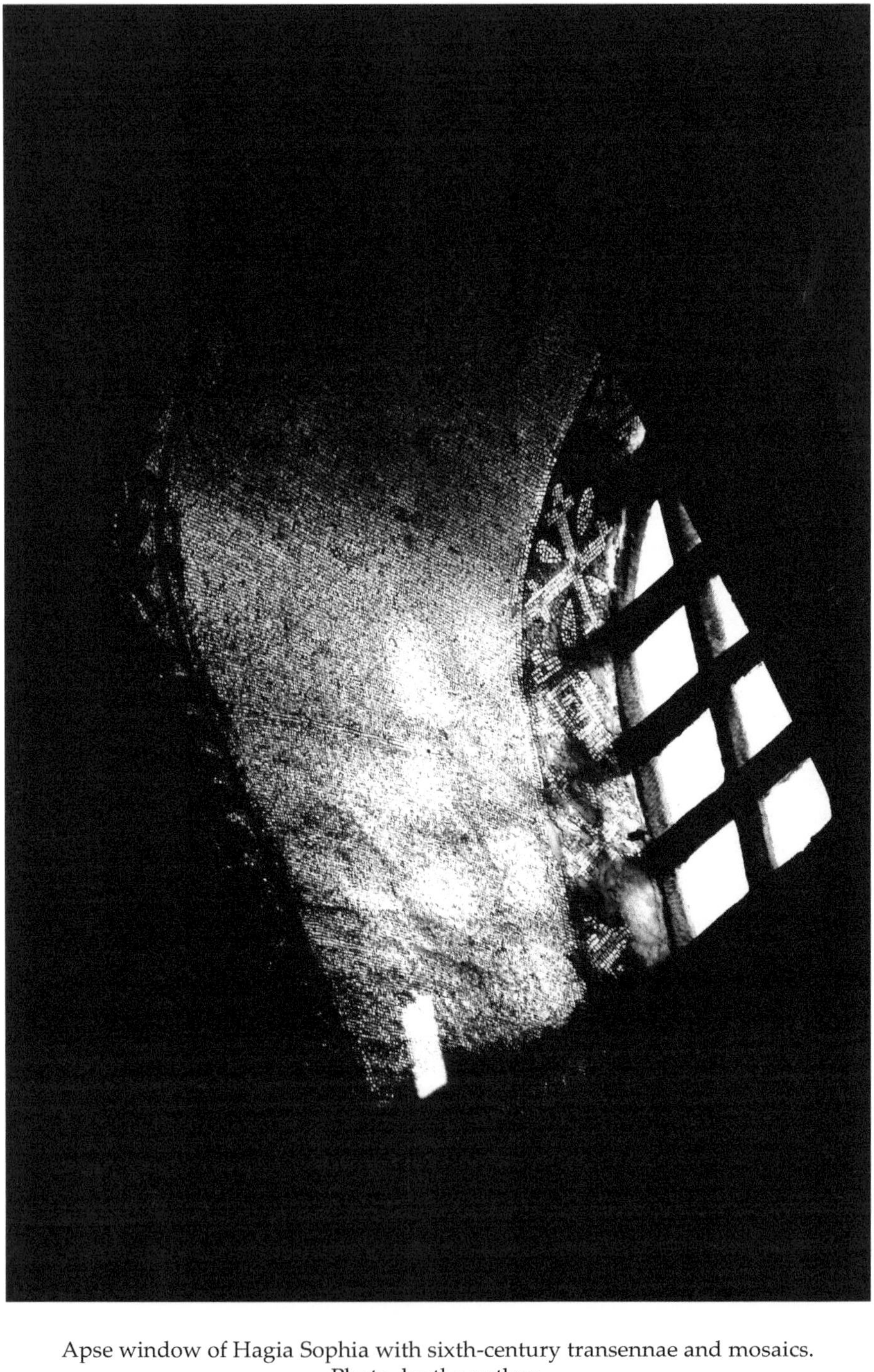

Apse window of Hagia Sophia with sixth-century transennae and mosaics.
Photo, by the author.

Contents

List of Illustrations

Note, all photographs by author unless otherwise stated.

Colour Plates

Black and White Figures

Acknowledgements

This book has its origin in my doctoral dissertation 'Light in Early Byzantium: The Church of Hagia Sophia in Constantinople' (University of Sussex, 2004). It evolved over many years, and progress was slow and often interrupted. In the intervening years, aesthetic approaches to ancient and Byzantine art have been salvaged from years of scholarly neglect, impacting on how we now interpret the art of the ancient and medieval worlds. This means that although 'light' as a central feature in the art and architecture of early Byzantium remains the underlying theme of this book, the focus has changed to that of aesthetic experience. In short, my dissertation has been utterly and repeatedly revised, and I hope that this has become a better book than what it would have been otherwise.

As the manuscript evolved over a long period of time, I have amassed great debts to many individuals and institutions that have continuously encouraged and supported me. My deepest gratitude is due to the two people who suffered most: my doctoral dissertation supervisor Professor Liz James who has supported this project throughout, read through various drafts and provided lots of ideas over the years – although she may very well not agree with some of the conclusions and the philosophical focus of this book; and Christian G. Specht, who painstakingly read the manuscript several times, contributing his invaluable scientific way of thinking and enthusiasm. He is also responsible for getting all the illustrations into publishable shape. This book would simply not have been possible without his constant help and encouragement; he kept me sane throughout the entire process.

Special thanks must be given to Jaś Elsner who read an earlier version of the manuscript and whose advice and constructive criticism are greatly appreciated. I would also like to thank the Dumbarton Oaks Research Library and Image Collection for permission to reproduce one of the photos on the study of light, and my colleagues from the Technische Universität Darmstadt, who granted me permission to use two of their digital reconstructions of Hagia Sophia: Lars Grobe, Oliver Hauck, Andreas Noback, Professor Rudolf

Stichel and Helge Svenshon. I would also like to thank a number of colleagues and friends whose expertise has helped to resolve specific issues, including Vassiliki Dimitropoulou, Scott Vanderbilt, Francesco Ventrella and Gabriel Wolfenstein.

This study would not have been possible without substantial financial support from the Getty Institute that provided a post-doctoral research fellowship for a year to get this project off the ground. Finally, I am grateful to the School of History, Art History and Philosophy at the University of Sussex for contributing funding for the book's colour reproductions.

List of Abbreviations

AJA	*American Journal of Archaeology*
AP	*Palatine Greek Anthology*
AT	*Antiquité Tardive*
BMGS	*Byzantine and Modern Greek Studies*
CFHB	Corpus Fontium Historiae Byzantinae
CH	*Celestial Hierarchy*
CSEL	Corpus Scriptorum Ecclesiasticorum Latinorum
CSHB	Corpus Scriptorium Historiae Byzantinae
DN	*Divine Names*
DOP	*Dumbarton Oaks Papers*
EH	*Ecclesiastical Hierarchy*
GNO	Gregorii Nysseni Opera
GRBS	*Greek, Roman and Byzantine Studies*
JAS	*Journal of Archaeological Science*
JGS	*Journal of Glass Studies*
JÖB	*Jahrbuch der Österreichischen Byzantinistik*
LSJ	Henry George Liddell, Robert Scott and Henry Stuart Jones. *A Greek-English Lexicon* (Oxford: Clarendon Press, 1940)
MT	*Mystical Theology*
NPNF	Nicene and Post-Nicene Fathers
ODB	Alexander P. Kazhdan, Alice-Mary Talbot, Anthony Cutler, Timothy E. Gregory and Nancy Patterson Ševčenko (eds.). *Oxford Dictionary of Byzantium* (New York and Oxford: Oxford University Press, 1991)
PG	Patrologia Graeca
RGZM	Römisch-Germanisches Zentralmuseum

For Christian

Introduction: Byzantine Aesthetics

> … to deny aesthetics is to deny art because no work of art can be produced, experienced, or judged without some kind of aesthetics. Aesthetics is critical thinking about the affective, cognitive, moral, political, technological, and other historical conditions constitutive of the production, experience, and judgement of art.
>
> Michael Kelly (2012), *A Hunger for Aesthetics: Enacting the Demands of Art*, xviii

The focus of this book is the conceptual dimension of the sixth-century church of Hagia Sophia in Constantinople as a work of art and as the result of a specific early Byzantine aesthetics. In acknowledging the link between aesthetics, by what I mean the sensation of art both in terms of its beauty and function and 'affective, cognitive, moral, political, technological, and other historical conditions', this study argues that multiple and interrelated aesthetic choices were constitutive of the sixth-century architecture and interior design of Hagia Sophia. Its unprecedented architectural structure and the unconventional interior decoration acquire meaning only within the particular aesthetic framework of late antique Byzantium. The architects created an ecclesiastical space within which the concept of divine immanence and transcendence could be apprehended in the material form of colour and light. In late antiquity, the perennial question of divine transcendence was necessarily identified with philosophical ontology and epistemology and embodied in the double-notion of φωτισμός, the at once physical and spiritual illumination. In other words, late antique Neoplatonic philosophy formulated an epistemology that was grounded in sense-perception (αἴσθησις) but that had as its goal the intelligible realm (νόησις), specifically aiming at knowledge about being, truth and ultimately about the divine itself.[1]

---

[1] Patricia Cox-Miller, *The Corporeal Imagination: Signifying the Holy in Late Ancient Christianity* (Philadelphia, PA: University of Pennsylvania Press, 2009), 3–7; Anthony Cutler 'Uses of luxury: On the functions of consumption and symbolic capital in Byzantine culture',

In viewing the sixth-century building of Hagia Sophia from the perspective of aesthetics, this study attempts to reconstruct the concepts of beauty and the function of art in late antique Byzantium. At a more fundamental level, it focuses on the perception of art and materiality in late antiquity. Insights into the concepts of visual perception and attitudes towards matter and materiality may provide clues to the nature and processes of artistic production and its motivating factors in the historical and cultural setting of sixth-century Byzantium.[2] The principal aim must be to understand the artistic practices of late antique Byzantium on its own terms. By exploring the early Byzantine ways of looking at the material world and at works of art, the investigation of aesthetics touches upon the very foundations of social and cultural norms and values. Aesthetics in this sense do not merely constitute the visuality of a culture but reflect the cultural identity of its people and contribute to maintaining or indeed transforming society.[3]

There exist three types of aesthetic data that are dealt with in this study: the material evidence present in the aesthetic object itself, the aesthetic values expressed in the responses to and evaluation of this object, and the ideas represented in pertinent philosophical and theological treatises.[4] In this book, I explore the aesthetic data enshrined in the sixth-century architecture and decoration of Hagia Sophia in Constantinople, in literary (ekphrastic) responses to the edifice, and in contemporary theological and philosophical debates about the material world as a manifestation of the transcendent divine. The church of Hagia Sophia (532–537 CE) is taken as a case study for the simple reason that the Great Church is undoubtedly one of the most influential buildings in world architecture. Its architectural structure and conceptual design may be unique in many respects, but Hagia Sophia is above all perhaps the most outstanding expression of early Byzantine aesthetics

in *Byzance et les images: Cycle de conférences organisé au Musée du Louvre par le service culturel du 5 octobre au 7 décembre 1992*, ed. André Guillou and Jannic Durand (Paris: La documentation Française, 1994), 307; Beate Regina Suchla, 'Verteidigung eines platonischen Denkmodells einer christlichen Welt. Die philosophie- und theologiegeschichtliche Bedeutung des Scholienwerks des Johannes von Skythopolis zu den areopagitischen Traktaten', *Nachrichten der Akademie der Wissenschaften in Göttingen I. Philologisch-historische Klasse* (1995): 2–3.

2 See, for example, Cox-Miller (2009), Introduction; Michael Kelly, *A Hunger for Aesthetics: Enacting the Demands of Art* (New York, NY: Columbia University Press, 2012), Preface.

3 Patricia Cox-Miller, '"The little blue flower is red": Relics and the poetizing of the body', *Journal of Early Christian Studies* 8 (2000); Cox-Miller (2009); Jaś Elsner, *Roman Eyes: Visuality & Subjectivity in Art & Text* (Princeton, NJ: Princeton University Press, 2007), 24–5; Matthew T. Kapstein, 'Rethinking religious experience: Seeing the light in the history of religions', in *The Presence of Light: Divine Radiance and Religious Experience*, ed. Matthew T. Kapstein (London and Chicago, IL: University of Chicago Press, 2004); James I. Porter, *The Origins of Aesthetic Thought in Ancient Greece: Matter, Sensation, and Experience* (Cambridge: Cambridge University Press, 2010), 10–15; Ellen Swift, *Style and Function in Roman Decoration* (Farnham: Ashgate, 2009), Introduction.

4 Bertram Jessup, 'The data of aesthetics', *Proceedings and Addresses of the American Philosophical Association* 29 (1955–1956).

and, by implication, early Byzantine identity.[5] I examine how Hagia Sophia's architectural and interior design is the result of a particular, metaphysical notion of aesthetics. It is an aesthetics that was in a way specific to the church of Hagia Sophia, but at the same time one that satisfied the sensibilities and expectations of sixth-century Byzantium at large. Numerous impressions of Hagia Sophia as expressed by Byzantine writers testify to its universal visual appeal. To corroborate that the aesthetic values of which Hagia Sophia is reflective was integral to artistic practices in the sixth-century world more generally, this study also draws on other contemporary monumental works of art and architecture such as the church of Hagios Polyeuktos, the monastery of Saint Catherine at Sinai and the church of San Vitale in Ravenna. These artistic examples reveal a similar taste for light and colour and, to a certain extent at least, a concern for spiritual epistemology.

Recent years have seen a renewed surge in scholarly interest in the aesthetics of the ancient world, trying to capture the aesthetic experience and perception of works of art from the viewpoint of its inhabitants, and thus to reinstate aesthetics as a valuable approach especially to late antique and Byzantine art.[6] Sensory experience was given particular emphasis in Bissera Pentcheva's recent phenomenological analysis of the Byzantine icon, in which she draws attention to the performative aspect of Byzantine art and the central role of animation in its aesthetic appreciation.[7] Pentcheva's book advocates a multi-sensory aesthetics of the Byzantine icon and thereby developed new ground in the study of Byzantine aesthetics. While following along similar lines of argument, in this study I concentrate on the primacy of the faculty of

[5] It is the combination of size and arrangement that is unique, but as Ćurčic has demonstrated, the construction of Hagia Sophia was preceded by a period of architectural experimentation. Robin Cormack, 'The Visual Arts', in *The Cambridge Ancient History. Late Antiquity: Empire and Successors, A.D. 425–600*, ed. Averil Cameron, Bryan Ward-Perkins, and Michael Whitby (Cambridge: Cambridge University Press, 2000); Slobodan Ćurčic, 'Design and structural innovation in Byzantine architecture before Hagia Sophia', in *Hagia Sophia*, ed. Robert Mark and Ahmet S. Çakmak (Cambridge: Cambridge University Press, 1992); Robert S. Nelson, *Hagia Sophia, 1850–1950: Holy Wisdom Modern Monument* (Chicago, IL: University of Chicago Press, 2004).

[6] Elizabeth S. Bolman, 'Late antique aesthetics, chromophobia, and the Red Monastery, Sohag, Egypt', *Eastern Christian Art* 3 (2006); Elizabeth S. Bolman, 'Painted skins: The illusions and realities of architectural polychromy, Sinai and Egypt', in *Approaching the Holy Mountain: Art and Liturgy at St Catherine's Monastery in the Sinai*, ed. Sharon E.J. Gerstel and Robert S. Nelson (Turnhout: Brepols, 2010); Cox-Miller (2000); Cox-Miller (2009); Jaś Elsner, *Art and the Roman Viewer: The Transformation of Art from the Pagan World to Christianity* (Cambridge and New York, NY: Cambridge University Press, 1995); Jaś Elsner, 'Late antique art: The problem of the concept and the cumulative aesthetic', in *Approaching Late Antiquity: The Transformation from Early to Late Empire*, ed. Simon Swain and Mark Edwards (Oxford: Oxford University Press, 2004); Gervase Mathew, *Byzantine Aesthetics* (London: J. Murray, 1963); Bissera V. Pentcheva, *The Sensual Icon: Space, Ritual, and the Senses in Byzantium* (University Park, PA: Pennsylvania State University Press, 2010); Bissera V. Pentcheva, 'Hagia Sophia and multisensory aesthetics', *Gesta* 50 (2011); Porter (2010); Ruth Webb, *Ekphrasis, Imagination and Persuasion in Ancient Rhetorical Theory and Practice* (Farnham: Ashgate, 2009).

[7] Pentcheva (2010).

sight in the aesthetic experience of early Byzantine art and on vision as the locus of religious epistemology.

The reason for this approach is that the aesthetic experience of early Byzantine ecclesiastical interiors was very much grounded in the perception and sensation of light both in physical as well as spiritual terms. This is what emerges from, for instance, sixth-century literary descriptions of Hagia Sophia that constantly draw attention to the phenomena of light. Light was highlighted as the quintessential object of aesthetic experience and the decisive element that established and shaped the visual and spatial impression of Hagia Sophia's ecclesiastical space. The ekphrastic images of light and material splendour control and condition the perception of Hagia Sophia in terms of its aesthetic value, but also in terms of its theological underpinnings. Sight, by extension, can be considered the medium of aesthetic experience *par excellence.* The purpose of the Byzantine *ekphrasis*, a literary device defined as a description of an event or object, was to evoke by verbal means the same effects that the actual visual experience would have elicited and to thus communicate meaning.[8] The ekphrasis is a re-enactment of the aesthetic reaction to the thing described, and because of the rhetorical nature of the ekphrasis the features that the author singles out can be considered the objects of aesthetic experience. This means that even though light may be a literary *topos* that reflects literary traditions as much as the subjective assignment of value, these ekphraseis give insights into late antique responses to the Great Church and disclose the aesthetic expectations and the cognitive processes involved in the assessment of the edifice as a work of art and its meaning at the time.[9] Whether real or present only in the author's mind, the aspects that stand out are those that have earned the author's attention for a good reason. Rhetorical conventions became conventions because they reflect cultural values.[10] Therefore, ekphraseis that describe works of art or architecture are vital sources for the reconstruction of the visual experience and responses to works of art, the assignment of aesthetic value, as well as for understanding the performative nature and Byzantine perception of art.

Under normal circumstances, light is merely an agent that illuminates objects and renders them visible. This property would appear to exclude light itself from any conscious aesthetic perception, if an aesthetic judgement were

---

8 Liz James and Ruth Webb, '"To understand ultimate things and enter secret places": Ekphrasis and art in Byzantium', *Art History* 14 (1991); Ruth Webb, 'The aesthetics of sacred space: Narrative, metaphor, and motion in ekphraseis of church buildings', *DOP* 53 (1999); Ruth Webb, 'Ekphrasis ancient and modern: The invention of a genre', *Word & Image* 15 (1999).

9 Elsner (2007), 24–5; Kapstein (2004); Swift (2009), 18–19; James Trilling, 'Medieval art without style? Plato's loophole and a modern detour', *Gesta* 34 (1995).

10 Leslie Brubaker, 'Perception and conception: Art, theory and culture in ninth-century Byzantium' *Word & Image* 5 (1989); Elsner (2007); James and Webb (1991); Henry Maguire, 'Truth and convention in Byzantine descriptions of works of art', *DOP* 28 (1974); Webb (2009).

to be defined in the post-*Enlightenment* Kantian sense as pure and disinterested, that is to say devoid of all other interests and purposes.[11] Prior to the eighteenth century, however, aesthetics had not been an independent philosophical discipline in its own right and with the criticism of art at its centre. Instead, aesthetic qualities had been intimately entwined with other philosophical and religious values such as moral, practical, intellectual or ontological and the sublime.[12] If therefore *aisthesis* is treated in the original sense of the word as sensation and perception, we arrive at the very core of the human visual experience. Then the significance of light as an object of aesthetic experience becomes clear. Light belongs first and foremost to the phenomenology of vision by bestowing colour and form onto matter and thus making it visible and comprehensible. In antiquity this capacity of light was closely linked with the acquisition of knowledge and cognitive processes more generally.[13] Entwined with this epistemological interpretation of light was a spiritual or religious symbolism that developed in different cultural and religious traditions.[14] In early Byzantium, light was connected to the notion of wisdom, while it simultaneously served as a very potent visual method that reconciled the paradox of divine immanence and transcendence. In the specific case of Hagia Sophia, light was instrumental in the representational construction of its ecclesiastical space by way of what Robert Nelson called the 'ancient logic of implication' without depending on figurative representations.[15]

I argue that it is not coincidental that the church dedicated to Holy Wisdom was praised for its extraordinary luminosity, and that by emphasising the phenomena of light, a range of mental processes were encouraged that relate to the spiritual and epistemological content of Justinian's Great Church. Light, beauty and wisdom are interwoven programmatic elements that can provide a conceptual framework for the interpretation and comprehension of the architectural structure and interior decoration of Hagia Sophia. A greater

[11] Henry E. Allison, *Kant's Theory of Taste* (Cambridge: Cambridge University Press, 2001), 85–97; Christopher Janaway, *Images of Excellence: Plato's Critique of the Arts* (Oxford: Clarendon Press, 1995), 192–3.

[12] Paul Guyer, *Values of Beauty: Historical Essays in Aesthetics* (Cambridge: Cambridge University Press, 2005); Stephen Halliwell, *The Aesthetics of Mimesis* (Princeton: Princeton University Press, 2002); Kai Hammermeister, *The German Aesthetic Tradition* (Cambridge: Cambridge University Press, 2002); Joseph P. Maguire, 'The differentiation of art in Plato's aesthetics', *Harvard Studies in Classical Philology* 68 (1964); Porter (2010), 32–4; James I. Porter, 'Is the sublime an aesthetic value?' in *Aesthetic Value in Classical Antiquity. Mnemosyne Supplements. Monographs on Greek and Latin Lnguage and Literature, 350*, ed. Ineke Sluiter and Ralph M. Rosen (Leiden and Boston, MA: Brill, 2012).

[13] The correlation of sight with intellectual perception and knowledge is reflected in the Greek language – οἶδα (I know) can be traced to its original meaning εἶδον (I have seen). Rudolf Bultmann, 'Zur Geschichte der Lichtsymbolik im Altertum', *Philologus* 97 (1948).

[14] Kapstein (2004).

[15] Robert S. Nelson, 'Byzantine art vs western medieval art', in *Byzance et le monde extérieur: contacts, relations, échanges: actes de trois séances du XXe Congrès international des études byzantines, Paris, 19–25 août 2001*, ed. Paule Pagès, *et al.* (Paris: Publications de la Sorbonne, 2005).

understanding of those components will not only clarify the conceptual content of the edifice, but also give new insights into the building's artistic uniqueness that derives ultimately from its dedication. The artistic application and underlying concepts of light in context of Hagia Sophia thus offer an ideal scope to explore the fundamental patterns of an emerging Byzantine aesthetic.[16]

What is the material evidence that light was indeed a defining constitutive feature in the design of Hagia Sophia? Although scholarly literature on Hagia Sophia usually does not fail to mention the impression of light and the visual effects within the church in one way or another,[17] the architectural and decorative features responsible for the spectacle of light that stimulated these aesthetic responses has up until now not been elucidated in detail. This book explores how light was artistically implemented in the design of Hagia Sophia by analysing the architectural and decorative components that contributed to or defined the illumination and luminosity of the building's interior. The traditional assumption that the church of Hagia Sophia was characterised by a conspicuous hierarchical distribution of light is challenged.[18] Hierarchical structures are what scholars were looking for in dependence on the late antique writings of Pseudo-Dionysius the Areopagite, who described the world in terms of ecclesiastical and celestial hierarchies. This interpretation, however, cannot be upheld based on the material evidence.

While the *Corpus Areopagiticum*, in which light and analogies of light feature prominently, is indeed an important contestant in the formulation of a Byzantine aesthetic, its interpretation is more complex than the simple postulation of a hierarchy. The aesthetic theory that the Pseudo-Dionysian treatises offer is

---

16 I disagree here with Piotrowski, who argued that the use of light to communicate prevalent theological ideas found its ultimate expression in middle Byzantine architecture and that early Byzantine church buildings were still far removed from this symbolic functioning of light. Andrzej Piotrowski, 'Architecture and the iconoclastic controversy', in *Medieval Practices of Space*, ed. Barbara A. Hanawalt and Michal Kobialka (Minneapolis, MN: University of Minnesota Press, 2000); Andrzej Piotrowski, 'Representational function of daylight in the Katholikon of Hosios Loukas' (paper presented at the Congress of Byzantine Studies, London, 21–24 August 2006).

17 Most recently, Pentcheva (2010), 45–56; Pentcheva (2011).

18 For the hypothesis of a hierarchical distribution of light see, for example, GA Andreades, 'Die Sophienkathedrale von Konstantinopel' *Kunstwissenschaftliche Forschungen* 1 (1931); Hubert Fänsen, 'Der "Lichtstil" in der mittelbyzantinischen Kreuzkuppelkirche', *Byzantinische Forschungen* 18 (1992); Walter Haug, 'Gab es eine mittelalterliche Ästhetik aus platonischer Tradition?', in *Neuplatonismus und Ästhetik: Zur Transformationsgeschichte des Schönen*, ed. Verena Olejniczak Lobsien and Claudia Olk (Berlin and New York, NY: Walter de Gruyter, 2007); Heinz Kähler, *Die Hagia Sophia* (Berlin: Gebr. Mann, 1967); W. Loerke, Anthony Cutler, and A. Kazhdan, 'Window', in *Oxford Dictionary of Byzantium* (New York: 1991); Konrad Onasch, *Lichthöhle und Sternenhaus: Licht und Materie im spätantik-christlichen und frühbyzantinischen Sakralbau* (Dresden and Basel: Verlag der Kunst, 1993); Lioba Theis, 'Lampen, Leuchten, Licht', in *Byzanz*, ed. C. Stiegemann (Paderborn: 2001); Wladimir R. Zaloziecky, *Die Sophienkirche in Konstantinopel und ihre Stellung in der Geschichte der abendländischen Architektur*, Studie di Antichita Cristiana 12 (Rome and Freiburg: Pontificio istituto di archeologia cristiana, 1936).

very intricate and cannot be isolated from the Pseudo-Dionysian ontology and metaphysics. As part of his metaphysical and ontological system, Pseudo-Dionysius considered light more in transcendental than in empirical terms. For Pseudo-Dionysius, the physical properties of light lent themselves perfectly to signify the divine immanence and transcendence and to exemplify spiritual enlightenment (φωτισμός) and the ascent and assimilation to the divine. Sensible light came to be viewed as a medium to convey absolute divine paradigms and as an agent of religious epistemology because it lay at the limits between the physical and spiritual. Pseudo-Dionysius' aesthetics owed much to the Greek patristic writings of the fourth century and especially the works of Gregory of Nyssa, while being deeply rooted in the philosophical tradition of late antique Platonism.[19] Hence, the early Byzantine aesthetic as formulated by Pseudo-Dionysius can be fully comprehended only against the Greco-Roman and Judeo-Christian background from which it developed and to which it responded. Pseudo-Dionysius appropriated the Platonic and Neoplatonic notions of beauty and art and transformed them into an aesthetic that accommodated a profoundly Christian (mystical) understanding of epistemology.

Pseudo-Dionysius frequently equates divine beauty with light, which when applied to the material world would seem to imply that luminous objects were considered more beautiful than objects that were less luminous. This was certainly true for the Byzantine perception of colour, which placed an emphasis on the brightness and purity of a colour rather than its specific hue.[20] The identification of light with beauty begs the question about its artistic implications. On answering this question, the focus must shift from the concept of beauty to that of art and its materiality. Although the *Corpus Areopagiticum* is quite explicit about beauty, it does not contain any specific discourse on the concept of art. Pseudo-Dionysius' principles of affirmative and negative theology, however, deal with issues of representation that offer a significant contribution to aesthetic thought.[21] Pseudo-Dionysius maintains that it is better to use negations instead of positive affirmations when talking about the divine. It is easier and more suitable to say what the divine is not than what the divine is, due to its ineffable nature. This negative theology and the Pseudo-Dionysian re-assessment of the material world as a manifestation and reflection of the divine are key for his aesthetic theory, which reveals the potential relationship between a work of art and a transcendental reality. The

---

19 See, for example, Jaś Elsner, 'The viewer and the vision: The case of the Sinai Apse', *Art History* 17 (1994); Colin Macleod, 'Allegory and mysticism in Origen and Gregory of Nyssa', *Journal of Theological Studies* 22 (1971); Colin Macleod, 'The preface to Gregory of Nyssa's Life of Moses', *Journal of Theological Studies* 33 (1982); Catherine P. Roth, 'Platonic and Pauline elements in the ascent of the soul in Gregory of Nyssa's dialogue on the soul and resurrection', *Vigiliae Christianae* 46 (1992); Suchla (1995).

20 Liz James, *Light and Colour in Byzantine Art* (Oxford: Oxford University Press, 1996); Kapstein (2004).

21 Moshe Barasch, *Icon: Studies in the History of an Idea* (London and New York, NY: New York University Press, 1992), 168–70.

imitation (*mimesis*) of this transcendental reality in the broadest possible sense was a fundamental criterion in antique reflections on artistic value and truth. Interesting in this context is Aristotle's view on the autonomy of art, granting art the capacity to imitate 'things as they were or are, things as they are said or thought to be, or things as they ought to be'.[22] This Aristotelian attitude towards mimesis is ultimately not so different from Plato's concept of the mimetic arts, and both were maintained and, in fact, merged in the Neoplatonic tradition, granting art a degree of autonomy as regards its representational functioning. Neoplatonic writings on art and the material world in terms of its ontological status and meaning in relation to an intelligible reality underlie the artistic practices in late antique Byzantium. In late antiquity, works of art functioned as paradigms for how things are or ought to be, representing the essence of things and universal values rather than individual qualities and outward appearances. The logical artistic consequence was a significant transformation in the representational arts from naturalism towards stylistically more abstract forms and symbolism.[23]

The question whether an architectural structure consistent with the Pseudo-Dionysian system of thought ought to be a 'cave of light' or a 'cave of darkness' has exercised art historians since Erwin Panofsky's seminal inquiry into the abbey church of Saint Denis and its dependence on Neoplatonic philosophy and scholasticism.[24] The approach endorsed in my study, in contrast, is not to impose a dualistic divide on the Pseudo-Dionysian philosophy and the art of early Byzantium, but to treat the seemingly contradictory evidence as unity that can be resolved into a complex, yet consistent aesthetic. This aesthetic is intimately connected with light, because light is both physical and could express visual beauty as well spiritual/cognitive and convey complex theologies. It is a metaphysical aesthetic of light that resolves the divine contradictions and intricacies that Pseudo-Dionysius expounded on in his apophatic (negative) and cataphatic (positive) theologies. Light offered an ideal paradigm to exemplify the conceptual properties of the divine, the beauty of Christian truth and reality, and the spiritual ascent of the soul. In the end, aesthetic values (beauty) converged on and were identified with the functional value of art and *vice versa*.

22 Aristotle, *Poetics*, 1460b: ἢ γὰρ οἷα ἦν ἢ ἔστιν, ἢ οἷά φασιν καὶ δοκεῖ, ἢ οἷα εἶναι δεῖ.

23 Cormack (2000); Kathleen Corrigan, 'Iconography', in *The Oxford Handbook of Byzantine Studies*, ed. Elizabeth Jeffreys, John Haldon, and Robin Cormack (Oxford: Oxford University Press, 2008); André Grabar, 'Plotin et les origines de l'ésthétique médiévale', *Cahiers Archéologiques* 1 (1945); Mathew (1963); John Onians, 'Abstraction and imagination in late antiquity', *Art History* 3 (1980).

24 Christoph Markschies, *Gibt es eine "Theologie der gotischen Kathedrale"? Nochmals: Suger von Saint-Denis und Sankt Dionys vom Areopag* (Heidelberg: Universitätsverlag Carl Winter, 1995); Onasch (1993); Erwin Panofsky, *Abbot Suger on the Abbey Church of St.-Denis and Its Art Treasures* (Princeton, NJ: Princeton University Press, 1946); Erwin Panofsky, *Gothic Architecture and Scholasticism* (Latrobe, Pennsylvania 1951); Otto von Simson, *The Gothic Cathedral: Origins of Gothic Architecture and the Medieval Concept of Order* (New York: Taylor & Francis, 1962, second edition).

Jaś Elsner has noted that by the fifth and sixth centuries CE the religious way of looking at art became divorced from and predominated over the aesthetic appreciation of art.[25] In my book a somewhat alternative viewpoint is adopted, arguing that this was not so much a shift away from the aesthetic to a religious attitude towards art, but rather a redefinition of the concept of beauty and the physical world in line with the Neoplatonic metaphysical system and ontology, what Patricia Cox-Miller termed 'the material turn' of the fourth century.[26] This novel understanding of matter and beauty resulted in an aesthetic experience in late antiquity that incorporated transcendental qualities and that necessarily engaged mystical and religious experiences. Aesthetic responses can for this reason not be isolated from the religious responses to art, at least as regards ecclesiastical forms of art.[27] Various pieces of aesthetic data across diverse art forms and material categories provide clear evidence for a common basis of the aesthetic expressions and experiences in sixth-century Byzantium. Aesthetic concepts and expectations are not universal and inevitably culturally conditioned. This means that aesthetic judgements are never neutral but loaded with culture-specific values that acquire meaning only in their particular cultural and historical setting. If it is accepted that aesthetics cannot be perceived independent of the historical and intellectual conditions of which they are a product, we can in turn extract important information about meaning, cultural values and conventions in late antiquity, and about how the world was perceived by its people by attending to aesthetic questions.[28] A further advantage of the fact that aesthetic sensibilities are culturally conditioned is that it becomes possible to draw extensive conclusions from a limited number of aesthetic responses.[29]

By integrating the available aesthetic data from philosophical treatises, literary sources and material evidence, it becomes possible to establish the distinctive traits of an early Byzantine aesthetics that is not confined to an individual work of art or any one social group, profession or artistic medium. The central intellectual challenge in aesthetics of the pre-modern world is a meaningful dialogue between artistic production and philosophical concepts at the time. While a dialogue between art and philosophy as part of a common cultural and intellectual environment can help to explore the mechanisms of perception that make sense of the conceptual content of art, a direct causal relationship between the two cannot be established. Instead, the approach

---

25 Elsner (1995); Jaś Elsner, *Art and Text in Roman Culture, Cambridge Studies in New Art History and Criticism* (Cambridge and New York: Cambridge University Press, 1996); Elsner (2007).

26 Cox-Miller (2009), 3–7.

27 For an excellent discussion of this matter see, e.g. Elsner (2007). Recently, James Porter discussed the sublime as an aesthetic value, observing 'Aesthetic value bleeds irresistibly into religious value in antiquity'. Porter (2012), 67.

28 Porter (2010), 15, 40–41.

29 Kapstein described this as the intersubjectivity of aesthetic experience. Kapstein (2004), 274–5.

advocated here is to focus on how the sixth-century beholder engaged with art and to start with the particulars and an in-depth analysis of the visual and literary evidence, before moving towards the philosophical concepts and problems of beauty and art. This book does this by beginning with a detailed study of contemporary textual aesthetic responses, followed by the close observation and examination of individual works of art and architecture. It concludes with the late antique pagan and Christian Neoplatonic theories regarding the concept of beauty and the symbolic interpretation of the material world that make possible a meaningful interpretation of the artistic production in late antique Byzantium.

The definition of aesthetics that this book then adopts concentrates on the concept of beauty and the function and formalism of art in relation to the reality it propounds. In antiquity, beauty was broadly defined to include sensuous, moral and cognitive values. Distinct from beauty were the theories of art as a social practice with a purpose, espousing the concepts of art as representation or as expression.[30] The value of art and how it relates to beauty depends on the conception of reality and the relationship between this reality and the artistic work. Contrasting presumptions about reality and truth necessarily result in very different kinds of art and different attitudes towards art. If, for example, reality is materialistically defined as the world of common sense, aspects of this reality can easily be represented artistically. If, on the other hand, reality is defined in transcendental terms, for example, in terms of an intelligible divine reality, the question arises to what extent this reality can ever be translated into and expressed by the material and visible form of a work of art. Hence, these two radically different notions of reality pose very different challenges to the work of art. In the most basic terms, the first concept demands a form of art that is committed to representing the material world in a mirror-like manner, while the latter results in a symbolic art purporting to provide access to a reality that lies outside the viewer's ordinary sensuous experience. In other words, the type of reality that art advocates has formal implications insofar as it can either strive for naturalistic rendering or for abstraction to convey the otherness of the transcendental reality. The formalism of art can in turn reveal the theory of reality that the work of art is grounded in. This reciprocity is highly complex, but once its mechanism is understood, the formalism of works of art can be better explained.[31]

In essence, my argument is that late antique philosophical and theological ontology and epistemology offer a mode of thought that reflects the conceptual framework within which contemporary artistic production and perceptions of art were situated. The fundamental principle of Platonic and Neoplatonic thought is the notion that beauty in sensible things is the manifestation of the

30 James W. Manns, *Aesthetics* (London and New York, NY: M.E. Sharpe, 1998).
31 Jaś Elsner has laid the groundwork for this approach. Elsner (1995).

Idea of Good, or in Christian terms, of God, and that beauty is more of an intelligible than it is a sensible quality. As a result beauty has the potential to lead to philosophical or religious truth. The means by which truth can be reached and the definition of this truth, however, were substantially redefined during late antiquity. In contrast to its Platonic heritage, discursive cognition and reason had lost their significance in the search for truth and the ascent of the soul. The Christian God of Gregory of Nyssa and Pseudo-Dionysius is known through unknowing and resides in divine darkness, as opposed to the Platonic realm of the ideas that was likened to a place in the sun. This indicates a fundamental shift away from the Classical notion of truth based on critical faculty and logic, and towards religious knowledge based on blind, unquestioning faith.

In the late antique Christian Neoplatonism of Gregory of Nyssa and Pseudo-Dionysius, the divine transcendence coincides with divine immanence, inevitably resulting in a symbolic interpretation of the material world.[32] Since beauty was understood as the prototypical divine paradigm that was by implication identified with being, everything was beautiful by virtue of its existence. This is why works of art necessarily have a share in beauty, too. This beauty, however, does not consist in the material, but is found predominantly in the idea of the divine that is reflected in the work of art. The preoccupation with divine beauty in relationship to the material reality of the church of Hagia Sophia is broached in the sixth-century descriptions of the building's interior. The objects of aesthetic experience highlighted in the two extant *ekphraseis* of Hagia Sophia include both objects perceptible to the senses as well as objects of thought. To salvage these objects of aesthetic experience from the highly rhetorical descriptions warrants a discussion of the literary conventions of the ekphrasis, which forms the starting point of this book. This is followed by a close examination of the materiality and artistic practices that underlie the architecture and interior design of Hagia Sophia and, for comparison, other late antique ecclesiastical structures and monumental decorations. I will concentrate particularly on light and illumination and the psychology of perception, to elucidate the prevailing light management and decorative systems. The study covers the entire range of artistic practices and materials from architectural design and architectural sculpture, to the marble revetment, mosaic decoration and the production of glass tesserae as well as the use of colours. The aesthetic data of the material culture are then contextualised within the intellectual environment of sixth-century Byzantium and the Neoplatonic philosophies of late antiquity. This necessitates the differential treatment of the concept of beauty and the performative nature of art, to consider the broader issues of how an understanding of the functional

[32] Eric D. Perl, *Theophany: The Neoplatonic Philosophy of Dionysius the Areopagite* (New York, NY: State University of New York Press, 2007), Chapter 2.

capacity of beauty and art can enrich our knowledge of artistic production and creativity in late antique Byzantium.

This study is intended as an inclusive account of the early Byzantine aesthetic experience, and in its critical function it demonstrates the need for an interdisciplinary approach to interpret the aesthetic data and to formulate the aesthetics of sixth-century Byzantium. It is important to stress once more that the clean break between aesthetic and other philosophical values such as ethical, epistemological and ontological that we owe to the eighteenth century poses a real limitation for the evaluation of ancient aesthetics. Exemplary of the problem with an *Enlightenment* approach is, for example, Michelis' comment that early Christian art is 'an art of the Sublime and not of the Beautiful'.[33] Michelis uses a distinction that did not exist in this form before the second half of the eighteenth century, when the sublime as an aesthetic criterion increasingly asserted its independence from beauty.[34] As the quote at the beginning of this chapter indicates, there is no art without aesthetics, and some kind of aesthetics is always integral to artistic strategies. In the following chapters it is my aim to clarify the many facets and principles of what constitutes the Byzantine aesthetics based on the church of Hagia Sophia. Aesthetic sensibilities are matters of cultural construction and can provide insights into the cultural identity of a people. This book is therefore not a strictly art-historical assessment of the forms and styles of the monuments. Instead, it takes a historical approach, assessing the transformations and innovations that took place during late antiquity and asking what the art and aesthetics of Hagia Sophia can tell us about early Byzantine civilisation.

---

[33] Panayotis A. Michelis, 'Neo-Platonic philosophy and Byzantine art', *The Journal of Aesthetics and Art Criticism* 11 (1952): 45. See also Panayotis A. Michelis, *An Aesthetic Approach to Byzantine Art* (London: Batsford, 1955).

[34] Developed, for instance, in the philosophies of Edmund Burke (1729–1797) and most notably Immanuel Kant. For the history of the sublime as a concept see, for example, Philip Shaw, *The Sublime* (London and New York, NY: Routledge, 2006).

1

Viewing Hagia Sophia through Sixth-Century Eyes

Famed for its 'marvellous beauty', the architectural structure and interior decoration of Hagia Sophia was not only innovative in its own time, but would prove paradigmatic for the architecture of later periods, while epitomising Byzantine identity.[1] Reaching for the sky, the edifice towers above the sixth-century city of Constantinople, combining sound proportion with faultless harmony.[2] The first impression of the building's interior is one suffused with light as:

> it abounds exceedingly in sunlight and in the reflection of the sun's rays from the marble. Indeed one might say that its interior is not illuminated from without by the sun, but that the radiance comes into being within it, such an abundance of light bathes this shrine.[3]

The east end recedes into the semi-circle of an apse, topped by two successive semi-domes, seemingly floating in mid-air and flanked by retreating exedras. The same arrangement can be found at the west end of the building. In the centre, four massive piers rise to a great height and support four arches on either side of the naos square, upon which rests a central dome. 'Yet it seems not to rest upon solid masonry, but to cover the space with its golden

---

1 Procopius I.1.27: Θέαμα τοίνυν ἡ ἐκκλησία κεκαλλιστευμένον γεγένηται. Robin Cormack, 'The visual arts', in *The Cambridge Ancient History. Late Antiquity: Empire and Successors, A.D. 425–600*, ed. Averil Cameron, Bryan Ward-Perkins, and Michael Whitby (Cambridge: Cambridge University Press, 2000); Jaś Elsner, 'Late antique art: The problem of the concept and the cumulative aesthetic', in *Approaching Late Antiquity: The Transformation from Early to Late Empire*, ed. Simon Swain and Mark Edwards (Oxford: Oxford University Press, 2004); Rowland J. Mainstone, *Hagia Sophia: Architecture, Structure and Liturgy of Justinian's Great Church* (London: Thames and Hudson, 1988); Robert S. Nelson, *Hagia Sophia, 1850–1950: Holy Wisdom Modern Monument* (Chicago, IL: University of Chicago Press, 2004).

2 Procopius I.1.27–29.

3 Procopius I.1.29–31: φωτὶ δὲ καὶ ἡλίου μαρμαρυγαῖς ὑπερφυῶς πλήθει. φαίης ἂν οὐκ ἔξωθεν καταλάμπεσθαι ἡλίῳ τὸν χῶρον, ἀλλὰ τὴν αἴγλην ἐν αὐτῷ φύεσθαι, τοσαύτη τις φωτὸς περιουσία ἐς τοῦτο δὴ τὸ ἱερὸν περικέχυται.

dome suspended from Heaven'.[4] It is a 'bewildering sight', and one does not know where to look first. Light reflects from the gold-covered ceilings, and the colonnaded aisles and galleries are simply beyond description. The polychromy of the church's interior is reminiscent of a meadow in full bloom. It is a marvel (*thauma*) of purple, green and crimson glows and white flashes, merging technical skill with divine providence.[5]

It is in these terms that the sixth-century court historian Procopius of Caesarea described the church of Hagia Sophia in Constantinople as part of his treatise *De Aedificiis* (*On Buildings*), the purpose of which was to celebrate and to preserve for posterity the architectural achievements of the emperor Justinian.[6] *De Aedificiis* is one of three historical works by Procopius, written in the tradition of classicising history and imperial panegyrics.[7] The work varies from elaborate descriptions of single buildings, fortifications and water supplies to mere cataloguing, and combines numerous literary genres, including panegyric, imperial biography, geography and ekphrasis.[8] Book I of the *De Aedificiis* opens with a detailed rhetorical description of the church of Hagia Sophia in Constantinople. Probably written around the middle of the 550s, Procopius' account of the Great Church is the only surviving historical source for the original Justinianic edifice before the collapse of its first dome in 558 CE.[9] While the text records some technical issues that arose during the construction process, it conveys above all a sixth-century response to the building. As outlined above, Procopius' narrative does not follow an obvious systematic sequence and does not always remain strictly factual. Instead, Procopius comments repeatedly on the subjectively felt

---

4 Procopius I.1.46: δοκεῖ δὲ οὐκ ἐπὶ στερρᾶς τῆς οἰκοδομίας διὰ τὸ παρειμένον τῆς οἰκοδομίας ἑστάναι, ἀλλὰ τῇ σφαίρᾳ τῇ χρυσῇ ἀπὸ τοῦ οὐρανοῦ ἐξημμένη καλύπτειν τὸν χῶρον.

5 Procopius I.1.27–78.

6 Procopius I.1.17–18; Judith Herrin, 'The Byzantine secrets of Procopius', *History Today* 38 (1988).

7 The limited information we have about Procopius the person stems from his own writings. He tells us that he was a native of Caesarea in Palestine, and we can assume that he received the standard secular education typical of late antiquity. Averil Cameron, *Procopius and the Sixth Century* (London: Duckworth, 1985), 7–9, 87–90.

8 Cameron (1985), 84–112; Jaś Elsner, 'The rhetoric of buildings in the *De Aedificiis* of Procopius', in *Art and Text in Byzantine Culture*, ed. Liz James (Cambridge: Cambridge University Press, 2007); Ruth Webb, 'Ekphrasis, amplification and persuasion in Procopius' *Buildings*', *AT* 8 (2000).

9 Procopius does not mention the collapse of 558 CE. For a pre-558 dating see Cameron (1985), 84–5; Glanville Downey, 'Notes on Procopius' *De Aedificiis* Book 1', in *Studies Presented to D. M. Robinson, vol. 2*, ed. G. Mylonas (St. Louis, MO: Washington University Press, 1953); G. Greatrex, 'The dates of Procopius' works', *BMGS* 18 (1994); James Howard-Johnston, 'The education and expertise of Procopius', *AT* 8 (2000); P. Rousseau, 'Procopius' buildings and Justinian's pride', *Byzantion* 68 (1998). Likewise, Evans argues for a pre-558 date with respect to the description of Hagia Sophia, while he maintains that the remainder of the *De Aedificiis* was added later. J. A. S. Evans, 'The dates of Procopius' works: A recapitulation of the evidence', *GRBS* 37 (1996). For a 560/561 date see Denis Roques, 'Les constructions de Justinien de Procope de Césarée', *AT* 8 (2000); Michael Whitby, 'Justinian's bridge over the Sangarius and the date of Procopius' *De Aedificiis*', *Journal of Hellenic Studies* 105 (1985).

experience, emphasising the marvel that skilfully combines the sacred with technological excellence and that escapes human comprehension. As such, Procopius' account corresponds to the ancient definition of an ekphrasis that goes beyond a simple technical description by commenting on the building's effects and visual impressions experienced by the orator and his audience.[10]

The definition of ekphrasis in antiquity is a complex one. In its most basic form, ekphrasis is a rhetorical technique that attempts to represent a material object or event through the medium of language and to verbalise what is originally non-verbal.[11] Ekphrasis is about visualisation and a direct expression of the ways of viewing rather than the technicalities of the perceived object or event.[12] An ekphrasis echoes the viewer's experience and perception, thereby creating an interpretative framework for the viewing process. The audience is invited to view the object (e.g. Hagia Sophia) through the mediation of the ekphrasis that points out 'the most notable features'.[13] In so doing, an ekphrasis pays attention to those properties to which aesthetic value was assigned by a Byzantine beholder. These objects of aesthetic experience, however, need not necessarily be material or visible. Rather, the ekphrasis promotes intelligent viewing by instructing the reader or listener how to look and what to see. Through an ekphrasis the audience can potentially gain access to the intelligible meaning (higher truths) that underlies the material reality of the ekphrasis and the artefact.[14] This chapter explores how the two extant ekphraseis of Hagia Sophia transformed the objects of sense perception

---

[10] Elsner (2007); Webb (2000).

[11] Ruth Webb, 'Ekphrasis ancient and modern: The invention of a genre', *Word and Image* 15 (1999).

[12] Page Dubois 'Reading the writing on the wall', *Classical Philology* 102 (2007); Jaś Elsner, *Art and the Roman Viewer: The Transformation of Art from the Pagan World to Christianity* (Cambridge and New York: Cambridge University Press, 1995); Simon Goldhill, 'What is ekphrasis for?', *Classical Philology* 102 (2007); Liz James and Ruth Webb, '"To understand ultimate things and enter secret places": Ekphrasis and art in Byzantium', *Art History* 14 (1991); Ruth Webb, 'Mémoire et imagination: Les limites de *l'enargeia* dans la théorie rhétorique grecque', in *Dire l'évidence (philosophie et rhétorique antiques): actes du colloque de Créteil et de Paris (24–25 mars 1995)*, ed. Carlos Lévy and Laurent Pernot (Paris: L'Harmattan, 1997); Ruth Webb, 'Accomplishing the picture: Ekphrasis, mimesis and martyrdom in Asterios of Amaseia', in *Art and Text in Byzantine Culture*, ed. Liz James (Cambridge: Cambridge University Press, 2007); A. Hohlweg, 'Ekphrasis', in *Reallexikon zur byzantinischen Kunst, Vol. 2* (Stuttgart: A. Hiersemann, 1971), 35; Ruth Webb, 'The aesthetics of sacred space: Narrative, metaphor, and motion in ekphraseis of church buildings', *DOP* 53 (1999); Ruth Webb, *Ekphrasis, Imagination and Persuasion in Ancient Rhetorical Theory and Practice* (Farnham: Ashgate, 2009).

[13] Procopius I.1.66: πραγμάτων ἀξιολογώτατα.

[14] Liz James, 'Art and lies: Text, image and imagination in the medieval world', in *Icon and Word: The Power of Images in Byzantium. Studies Presented to Robin Cormack*, ed. Antony Eastmond and Liz James (Aldershot: Ashgate, 2003); Verity Platt, 'Virtual visions: Phantasia and the perception of the divine in The Life of Apollonius of Tyana', in *Philostratus*, ed. E. Bowie and Jaś Elsner (Cambridge: Cambridge University Press, 2009); Webb (1999); Webb (2009).

(*aisthesis*) into potential objects of intellection (*noesis*),[15] and how Procopius and Paul the Silentiary transcended the material reality (materiality) of the building of Hagia Sophia into a monument of wisdom (*sophia*).

Visualising Hagia Sophia through the Agency of Light

As a rhetorical device, an ekphrasis could be employed in a variety of contexts, and the two sixth-century ekphrastic accounts of Hagia Sophia, one by Procopius and the other by Paul the Silentiary, indeed differ in purpose and structure. Both authors wrote in a classicising style with a 'flowery language' and abundant use of archaisms and metaphors reminiscent of Homeric vocabulary.[16] The difference between the two is that Procopius set out to preserve the memory of the emperor Justinian's accomplishments for generations to come in the classical tradition of historiography,[17] while Paul the Silentiary wrote an ekphrastic poem to be recited for a specific occasion, namely the celebrations of the church's re-consecration in 562/563 CE.[18] In other words, the two ekphraseis differ significantly in terms of the historical backdrop against which they were composed as well as in terms of the relationship between the audience and the described object. Procopius focused on the early and glorious years of Justinian's reign and the construction of the emperor's architectural masterpiece. Paul the Silentiary's poem, on the other hand, followed the collapse of the main dome of Hagia Sophia, at a time when Justinian's long and eventful (and not always successful) reign was drawing near its close.[19] In the case of Procopius' *De Aedificiis*, it is a classicising historical work aimed at a readership/audience that was not necessarily present on site

15 LSJ: αἴσθησις = sense-perception, sensation; νόησις = intelligence, under-standing.

16 Gianfranco Agosti, 'Niveaux de style, littérarité, poétiques: Pour une histoire du système de la poésie classicisante au VIe siècle', in *Doux remède: Poésie et poétique à Byzance. Actes du IVe colloque international philologique Paris, 23–24–25 février 2006. Dossiers byzantines, 9*, ed. P. Odorico, P. Agapitos, and M. Hinterberger (Paris: Centres d'études byzantines, néo-helleniques et sud-est européennes, École des hautes études en sciences sociales, 2009); Cameron (1985), 99; Maria Luigia Fobelli, *Un tempio per Giustiniano: Santa Sofia di Constantinopoli e la Descrizione die Paolo Silenziario* (Rome: Viella, 2005), 9; Bissera V. Pentcheva, 'Hagia Sophia and multisensory aesthetics', *Gesta* 50 (2011).

17 Procopius I.1.17–18; compare, for example, the Homeric and Herodotean conception of history; Henry R. Immerwahr, 'Ergon: History as a monument in Herodotus and Thucydides', *The American Journal of Philology* 81 (1960).

18 As we learn from Agathias of Myrina, a close associate of Paul the Silentiary, Paul was a poet, lawyer and bureaucrat of senatorial rank in Constantinople during the reign of Justinian and famous for some 80 epigrams and above all his detailed description of Hagia Sophia and its furnishings. Agathias, *Historiae*, V.9.7–9; Fobelli (2005), 9–12; Ruth Macrides and Paul Magdalino, 'The architecture of ekphrasis: Construction and context of Paul the Silentiary's poem on Hagia Sophia', *BMGS* 12 (1988); Mary Whitby, 'Procopius' *Buildings*, Book I: A panegyrical perspective', *AT* 8 (2000).

19 Cameron (1985), 9–11; Averil Cameron, 'Images of authority: Elites and icons in late sixth-century Byzantium', *Past & Present*, 84 (1979).

and that may in fact not have had personal knowledge of the monument at all. Procopius' main task was therefore to convincingly create a vision of the edifice in the minds of his audience, a problem of which he himself was acutely aware when he exclaims that 'the church has become a spectacle of marvellous beauty, overwhelming to those who see it, but to those who know it by hearsay altogether incredible'.[20] Paul's poem, in contrast, was recited in close proximity to the church (at least in the first instance) and in front of an audience who were familiar with the building and who had the subject matter (Hagia Sophia) literally before their eyes.[21] Given the ancient definition of ekphrasis as 'a descriptive speech which vividly (*enargos*) brings the subject shown before the eyes',[22] Paul's ekphrasis ran the risk of being superfluous, because the very thing he was meant to 'bring before the eyes' of his audience was precisely there, in front of his audience.[23] Hence, Paul was faced with a different problem to that of Procopius. Paul himself concedes that trying to rival the beauty and greatness of Hagia Sophia in words was an impossible task, but that it was nonetheless worth trying, as sight and words would complement each other.[24] Even though the author's claim of inadequacy to capture the monument in words has to be considered as a rhetorical *topos*, Paul's comment also implies that an ekphrasis can supplement the visual experience by explicating values and meanings that go beyond the strictly visible.[25] Whereas Procopius' ekphrasis of Hagia Sophia was a means to evoke a visual experience in the minds of those who had not seen the edifice, Paul the Silentiary's poem served as a guide to intelligent viewing. Paul

---

[20] Procopius I.1.27: Θέαμα τοίνυν ἡ ἐκκλησία κεκαλλιστευμένον γεγένηται, τοῖς μὲν ὁρῶσιν ὑπερφυές, τοῖς δὲ ἀκούουσι παντελῶς ἄπιστον.

[21] The actual date of recitation is a matter of dispute. It is usually placed either on 6 January 563 CE, the day of Epiphany (the feast of the light) or on 31 December 562 CE, the commemoration day of David. Macrides and Magdalino (1988), 63–7; Mary Whitby, 'The occasion of Paul the Silentiary's ekphrasis of S. Sophia', *Classical Quarterly* 35 (1985): 216–17. For new archaeological evidence as regards the precise location of the poem's delivery, see Jan Kostenec and Ken Dark, 'Paul the Silentiary's description of Hagia Sophia in light of new archaeological evidence', *Byzantinoslavica – Revue internationale des Études Byzantines* 69 (2011).

[22] Theon, *Progymnasmata* 118.6; translated in Webb (2009), 197–204. Four *progymnasmata* survive that display a remarkable consistency in form and content, pointing to a static definition of an ekphrasis. Theon's version is assumed to be the earliest extant definition of ekphrasis and dates to the first century CE. Virtually the same definition can be found in the versions of Hermogenes (third century), Aphthonios (fourth century) and Nikolaos (fifth century). Elsner (1995), 24–5; Paul Friedländer, *Johannes von Gaza und Paulus Silentiarius: Kunstbeschreibungen justinianischer Zeit* (Leipzig and Berlin: Teubner, 1912), 84; James and Webb (1991), ft. 23; Romilly J.H. Jenkins, 'The Hellenistic origins of Byzantine literature', *DOP* 17 (1963), 43; Goldhill (2007).

[23] Webb (2009), 172–4.

[24] Paul the Silentiary verses 100–125; English translations in Peter N. Bell, *Three Political Voices from the Age of Justinian: Agapetus, Advice to the Emperor; Dialogue on Political Science; Paul the Silentiary, Description of Hagia Sophia* (Liverpool: Liverpool University Press, 2009), 189–212; Cyril Mango, *The Art of the Byzantine Empire 312–1453: Sources and Documents* (Toronto: University of Toronto Press, 1972, reprint 1986), 80–102.

[25] Webb (2009), 174–5.

controlled and directed the ways of perception by highlighting much more the spiritual and ideological significance of Hagia Sophia in its cultural and religious setting, reflecting the intensely ecclesiastical context of the poem's delivery. Ultimately, however, both ekphraseis were designed to influence the audience and to focus the attention of the spectator so as to structure the viewing process of the church.

Before addressing questions about the ideological and psychological implications of Paul the Silentiary's and Procopius' descriptions, I would like to return to the materiality of the two ekphraseis to identify those architectural and decorative features of Hagia Sophia that were singled out as the objects of aesthetic experience, or, in Procopius' words, as 'the most notable features (πραγμάτων ἀξιολογώτατα)'.[26] All descriptions are inevitably interpretative and selective, subject to the author's agenda and the purpose of the description.[27] In relation to ancient descriptions it can furthermore be assumed that the author's choice reflects the expectations of his audience, because for the ekphrasis to be effective, the author and audience need to share in the same cultural values and conventions.[28] Byzantine ekphrasis at once documents and sustains the aesthetic preferences of the Byzantine beholder. This is why, through the conditioning filter of the two ekphraseis, we can gain a sense of the sixth-century reflections on the aesthetics embodied in the church of Hagia Sophia.

Paul the Silentiary and Procopius essentially organise their descriptions along the two main architectural dimensions that shape the spatial impression of Hagia Sophia. Both commence with a description of the apse in the east, the exedras and semi-domes, then move on to the western end of the building and thereby emphasise the east-west as well as the vertical axes of the church.[29] Neither Paul nor Procopius follow a strictly linear sequence: both descriptions jump from east to west and back to the central space from bottom to top and back again. This sense of disarray exemplifies the visual experience of the spectator who is overwhelmed by the intricacies of the architectural details, each of which, according to Procopius, 'attracts the eye and draws it on irresistibly to itself, so the vision constantly shifts suddenly'.[30] Paul similarly exclaims, 'Whither am I driven? (πῆι φέρομαι;)', expressing his surprise when he realises that he had been distracted by secondary structures (doors and the narthex) and has accidentally passed over the most important feature of the church (the naos).[31] This figure of speech interrupts the narrative and thus invokes

26 Procopius I.1.66.

27 Jaś Elsner, 'Art history as ekphrasis', *Art History* 33 (2010).

28 Webb (2009), Chapter 5.

29 Procopius I.1.32–37; Silentiary verses 354–410.

30 Procopius I.1.48: μεθέλκει τὸν ὀφθαλμὸν ἕκαστον, καὶ μεταβιβάζει ῥᾷστα ἐφ' ἑαυτό.

31 Silentiary verses 444–445; Paul makes the same exclamation again when describing the silver furnishings (verse 755).

the feeling of authenticity by appearing improvised, and simultaneously stirs and directs the attention of the audience.[32] The bewildering effect of the edifice on the spectator, appearing as a dynamic sequence of different structures and spaces, highlights the need for guidance. Without the ekphrasis that focuses the attention of the audience, the listener finds him- or herself in a state of confusion and ignorance. By leading the spectator around (*periegesis*), the ekphrasis elaborates on the individual sights and achieves vividness while 'adding order and meaning to the undifferentiated mass of sights'.[33] The rhetorical technique of *periegesis* helps to visualise the spatial impression and provides the explanatory context for how the audience is supposed to relate to the sacred space. It is a deliberate collection of those features, which the authors thought would best conjure up the nature of the building, both as an architectural masterpiece and as a place that transforms human experience and constructs an early Byzantine identity.[34]

The selectivity and accumulation of visual impressions that seemingly eschew any structural logic emphasise the building's visual impact on the beholder and its dynamic qualities. The architecture has become deeply imbued with the image of a moving force. Procopius describes how the architectural parts curve, recede and retreat, how the domes float in mid-air and the columns dance (*chorós*) and how the piers rise to soaring heights from which the arches spring.[35] Paul similarly relates springing spheres, a wheeling synthronon and exedras that welcome the visitor 'like bent arms stretched out to embrace'.[36] As Ruth Webb has noted, this visual animation was an effective rhetorical tool meant to create a vivid fantasy of the spatial experience.[37] The rhetorical technique makes the building come alive and

---

32 Nicoletta Isar, '"Xopos of light": Vision of the sacred in Paulus the Silentiary's poem Descriptio S. Sophia', *Byzantinische Forschungen* 28 (2004): 227.

33 Webb (2009), 54. Webb has shown that the *periegesis* was the most frequently used technique in ekphrasis to effect a dynamic impression. Webb (1999), 64–8.

34 For the rhetorical and structural implications of *periegesis* see Jaś Elsner, 'Structuring "Greece": Pausanias's Periegesis as a literary construct', in *Pausanias: Travel and Memory in Roman Greece*, ed. Susan E. Alcock, John F. Cherry, and Jaś Elsner (Oxford: Oxford University Press, 2001).

35 Procopius I.1.32–36: οἰκοδομία τις ἐκ γῆς ἀνέχει, οὐκ ἐπ' εὐθείας πεποιημένη, ἀλλ' ἐκ τῶν πλαγίων ὑπεσταλμένη κατὰ βραχύ, καὶ κατὰ τὰ μέσα ὑποχωροῦσα, ἐπὶ σχῆμά τε κατὰ ἥμισυ τὸ στρογγύλον ἰοῦσα, ὅπερ οἱ περὶ τὰ τοιαῦτα σοφοὶ ἡμικύλινδρον ὀνομάζουσιν, ἐς ὕψος ἀπότομον ἐπανέστηκεν. ἡ δὲ τοῦ ἔργου τούτου ὑπερβολὴ ἐς σφαίρας τεταρτημόριον ἀποκέκριται, ὕπερθέν τε μηνοειδές τι αὐτῇ ἕτερον τοῖς προσεχέσι τῆς οἰκοδομίας ἐπῆρται, τῇ μὲν εὐπρεπείᾳ θαυμάσιον, τῷ δὲ σφαλερῷ τῆς συνθέσεως δοκοῦντι εἶναι φοβερὸν ὅλως. δοκεῖ γάρ πη οὐκ ἐν βεβαίῳ ἐπηωρῆσθαι, ἀλλ' ἐπικινδύνως τοῖς ἐνθάδε οὖσι μετεωρίζεσθαι … ἀλλ' εἴσω κατὰ σχῆμα τὸ ἡμίκυκλον ὥσπερ ἐν χορῷ ἀλλήλοις ὑπεξιστάμενοι, καὶ αὐτῶν ὑπεράνωθεν οἰκοδόμημα μηνοειδὲς ἀποκρέμαται. Nicoletta Isar discussed the concept of *chorós* (dance) in context of Paul the Silentiary's ekphrasis, observing that *chorós* and its cognates commonly imply circular movement and reflect Neoplatonic influences on Paul especially as regards his description of the nocturnal lighting installations in Hagia Sophia. Isar (2004).

36 Silentiary verses 353, 367 and 374.

37 Webb (1999), 68–9.

arouses the feeling of an active force that is literally built into the architectural structure. Both ekphraseis draw the listeners into the aesthetic experience of the awe-inspiring sacred space so that the dominant impression with which the audience is left is not one of an inert dead monument but of materialised dynamic motion. The visual experience of animated matter is best captured by Paul the Silentiary's description of 'the marble meadows gathered upon the mighty walls':

> … the speckled Phrygian stone, sometimes rosy mixed with white, sometimes gleaming with purple and silver flowers. There is a wealth of porphyry stone, too, besprinkled with little bright stars … You may see the bright green stone of Laconia and the glittering marble with wavy veins … of the Iasian peaks, exhibiting slanting streaks of blood-red and livid white; the pale yellow with swirling red from the Lydian headland; the glittering crocus-like golden stone … of the Moorish hills; that of glittering black upon which the Celtic crags, deep in ice, have poured here and there an abundance of milk; the pale onyx with glint of precious metal; and that which the land of Atrax yields … in parts vivid green not unlike emerald, in others of a darker green, almost blue. It has spots resembling snow next to flashes (marmaryges) of black so that in one stone various beauties mingle.[38]

The message in Paul the Silentiary's detailed description of the marble revetment is twofold: that the Byzantine Empire is vast and its emperor great and that the visual qualities of the marble, its variation (*poikilia*), vibrant colours, brilliance and motion are aesthetically pleasing. The marble surfaces are defined as gleaming, bright, sparkling, glittering, shiny and shimmering as well as speckled, besprinkled, wavy, slanting and swirling. Paul the Silentiary describes the marble revetment in terms of its kinetic effects as animated matter that is directly dependent on the transformative power of light. The appearance of animated surfaces, of movement and change, is produced by the optical properties of the marble that is literally brought to life by the effects of light. Paul deliberately draws the attention of his audience to these perceptual qualities through a series of metaphors and attributes of movement such as silvery flowers, blood-red and livid white, swirling red and crocus-like gold, vivid green and flashes of snow.[39] In so doing, Paul's account of the marble revetment reveals the late antique taste for *poikilia* and animation. Both *poikilia* and animation were major aesthetic principles that shaped the composition of late antique poetry and artistic practices alike.[40] As rhetorical motifs they are found in Paul's and Procopius' ekphraseis of Hagia

38 Silentiary verses 617–646.

39 Bissera Pentcheva discussed similar sentiments in the context of Paul's description of the solea. Pentcheva (2011), 95–6.

40 Sandrine Dubel, 'Colour in Philostratus "Imagines"', in *Philostratus*, ed. E. Bowie and Jaś Elsner (Cambridge: Cambridge University Press, 2009); Pentcheva (2011); Michael Roberts, *The Jeweled Style: Poetry and Poetics in Late Antiquity* (Ithaca, NY: Cornell University Press, 1989), 38–65.

Sophia, and they are materialised in the luminous colours, patterns and veins of the actual marble surfaces in Hagia Sophia that gave rise to the ekphrastic poems in the first place.

Procopius similarly describes the interior of Hagia Sophia as a meadow of scintillating colours 'with its flowers (*anthae*) in full bloom'.[41] In the rhetorical tradition of late antiquity, the Greek term for flower (*anthae*) employed here by Procopius, as well as by Paul in several contexts,[42] also designates brilliant colours and has a rhetorical and an aesthetic dimension. From a rhetorical point of view, the chromatic variability and the metaphor of a meadow of flowers/colours heightens the sense of vividness (*enargeia*), conjuring up vivid images of the ecclesiastical interior in the audience's mind and thus complying with the rhetorical requirements of an ekphrasis. The specificity of the colours in Paul's description of the marble revetment, for instance, evokes visual immediacy. This is further enhanced when Paul implicates his audience in the viewing process directly by stating at the beginning of his enumeration of the marbles 'you may see'.[43] All this renders the experience of Hagia Sophia visual and vivid in the audience's imagination through the notion of bright colours and a series of familiar images. The colours of the marble surfaces literally transform the ecclesiastical space into a blossoming meadow in spring[44] inasmuch as in Byzantine belief colour is the very element that gives identity and meaning to an object.[45] Hagia Sophia's sacred interior is a symbol of vernal renewal (Hagia Sophia had, after all, been rebuilt) and of nature's diversity on account of its polychromy. Aesthetically, the blossoming meadow reflects the Byzantine taste for all things living, for colours, light and contrasts. In Paul's ekphrasis the colours are typically given as opposites: blood-red is contrasted with livid white, glittering black is interspersed with milk-white and spots of snow appear next to flashes of black. These contrasts not only reinforce the rhetorical principle of diversity (*poikilia*) and the aesthetics of contrasts united in 'a spectacle of marvellous beauty',[46] but the antithesis also highlights the quality of brilliance and iridescence for which colours were particularly admired in Byzantium.[47] The dichotomy of dark and light and variegated surfaces that differentially absorb and

41 Procopius I.1.59.

42 Silentiary verses 388, 879.

43 Silentiary verse 620.

44 Paul the Silentiary explicitly compares the light from the gold mosaics to 'the midday sun in spring' (verses 668–672).

45 Dubel (2009); Liz James, *Light and Colour in Byzantine Art* (Oxford: Oxford University Press, 1996); Liz James, 'Color and meaning in Byzantium', *Journal of Early Christian Studies* 11 (2003).

46 Procopius I.1.27; Dubel (2009), 315–16.

47 Dubel (2009); Rico Franses, 'When all that is gold does not glitter: On the strange history of looking at Byzantine art', in *Icon and Word: The Power of Images in Byzatnium*, ed. Antony Eastmond and Liz James (Aldershot and Burlington, VT: Ashgate Publishing, 2003); James (1996); James (2003).

reflect light is highly valued by both Procopius and Paul the Silentiary. The marble revetment thus comes to life through the play of light. Without light, the decoration loses a fundamental aspect of its aesthetic appeal. Brilliance had long been associated with movement and temporality in ancient Greek poetry,[48] and it illustrates once more that the aesthetic experience of Hagia Sophia's sacred space is founded on the dynamic quality of its architectural structure and interior decoration animated through light and colour.

Nowhere is this aesthetics of light made more explicit than in the description of Hagia Sophia's illumination by day (Procopius) and by night (Paul the Silentiary). Upon turning to the impression of the building's sacred interior almost in the opening scene of his ekphrasis, Procopius elaborates at considerable length on the theme of light, describing how '… it abounds exceedingly in sunlight and in the reflection of the sun's rays from the marble (*marmarygais*). Indeed one might say that its interior is not illuminated from without by the sun, but that the radiance comes into being within it, such an abundance of light bathes this shrine'.[49] Paul the Silentiary's ekphrasis, on the other hand, culminates in a detailed description of the nocturnal lighting of Hagia Sophia. He marvels:

> Thus is everything clothed in beauty, everything fills the eye with wonder. But no words are sufficient to describe the illumination in the evening: you might say that some nocturnal sun filled the majestic temple with light (806–811) … Thus the evening light revolves around the temple, brightly shining … so that the darkness is made to flee (834–838).[50]

The emblematic motif of light occurs at very strategic points in both ekphraseis, at the beginning of Procopius' and in the closing parts of Paul the Silentiary's account. Combined with numerous references to the light-bearing quality of the interior and its decorative materials scattered throughout both texts, the image of light very much controls the visualisation and audience's experience of the Great Church. Both ekphraseis, for instance, recognise that the opulence of the colours and the materials is actualised through the agency of light. Procopius specifically notices the effects of *marmaryge*. The term signifies the vibrant play of light on the marble surfaces.[51] As Pentcheva discussed in great detail, in Greek literature *marmaryge* and its cognates traditionally convey motion and the sparkling effect of light on reflective

48 Dubel (2009); Eleanor Irwin, *Colour Terms in Greek Poetry* (Toronto: Hakkert, 1974), appendix II, 213–15.

49 Procopius I. 1. 29–31: φωτὶ δὲ καὶ ἡλίου μαρμαρυγαῖς ὑπερφυῶς πλήθει. φαίης ἂν οὐκ ἔξωθεν καταλάμπεσθαι ἡλίῳ τὸν χῶρον, ἀλλὰ τὴν αἴγλην ἐν αὐτῷ φύεσθαι, τοσαύτη τις φωτὸς περιουσία ἐς τοῦτο δὴ τὸ ἱερὸν περικέχυται.

50 Silentiary verses 806–920. Paul provides a detailed account of the different lighting devices from which it is possible to gain some idea about the lighting system of Hagia Sophia in the sixth century.

51 Procopius I.1.29. LSJ: μαρμαρυγή = flashing, sparkling, gleaming.

materials (the sea, metals). In late antiquity, the term *marmaryge* acquires a metaphysical connotation and describes the transformative potential of light to animate matter so that it becomes alive (*empsychos*).[52] As an expression of truly animated matter, the concept of *marmaryge* is reminiscent of the Pseudo-Dionysian concept of light as a divine attribute and divine illumination.[53] The transformative effect of light has become a dominant and deliberate aesthetic principle that constitutes the notion of space and animation in the two sixth-century descriptions of Hagia Sophia. Light was evidently considered the fundamental structural and visual feature of the edifice.

The recurring imagery of light and the use of metaphors of light in both ekphraseis not only helps to satisfy the rhetorical requirement of *enargeia* (vividness), but light and its effects are the most visible manifestation of the active force that vigorously strikes the eye of the spectator and that 'makes the darkness flee'. Paul describes how the 'glittering stream of golden rays [that] pours abundantly strikes men's eyes with irresistible force',[54] emphasising the effectiveness and visual appeal of the light that has been transformed through the agency of the edifice and its decoration. Light is the actual embodiment of power (divine force) and the all-prevailing image of light serves as a vehicle for a decisively theological message.[55] This theological dimension is introduced in the preface of Paul's poem, when he recounts how 'the night of sorrows waned and the bright gleam of joy spread over everyone' on the day of Hagia Sophia's re-consecration.[56] This sentiment, as we have just seen, is repeated in his description of the artificial lighting of the edifice that illustrates the transcendental potential of light to drive out the darkness of night and with it the sorrows of the people. Hagia Sophia is even compared to the tower of Pharos, guiding the traveller not by means of its physical light alone, but above all with the 'help of the living God'.[57]

The divine within Hagia Sophia, then, is represented in and perceived through the form of light. As the true manifestation of the divine, the physical presence of light facilitates what can be considered 'an epiphanic viewing experience'.[58] The phenomenon of light underlies at once the visual (aesthetic)

---

52 LSJ: ἔμψυχος = having life in one, animate; Pentcheva (2011).

53 According to Pseudo-Dionysius, the 'transcendent rays prefer to give off the fullness of their splendour (μαρμαρυγῶν) more purely and more luminously in mirrors made in their image'. Pseudo-Dionysius, EH III(3).10.440B.

54 Silentiary verses 668–671.

55 Macrides and Magdalino defined a spiritual, cyclical and anagogical structure of the poem. Macrides and Magdalino (1988), 58–60.

56 Silentiary verses 324–325.

57 Silentiary verses 906–920: πάντας ἐπαυγάζει σέλας ἱερόν … ἀλλά καί εὐδώροισι θεοῦ ζώοντος ἀρωγαῖς; for a German translation see Otto Veh, *Prokop Bauten. Bescrheibung der Hagia Sophia*, trans. Otto Veh (Munich: Heimeran, 1977). The Pharos of Alexandria was believed to be the oldest lighthouse in the world. R. J. Forbes, *Studies in Ancient Technology: Light*, vol. VI (Leiden, 1966), 182–5.

58 Verity Platt convincingly argues for the connection of light, viewing and the quest for wisdom in context of Philostratus' *Life of Apollonius of Tyana*. Platt (2009).

splendour as well as the spiritual and epistemological significance of the church of Hagia Sophia. This is further exemplified in Paul the Silentiary's use of the term *noein* that implies both sensuous as well as intellectual perception whenever the audience is invited to *see*.[59] By inviting his audience to see *and* apprehend, Paul encourages his audience to look beyond the materiality of Hagia Sophia and to grasp the epiphanic character of the edifice. Hagia Sophia becomes the material manifestation of divine revelation. The process of this revelation and transformation through sight is spelled out in Procopius' statement that 'whenever anyone enters this church to pray … his mind is lifted up toward God and exalted, feeling that He cannot be far away, but must especially love to dwell in this place which He has chosen'.[60] On account of an ever-present divine immanence, the edifice was understood to be endowed with an anagogical capacity in the Neoplatonic sense, whereby the divine was made accessible through the material reality of the edifice. The sixth-century Byzantine viewer saw the presence of the divine in the physical light that pervaded the interior and that created the impression of an active force, representing the divine torch that guides the faithful (and the sea farer).[61] Just as light, so too is the divine recognised as an intrinsic part of Hagia Sophia's very fabric and beauty.

The central meaning brought out by both ekphraseis is the manifestation of the immaterial divine essence in the luminous aesthetic beauty of Hagia Sophia. They make explicit what is implicit in the physical nature of the church. The material reality of the viewer's ordinary world is transcended through the mediation of the ekphrastic language and the imagery of light.[62] The visual (aesthetic) experience of the monument gives rise to a deeper religious and by extension philosophical understanding.[63] The initial reaction is one of confusion (*aporia*), followed by the ekphrastically guided (intelligent) viewing experience that eventually results in the recognition of divine immanence in the visible shape of light. This phenomenological process is mirrored in the ekphrastic accounts of Hagia Sophia. At the beginning of his description, Procopius comments on how Hagia Sophia's beauty is simply overwhelming and altogether incredible, while Paul the Silentiary adopts the role of a confused poet, asking 'Whither am I driven?' twice interrupting his narrative.[64] This sense of *aporia* neatly ties into the rhetorical tradition of

[59] For example Silentiary verses 389, 417, 532, 609, 621, 846; Macrides and Magdalino (1988), 60.

[60] Procopius I.1.61–62: ὁπηνίκα δέ τις εὐξόμενος ἐς αὐτὸ ἴοι, ξυνίησι μὲν εὐθὺς ὡς οὐκ ἀνθρωπείᾳ δυνάμει ἢ τέχνῃ, ἀλλὰ θεοῦ ῥοπῇ τὸ ἔργον τοῦτο ἀποτετόρνευται· ὁ νοῦς δέ οἱ πρὸς τὸν θεὸν ἐπαιρόμενος ἀεροβατεῖ, οὐ μακράν που ἡγούμενος αὐτὸν εἶναι, ἀλλ' ἐμφιλοχωρεῖν μάλιστα οἷς αὐτὸς εἵλετο.

[61] Bell (2009), 93–4; Elsner (2007), 48–9.

[62] Webb (1999), 68–70.

[63] For an excellent discussion of the connection between vision and knowledge in context of ekphrasis see Platt (2009).

[64] Procopius I.1.27; Silentiary verses 444, 755.

acknowledging the limitations of language to capture a visual experience.[65] Language, according to Paul the Silentiary, must necessarily fall short of the perfection of Hagia Sophia, but language, he explains, can nonetheless provide a useful commentary.[66] Literary commentaries can promote informed viewing, without which the experience of Hagia Sophia would remain elusive. Neither language nor sensuous perception on its own suffices to adequately comprehend the beauty of Hagia Sophia. Instead, textual exegesis complements the visual experience and *vice versa*. Only the combination of word and vision adequately communicates the underlying religious and epistemological dimensions of the Great Church and provides the basis for the recognition of divine immanence.

The experience of Hagia Sophia inspired indescribable wonder (*thauma*) in the sixth-century beholder, and it is this marvel that the two ekphraseis are trying to convey.[67] Traditionally *thauma* anticipates the moment of divine epiphany, and *thauma* is the origin of philosophy in the quest for truth and knowledge.[68] As a key ekphrastic category, the concept of *thauma* had often been employed for natural phenomena.[69] In the case of Hagia Sophia, *thauma* is caused by a work of art that rivals and surpasses in beauty and luminosity nature, and even heaven. The edifice is said to match the sky and to outshine the light of the sun, and while everybody would soon get tired of looking at the heaven, craving for the colours of the world, the beauty of Hagia Sophia is such that no one would ever have a surfeit.[70] By comparing the building to nature and the divine creation, the two ekphraseis highlight the cosmological sublime quality of the edifice.[71] This intimate connection with nature and the sublime elevates the church of Hagia Sophia as a work of art onto an ontological level within the hierarchy of being similar to, if not higher than, nature, acknowledging once more the symbolic and anagogic function of the church.

The impression of the sublime is underscored by the inadequacy of the human mind to fully grasp the architectural marvel, because Hagia Sophia really

---

65 As Elsner has pointed out, Achilles Tatios found himself 'dazed and dissatisfied by the marvel of a spectacle on which his eyes can never comfortably rest'. Elsner (2007), 40.

66 Silentiary verses 95–125.

67 For example, Silentiary verses 201, 392, 399, 447, 807; Procopius I.1.27, 33, 60.

68 Andrea Wilson Nightingale, *Spectacles of Truth in Classical Greek Philosophy: Theoria in its Cultural Context* (Cambridge and New York: Cambridge University Press, 2004), 12, 253–4; Verity Platt, *Facing the Gods: Epiphany and Representation in Graeco-Roman Art, Literature and Religion* (Cambridge: Cambridge University Press, 2011), 64.

69 For example, in Posidippus' ekphrastic epigrams, see e.g. Peter Bing, 'The politics and poetics of geography in the Milan Posidippus section one: On stones (AB 1–20)', in *The New Posidippus: A Hellenistic Poetry Book*, ed. Kathryn Gutzwiller (Oxford: Oxford University Press, 2005).

70 Silentiary verses 286–300; Procopius I.1.27–30, 61–63.

71 According to Longinus, 'art is only perfect when it looks like nature'. Longinus, *On the Sublime*, 22; for a discussion of the technique to achieve the sublime, see Ulrich J. Beil, 'Rhetorische "Phantasia": Ein Beitrag zur Archäologie des Erhabenen', *Arcadia* 28 (1993); Timothy M. Costelloe, *The Sublime: From Antiquity to the Present* (Cambridge: Cambridge University Press, 2012), 251–4.

is beyond description and beyond human comprehension. Procopius is quite specific about this, defining the building as a 'bewildering sight (ὄψιν ἀμηχανίᾳ)', which implies that there is no natural explanation that could do justice to the effect of the building on the beholder.[72] This repeated wonder of Hagia Sophia that cannot be expressed in human terms serves as a constant reminder that the church cannot be perceived by the senses alone and that the visual experience cannot be translated into intelligible language, thus contributing to the sense of the sublime. The aim of both ekphraseis is to make accessible the in-expressible nature of the sacred space by depicting it as a sight that transcends common human experience and that testifies to divine immanence.[73]

The ideology of vision and divine revelation coalesces around the image and metaphors of light. Scattered throughout the two texts are numerous references to the visual appeal of light in the form of natural and artificial light, and particularly the light that is reflected from the colourful surfaces or inherent in the brilliance of the colours themselves. Procopius even claims that the admission of sufficient natural light had determined the layout and precariousness of the original dome.[74] However, the aesthetic appreciation of light was not the only factor. Rather, the contemporary descriptions recognise above all a spiritual and epistemological dimension in the phenomenon of light. Justinian's ingenuity, for example, is explained through divine illumination that endowed him with a clear intellect.[75] It is through the abundance of light ever present within Hagia Sophia that the mind is lifted up and transcended. The brightness of the building represents the divine light that shines for all, drives out sorrow and guides the seafarer to reach a safe haven. In this sense, the aesthetic (visual) appreciation of light exhibited in the two ekphraseis is intimately linked to a series of beliefs, conventions and expectations through which we can gain a sense of how the church of Hagia Sophia was perceived in the sixth century.[76] The building embodies a sense of light that transcends the aesthetic experience of the edifice and transfigures the sacred space into a self-contained divine reality. The aesthetic significance of light is intrinsically grounded in its metaphysical association with the divine. As such, physical light, transformed through the edifice, reflects the immaterial cause and source of all being and, in juxtaposition with the church of Hagia Sophia, operates as a symbol for the quest for wisdom and the perception of the divine. It is no coincidence, so Procopius insists, that the people of Byzantium call the church Sophia, which is the most appropriate epithet (ἐπώνυμος) for God and thus

72 Procopius I.1.49; Rousseau (1998), 122.

73 Webb (1999).

74 Procopius, I.1.41–43.

75 For example, Procopius I.1.24–25, 71; Silentiary verse 300. Zaga Gavrilovic, 'Divine wisdom as part of Byzantine imperial ideology: Research into the artistic interpretations of the theme of medieval Serbia', *Zograf* 11 (1982): 45.

76 Porter aptly discusses the interrelation of aesthetic appreciation and social processes and conventions. James I. Porter, *The Origins of Aesthetic Thought in Ancient Greece: Matter, Sensation, and Experience* (Cambridge: Cambridge University Press, 2010), 13–15, 40.

the most befitting name for the church that is suffused with light and a place where God loves to dwell.[77]

The idea of the divine reflected in these early Byzantine sources is deeply rooted in the belief that there is much that escapes human understanding.[78] This is what the architecture and interior decoration of Hagia Sophia stand for and what the two ekphraseis eloquently mirror. The light-suffused ecclesiastical space creates a sense of the unknown, of something that the human mind cannot fully grasp. Procopius and Paul the Silentiary turn this notion of incomprehension into a rhetorical discourse that fulfils a dual purpose. Through the careful collection and selection of visual impressions, they construct an image of Hagia Sophia that is as much ideological as it is factual. The ekphraseis, by reflecting on the impression of the church as a whole, offer a framework for how the spectator is to relate to the sacred building. The authors take their audience from the material to the immaterial divine that inhabits the architectural structure of Hagia Sophia. The ecclesiastical space is a place where the divine becomes manifest in the form of light, not simply in the form of the physical light of the sun, but light transformed through the mediation of Hagia Sophia as it interacts with the architecture and is reflected off the surfaces. The architectural structure and interior decoration of Hagia Sophia are such that by sublimating their material nature they transcend human experience.[79] It is not any specific material aspect of the building alone that is associated with a transformative potential. Instead, it is the experience of the sacred space as a whole infused with light and divine immanence that has the capacity to lead the soul upward and present a glimpse of the divine mysteries. Viewing Hagia Sophia through sixth-century eyes is to succumb to this aesthetics of light grounded in an ideology of vision that allows for uncertainties and that requires the intellectual engagement of the viewer's mind.[80] The visual and the intellectual are thus merged in order to reach beyond mere surface appearances and to open up for spiritual and philosophical contemplation of the divine immanence manifest in the material reality of Hagia Sophia.

Making Listeners into Spectators – The Concept of Enargeia

Through their rhetorical descriptions, Procopius and Paul the Silentiary present us with an ideology of vision and visualisation that problematises the

[77] Procopius I.1.21; Cameron does not agree that this statement reflects the significance of the name. However, it is part of the argument of this book that the name *Sophia* is programmatic. Averil Cameron, 'Procopius and the church of St. Sophia', *Harvard Theological Review* 58 (1965, Variorum Reprints 1981).

[78] Franses (2003); V. Lossky, *The Mystical Theology of the Eastern Church* (Crestwood, NY: St. Vladimir's Seminary Press, 1976), 23–43.

[79] Webb (1999), 69.

[80] Robert S. Nelson, 'To say and to see: Ekphrasis and vision in Byzantium', in *Visuality Before and Beyond the Renaissance*, ed. Robert S. Nelson (Cambridge: Cambridge University Press, 2000).

representation and perception of the divine.[81] Extraordinarily, the ekphrastic representations of Hagia Sophia hint at the revelatory potential of the building through the faculty of sight. Perceiving the divine through sight, seeing what in Byzantine belief cannot be seen, seems paradoxical. Yet, this paradox is resolved through the image of light that animates and transcends the material reality of the edifice, and in so doing links visual perception with the spiritual. The sense of divine immanence and transcendence is transmitted from the physical light of the sun or the light of the candles and oil lamps, transformed through the building's architectural structure and decoration, perceived through the eyes of the beholder and grasped by the minds of those who have learnt to view intelligently with the help of the ekphraseis. By their very nature as a rhetorical device, their use of visual images and the evocations of the conceptual properties of the divine, the ekphraseis directly express a series of Byzantine assumptions and expectations as to how to acquire insights into the 'sacred mysteries' of the divine. Since ekphraseis acted upon the mind of the audience by contriving mental images through the power of language, an ekphrastic account is not only a rhetorical exercise but also a reflection of ancient visuality and psychology.[82] Understanding the rhetorical and literary techniques employed in an ekphrasis can therefore add a crucial psychological dimension to the study of aesthetics in that they touch upon some of the most basic questions of sensation and perception.

According to first- to fourth-century CE rhetorical handbooks (the so-called *progymnasmata*), key to an ekphrasis is clarity (σαφήνεια) and vividness (ἐνάργεια), in order to visualise what is described without lingering over useless (ἀχρεῖος) aspects.[83] This notion of ekphrasis points to some crucial issues of ancient theories about visualisation, imagination and epistemology. Unlike a modern technical description of a work of art, for example, an ekphrasis implicates the audience in the experience of the subject matter by contextualising it and giving a full account that goes far beyond what is technically visible.[84] The defining aspect that distinguishes an ekphrasis from narration (*diegesis*) is that of vividness (*enargeia*).[85]

81 For an excellent discussion of the iconoclastic debate revolving around the visualisation of the divine and how it implicates the viewer, see Charles Barber, *Figure and Likeness: On the Limits of Representation in Byzantine Iconoclasm* (Oxford and Princeton, NJ: Princeton University Press, 2002); Hans Belting, *Bild und Kult: Eine Geschichte des Bildes vor dem Zeitalter der Kunst* (Munich: C.H. Beck, 1991), Chapter 8.

82 Webb (2009), 5, 10, 27.

83 Elsner (1995); Friedländer (1912); James and Webb (1991); Jenkins (1963); Webb (2009), 198. The *progymnasmata* that survive are of Aelius Theon (first century CE), ps.-Hermogenes (possibly third century CE), Aphthonios (late fourth century CE), and Nikolaos Rhetor (fifth century CE).

84 Elsner (1995); Webb (1999).

85 Sandrine Dubel, '*Ekphrasis* et *enargeia*: la description antique comme parcours', in *Dire l'évidence (philosophie et rhétorique antiques): actes du colloque de Créteil et de Paris (24–25 mars 1995)*, ed. Carlos Lévy and Laurent Pernot (Paris: L'Harmattan,1997), 254; Webb (2009), 87–106.

Unfortunately, the *progymnasmata* do not give any information about how *enargeia* is attained.[86] As a concept, however, *enargeia* had been vital in rhetorical theory since the time of Aristotle in the form of πρὸ ὀμμάτων ποιεῖ. In the discussion of metaphor in his *Rhetoric*, Aristotle claims explicitly that animated subjects appear more vivid (πρὸ ὀμμάτων).[87] Hence, the concept of *enargeia* seems to have been closely associated with movement and its rendering of space through time.[88] Movement and animation, as we have already seen, are central themes in both ekphraseis of Hagia Sophia, and this impression of animated matter was achieved mainly through the use of images of light. The very nature of light is such that its effects are temporal, recapitulating the temporality of the aesthetic experience of Hagia Sophia. In this sense, the rhetorical (ekphrastic) representation of Hagia Sophia is an imitation of the visual (artistic) experience of the building, confirming the deep affinity between the visual arts and rhetoric that Sardianos highlighted in his ninth-century commentary on Aphthonios' *progymnasmaton* where he states that '*enargeia* imitates [the actions and effects of] the art of painting'.[89]

For Nikolaos in the fifth century, *enargeia* was particularly relevant to ekphrastic renderings of works of art. Nikolaos' *progymnasmaton* is the only one that makes explicit reference to 'statues, for example, or paintings or things of this sort' as a specific subject matter for ekphrasis. He states that when describing works of art it is important to add reasons (*logismoi*) and emotion (*pathos*) to produce a vivid account.[90] By extension, an ekphrasis is distinguished from a simple exposition of facts through 'those elements that create *enargeia* [and that] bring the subjects of the speech before the eyes and almost make the audience into spectators'.[91] Nikolaos' characterisation of ekphrasis is reminiscent of Quintilian's distinction between a plain statement of facts (*narratio*) and a vivid account related with *enargeia* that is the difference between simply narrating a story and exhibiting a story.[92] Since the discussion of *enargeia* in Quintilian's *Institutio Oratoria* (first century CE) is strikingly similar to the concept of ekphrasis and because the Greek *progymnasmata* fail to give sufficient explanation, it is extremely useful to look at Quintilian's text for additional information.[93] Quintilian insists on the need of *evidentia*

86 *Enargeia* became an essential technical term in Hellenistic literary criticism (second century BCE). Goldhill (2007); Alessandra Manieri, *L'immagine poetica nella teoria degli antichi: phantasia ed enargeia* (Pisa: Istituti editoriali e poligrafici internazionali, 1998), 97–104; Anne Sheppard, 'The role of imagination in aesthetic experience', *Journal of Aesthetic Education* 25 (1991); G. Zanker, 'Enargeia in the ancient criticism of poetry', *Rheinisches Museum für Philologie* 124 (1981).

87 Aristotle, *The Art of Rhetoric*, 3.10.7.

88 Webb (2009), 84–6.

89 Sardianos, *Commentarium*, II.3–6; quoted in Webb (2009), 83.

90 Nikolaos, *Progymnasmata*, 69; quoted and translated in Webb (2009), 203.

91 Webb (1997); Dubel (1997); Nikolaos, *Progymnasmata*, 70, II. 2–3; translated in Webb (2009), 203.

92 Quintilian, VI.2.32.

93 Manieri (1998), 140–49; Webb (2009), 72–4.

'which the Greeks call *enargeia* ... when a truth requires not merely to be told, but to some extent obtruded'.[94] Elsewhere, he explains how *enargeia* results from *phantasia*, which are 'images of absent things [that] are presented to our imagination with such extreme vividness that they seem actually to be before our very eyes'.[95] For Quintilian, the effective use of *enargeia* has the power to penetrate the emotions of the audience.[96] As a rhetorical device, *enargeia* aims at exploiting the emotions of the audience by activating its imagination through descriptive discourse and thereby creating the illusion of seeing rather than listening to a technical description of it. If employed successfully, the audience will be fully persuaded by the account independent of the facts, 'bypassing the intellect and critical faculties'.[97] The implication is that *enargeia* appeals to the non-rational faculties and reaches deeply into the audience's minds. For this reason a vivid (ekphrastic) narrative is more about persuasiveness and emotional effects than it is about factual exposition of objective truths or material realities.

The question of truth is quite a different matter, as Quintilian himself notes, and false things can appear truthful especially when related persuasively by means of *enargeia*.[98] An account is credible, according to Quintilian, as long as it obeys the laws of nature and follows a 'natural sequence and coherence'.[99] This notion of natural credibility extends to both true and false statements. The purpose of an ekphrasis was to represent its subject matter credibly and convincingly. To be credible and convincing, the rhetorician had to engage imagery familiar and acceptable to his audience. In other words, the ekphrasis needed to conform to cultural conventions and the audience's expectations.[100] An ekphrasis can in turn offer insights into these conventions and expectations as well as the concepts of verisimilitude. For example, Byzantine descriptions of works of art usually emphasise the realism of the art and appear to lack any awareness of the art's increasing tendency towards abstraction. The reason for this inconsistency between artistic production and its description during the Byzantine period was generally associated with the fact that Byzantine ekphraseis followed a literary tradition and essentially copied ancient models, without paying much attention to the work of art at hand.[101] Even though Byzantine ekphraseis do indeed frequently employ highly rhetorical

94 Quintilian, IV.2.63–64: sunt qui adiiciant his evidentiam, quae ἐνάργεια Graece vocatur ... cum quid veri non dicendum, sed quodammodo etiam ostendendum est.

95 Quintilian, VI.2.29: quas φαντασίας ... per quas imagines rerum absentium ita repraesentantur animo, ut eas cernere oculis ac praesentes habere videamur.

96 Quintilian, VIII.3.67.

97 Goldhill (2007), 7.

98 Quintilian, IV.2.34 and IV.2.64–65.

99 Quintilian, IV.2.52–53.

100 Ruth Webb, 'Imagination and the arousal of the emotions in Greco-Roman rhetoric', in *The Passions in Roman Thought and Literature*, ed. Susanna Morton Braund and Christopher Gill (Cambridge: Cambridge University Press, 1997); Webb (2007); Webb (2009), 122.

101 Cyril Mango, 'Antique statuary and the Byzantine beholder', *DOP* 17 (1963): 65–6.

clichés and ancient quotations, these topoi reveal the type of reality that both the ekphrasis as well as the work of art are grounded in.[102] The discrepancy between the increasingly abstract and symbolic nature of early Byzantine art and its continuous description as realistic and true to life can be explained through a concept of reality that was not founded on the material world alone but that was an expression of a divine reality. This is why an ekphrasis that imitates the process of perception and serves to elucidate aspects of a work of art whose meaning and significance are not necessarily visible may not be immediately accessible to the modern beholder.[103]

In early Byzantine belief, the phenomenal universe was simply a self-revelation of the divine, and only the divine was considered real being. Hence, the material reality was no more than a reflection of this divine reality that is beyond human perception and comprehension.[104] The ekphrastic accounts of Procopius and Paul the Silentiary, for example, testify to the idea of universal divine immanence as an intrinsic part of the beauty and architectural structure of Hagia Sophia. Its sacred space filled with light was the visible manifestation of divine light through which Hagia Sophia provided direct access to the divine reality. As we have seen in Procopius' ekphrasis, the edifice inspired the soul's ascent to the divine, a process that the Neoplatonists call *anagoge*.[105] The verbal (ekphrastic) commentary to the visual (aesthetic) experience accordingly reaches beyond the surface appearances and appeals to the faculty of the mind. This imaginative visualisation ultimately leads to a higher (truer) reality that is different from the materiality of this world. In practical terms, this means a four-step sequence starting with the formation of a mental image in the artist's mind, its realisation in the work of art, the verbalisation of this image by the rhetorician who transmits the image to an audience, which in turn prompts the construction of yet another image in the mind of the audience. When applied to Hagia Sophia, this process corresponds to the initial divine inspiration (illumination) of the emperor, the conversion of this idea into the architectural masterpiece that is Hagia Sophia and its ekphrastic rendition by Paul the Silentiary and Procopius that aim to evoke these images in the minds of their audiences. These mental images are *phantasiai*.[106] *Phantasia* here may be defined as imagination or intuitive insight.[107] As a technical rhetorical term *phantasia* was an essential element of

---

[102] Elsner (1995), 22–8; Jaś Elsner, *Roman Eyes: Visuality and Subjectivity in Art and Text* (Princeton, NJ: Princeton University Press, 2007); Henry Maguire, 'Truth and convention in Byzantine descriptions of works of art', *DOP* 28 (1974).

[103] Webb (1997); Webb (1999); Webb (2009), 127–8.

[104] Moshe Barasch, *Icon: Studies in the History of an Idea* (London and New York: New York University Press, 1992), 158–81.

[105] Pseudo-Dionysius, *DN*, 705B; *EH*, 373B; *CH*, 124A.

[106] 'images of absent things' according to Quintilian, VI.2.29–32.

[107] For example, Platt (2009); Gerard Watson, *Phantasia in Classical Thought* (Galway: Galway University Press, 1988), Chapter 4.

enargeia that enabled the audience to visualise the unseen. Since an ekphrasis tries to capture and verbalise the *phantasia* embodied in a work of art, it is possible to reconstruct the *phantasia* that gave rise to the ekphrasis in the first place.[108] The sixth-century *phantasia* that underlies the church of Hagia Sophia and its ekphraseis is one of divine splendour and beauty constructed through colour and light. To the Byzantine beholder, it is a vision of the heavenly realm that is 'pure gold, clear as glass' and that 'has no need of sun or moon to shine on it, for the glory of God is its light'.[109]

Phantasia and the Perception of the Divine

Phantasia in late antiquity had multi-layered meanings that contribute important moral and epistemological dimensions to the assessment of ekphraseis and by extension the work of art under consideration. Since these *phantasiai* or mental images underlie the creative process as well as the aesthetic and psychological effect of a work of art, they are a vital source for how art was perceived and for the art's intrinsic aesthetic values.[110] The concept of *phantasia* is furthermore closely related to rhetorical *enargeia* as evident from Longinus' work *On the Sublime* (*Peri Hypsous*) dated possibly to the first century CE.[111] Here, Longinus explains that 'the term phantasia is used generally for anything that in any way suggests a thought productive of speech; but the word has also come into fashion for the situation in which enthusiasm and emotion make the speaker see what he is saying and bring it visually before his audience'.[112] *Phantasiai* then are mental images that exploit the emotional and excitatory sensibilities of the audience in order to create *enargeia*. Here, Longinus' distinction between the rhetorical and the poetical use of *phantasia* is important. Although both aim at emotion (*pathos*) and excitement (*kinesis*), poetry aims at astonishment (*ekplexis*), while the intended effect of *phantasia* in prose is vividness (*enargeia*). What is more, in prose *phantasia* has the power not merely to persuade but to enslave (*douloutai*) the audience when it is

108 Elsner (1995), 26–7; Webb (2009), 96–7.

109 Revelation 21:18 and 22.

110 Philostratus in the early third century, for example, claims that *phantasia* is the creative force of skilled craftsmen. Ella Birmelin, 'Die kunsttheoretischen Gedanken in Philostrats Appolonios', *Philologus* 88 (1933); Göran Sörbom, 'The classical concept of mimesis', in *A Companion To Art Theory*, ed. Paul Smith and Carolyn Wilde (Oxford: Blackwell Publishing Company, 2002).

111 Longinus, sometimes called Pseudo-Longinus, is in fact the anonymous author of *On the Sublime* (*Peri Hypsous*). It is traditionally ascribed to the first century CE, but could date as late as the third century CE. Donald Andrew Russell, *'Longinus' On the Sublime* (Oxford: Clarendon Press, 1964), XXII ff.

112 Longinus, *On the Sublime*, 15.1: καλεῖται μὲν γὰρ κοινῶς φαντασία πᾶν τὸ ὁπωσοῦν ἐννόημα γεννητικὸν λόγου παριστάμενον: ἤδη δ ἐπὶ τούτων κεκράτηκε τοὔνομα, ὅταν ἃ λέγεις ὑπ ἐνθουσιασμοῦ καὶ πάθους βλέπειν δοκῇς καὶ ὑπ ὄψιν τιθῇς τοῖς ἀκούουσιν. Translated in Goldhill (2007), 6.

paired with factual argument.[113] In this case, the orator sways the audience into believing that they are not simply listening to a plain statement of facts but that they actually witness the event themselves. Longinus' definition of *phantasia* to stir up a strong psychological experience through visualisation is conspicuously similar to what an ekphrasis was meant to achieve. It is a rhetorical device that basically seeks to emotionally manipulate the audience.

Phantasia was not only a literary tool exploited to control the emotional response of the audience. In philosophical contexts, *phantasia* was considered a criterion of truth that was intimately connected to Stoic epistemology.[114] Intriguingly, this philosophical connotation of *phantasia* coheres with one of the definitions of *enargeia* found in the tenth-century Byzantine dictionary of the *Suda*. Here, μετ' ἐναργείας is given as μετ' ἀληθείας, meaning 'with truth' (*cum veritate*).[115] To understand how and why rhetorical *enargeia* operated in moral and epistemological terms and how this relates to the aesthetic aspects of representation, the role of *phantasia* in the process of human thought and cognition is revealing. In the tradition of Stoic epistemology, knowledge had its origin in the senses (*aisthesis*) but required *phantasia* to enable the apprehension of these sense perceptions.[116] The Stoic *phantasia* was understood as an imprint of an external object on the soul. Human beings accumulate these impressions throughout their lifetime and build up a repertoire of memory images with which newly incoming stimuli can be compared, verified and identified. This enables the capacity to assent or to withhold assent to impressions. From a collection of similar individual impressions a more general, systematic whole can then be constructed.[117] The type of *phantasia* that involves assent and the grasping of sense-impressions is defined as *phantasia kataleptika* (cognitive *phantasia*). These cognitive *phantasiai* are the foundation of cognition (that is assent to a cognitive *phantasia*) and eventually of episteme (that is a firm cognition that is unchangeable by reason).[118] For the Stoics, *phantasia* was a criterion of truth because it originated from an external object that it reproduced with absolute accuracy, 'imprinted seal-fashion and stamped upon the mind'.[119] *Phantasia* was true for the simple reason that it was self-evident (*enargeia*) and known through itself (*autothen*) because a *phantasia* was

113 Longinus, *On the Sublime*, 15.2 and 15.9.

114 Goldhill (2007); Watson (1988), particularly Chapters 3 and 4.

115 Suda, Adler entry mu 761; Papaioannou argues that this is the definition how *enargeia* is predominantly used in most middle Byzantine writing. Stratis Papaioannou, 'Byzantine enargeia and theories of representation', *Byzantinoslavica – Revue internationale des Études Byzantines* 69 (2011).

116 Anna-Maria Ioppolo, 'Presentation and assent: A physical and cognitive problem in early Stoicism', *The Classical Quarterly* 40 (1990); Manieri (1998), 43–7; Watson (1988), 44–7.

117 Diogenes Laertius, VII.1.46–54; Jeffrey Barnouw, *Propositional Perception: Phantasia, Predication, and Sign in Plato, Aristotle, and the Stoics* (Lanham, MD: University Press of America, 2002), 189.

118 Sextus Empiricus, LS 41C/M 7.151; Ioppolo (1990), 436–7.

119 Diogenes Laertius, VII.46, VII.49; Gisela Striker, *Essays on Hellenistic Epistemology and Ethics* (Cambridge and New York: Cambridge University Press, 1996), 51.

at once the passive imprint of sense perception on the soul and the active operation of the mind that interpreted this impression.[120] Hence, cognitive *phantasia* were unmediated and not prone to distortions.

This is exactly the ekphrastic claim to truth, namely to relate the truth of the aesthetic and, in the case of Hagia Sophia, the spiritual experience through *enargeia* in an unmediated fashion rather than through reasoning and technical descriptions. It is in this tradition that *enargeia* was used for theological purposes. This is, for instance, expressed in Philo of Alexandria's comment that God is 'only perceived through *enargeia* not through discursive argument (λόγον ἀπόδειξει)'.[121] One of the Byzantine rhetorical techniques to visualise something that by itself escapes any visual or verbal representation (for example the divine or, in fact, the beauty of Hagia Sophia) is to acknowledge these very limitations of the human rational faculties. As Warnock explained, it is this 'very inadequacy to form an image of the idea suggested by the object which constitutes our sense of the sublime'.[122] Procopius and Paul the Silentiary frequently revert to the trope of *aporia* in order to express the conceptual challenges posed by the ineffable wonder of Hagia Sophia that leaves the beholder, the authors included, overwhelmed and speechless.[123] Indeed, the literary trope of *aporia* attests to the metaphysical and sublime dimension of the building's beauty that, similar to the divine, cannot be perceived by the human mind and cannot be described in normal meaningful language (λογική).[124] This reinforces the divine quality of Hagia Sophia and marks the integration of the aesthetic experience with its spiritual and epistemological operations. The unspeakable beauty of Hagia Sophia literally paves the way for the pursuit of *Sophia* in the widest sense.

Given the theories of *phantasia* and *enargeia* within the framework of ekphrastic representation and perception, how can *enargeia* (vividness/truth) be achieved when relating something that does not arise directly from sense perceptions? In other words, how can an image of divine immanence and transcendence be created in the mind of the listener? The notion of *phantasiai ouk aisthetikai*, meaning images without sense perception of any existing external source that are brought about instead through reason (*noesis*),[125] suggest a possible solution for the rhetorical representation of the unseen and ineffable. These *phantasiai ouk aisthetikai* were indirectly formed by way of *metabasis* that works through resemblance, analogy, transposition, and

120 Sextus Empiricus, M 7.257; Ioppolo (1990); Barnouw (2002), 167, 192.

121 Philo of Alexandria, *De Posteritate Caini*, 167; Papaioannou (2011).

122 Sheppard (1991); Mary Warnock, *Imagination* (Berkeley and Los Angeles, CA: University of California Press, 1976), 57.

123 Elsner (2007), 40–43.

124 Being *logike* (i.e. expressible in meaningful language) is central to the Stoic definition of *phantasia*. Goldhill (2007); Watson (1988), particularly Chapters 3 and 4.

125 Manieri (1998).

composition or by contrariety.[126] *Phantasia's* philosophical and rhetorical significance as a representation of something that is conceived by *metabasis* is synthesised most clearly by Philostratus in the early third century CE. In the *Life of Apollonius of Tyana*, Philostratus contrasts artistic *mimesis* with *phantasia*, claiming that *phantasia* 'is wiser than *mimesis*. For imitation will represent that which can be seen with the eyes while *phantasia* will represent that which cannot, for the latter proceeds with reality as its basis'.[127] Detaching *phantasia* from *aisthesis* (sense-perception), Philostratus claims that *phantasia* has access to a reality beyond the world of common sense.[128] *Phantasia* independent of sensation helps to explain two basic ideas about visualising or thinking the unseen and about *phantasia's* rhetorical claim to truth and reality. Firstly, these *phantasiai ouk aisthetikai*, albeit not true to the material reality of any external object, were grounded in an intersubjective reality. They reflected cultural memory, common knowledge and the expectation of their target audience. Secondly, if *phantasiai* of the unseen can be constructed through *metabasis* then it is possible to construct an epiphanic vision of the divine by the same means. As Verity Platt suggested, *phantasia* is 'the ultimate form of *theoria* – the power of the mind itself to visualise and communicate with God'.[129] Still, to construct *phantasiai ouk aisthetikai*, the human mind ultimately relies on the sphere of sensation. Any imaginative perception starts with the collection of memory images of material objects that can be perceived by the senses and that leave an impression upon the soul.

These philosophical concepts of *phantasia* have far-reaching consequences for the use and interpretation of late antique ekphraseis that tap into the depository of memory images of their audience to create a simulacrum of the act of perception. As Ruth Webb observed, ekphrasis imitates the act of seeing and does not attempt a mimesis of the object itself.[130] Accordingly, the ekphraseis of Paul the Silentiary and Procopius operated within the context of aesthetic experience and the *phantasiai* associated with these experiences. The activation of a specific imagination through their ekphraseis bears witness to the aesthetic as well as psychological effects of Hagia Sophia on the sixth-century beholder. The ekphraseis of the sacred space of Hagia Sophia therefore bridge the gap between perceptual aesthetics and its spiritual and epistemological potential. Paul and Procopius exploit perceptual experiences to target the metaphysical dimension underlying the ecclesiastical edifice, visualising divine immanence and transcendence through analogy (*metabasis*) to the physical light that pervades the sacred space. The spiritual and

[126] Diogenes Laertius, VII.51–53; Barnouw (2002), 192; Ioppolo (1990); Watson (1988), 48–50.

[127] Philostratus, *Life of Apollonius of Tyana*, VI.19; translated in Elsner (1995), 26; Watson (1988), Chapter 4.

[128] Elsner (1995), 26–7.

[129] Platt (2009), 151–2.

[130] Pentcheva (2011); Webb (2009), 107–30.

epistemological quality of the building is translated into the language of *enargeia* through metaphors and the phenomena of light. Light, in the form of sunlight as well as artificial light, is described as an active force that illuminates the space and enlightens the beholder in an aesthetic as well as an epistemological sense. Using the image of φωτισμός (illumination/light), Paul the Silentiary and Procopius impress the two-fold connotations of illumination and enlightenment upon their audience. The ecclesiastical interior suffused with light represents an epiphanic vision of divine beauty and divine light that is said to even outshine the light of the sun.[131] Light even becomes the cause of salvation when it literally makes the darkness flee.[132] The emphasis on the image of light transcends the materiality of Hagia Sophia and epitomises the *theoretic* process, the quest for the supreme form of wisdom and metaphysical truth.[133] Evoking the traditional associations between light and episteme as well as between light and the divine, Procopius and Paul the Silentiary invite their audiences to look beyond the merely visible materiality of Hagia Sophia and to contemplate the building's performative nature. Viewing its light-filled sacred space is ultimately an activity of *theoria,* a means of reaching spiritually higher grounds. The building's awe-inspiring quality frequently emphasised in the two ekphraseis creates a feeling of permanent divine presence. Both authors engage rhetorical techniques to construct vivid mental images to make the building come alive in the minds of their audience.

By appealing to the imaginative faculty, ekphrasis mirrors human perception. The evidence from the rhetorical handbooks and related works emphasises the need for vividness (*enargeia*) through mental visualisation (*phantasia*) in order to transform the listeners into spectators. It is the ekphrasis' highly rhetorical nature and its close affinity with the concepts of *phantasia* and *enargeia* that offers insights into Byzantine theories of representation (mental and real). What is more, the rhetorical techniques *enargeia* and *phantasia* are culture-specific. Consequently, an ekphrasis reflects cultural memory and expectations as well as beliefs about the world and reality. The verisimilitude of an ekphrasis is consistent with the truths and cultural values shared by the artist, the author and the audience. It is therefore a vital source not only for how Byzantine art was viewed and its aesthetic values, but also for the cultural identity of its people. The significance of light (*photismos*) in the sense of illumination and enlightenment is evident from both sixth-century descriptions of Hagia Sophia. It seems feasible to assume that the dedication of Hagia Sophia to Holy Wisdom was an expression of this twofold implication of light. That this interpretation is genuine is testified memorably by an anonymous inauguration hymn (*kontakion*) that, like Paul

131 Procopius I.1.27–30.

132 Silentiary verse 838.

133 This is in fact the definition of *theoria* in ancient Greek thought. Nightingale (2004), Introduction; Platt (2009).

the Silentiary's poem, was composed for the celebration of Hagia Sophia's rededication on 24 December 562 CE.

'A Sanctuary of Wisdom'

The *kontakion* entitled τῶν ἐγκαινίων ὁ ὕμνος[134] is generally understood to be the popular counterpart to Paul the Silentiary's intellectual and classicising ekphrasis that had been commissioned for the very same occasion but recited a few days later.[135] The genre of the *kontakion* was introduced into Byzantine liturgy at the beginning of the sixth century to be chanted on special occasions. The themes of the *kontakion* usually pertained to the Bible passages that were being read and thus provide an exegesis of these.[136] The *kontakion* for Hagia Sophia's inauguration has many themes in common with the two ekphraseis. It is, however, much more explicit about the theological and symbolic significance of the Great Church and can thus help to make explicit what is only implicit in the ekphrastic descriptions.[137]

The inauguration hymn of Hagia Sophia follows the general structure of a *kontakion* with eighteen strophes (so-called *oikoi* from the Syriac tradition) preceded by a proemium. The proemium celebrates the building as the dwelling place of the divine that rivals in beauty the heavenly firmament. The chorus line (ἐφύμνιον), 'the life and resurrection of all',[138] connects the proemium with the first *oikos* and concludes every *oikos*.[139] The theme of the incarnation plays an essential role throughout the *kontakion*, repeatedly equating the incarnate figure of Christ with *logos* and *sophia*. The process of incarnation is linked to divine illumination and divine wisdom, all of which is beyond human comprehension. Owing to the Incarnation the '*Logos* consents ... to reside in temples built by hand' (*oikos* 4). Yet, only an architectural masterpiece that 'surpasses the whole of mankind's knowledge of architectural technology' (*oikos* 5) is worthy of God. As the poet asserts, the church of Hagia Sophia is a 'sanctuary of Wisdom' and a 'divine palace' (*oikos* 2), because of the building's architectural pre-eminence, beauty and luminosity. This sentiment is most clearly expressed in the sixth *oikos*, in which the image of light and its relationship with knowledge and wisdom is most fully explored:

134 The *kontakion* was edited by C. A. Trypanis, 'Fourteen early Byzantine cantica', *Wiener Byzantinische Studien* 5 (1968) and translated in Andrew Palmer and Lyn Rodley, 'The inauguration anthem of Hagia Sophia in Edessa: A new edition and translation with historical and architectural notes and a comparison with a contemporary Constantinopolitan kontakion', *BMGS* 12 (1988): 140–44.

135 Macrides and Magdalino (1988), 76–8; Palmer and Rodley (1988), 140–44; Trypanis (1968); Whitby (2000), 47–8.

136 Constantin Floros, 'Das Kontakion. Mit 2 Abbildungen und einem Notenanhang', *Deutsche Vierteljahrsschrift für Literaturwissenschaft und Geistesgeschichte* 34 (1960): 85.

137 Macrides and Magdalino (1988), 76–8.

138 ἡ πάντων ζωή καί ἀνάστασις.

139 Floros (1960), 85.

> This sacred church of Christ evidently outstrips in glory even the firmament above, for it does not offer a lamp of merely sensible light, but the shrine of it bears aloft the divine illumination of the Sun of Truth (τὸν ἥλιον τῆς ἀληθείας) and it is splendidly illumined throughout by day and by night by the rays of the Word of the Spirit (τὸν λόγον τοῦ πνεύματος), through which the eyes of the mind (τὰ ὄμματα τῆς διανοίας) are enlightened (καταυγάζει) by him [who said] 'Let there be light!' God.[140]

In this passage, the beauty of the church of Hagia Sophia is perceived as being superior to the firmament, because it is not only illuminated by the light of the sun but above all by the light of the 'sun of truth' and the transcendent light of the 'word of the spirit'. The author unmistakably sets forth the equation of the physical light within the sacred space and the divine light that enlightens the 'eyes of the mind'. The visual experience of light is thus complemented by the engagement of the faculty of the mind that in turn ascertains the acquisition of a deeper religious (and philosophical) understanding on the part of the faithful. While the ekphrastic accounts of Procopius and Paul the Silentiary anticipated the religious and philosophical implications of Hagia Sophia and the light within, the *kontakion* presents us with a much more elaborate spiritual and epistemological interpretation, unequivocally identifying sensible light with divine illumination.[141] In principle, the *kontakion* follows an ancient tradition of associating light with cognition as well as the experience of aesthetic and moral (spiritual) values.[142] Here, however, light is not a mere metaphor. Rather, the physical light within Hagia Sophia is the divine presence made palpable; it is the perceptible manifestation of the divine essence that pervades the sacred space. The process of epistemology and divine revelation is communicated in aesthetic terms through the beauty of the light-filled space of Hagia Sophia.

Continuing the theme of light as the source of epistemology, the *kontakion* contrasts the dark 'clouds of human failings (νέφη πταισμάτων)' (*oikos* 8) with the 'spiritual luminaries (φωστῆρας) … of prophets and apostles and teachers … enlightening (καταυγάζοντας) in the night of life those drifting about on the ocean of sin' with the 'lightning (ἀπαστράπτοντας) of their doctrines' (*oikos* 9). The implication of the metaphors of light is clear: the kontakion imbues the image of light with divine wisdom symbolised by the sun of truth that is indicative of life and the salvation of mankind though the agency of the Holy Scriptures. The epiphanic potential of light is contrasted with the evils of the dark waters and the shadows of clouds that signify human

140 Trypanis (1968), 143, translated in Palmer and Rodley (1988), 141.

141 Palmer pointed out the quotation of God's first recorded words at the end of the strophe and the train of thought this reference might have initiated in Byzantium, namely the equation of divine wisdom with the first of God's creations, which in analogy with Proverbs 8.22–31, was the creation of light itself. Palmer and Rodley (1988), 147.

142 Rudolf Bultmann, 'Zur Geschichte der Lichtsymbolik im Altertum', *Philologus* 97 (1948); Dorothy Tarrant, 'Greek metaphors of light', *Classical Quarterly* 10 (1960).

ignorance and perdition. This juxtaposition of divine light and the darkness of human ignorance is suggestive of Gregory of Nyssa's mysticism of the spiritual and epistemological ascent of the soul that follows a path from the darkness of human sin and unknowing into the discursive light of truth and knowledge, which in turn gives way eventually to a mystical divine darkness beyond knowledge.[143] Accordingly, it is precisely through divine illumination manifest in the physical light of the senses that the church of Hagia Sophia has been transformed into 'a worthy dwelling-place of knowledge' (*oikos* 1). The sacred interior of the Great Church suffused with light epitomises divine revelation and the acquisition of wisdom. The nature of Hagia Sophia that is intrinsically luminous is the ideal environment to accommodate the *theoric* experience of raising the spirit to a higher level.

The wisdom and supremacy of the church of Hagia Sophia is developed further throughout the following strophes of the kontakion. The conceptual structure of *oikoi* 7–16 recounts the prophecy and the fulfilment of the Incarnation, beginning with the divine creation (*oikoi* 7–9), Moses' provisional covenant (*oikoi* 10–11), Solomon's wisdom despite the erring traditions of the Israelites (*oikoi* 12–13) and culminating in the wisdom of the Christian faith embodied in the church of Hagia Sophia (*oikoi* 14–16). Strophes 10 and 11 invoke the construction of Moses' provisional tabernacle through Bezalel, who had been 'endowed with the wisdom of God' in order to complete this feat. But as we learn from the twelfth *oikos*, the Incarnation made the tabernacle and the ancient laws redundant. The Byzantine basileus superseded Bezalel as an agent of divine wisdom.[144] It is he who built 'this divinely constructed temple' (*oikos* 12) that 'transcends everything' (*oikos* 14) and that surpasses even the splendours of the temple of Solomon (*oikos* 13), for it is a mirror image of heaven (*oikos* 17). This passage draws a direct parallel between the divine creation of nature and Justinian's 'demiurgic' creation of the architectural masterpiece. The inauguration hymn invites the audience to view Hagia Sophia as a divine creation mediated by the emperor. As such, the kontakion promotes an elaborate imperial ideology similar to that of Procopius' and Paul the Silentiary's ekphraseis.[145] It varies in its approach from the rhetorical treatment of the building, focusing much more on the exegetic significance of the church as a symbol of God's omnipotence and omnipresence.[146]

The notion of God as wisdom is one of the leading themes of the inauguration hymn, and it is consistently linked with the image of light in

[143] Martin Laird, 'Gregory of Nyssa and the mysticism of darkness: A reconsideration', *The Journal of Religion* 79 (1999).

[144] This is the only reference to Justinian in the *kontakion*; compare to Exodus 31, 1–3: And the Lord spoke unto Moses, saying, see I have called by name Bezaleel … and I have filled him with the spirit of God, in wisdom, and in understanding, and in knowledge, and in all manner of workmanship.

[145] Palmer and Rodley recognised this panegyric tendency throughout the hymn. Palmer and Rodley (1988), 144–9.

[146] Macrides and Magdalino (1988), 76–8; Whitby (2000), 48.

terms of a metaphysical analogy. The experience of light is defined in terms of beauty (aesthetic) and in terms of the divine (epistemological, spiritual). Through the constant juxtaposition of the sensible and the intelligible, the kontakion asserts the status of the church of Hagia Sophia as a space of symbolic significance. The images of light evoke specific associations to arouse the notion of a transcendent reality that is reminiscent of the Platonic and Neoplatonic concepts of light and illumination as the source of epistemology. This is why only an exceptionally bright and luminous 'sanctuary of wisdom' (τῆς Σοφίας τὸ ἁγίασμα) satisfies the requirements for a worthy dwelling place of the divine as 'it is not right for the King to enter a rude cave' (*oikos* 2). With this reference to the Platonic cave, the kontakion disposes once and for all with the wisdom of ancient philosophy (the wisdom of words).[147] The final goal of the enlightenment offered through the agency of Hagia Sophia is 'the wisdom of faith' (*oikos* 12) that had been fulfilled in the incarnate Christ.[148] Hagia Sophia is explicitly not a Platonic cave of cognition; instead, it is a *sanctuary of wisdom*.

Conclusion

The kontakion provides the conceptual implications of light in the context of the church of Hagia Sophia in the sixth century. It yokes together light/illumination and wisdom, and in so doing, elucidates the symbolic significance of the theme of light in the two sixth-century ekphraseis. By combining the visual with the intellectual and spiritual, both light and wisdom are metaphors for the complexities of the Christian faith. It is the physical light of the church that guides the faithful towards salvation because it offers some insight into divine wisdom and spiritual reality.

The differences between the ekphraseis and the kontakion can be ascribed to the difference in purpose and in the target audience. Procopius and Paul the Silentiary closely followed classical rhetorical conventions, providing a vivid textual equivalent to the material object. In line with this tradition, they focused on the magnificence and splendour of the building and on the sensuous effects of the sacred space, employing imagery and a classicising style that would have been familiar to their predominantly aristocratic audience. In that the ekphraseis imitate the process of perception and visualisation, they present a vital source for the aesthetic qualities that were appreciated by a Byzantine beholder in the sixth century. The attention paid to the effects of light within Hagia Sophia shows that the building's luminosity was perceived as exceptional and that aesthetic pleasure was derived from this experience

147 I Cor. 1, 17–24.

148 Gavrilovic (1982); John Meyendorff, 'Wisdom – Sophia: Contrasting approaches to a complex theme', *DOP* 41 (1987).

of light. A contemplative perception of divine immanence accompanies the aesthetic appreciation of light and is indicative of a metaphysical notion of light. In its role as an inauguration hymn, the kontakion was aimed at the more common Byzantine viewer and makes much more explicit what is implicit in the ekphraseis. It uses images of light and wisdom to clearly articulate divine qualities that are intrinsic to the design of Hagia Sophia. Through this, it signals the religious symbolism of light and highlights the role of light in the pursuit of an epiphanic viewing experience. The kontakion forges the link between these symbolic implications and the architectural structure of Hagia Sophia, thus relating aesthetic vision to the intellectual or contemplative quest for *Sophia*. The *kontakion* thus lends support to the interpretation of the light in Hagia Sophia as an essential constituent that reflects common aesthetic sensibilities.

The architecture of Hagia Sophia with its luminous interior is seen as the material manifestation of divine wisdom – just as God's wisdom is beyond human comprehension, so too the edifice's architectural technology and luminosity surpass human knowledge. It is truly a sanctuary of wisdom 'wondrous to all who see it'. Light is identified as an essential aesthetic feature in the sensuous experience of the building, but light is also equated with divine wisdom. In early Byzantium wisdom, the good and beauty are divine paradigms that necessarily go together, all of which can be represented in the form of physical light. The experience of light is thus as much aesthetic (in terms of beauty) as it is spiritual and epistemological. The authors of the ekphraseis and the kontakion ultimately seek to portray Hagia Sophia's intelligible content rather than the fabric of the building as such. They literally transform the material reality of the edifice into an object of intellection. This would seem to render the actual edifice secondary. Still, the texts (at least the ekphraseis) convey the experience and perception of Hagia Sophia's sacred space that is inextricably linked with its architectural structure, interior decoration and with light that was conceived as a central aesthetic element of the edifice.[149] The constant reminder of the abundance of light within Hagia Sophia both in the kontakion as well as in the ekphraseis confirms that light was indeed seen as an intrinsic part of the church dedicated to holy wisdom.

[149] Webb has pointed out that in Byzantine ekphraseis the distinction between the sensible and intelligible qualities of the buildings become unimportant. Webb (1999), 53.

2

Animation and Illumination of Hagia Sophia's Architectural Structure

The sixth-century literary sources discussed in Chapter 1 emphasised the dynamic quality of the church of Hagia Sophia and the impression of light within its sacred space. Even though these rhetorical accounts cannot be taken as objective factual descriptions of the edifice, they have important historical value in that these texts record visual experiences and aesthetic responses that the building inspired in its viewers.[1] In constantly drawing the audience's attention to the phenomena of light, the literary sources reinforce the sense of an exceptional presence of light that exceeds purely practical requirements. The clearest evidence that in the sixth century the physical light in sacred buildings was more widely recognised as a potent agent in spiritual as well as metaphysical terms is found in a letter written by Hypatius, archbishop of Ephesus from 531 to about 538 CE and one of emperor Justinian's theological advisors. In a letter addressed to bishop Julian of Atramytium,[2] Hypatius expounds on the use of religious images and sculptures for educational purposes.[3] He states that 'some people are guided even by these [material embellishments] towards the intelligible beauty and from the abundant light in the sanctuaries to the intelligible and immaterial light'.[4] Hypatius reiterates that the divine is beyond visual depiction because 'the divine being is not at all

[1] Henry Maguire, 'Truth and convention in Byzantine descriptions of works of art', *DOP* 28 (1974); Ruth Webb, 'The aesthetics of sacred space: Narrative, metaphor, and motion in ekphraseis of church buildings', *DOP* 53 (1999).

[2] The fragment is transmitted in a manuscript (*Parisinus* gr. 1115, fol. 254v-255v) written in 1276. Franz Diekamp, ed. *Analecta Patristica (Orientalia Christ. Analecta, 117)* (Rome: 1938), 127–9.

[3] Paul J. Alexander, 'Hypatius of Ephesus: A note on image worship in the sixth century', *The Harvard Theological Review* 45 (1952); Jean Gouillard, 'Hypathios d'Ephèse ou du Pseudo-Denys à Théodore Studite', *Revue des études byzantines* 19 (1961).

[4] Adapted from Alexander (1952), 180; Greek text in Hans Georg Thümmel, 'Hypatios von Ephesos und Iulianos von Atramytion zur Bilderfrage', *Byzantinoslavica – Revue internationale des Études Byzantines* 44 (1983): 168 (61–3): ὥς τινων καὶ ἀπὸ τούτων ἐπὶ τὴν νοητὴν εὐπρέπειαν χειραγωγουμένων καὶ ἀπὸ τοῦ κατὰ τὰ ἱερὰ πολλοῦ φωτὸς ἐπὶ τὸ νοητὸν καὶ ἄϋλον φῶς.

identical or the same or similar to any of the existing things'.[5] He nonetheless recognises that the splendour of sacred buildings and above all the visible light within has the potential to enlighten those that cannot learn otherwise (the illiterate).

Even though Hypatius' letter may have been modified in the eighth century in line with the iconophile cause, the overall sentiment, namely that material objects can aid in the contemplation of the spiritual and the ascent of the soul (*anagoge*), does certainly correspond to the Neoplatonic thought of the sixth century and earlier.[6] A similar apology for the use of images, for instance, is the subject of a cycle of sixth-century epigrams by Agathias Scholasticus of Myrina (531/2–c. 580)[7] on the archangel Michael, in which Agathias justifies the making and use of images:

> Greatly daring was the wax that formed the image of the invisible Prince of the Angels, incorporeal in the essence of his form. But yet it is not without grace; for a man looking at the image directs his mind to a higher contemplation. No longer has he a confused veneration, but imprinting the image in himself he fears him as if he were present. The eyes stir up the depths of the spirit, and art can convey by colours the prayers of the soul.[8]

The theological justification of the use of art in Agathias' poem mirrors the same anagogical capacity of art found in the letter of Hypatius. Both authors approve of the use of images as spiritual aid as a concession to the weakness of the human mind. Agathias' epigram expands on and thereby clarifies the psychological effect of art that affects the non-rational faculties and stirs up the soul. It is the immediate visual (aesthetic) effect of colours and light that brings about a spiritual and, by extension, an epistemological change. I should note that the concept that sensual stimuli induce a psychological and revelatory effect is not novel. Already in the early fifth century, Paulinus of Nola famously proclaimed the richly embellished sacred interiors as 'a marvel

5 Alexander (1952), 181; Greek text in Thümmel (1983), 168 (81–2): ὡς οὐδενὶ τῶν ὄντων ἐστὶ καθόλου τὸ θεῖον ἤ ταὐτὸν ἤ ἰσον ἤ ὅμοιον.

6 The text is corrupt and doubts have been raised about its authenticity. Arguments have been made that the letter uses ideas and language reminiscent of the iconoclastic controversy and is to be dated to the eighth century instead. Stephen Gero, 'Hypatius of Ephesus on the cult of images', in *Christianity, Judaism and other Greco-Roman Cults. Part II. Christianity*, ed. Jacob Neusner (Leiden: Brill, 1975); Paul Speck, "ΓΡΑΦΑΙΣ Η ΓΛΥΦΑΙΣ. Zu dem Fragment des Hypatios von Ephesos über die Bilder mit einem Anhang zu dem Dialog mit einem Juden des Leontios von Neapolis', *Varia* 1 (1984); Hans Georg Thümmel, *Die Frühgeschichte der ostkirchlichen Bilderlehre, Texte und Untersuchungen zur Geschichte der altchristlichen Literatur* (Berlin: Academie Verlag, 1992), 103–17.

7 Averil Cameron and Alan Cameron, 'The Cycle of Agathias', *The Journal of Hellenic Studies* 86 (1966).

8 Agathias, *On Another on the Island of Platé*, in AP I.34: ἄσκοπον ἀγγελίαρχον, ἀσώματον εἴδεϊ μορφῆς, ἆ μέγα τολμήεις κηρὸς ἀπεπλάσατο: ἔμπης οὐκ ἀχάριστον, ἐπεὶ βροτὸς εἰκόνα λεύσσων θυμὸν ἀπιθύνει κρέσσονι φαντασίῃ: οὐκέτι δ᾽ ἀλλοπρόσαλλον ἔχει σέβας, ἀλλ᾽ ἐν ἑαυτῷ τὸν τύπον ἐγγράψας ὡς παρεόντα τρέμει: ὄμματα δ᾽ ὀτρύνουσι βαθὺν νόον οἶδε δὲ τέχνη χρώμασι πορθμεῦσαι τὴν φρενὸς ἱκεσίην. Thümmel (1992), 114.

for the eyes' (*mirum oculis*).[9] The splendour of the multi-coloured decoration, he states, 'might seize the beguiled minds (*adtonitas mentes*) of the rustics (*agrestes*) through their wondrous appearance (*spectacula*)'.[10] Paulinus clearly anticipates the didactic role of art that emerges more explicitly and frequently in later centuries. What is missing, however, is the metaphysical dimension that implicates the soul's ascent (anagoge) to higher spiritual levels through the sensual experience of the 'abundant light in the sanctuaries' as Hypatius puts it.

Hypatius' and Agathias' statements give great value to the faculty of vision and the appropriate stimulation of the senses through the agency of the ecclesiastical space to transform the visual experience into a spiritual state. It is important here to realise that at the most fundamental level of human sensory perception, light and, to a certain extent, movement pertain to the basic human visual experiences. Light and animation may therefore convey universal aesthetic ideals shared across societies and cultural media (art and architecture, literature, philosophy) and can serve as powerful and expressive architectural symbols.[11] An evaluation of these basic objects of vision is particularly pertinent because they establish the physical (spatial) and psychological framework for the visual experience of Hagia Sophia. If architecture is concurrently considered to be 'a form of social language' and an expression of social identity, then it should furthermore be possible to reconstruct the ideological or cultural ideas that the building tries to communicate.[12] The focus must therefore turn to the architecture itself. A detailed investigation of the architectural evidence enables us to evaluate the structural and decorative implications of the aesthetics of light and animation in architectural terms, and the main message that the ecclesiastical space of Hagia Sophia sought to convey.

Although there have been individual studies on the architecture of Hagia Sophia and the underlying geometrical principles, most notably the seminal work by Rowland Mainstone (1988), there has never been a systematic attempt to evaluate the architectural structure and decoration of the Great Church

9 Paulinus of Nola, *Carmen* 28.43.

10 Paulinus of Nola, *Carmen* 27.580–91; English translation in Dennis E. Trout, *Paulinus of Nola: Life, Letters, and Poems* (Berkeley, CA: University of California Press, 1999), 182–3; Carola Jäggi, 'Das kontrollierte Bild. Auseinandersetzungen um Bedeutung und Gebrauch von Bildern in der christlichen Frühzeit und im Mittelalter', in *Alles Buch, Studien der Erlanger Buchwissenschaft XXXIII*, ed. Ursula Rautenberg and Volker Titel (Erlangen-Nürnberg: Buchwissenschaft, 2009).

11 As Arnheim has stated 'the most powerful symbols derive from the most elementary perceptual sensations'. Rudolf Arnheim, *The Dynamics of Architectural Form* (London, Berkeley and Los Angeles, CA: University of California Press, 1977), 207–9; James I. Porter, *The Origins of Aesthetic Thought in Ancient Greece: Matter, Sensation, and Experience* (Cambridge: Cambridge University Press, 2010), 4; Semir Zeki, *Inner Vision: An Exploration of Art and the Brain* (Oxford: Oxford University Press, 1999).

12 Arnheim (1977), 20–21; Edmund Thomas, *Monumentality and the Roman Empire: Architecture in the Antonine Age* (Oxford: Oxford University Press, 2007), Introduction.

from the perspective of its psychological effects, light and illumination.[13] Numerous scholars recognised light as a crucial aesthetic component of the edifice, but most analyses remained confined to the simple identification of a hierarchical distribution of light within the building, in analogy to the Pseudo-Dionysian ecclesiastical and celestial hierarchies.[14] This idea of a hierarchy of light is challenged here. The present chapter aims to piece together the sixth-century illumination of Hagia Sophia based on the combined evidence from the architectural structure as originally intended (including orientation, dome configuration, fenestration) and from the building's artificial lighting installations. The phenomenon of light, as will be shown, is at the very heart of the architectural design, constituting a crucial architectural and aesthetic component. The examination of the architectural evidence will allow us to

[13] See, for example, Hans Buchwald, 'Saint Sophia, turning point in the development of Byzantine architecture?', in *Die Hagia Sophia in Istanbul: Akten des Berner Kolloquiums vom 21. Oktober 1994*, ed. Volker Hoffmann (Bern and New York: P. Lange, 1997); Lawrence E. Butler, 'Hagia Sophia's nave cornices as elements of its design and structure', in *Hagia Sophia*, ed. Robert Mark and Ahmet S. Çakmak (Cambridge: Cambridge University Press, 1992); Slobodan Ćurčić, 'Design and structural innovation in Byzantine architecture before Hagia Sophia', in *Hagia Sophia*, Robert Mark and Ahmet S. Çakmak (Cambridge: Cambridge University Press, 1992); Rowland J. Mainstone, *Hagia Sophia: Architecture, Structure and Liturgy of Justinian's Great Church* (London: Thames and Hudson, 1988); Robert Mark and Ahmet S. Çakmak, eds, *Hagia Sophia from the Age of Justinian to the Present* (Cambridge: Cambridge University Press, 1992); Marcell Restle, 'Die Hagia Sophia Kaiser Justinians in Konstantinopel', in *Die Hagia Sophia in Istanbul. Bilder aus sechs Jahrhunderten und Gaspare Fossatis Restaurierung der Jahre 1847–1849*, ed. V. Hoffmann (Bern: P. Lang, 1999); Emerson Howland Swift, *Hagia Sophia* (New York, NY: Columbia University Press, 1940); Robert S. Nelson, *Hagia Sophia, 1850–1950: Holy Wisdom Modern Monument* (Chicago, IL: University of Chicago Press, 2004); Volker Hoffmann and Nikolaos Theocharis, 'Der geometrische Entwurf der Hagia Sophia in Istanbul: Erster Teil', *Istanbuler Mitteilungen* 52 (2002). Some preliminary results have been published in Nadine Schibille, 'The use of light in the church of Hagia Sophia in Constantinople: The church reconsidered', in *Current Work in Architectural History – Papers Read at the Annual Symposium of the Society of Architectural Historians of Great Britain, London, 2004*, ed. Peter Draper (London: Society of Architectural Historians of Great Britain, 2005); Nadine Schibille, 'Astronomical and optical principles in the architecture of Hagia Sophia in Constantinople', *Science in Context* 22 (2009); Nadine Schibille, 'A quest for wisdom: The sixth-century mosaics of Hagia Sophia in Constantinople and late antique aesthetics', in *New Light on Old Glass: Recent Research on Byzantine Glass and Mosaics*, ed. C. Entwistle and L. James (London: British Museum Press, 2013); Nadine Schibille, 'Light as an aesthetic constituent in the architecture of Hagia Sophia in Constantinople', in *Manipulating Light in Pre-modern Times / Manipolare la luce in epoca premoderna*, ed. D. Mondini and V. Ivanovici (Mendrisio: Mendrisio Academy Press / Silvana Editoriale Cinisello Balsamo, 2014); Helge Svenshon, 'Das Bauwerk als "Aistheton Soma"', in *Byzanz – das Römerreich im Mittelalter, Teil 2, 1 Schauplätze*, ed. Falko Daim and Jörg Drauschke (Mainz: RGZM, 2010).

[14] GA Andreades, *Die Sophienkathedrale von Konstantinopel* (Frankfurt: Frankfurter Verlags-Anstalt, 1931); Hubert Fänsen, 'Der "Lichtstil" in der mittelbyzantinischen Kreuzkuppelkirche', *Byzantinische Forschungen* 18 (1992); Heinz Kähler, *Die Hagia Sophia* (Berlin: Gebr. Mann, 1967); Konrad Onasch, *Lichthöhle und Sternenhaus: Licht und Materie im spätantik-christlichen und frühbyzantinischen Sakralbau* (Dresden and Basel: Verlag der Kunst, 1993); Lioba Theis, 'Lampen, Leuchten, Licht', in *Byzanz. Das Licht aus dem Osten. Kult und Alltag im byzantinischen Reich vom 4. bis 15. Jahrhundert. Katalog der Ausstellung im Erzbischöflichen Diözesanmuseum Paderborn*, ed. C. Stiegemann (Mainz: Verlag Philipp von Zabern, 2001); Wladimir R. Zaloziecky, *Die Sophienkirche in Konstantinopel und ihre Stellung in der Geschichte der abendländischen Architektur* (Studie di Antichità Cristiana, 12) (Rome and Freiburg: Pontificio istituto di archeologia cristiana, 1936).

define a distinctive and conscious light management system against which contemporary aesthetic theories can then be evaluated. To better understand the aesthetic significance of Hagia Sophia for its contemporaries, the building's original architectural structure and illumination need to be reconstructed and assessed in relation to the wider developments in ecclesiastical architecture in Byzantium during and preceding the first half of the sixth century CE. This reveals to what degree the sixth-century illumination of Hagia Sophia was innovative and unique within the early Byzantine context, and to what degree its architecture and illumination fits in with the sixth-century developments of a specifically Byzantine aesthetics.

Constructing a Sacred Space

From the exterior, the monumentality of an edifice depends above all on its setting and the surrounding structures, or, as Arnheim put it, whether 'the building appears as a pinnacle or an inconspicuous attendant'.[15] In this sense, the church of Hagia Sophia has been an exceptionally outstanding building throughout its 1,500 years of history (Figure 2.1). Situated on the European promontory of present-day Istanbul where the Sea of Marmara narrows into the Bosporus, Hagia Sophia is visible for miles across the sea and dominates the skyline of the city to this day.[16] In the sixth century, Hagia Sophia was by far the largest and most magnificent architectural structure in Constantinople, with its cascade of soaring dome, semi-domes and arches.[17] Today, the exterior of Hagia Sophia is a hodgepodge of minarets and reinforcements that have been added over the centuries. Underneath these later modifications, we are left with the original sixth-century structure, consisting of the main dome rising on a square base to a height of about 60 m (Figure 2.2).[18] Adjacent to the east and west are a series of semi-domes. To the west the vaulting system terminates in a large, almost semicircular window, corresponding with the apse semi-dome in the east.[19] Massive buttress piers that continue above the gallery roofs frame the tympana screens on the north and south sides of the dome base. These sixth-century buttress piers connect with the backs of the main piers that form the corners of the square dome support almost at the height of the springing of the dome. Below the tympana and the great west window bulge the lead covered roofs of the galleries. Gallery

15 Arnheim (1977), 93; Thomas (2007).

16 In its entirety, the edifice can best be seen from either the Bosphorus to the east, the Sea of Marmara to the south or the elevated sections of Galata across the Golden Horn to the north. Nelson discusses the preferred views of Hagia Sophia extensively in his book. Nelson (2004), 3–5, Chapter 4; Mainstone (1988), 9, 21.

17 With the possible exception of the church of St. Polyeuktos built around 524–527 CE by Anicia Juliana.

18 Based on Mainstone (1988).

19 It is the largest surviving single window of the building. Mainstone (1988), 21.

2.1 Skyline of Istanbul looking south from Galata across the Golden Horn.

access ramps project beyond three corners of the building's main rectangle. There might have been a fourth access ramp at the southeast corner as well, but clear evidence is lacking. An outer narthex precedes the building to the west, somewhat squeezed in between the substructures of the two western minarets. Originally a large enclosed courtyard (atrium) extended westward from this outer narthex.[20] Without the later additions (minarets, additional buttresses, Islamic imperial tombs), the church of Hagia Sophia would have appeared to its contemporaries in the sixth-century in an exalted location, surrounded by open courtyards and 'bathed all round by the bright light of day'.[21]

The building's external isolation was an important feature in the sixth-century. It ensured not only the building's imposing monumentality especially when seen from afar, but it also guaranteed an unobstructed illumination with natural light. Byzantine writers are largely silent on the subject of the building's exterior. At one level, this is partially due to the fact that the complex architectural structure would not have been immediately comprehensible from up close. More importantly, though, this omission signals the exterior's relative inconsequence as regards the edifice's aesthetic and symbolic significance. On the outside, the solid architectural form was very much grounded in the material reality of human every-day life, while it enclosed and screened off the sacred interior.[22] This is why Byzantine writers

[20] For a detailed discussion of the architectural phases see Mainstone (1988), 102–4, 122.

[21] Procopius I.1.27; Silentiary verses 612–615: ὄφρα φανείη φέγγεσιν εὐγλήνοισι περίρρυτον ἠριγενείης.

[22] Leach showed how in many cultures the entrance to sacred buildings represents the threshold between this world and the other i.e. heaven or hell and that consequently,

2.2 Exterior of Hagia Sophia seen from the south.

frequently describe the moment of crossing the threshold into the church in theatrical terms.[23] Paul the Silentiary, for instance, relates how on the day of the re-inauguration of Hagia Sophia, the congregation gathered outside the doors of the church and requested entrance from the priests.[24] Entering the church of Hagia Sophia was evidently conceived not simply as a transition from the exterior to the interior, but just as much as a transition from the material to the immaterial, from the human to the divine. The exterior of Hagia Sophia is thus only secondary to its interior, even though its monumentality has shaped the urban landscape of Constantinople ever since. The exterior is merely the shell that encloses a sacred space of high symbolic and aesthetic value. As the textual evidence has highlighted, Hagia Sophia's ecclesiastical interior is the spatial representation of the immaterial divine in the form of light and animation.

the exterior was seen as part of this world. This also means that the entrances often obtained a special architectural treatment. Edmund R. Leach, 'The gatekeepers of heaven: Anthropological aspects of grandiose architecture', *Journal of Anthropological Research* 39 (1983).

23 Webb (1999), 68.

24 Silentiary verses 350–352.

Discussion of the innovative and dynamic character of Hagia Sophia's sixth-century design must begin with the history of the building and a survey of the structural alterations the building underwent over the centuries. The building's highly innovative and unprecedented architectural design has astounded visitors throughout the centuries, especially because the church was built in less than six years, between February 532 CE and December 537 CE.[25] Justinian's church was in fact the third building on this site; its two predecessors had both fallen victim to fire. The first church dedicated under Constantius in 360 CE was damaged in 404 CE, and the Theodosian church rededicated in 415 CE was largely destroyed during the Nika revolt of January 532 CE. According to the *Chronographia* of Leo Grammaticus, written in the late tenth or early eleventh century, work on the Justinianic building had already begun by 23 February 532.[26] There can be no doubt that a complex architectural structure such as that of Hagia Sophia was the result of extensive planning and design prior to the onset of construction, which is why many scholars believe that Justinian might have contemplated a re-building of the church well before the fire of 532 CE.[27] That the architects of Hagia Sophia, Anthemius of Tralles and Isidorus of Miletus, were highly educated in the mathematical and astronomical sciences and that they employed this knowledge in the architectural structure and layout of the Great Church has been established elsewhere.[28] Some written remains, and above all the complex architectural design of Hagia Sophia, testify to the architects' competence in mathematical design and may reflect an intellectual connection with the supposed centre of architectural knowledge and education in Alexandria (Egypt).[29]

Little more than twenty years after Hagia Sophia's completion, on 7 May 558 CE, the dome and parts of its supporting structural system collapsed following a series of earthquakes.[30] The building was restored and fitted with a modified dome structure by Isidorus the Younger, nephew of the

25 Particularly the original dome structure is considered to be innovative and experimental. Ahmet S. Çakmak, Rabun M. Taylor, and Eser Durukal, 'The structural configuration of the first dome of Justinian's Hagia Sophia (A.D. 537–558): An investigation based on structural and literary analysis', *Soil Dynamics and Earthquake Engineering* 29 (2009). For an overview of how Hagia Sophia was perceived throughout the ages, see Nelson (2004).

26 Leo Grammaticus, *Chronographia*, 126; Cyril Mango, 'Byzantine Writers on the Fabric of Hagia Sophia', in *The Hagia Sophia: From the Age of Justinian to the Present*, ed. Robert Mark and Ahmet S. Çakmak (Cambridge: Cambridge University Press, 1992), 51.

27 W. Eugene Kleinbauer, *Saint Sophia at Constantinople: Singulariter in Mundo* (Dublin and Peterborough, NH: William L. Bauhan, 1999), 14; Mainstone (1988), 151.

28 Nadine Schibille, 'The profession of the architect in late antique Byzantium', *Byzantion* 79 (2009b); Schibille (2009a).

29 Judith McKenzie discussed the evidence of architectural planning and design in late antique Alexandria. Judith McKenzie, *The Architecture of Alexandria and Egypt 300 BC–AD 700* (London and New Haven, CT: Yale University Press, 2007), Chapter 12; Svenshon (2010).

30 According to the sixth-century chronicle of Malalas (708–709) and the histories of Agathias (V.9.1–5); see also the eighth- and ninth-century chronicle of Theophanes (480, 509). Çakmak, Taylor, and Durukal (2009).

original architect Isidorus of Miletus. The festivities of the re-consecration allegedly lasted for numerous days from 24 December 562 CE until the Feast of Epiphany on 6 January 563.[31] It is in this context that Paul the Silentiary's ekphrasis and the inauguration hymn were composed and recited. It is well known from primary sources that the new dome altered the visual experience and spatial impression of the central space beneath the dome considerably.[32] It is this re-built architectural structure that is largely preserved to this day. Further repairs of two partial collapses of the dome in 989 CE and 1346 CE were restricted to the damaged areas. Some alterations can be traced in the north and south tympana and supporting gallery colonnades. Numerous buttresses were added to the original structure of the building in three consecutive repair and strengthening campaigns in 1317, 1573 and 1847.[33] No doubt, these additions and structural reinforcements have had a decisive effect on the lighting of the interior, due to the obstruction of numerous window openings.

The Spatial Impression

Approaching from the atrium in the west, Hagia Sophia presents itself as a relatively closed off structure with only three doors opening into the three central bays of the outer narthex (Figure 2.3A).[34] From here, five doors in alternate bays lead to the inner narthex and nine entrances finally give way into the church. Only the central doors are aligned. This unaligned sequence of openings and differently articulated spaces create a gradient of increasing openness and expanding space. The transition from the material world on the outside to the immaterial sacred space is exaggerated architecturally and aesthetically: from the humble and earth-bound solid mass of the outer narthex,[35] to a much more impressive inner narthex that is higher, wider and richly decorated, and finally to the vast church interior with its soaring dome structures. The two narthexes thus mediate between the exterior and the interior, preparing the faithful and offering a gradual initiation before entering the sacred space itself. Once inside the church, the architectural spaces and shapes finally unfold. The luminous emptiness of Hagia Sophia's

[31] Malalas suggested that the 12-day long Christmas festivities (Christmas Eve until Epiphany) already existed during Justinian's reign. Malalas, *The Chronicle*, 296.

[32] Agathias, *The Histories*, V.9.1–5; Malalas, *The Chronicle*, 297, 303.

[33] For a detailed discussion of the architectural structure and changes throughout the centuries see Rowland J. Mainstone, 'The reconstruction of the tympana of St. Sophia at Istanbul', *DOP* 23, 24 (1969–1970); Mainstone (1988), 91–104.

[34] Two further doors probably linked the two end bays originally to the atrium arcades. Mainstone (1988), 29.

[35] The outer narthex consists of a series of nine unembellished domical cross vaults that are approximately as high as they are wide, thus creating a space that is still very much bound to the earth.

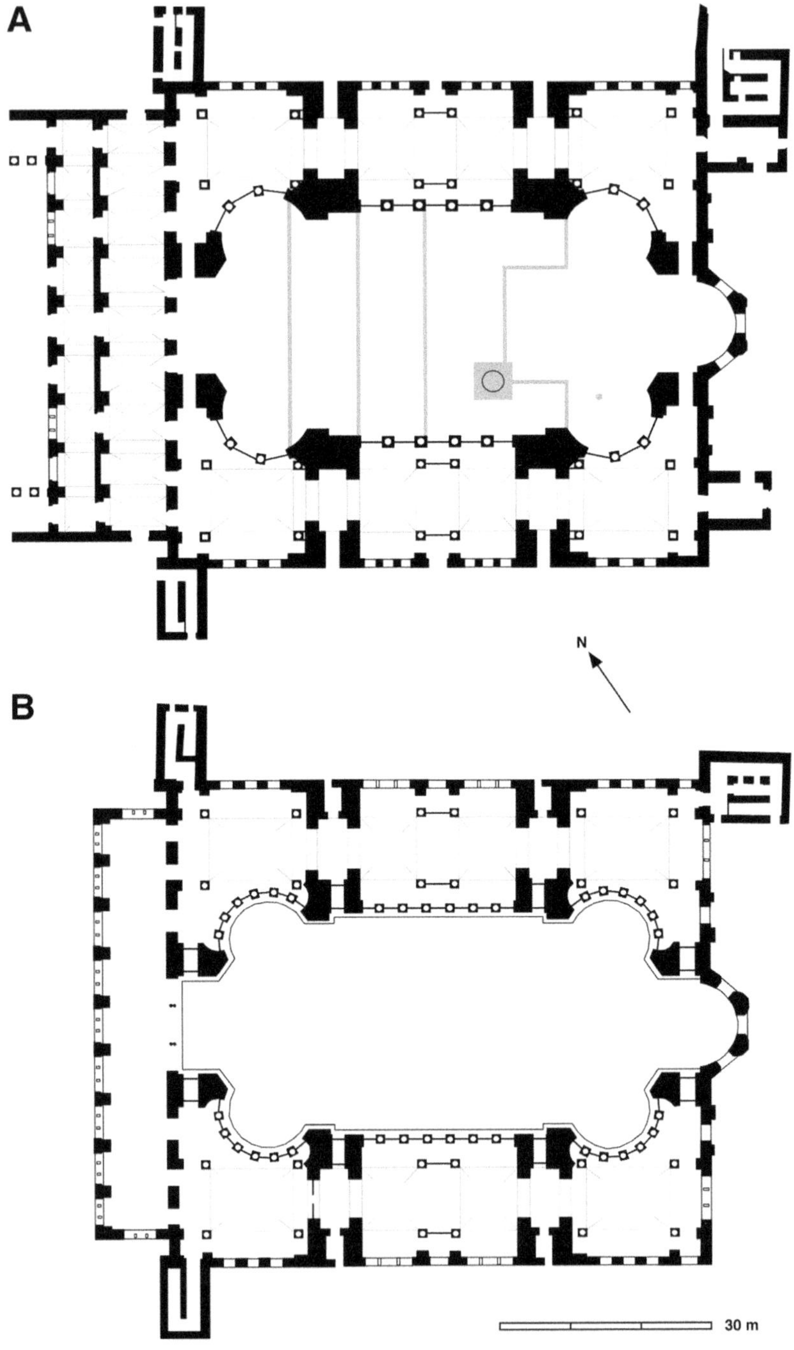

2.3 Plan of ground floor (A) and the gallery level (B) of Hagia Sophia (adapted from Mainstone 1988).

sacred interior conveys the essence of the edifice's meaning; the light-filled space is the visible yet immaterial manifestation of the divine (Plate 1).[36]

The structural system of Hagia Sophia is surprisingly simple. Four huge piers mark the corners of a square with a side length of almost exactly 31 m (99 Byzantine feet).[37] This four-corner support constitutes the core design of Hagia Sophia and was to become one of the most fundamental structural principles of Byzantine architecture.[38] Four arches swing across each side of the naos square. Together with the pendentives, they create the topmost cornice at a height of approximately 41 m, above which the main dome rises to about 56 m. The dome shell is scalloped by 40 ribs, which die out towards the apex of the dome. Forty windows pierce the dome base between the ribs, creating a continuous ring of light.[39] While the main arches to the north and south enclose large fenestrated tympana, the arches to the east and west are freestanding, merging into the two main semi-domes, thus making the central space about twice as long as it is wide and emphasising the building's longitudinal axis. The semi-domes rest on the main piers and two pairs of subsidiary piers, which flank the bema and the entrance. A barrel vault projects on the longitudinal axis from the main semi-domes, opening once more into the apse semi-dome and the semi-circular apsidal bema in the east and terminating in a semi-circular great window and the narthex wall to the west. Smaller semi-domes crown the four exedras that open diagonally slightly off-centre onto the naos.

Hagia Sophia's design along the vertical and longitudinal axes manifests itself best from the centre of the naos.[40] The building skilfully combines the longitudinal orientation of a basilica with the verticality of a centralised domed

---

36 As Sir Edmund Leach argued, the divine is represented in many religious cultures in the form of immaterial space, and sacred spaces thus become 'works of art' in their own right. Leach (1983).

37 For an interesting discussion in favour of 99 Byzantine feet instead of 100 feet for the sides of the square based on geometry, see Helge Svenshon and Rudolf H. W. Stichel, 'Systems of Monads' as design principle in the Hagia Sophia: Neo-Platonic mathematics in the architecture of late antiquity', *Nexus* 6 (2006); Svenshon (2010). There is still uncertainty about the exact conversion of the Byzantine foot into metres. Svenshon calculates one Byzantine foot to be equivalent to 0.3131 m, while Antoniadis and Mainstone define the Byzantine foot as 0.312 m.

38 The origins and development of the four-corner support were extensively studied by Sedlmayr, who called it the *Baldachinprinzip*. Ćurčić (1992); Hans Sedlmayr, 'Das mittelalterliche Architektursystem', *Kunstwissenschaftliche Forschungen* 2 (1933).

39 Robert L. van Nice, *Saint Sophia in Istanbul: An Architectural Survey* (Washington, DC: The Dumbarton Oaks Centre for Byzantine Studies, 1986), plates 1, 4, 29, 30.

40 Richard Krautheimer, *Early Christian and Byzantine Architecture*, Pelican History of Art (New Haven, CT: Yale University Press, 1965, 4th edition, 1986), 206–13. The central space beneath the dome is relatively independent of the enveloping aisles and galleries. The aisles and galleries consist of a succession of groined vaulted bays in alteration with smaller barrel vaults. One larger elongated groined vaulted bay bends around the exedras at each end of the galleries and the aisles. A simple barrel vault roofs the western gallery over its entire length. Compared to the aisles, the height of the galleries is considerably reduced, which gives a greater emphasis to its width, increasing its perceived spaciousness and luminosity. Mainstone (1988), 56.

form. This combination gives the edifice a distinctly dynamic quality further strengthened by the exedras that are turned towards the naos but not towards its centre.[41] The viewer is presented with two competing visual centres and psychological experiences. On the one hand, the architectural structure has the visual and psychological properties of the longitudinal nave (linear path/progress), while on the other hand, the articulation of its centre conveys the impression of a dwelling place.[42] The ambiguity in its most basic structural arrangement evokes at once a sense of serenity and animation and imparts an animated character to the building that is reminiscent of Procopius' statement that 'the vision constantly shifts suddenly, for the beholder is utterly unable to select which particular detail he should admire more than all the others'.[43] The architecture of Hagia Sophia can only be experienced in sequence and through movement. It is this very movement of the eyes, the head or the entire body that repositions the viewer in relation to the architecture, thereby imparting the quality of an animated, rather than of an inert and static, object to the edifice.[44]

As the most impressive architectural feature, the main dome introduces the vertical element into the architectural design. The viewer's gaze is drawn upward, simulating a visual ascent along the lateral arcades and exedra semi-domes to the larger semi-domes and culminating in the main dome. The columns and arches flanking the naos to the north and south sustain this verticality, while simultaneously introducing a horizontal structuring element in the form of the cornices and marble revetment. The arcades are adapted to the vertical dimension by the deeply undercut swirling acanthus leaf patterns that cover the capitals and vertical surfaces between the arches (spandrels), and in so doing obscure the transition from columns to wall. The arcades flanking the naos consist of five intercolumniations surmounted by gallery arcades of seven bays (Figure 2.3B). This practice of placing columns 'over empty air',[45] is further pronounced in the exedras, where triple arcades at ground level support seven openings at gallery level. This lack of correspondence between the ground floor and the gallery arcades creates a vertical gradient of diminishing height, visually enhanced through the larger number and reduced size of the columns and intercolumniations at gallery level. Optically, this has the effect of perspective foreshortening, thus producing the illusion of greater overall height.

The cascading structures of dome and semi-domes – all of which were originally extensively fenestrated – contribute to the dynamic quality of Hagia Sophia's naos. Previous assumptions that the main semi-domes merely

41 Svenshon (2010), 60–61.

42 Arnheim (1977), 89–91.

43 Procopius I.1.48–49: ἀγχίστροφός τε ἡ τῆς θέας μεταβολὴ ἐς ἀεὶ γίγνεται, ἀπολέξασθαι τοῦ ἐσορῶντος οὐδαμῆ ἔχοντος ὅ τι ἄν ποτε ἀγασθείη μᾶλλον τῶν ἄλλων ἁπάντων.

44 Arnheim (1977), 129–30.

45 Silentiary verse 394: οὐδὲ βάσιν κενεοῖο κατ᾽ ἠέρος ἔτρεσε πῆξαι.

served a structural function have since been refuted. They clearly constitute aesthetic elements to enhance the spatial effect of the naos,[46] while the diagonal planning of the exedras with their semi-domes literally envelop the central space and provide a visual continuum between viewer and architecture, due to their smaller size. The gaze of the viewer is concurrently drawn into the light-filled aisles and galleries, creating an impression of overlapping views and spatial units. It is the fusion of the numerous spherical shapes and the abundance of light entering through a multitude of windows that unify the architectural system (Plate 2).[47] The whole structure is held together visibly through the agency of the spherical shapes and light, which are both genuine metaphors for the power of the divine.[48] The profusion of natural light within Hagia Sophia, falling through the windows in the dome, semi-domes and tympana, provokes a profound perceptual sensation that in turn evokes a sense of spiritual and intellectual enlightenment as expressed in the sixth-century ekphrastic descriptions.

Originally, all spatial units of Hagia Sophia were illuminated directly and indirectly through a large number of light sources. Natural light would have entered through multiple openings in the dome (40 windows) and semi-domes (35 windows), as well as a series of windows in the south and north tympana and on all four outer facades of the building. Unfortunately, the building's sixth-century luminosity has since been lost because of the total or partial closure of many openings or the obstruction of the light path. For example, the pair of flying buttresses at the east end (north and south of the apse) that was possibly added in the thirteenth or fourteenth century cut out direct light from the lateral apse windows (Figure 2.4). Similarly, the central buttresses to the north and south of the building (ninth/tenth century) obstruct numerous windows in the aisles.[49] The aisles have generally suffered more acute changes than the galleries, best exemplified by some of the Ottoman fittings in the

---

46 Anthony Cutler, 'Structure and aesthetic at Hagia Sophia in Constantinople', *The Journal of Aesthetics and Art Criticism* 25 (1966). Pentcheva called the architectural structure of Hagia Sophia's interior the 'ideal chora'. Bissera V. Pentcheva, *The Sensual Icon: Space, Ritual, and the Senses in Byzantium* (University Park, PA: Pennsylvania State University Press, 2010), 49.

47 It is generally assumed that the first dome had a ring of 40 windows along its rim similar to the ones today, and that the semi-domes were pierced by five windows each (i.e. 35 windows in total). Çakmak *et al.* argue that it is unlikely that the Byzantines would have introduced the windows only in the rebuilt version that was supposed to be less prone to destruction. Çakmak, Taylor, and Durukal (2009).

48 The form of the sphere was traditionally associated with the image of the cosmos and the architectural dome with the vault of heaven or the natural sky. Louis Hautecoeur, *Mystique et architecture: Symbolisme du cercle et de la coupole* (Paris: A. et J. Picard, 1954); Karl Lehmann, 'The dome of heaven', *The Art Bulletin* 27 (1945); Thomas (2007), Chapter 3, particularly 53–6. In the sixth century, a monumental mosaic cross seems to have decorated the main dome and controlled the experience of the sacred interior in the same way. Silentiary verses 506–508.

49 Mainstone (1988), 104–5. The massive southeast buttresses can be attributed to the reign of Andronicus II, sometime after 1317. See reference in Nicephorus Gregoras, *Byzantina Historia*, I. 273; translated in Mango (1992), 54.

2.4 Exterior of the apse of Hagia Sophia seen from the east.

south aisle. This has obviously a decisive impact on the distribution of light and the aesthetic experience of the interior as a whole. The impression of brightness would have been furthermore enhanced through the decoration of the surfaces and vaults with highly reflective materials such as polished marble and gold-ground mosaics, which are now either missing, covered in paint and plaster or have become dull. Hence, in order to gain a sense of the building's visual properties and the nature of its illumination as the architects had originally intended, all these structural and decorative modifications need to be considered. In so doing, the aesthetic significance of light and its meaning can be reconstructed, thus bringing to light the innovative character of the edifice.

A Canopy of Heaven

The crowing architectural feature of Hagia Sophia is its main spherical dome that, according to Procopius, 'makes the structure exceptionally beautiful'.[50] Given its decisive role in the aesthetic experience and luminosity of Hagia Sophia's interior, the structural and visual properties of the original dome (537–

[50] Procopius I.1.45–46: τούτου δὲ τοῦ κυκλοτεροῦς παμμεγέθης ἐπανεστηκυῖά τις σφαιροειδὴς θόλος ποιεῖται αὐτὸ διαφερόντως εὐπρόσωπον.

558 CE) as devised and built by Anthemius of Tralles and Isidorus of Miletus need to be reconstructed. As no archaeological remains or reliable written technical accounts are preserved, the possible original vaulting system needs to be pieced together from the fragmentary comments found in contemporary chronicles, and from structural as well as aesthetic considerations. According to the sixth-century historian Malalas (c. 491–578 CE), the reconstructed dome was raised by 20 or 30 Byzantine feet.[51] Agathias Scholasticus furthermore states that the new dome was more regular in shape and that because it was narrower and higher, it was more secure and consequently less impressive than the original dome.[52] Although these written sources with their internal discrepancies cannot be taken at face value, they evidently agree on one important aspect, namely that the first dome was notably lower than the one rebuilt after 558 CE.

Following these literary sources, different dome profiles have been proposed in the past.[53] While compelling, in particular the reconstruction by Mainstone, none of these models is entirely satisfactory. For example, Çakmak and Taylor argued in favour of a substantial drum with a height of 20 Byzantine feet at the base of the dome. Mainstone's reconstruction similarly envisaged a 'low drum-like' section. However, in aesthetic, geometrical and structural terms, the ideal profile would have been that of a continuous pendentive dome, where the diameter of the dome sphere is the same as the diagonal of the square of the naos (Figure 2.5).[54] Continuous pendentive domes had been around since the first century BCE and manuals for the calculations of volumes and shapes were likewise readily available.[55] Therefore, in principle there is no reason why Hagia Sophia could not have been equipped with a continuous pendentive dome or a variation of such an ideal profile.

It is widely assumed, probably correctly, that the first version of the dome had a cornice similar to the one today.[56] To accommodate a cornice, the

---

51 Malalas, *The Chronicle*, 297, 303; Theophanes the Confessor (d. 818 CE), who is known to have copied passages from Malalas, later quotes the value of 20 feet. Theophanes, *Chronographia*, 233; translated in Theophanes Confessor, *The Chronicle of Theophanes Confessor*, ed. Cyril Mango and Roger Scott (Oxford: Clarendon Press, 1997), 341.

52 Agathias, *The Histories*, V. 9. 2–5.

53 Antoniades suggested a part-circular dome without ribs, Conant proposed a three-zoned profile, while Taylor and very recently Çakmak *et al.* argued in favour of a fenestrated drum. Mainstone's first dome shares its radius and curvature with the pendentives, but he proposes that the centre of curvature of the dome was about 2 m higher than that of the pendentives. Eugenios Michael Antoniades, *Έκφρασις της Αγίας Σοφίας, ήτοι μελέτη συνθετική και αναλυτική υπό έποψιν αρχιτεκτονικήν, αρχαιολογικήν και ιστορικήν του πολυθρυλήτου τεμένους Κωνσταντινουπόλεως/Ευγενίου Μ. Αντωνιάδου τ. 2* (1908), Vol. III, 103–4; Çakmak, Taylor, and Durukal (2009); Kenneth John Conant, 'The first dome of St. Sophia and its rebuilding', *The Bulletin of the Byzantine Institute* 1 (1946); Mainstone (1988), 127, 209–12; R. Taylor, 'A literary and structural analysis of the first dome of Justinian's Hagia Sophia, Constantinople', *The Journal of the Society of Architectural Historians* 55 (1996).

54 Ćurčić (1992); Robert Mark, *Light, Wind, and Structure: The Mystery of the Master-Builders* (London and Cambridge, MA: MIT Press, 1990), 49–67, 79–89; Ramsay Traquair, 'The origin of the pendentive', *Journal of the Royal Institute of British Architects* 35 (1928).

55 McKenzie (2007), 324; Schibille (2009a, b).

56 Procopius explicitly described how the upper edges of the pendentive form the segment of a circle, upon which the dome rests (I.1.41–47). In a continuous pendentive

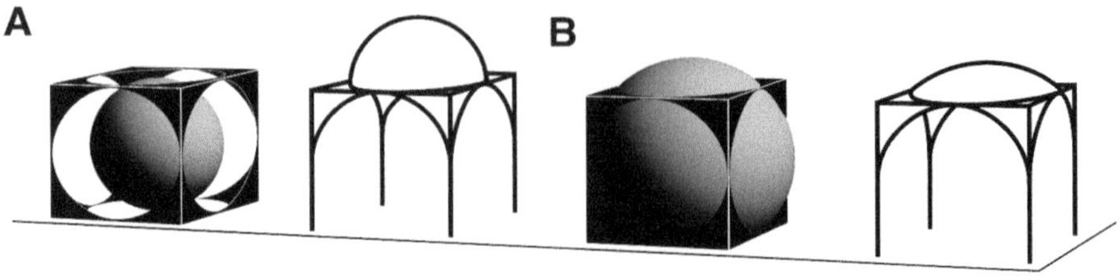

2.5 Schematic dome configurations: current dome (A) and the ideal configuration of a pendentive dome (B).

most likely profile then is a near-continuous pendentive dome with a radius slightly greater than that of the pendentives. If we consider a diameter for the pendentives of 140 Byzantine feet and we assume that Hagia Sophia's architectural design was based on strict mathematical principles and rational numbers,[57] it follows that the diameter of the original dome must have been 147 feet.[58] The increase in the diameter would effectively set back the springing of the dome-shell behind the edge of the cornice by about 3–4 feet thus providing sufficient space for a cornice similar to the present one.[59] This dome configuration would make the original vaulting system about 7.5 m (about 24 Byzantine feet) lower than the present dome and visibly shallower. While the current dome describes almost a complete hemisphere, subtending an angle of 163 degrees between the sphere centre and the base of the dome,[60] the proposed original curvature would correspond roughly to the quadrant of a sphere (subtending an angle of ~ 90 degrees) and appear more like a canopy when seen from below (Figure 2.6).[61]

This proposed original vaulting system, combining a precariously shallow and innovative profile with an unprecedented span of 31 m, satisfies the spatial and visual effect that is echoed in the contemporary descriptions.

dome, these circle segments would not be apparent, which seems to indicate that there was a cornice in the first church as well. Another piece of evidence is the significance of artificial light installations for which a cornice would have been indispensable. See Paul the Silentiary's description of light installations (verses 809–814). Mainstone (1988), 127, 209–12; Onasch (1993), 31–3, 132–3; Theis (2001), 59.

57 Svenshon has convincingly demonstrated that architectural design and planning in late antiquity was grounded in *geodaisia* i.e. the numerical system expressible in rational numbers. Svenshon (2010).

58 Heron of Alexandria demonstrated the calculations for relating a sphere to a cube where the diameter of a sphere is the same as the diagonal of a square. The calculations in Heron's *Metrica* are independent of units and are based on numerical values for the diameter of the sphere that would result in rational numbers when divided by the denominator 7, because the approximate value of π used was 22/7. McKenzie (2007), 323–5; Svenshon (2010), 68.

59 Svenshon (2010), 85–6.

60 Onur Gürkan, Serhat Camlidere, and Mustafa Erdik, 'Photogrammetric studies of the dome of Hagia Sophia', in *Hagia Sophia*, ed. Robert Mark and Ahmet S. Çakmak (Cambridge: Cambridge University Press, 1992); Mainstone (1988), 216–17.

61 Schibille (2005).

2.6 Cross section of Hagia Sophia along its longitudinal axis as seen from south (adapted from Grobe *et al.* 2010, Plate 2). Note the height of the dome has been reduced to approximate the profile of a pendentive dome as it is assumed to have existed in the original sixth-century configuration (compare Plate 3).

Both Agathias and Malalas commented on the notably lower rise of the first dome, which Agathias explicitly characterised as more imposing.[62] Procopius, whose ekphrasis is the only description of Hagia Sophia's first dome, likewise marvelled at the seemingly floating vaulting system:

> Upon the crowns of the arches rests a circular structure, cylindrical in shape; it is through this that the light of day always first smiles. For it towers above the whole earth, as I believe, and the structure is interrupted at short intervals, openings having been left intentionally, in the spaces where the perforation of the stone-work takes place, to be channels for the admission of light in sufficient measure … And upon this circle rests the huge spherical dome which makes the structure exceptionally beautiful. Yet it seems not to rest upon solid masonry, but to cover the space with its golden dome suspended from heaven. All these details, fitted together with incredible skill in mid-air and floating off from each other and resting only on the parts next to them, produce a single and most extraordinary harmony in the work …[63]

[62] Çakmak and colleagues argue correctly that neither Agathias nor Malalas explicitly specify a change in the overall absolute height of the building, but I contend that the original dome was a pendentive dome and not a dome upon a drum. Çakmak, Taylor, and Durukal (2009).

[63] Procopius I.1. 41–47: ὕπερθεν δὲ αὐτῶν κυκλοτερὴς οἰκοδομία ἐν στρογγύλῳ ἐπῆρται· ὅθεν ἀεὶ διαγελᾷ πρῶτον ἡ ἡμέρα. ὑπεραίρει γάρ, οἶμαι, τὴν γῆν ξύμπασαν,

Çakmak and Taylor maintain that Procopius' 'circular structure' must have been a fenestrated drum upon which a shallow dome segment rested.[64] However, an ekphrastic description with all its deliberate rhetorical effects hardly lends itself to an accurate reconstruction of a work of art or architecture. As discussed in the first chapter, an ekphrasis is not a technical description of actuality or realism. Instead, an ekphrasis recreates the visual experience and consequently reveals the aesthetic properties of an architectural structure. Accordingly, four main aesthetic qualities emerge from Procopius' ekphrastic account. Procopius emphasises the importance of light, the impression that the dome and semi-domes float in mid-air, the extraordinary harmony and finally, the innovative character of the whole design. To Procopius, the dome configuration of Hagia Sophia appeared bright and weightless. This sentiment is later spelled out by Agathias when he describes the second dome as more firmly arranged. This confirms, I believe, that the original dome was indeed an exceedingly shallow spherical segment that simply seemed to hover above the main space without exposing its downward thrusts, due to its flatness. The 'circular structure' mentioned by Procopius may refer to the cornice and the ring of windows in the lower part of the dome. The first dome was most likely fenestrated with the same number of windows as today (40).[65] Procopius states that the window 'openings have been left intentionally', suggesting that the original vaulting system of Hagia Sophia was based to a large extent on visual and optical principles.[66] The innovative character attested by the written sources is also an argument against a drum, because this was the conventional configuration in Roman and early Byzantine architecture.[67] The visual effect of Hagia Sophia's initial design was novel due to the combination of a large circular dome, seemingly suspended from heaven, on a square base with abutting semi-domes to the east and west, creating a nave with a span of 67 m along its longitudinal axis.[68]

The dome forms part of a larger unit, and it is plausible that its original structure ultimately followed the geometry of the overall architectural system of Hagia Sophia. This is true even for the reconstructed dome, whose curvature fits well with the structures and curves of the semi-domes. This shows that the present dome derived its shape from existing architectural features, because

καὶ διαλείπει τὸ οἰκοδόμημα κατὰ βραχύ, ἐξεπίτηδες παρειμένον τοσοῦτον, ὅσον τοὺς χώρους, οὗ δὴ τὸ διῃρημένον τῆς οἰκοδομίας συμβαίνει εἶναι, φέγγους διαρκῶς ἀγωγοὺς εἶναι … τούτου δὲ τοῦ κυκλοτεροῦς παμμεγέθης ἐπανεστηκυῖά τις σφαιροειδὴς θόλος ποιεῖται αὐτὸ διαφερόντως εὐπρόσωπον. δοκεῖ δὲ οὐκ ἐπὶ στερρᾶς τῆς οἰκοδομίας διὰ τὸ παρειμένον τῆς οἰκοδομίας ἑστάναι, ἀλλὰ τῇ σφαίρᾳ τῇ χρυσῇ ἀπὸ τοῦ οὐρανοῦ ἐξημμένη καλύπτειν τὸν χῶρον. ταῦτα δὲ πάντα ἐς ἄλληλά τε παρὰ δόξαν ἐν μεταρσίῳ ἐναρμοσθέντα, ἔκ τε ἀλλήλων ἠωρημένα καὶ μόνοις ἐναπερειδόμενα τοῖς ἄγχιστα οὖσι, μίαν μὲν ἁρμονίαν ἐκπρεπεστάτην τοῦ ἔργου ποιοῦνται …

64 Çakmak, Taylor, and Durukal (2009); Taylor (1996).

65 Çakmak, Taylor, and Durukal (2009).

66 Schibille (2009a).

67 Çakmak, Taylor, and Durukal (2009).

68 McKenzie (2007), 344–9.

the building was treated as a single entity. It would be surprising if the first dome had not similarly been governed by mathematical principles that were closely related to the rest of the building. Visually and geometrically, a simple continuation of the pendentives would have provided the ideal solution. How exactly the cornice would have been fitted must remain open, but this may have been accomplished by raising the dome shell either through a higher centre of curvature, as suggested by Mainstone,[69] or through a somewhat greater radius of curvature, as argued before. As a result of such a profile, the fenestration could then have followed the system of the semi-domes. The windowsills and soffits in the main semi-domes used to be consistently inclined at about 30 degrees throughout the semi-dome windows.[70] The windows in a continuous pendentive dome would similarly have been carried at an angle of about 50 degrees from the centre of curvature as regards the upper edge of the opening, with sloping window soffits and sills at approximately 30 degrees from the horizontal and a window-height of about 2.3 m. This configuration would have fitted perfectly with the fenestration in the main semi-domes.[71] In the current dome, this pattern is broken. Nowadays the windows of the main dome are inserted at a height of about 1.7 m above the dome cornice at an inclination of about 9 degrees. While the windowsills are inclined by about 37 degrees, the soffits have an inclination of only about 10 degrees.

These changes in the geometry of the dome window openings have a severe impact on the illumination of the naos below, because the arches above the windows (window soffits) can potentially reflect a substantial amount of light toward the interior of the church, and the windowsills reflect light into the dome shell. This depends on the angle at which the openings are cut into the spherical dome shell: the shallower the dome profile, the wider the window soffits. The efficacy of light reflection lies in the balance between the inclination and the width of the arched window soffits. In case of correspondingly sloped windowsill and soffit either one of them would catch and reflect direct sunlight throughout the day, provided they were covered with reflective material.[72] As is generally assumed, the dome including the window openings were probably decorated with gold-ground mosaics that would have been sufficient to reflect the light towards the dome and ultimately downward to the beholder, creating a strongly radiant dome shell and contributing an ethereal, hovering impression.[73]

69 Mainstone (1988), 163–4, 209–12.

70 The present window openings in the eastern semi-dome date from the Fossati restorations (mid-nineteenth century). Cyril Mango and Ernest J. W. Hawkins, 'The apse mosaics of St. Sophia at Istanbul: Report on work carried out in 1964', *DOP* 19 (1965): 135–6.

71 Schibille (2005).

72 Potamianos suggested that reflectors might even have been installed on the windowsills to reflect light up into the dome shell. Iakovos Potamianos, 'Light into Architecture: Evocative Aspects of Natural Light as Related to Liturgy and Byzantine Churches' (PhD, University of Michigan, 1996), 161–3; Schibille (2005).

73 Procopius, I.1.54–55: χρυσῷ μὲν ἀκιβδήλῳ καταλήλειπται ἡ ὀροφὴ πᾶσα, κεραννῦσα τὸν κόμπον τῷ κάλλει, νικᾷ μέντοι ἡ ἐκ τῶν λίθων αὐγὴ ἀνταστράπτουσα

The proposed original design of Hagia Sophia's dome would necessarily appear more luminous, due to a more advantageous window to surface ratio. As I have demonstrated elsewhere, the present dome has a window to total surface ratio of approximately 7.5 per cent ($\frac{120m^2}{1600m^2}$), while the ratio in the proposed model would have been 9.5 per cent ($\frac{104m^2}{1100m^2}$).[74] Hence, the surface to be illuminated was significantly smaller relative to the window openings even though the windows would have been somewhat smaller as well. A flatter spherical dome segment would furthermore be much more evenly illuminated, thus generating a strong radiance. Assuming that 40 windows were arranged at regular intervals around the 360 degree circumscription, up to nine windows received direct sunlight at any given time of the day, disregarding the position of the sun.[75] The dome was then continuously illuminated throughout the day and the seasons, representing a vital constituent in the direct and indirect lighting of Hagia Sophia's main space.

Natural Light as Formative Principle

Justinian's two architects, Anthemius and Isidorus, undeniably contrived an architectural monument whose interior was extensively lit from all sides. In the morning, the individual windows of the dome and eastern semi-domes are successively lit, due to their arrangement around the curvature of the sphere. As they are cut perpendicularly into the dome shell, the windows direct the sunlight towards the spaces below. Skylight entering through substantially larger window openings in the tympana and the auxiliary spaces augmented the illumination of the central space indirectly. The windows in Hagia Sophia evidently form an integral part of a homogeneous architectural system. As the structural components of the building, the openings fulfil a constitutive as well as an aesthetic role.[76] They do not stand out as independent shapes from the background; rather, the transition between the openings and surrounding walls is typically fluent and not demarcated by architectural frames.[77] This

τῷ χρυσῷ. Mango's translation appears closer to the Greek text than the Loeb edition: 'The entire ceiling has been overlaid with pure gold which combines beauty with ostentation, yet the refulgence from the marble prevails, vying as it does with that of the gold'. Cyril Mango, *The Art of the Byzantine Empire 312–1453: Sources and Documents* (Toronto: University of Toronto Press, 1972, reprint 1986), 76.

74 Schibille (2005).

75 Thomas Whittemore, *Notes on Light in Hagia Sophia, Istanbul, 26 January 1945, Dumbarton Oaks, Byzantine Photograph and Fieldwork Archives* (Washington, unpublished).

76 For the window as a 'Baumotiv' see Francesca Dell'Acqua, 'Enhancing luxury through stained glass, from Asia Minor to Italy', *DOP* 59 (2005); Roland Günter, 'Wand, Fenster und Licht in der spätantik-frühchristlichen Architektur' (PhD, Ludwig-Maximilians-Universität, 1965), 34–40.

77 Arnheim discusses how the window in a traditional masonry wall is the 'picture' against the background of the wall. However, this depends, I believe, on the extent of the fenestration and the ratio of wall to window surface. Arnheim (1977), 226.

is true for the windows in the dome, semi-dome and tympana as well as the large window screens in the aisles and galleries. Not only was the original dome shell more efficiently illuminated and more radiant, the windows of the semi-domes used to be taller as well. During the conservation of the apse mosaics in 1964, it was found that the steeply inclined windowsills in the apse semi-dome and main eastern semi-dome dated from the Fossati restorations. Yet, mason's marks on the transennae allow for an unequivocal attribution to the sixth century. Although the marble transennae in the semi-dome windows are of Justinianic date, there used to be a further row of lights at the bottom, making the windows up to 0.4 m or 0.5 m taller, bringing the openings to 2.2 m or 2.3 m in total height.[78] The seemingly random sizes of the windows in the exedra semi-domes (ranging from 2.1 m to 2.4 m) suggest that they have undergone similar modifications.

During afternoon hours, and depending on the altitude of the sun (the season), the windows of the south tympanum, gallery or the aisle take over the direct illumination of the naos. At present, the tympana contain two rows of windows, five in the upper zone and seven in the lower, above a row of seven shallow niches aligned with the lower range of windows.[79] The tympana were entirely reconstructed after the gallery arcades had been re-erected, presumably shortly after the earthquake of 869 CE. Nonetheless, architectural evidence suggests that they basically follow the original structure, except for the fenestration.[80] Mainstone explored the extremities of the tympana and found the springings of the original window arches at the height of the lower range of windows just inside the soffits of the main tympanum arches. Based on these remains, he concluded that there must have been a row of seven windows in the lower part of each tympanum, corresponding, as today, with the intercolumniations of the gallery arcades below. Since Paul the Silentiary mentions in his ekphrasis a total number of eight windows,[81] Mainstone assumed that there was a single, large window similar to the great west window in the upper part.[82] The inconsistency with Paul's two rows of four windows can easily be dismissed, because it has proven impossible in the past to use an ekphrasis for reconstructing the precise details of a lost architectural feature, given the rhetorical nature of the text. Paul's description of 'twice four' windows could be interpreted in the sense of the French 'quatre-vingts' and simply mean *eight*, especially because from

78 Mango and Hawkins (1965), 134–5.

79 van Nice (1986). The southern tympanum measures 10.6 m to 22.2 m (height to width) on the exterior above the gallery roof. The central window of the upper row measures 4.6 m to 1.8 m; the flanking windows are 3.6 m to 1.2 m and the lateral ones measure 2.5 m to 1.1 m. The windows of the lower row are all roughly the same size with a height of 2.3 m and a width of 1.1 m.

80 Mainstone (1969–1970), 365–8.

81 Paul the Silentiary states that 'it is illuminated by twice four (τετϱάκι δοιαῖς) windows' (verse 536).

82 Mainstone (1969–1970), 364–9; Mainstone (1988), 125.

a geometric point of view, two rows of four windows seems a highly unlikely configuration for a round-headed tympanum wall. Presuming then that the total number of windows is accurate, one large thermal window resembling the great west window filling the apex of the tympana on top of a row of seven smaller windows seems a perfectly possible solution. However, other arrangements may also be considered. For example, it is equally feasible that the lower register of windows consisted of four coupled two-light windows slightly displaced with respect to the gallery arcades below and repeating the structural discrepancy between the arcades of the gallery and ground floor. The window arches would then continue the vertical and overlapping gradient of diminishing size from the ground floor to the gallery and finally to the small arched double-windows in the tympanum walls.[83] Independent of the exact arrangement, however, the tympana were undoubtedly extensively fenestrated in the sixth century, admitting an abundance of natural light into the naos, particularly during the afternoon hours, when the sun has moved towards the southern reaches of the sky.[84]

Additionally, large window screens and lunette windows pierce the exterior walls of the aisles and galleries. Structural reinforcements on the outside now block many of these windows, particularly in the aisles, and the original lighting is lost. What the lighting must have been like in the sixth century can be observed on a sunny afternoon when the south gallery is bathed in gleaming sunlight. Although the aisles nowadays appear rather gloomy in comparison, in the sixth century the level of luminance of the aisles most certainly equalled that of the respective gallery. This is evident from a comparison of the total window area that originally amounted to an estimated 165 m^2 in the aisles compared to about 140 m^2 at gallery level. The difference in the total window area compensates for the difference in height between aisle (about 12.5 m) and gallery (about 9.5 m). This indicates that the aisles used to be just as brightly lit as the galleries, and that both spaces indirectly supplemented the light in the naos.[85] The original sixth-century illumination of Hagia Sophia has recently been modeled by means of a computer simulation that confirmed that during the afternoon hours the south aisle and gallery were flooded with an abundance of natural light (Plate 2).[86] As a result, light was spread more evenly throughout the building, dissolving the boundaries between the spatial units.

83 Nadine Schibille, 'Light in Early Byzantium: The Church of Hagia Sophia in Constantinople' (PhD, University of Sussex, 2004), 78–87.

84 The present window area of the tympana has furthermore been significantly reduced during Ottoman times to about half to a third of its initial ninth-century size, further impeding the natural illumination of Hagia Sophia's interior. Mainstone (1988), 99.

85 Schibille (2014).

86 Lars O. Grobe, Oliver Hauck, and Andreas Noback, 'Das Licht in der Hagia Sophia – eine Computersimulation', in *Byzanz – das Römerreich im Mittelalter, Teil 2, 1 Schauplätze*, ed. Falko Daim and Jörg Drauschke (Mainz: RGZM, 2010).

The most distinguishing feature of Hagia Sophia's interior space was its abundant and even illumination resulting from a multitude of windows. There are window openings on all planes and depths encircling the building and creating an optical continuum and homogeneity through a well-balanced illumination. The traditional claim that the distribution of light within Hagia Sophia followed hierarchical patterns, reflecting the differential liturgical and religious significance of the spatial units cannot be confirmed. According to the hierarchy claim, more light identified a specific spatial unit as religiously more significant, which is why the naos must necessarily be much brighter than the aisles and galleries.[87] As Fänsen explained, the naos of Hagia Sophia was suffused with light 'seemingly expanding into the metaphysical realm', while the auxiliary spaces were shrouded in twilight.[88] The original window configuration of Hagia Sophia provides ample evidence to the contrary. Several equally significant light sources perforate all the exterior walls of the building and originally flooded the sacred space with light from all sides.[89] Intriguingly, the lack of an unambiguous light source results in multiple shadows generated by one and the same object at certain times of the day (in the afternoon) similar to a football stadium at night under floodlight instead of casting one well-defined shadow. Streams of bright light through the lateral windows are set against the darkness of the structural features such as the window transennae or the columns of the side arcades, thus producing a vivid intermingling of light and dark architectural elements. This neutralises the three-dimensional shaping of the interior and contributes to the unifying effect.[90] Even today, the tympana appear as perforated membranes, an impression that must have been stronger with the original fenestration in place. The exterior walls of Hagia Sophia are transformed into walls of light, forfeiting their substantiality.[91] Light has become a crucial structural and aesthetic element of Hagia Sophia's architecture; it constitutes space and affects the ways in which we perceive and experience the building's interior.

The influx of light into the interior is directly dependent on the orientation of the building in relation to the path of the sun along the horizon. Interestingly, Hagia Sophia's longitudinal axis (approximately 123.5 degrees clockwise from north) is aligned with the azimuth (the horizontal angle from north) of the sun on the shortest day of the year (winter solstice). As a result of Hagia Sophia's specific orientation, the morning light falls through the windows in the apse and eastern semi-domes, illuminating the interior along its east-west

87 See for example *ODB*, 2198–2199; Andreades (1931), 44–9; Fänsen (1992), 189; Kähler (1967), 40–41; Onasch (1993); Theis (2001), 55–6; Zaloziecky (1936), 50–51.

88 Fänsen (1992), 189.

89 Light measurements confirm these observations. Schibille (2014).

90 Paul Hills, *Venetian Colour: Marble, Mosaic, Painting and Glass 1250–1550* (London and New Haven, CT: Yale University Press, 1999), 16.

91 Günter described this as a transcendental transformation of the architectural structure into walls and eventually spaces of light. Günter, (1965), 58–9.

axis throughout the year.[92] Whittemore, in a comprehensive study of Hagia Sophia's illumination during restoration work carried out by the Byzantine Institute between 1931 and 1949, observed that the period of utmost floor illumination is when direct sunlight falls in planes parallel to the longitudinal axis of the nave.[93] This occurred, according to Whittemore, between 8.30 am (winter) and 11.00 am (summer) and may have served the amplification of the liturgical celebrations. He noted that sunbeams entered successively through the individual windows in the eastern semi-domes and main dome, describing a path over the pavement from the south and southwest pavement to the major axis of the naos and finally to the northeast, where they eventually vanished (Plate 1). Twenty-seven out of 40 dome windows (five to nine windows at once) took part in the direct illumination of the naos during spring and summer. Diffuse skylight concurrently entered through all windows, slightly increasing towards noon and decreasing again in the afternoon.

Whittemore's observations can be largely confirmed by calculations of the sun's orbit in relation to the orientation of the building and its window openings.[94] Evidence about the architectural training and astronomical manuals in circulation in the sixth century confirm that the architects of Hagia Sophia were perfectly capable of calculating the position of the sun to this exactitude.[95] Notwithstanding the astronomical testimony, it is the architectural layout of Hagia Sophia in its entirety, its orientation together with its architectural system of fenestrated dome, semi-domes and exterior walls that ensure that the building is optimally illuminated independent of the time of day or the season. It follows that it was not the lighting of the sanctuary exclusively during liturgical hours or on specific celebration days that motivated the orientation of the building towards the sunrise on the winter solstice. Instead, it is the universal illumination of the interior as a whole throughout the day and the year, which underlies the architectural and structural design of Hagia Sophia. Natural light, and by extension the windows of Hagia Sophia not only serve a practical function, but the amount of light clearly exceeds this requirement, suggesting that light has meaning and is symbolically (semantically) and/or aesthetically important. On account of its all-pervading and unifying properties, light was associated with the omnipotence and transcendence of the divine. In the sixth century, the abundance of light within Hagia Sophia was intimately associated with a profound experience of the divine. Light was seen as the visible manifestation

---

92 For different theories on Hagia Sophia's orientations see, for example, Antoniades (1908), Vol. I, 73; William R. Lethaby and Harold Swainson, *The Church of Sancta Sophia Constantinople: A Study of Byzantine Building* (London and New York, NY: Kessinger Publishing, 1894, reprint 2004), 17; Potamianos, (1996), 180, 230; Whittemore (unpublished).

93 Whittemore (unpublished).

94 Schibille (2005); Schibille (2014).

95 Schibille (2005); Schibille (2009 a, b).

of the divine that conveyed a sense of intellectual and spiritual enlightenment. This awareness of divine immanence has a physiological basis inasmuch as the perception of light is one of the most basic human experiences and has the intense immediacy of unmediated sensation.

Natural light clearly formed part of the original architectural design and was meant to flood the sacred space with light all around, and although the amount of light entering the building is significantly reduced, the effect is still noticeable today. In 1913, Soisson noted about Hagia Sophia that 'there is such a profusion of light that under its influence the rich hues of mosaics look faded, strange as it seems, and as if sprinkled with grey ashes' and that the glow of coloured mosaics was effective only in diffuse twilight.[96] Even though there is some truth in this observation, it identifies above all a fundamental problem in the evaluation of the original brightness and quality of light within Hagia Sophia because of the lack of any archaeological remnants of original window materials. While many of the sixth-century marble transennae with rectangular openings (between 30 cm and 40 cm side length) are still preserved, it remains uncertain what type of window material they were destined to hold.[97] It has often been assumed in the past that Hagia Sophia's windows might have been closed with thin alabaster panes or similar highly absorbent materials that created a more sombre and diffused light impression.[98] No alabaster, however, was ever found in the immediate vicinity of the building, and there is no reason to believe that the architects chose anything other than window glass in the sixth century.[99]

At the time of Hagia Sophia's construction, the use and production of window glass had long been established.[100] Comparative late antique archaeological finds provide evidence for the widespread use of window

---

[96] Count de Soisson, 'The aesthetic purpose of Byzantine architecture', *Contemporary Review* 103 (1913): 98.

[97] Heinrich Gerhard Franz, 'Transennae als Fensterverschluss: Ihre Entwicklung von der frühchristlichen bis zur islamischen Zeit', *Istanbuler Mitteilungen* 8 (1958): 69; Mango and Hawkins (1965), 134–5.

[98] Mango pointed out that in the late seventeenth century, Covel and Grelot reported alabaster or some other translucent stone to form part of the marble work of the second window from the south on the west gallery, which Antoniades confirmed at the beginning of the twentieth century. However, this does not prove that alabaster windows formed part of the original design. Cyril Mango, *Materials for the Study of the Mosaics of St. Sophia at Istanbul* (Washington, DC: The Dumbarton Oaks Research Library, 1962), 43; Wolfgang Schöne, *Über das Licht in der Malerei* (Berlin: Gebr. Mann, 1954).

[99] Schibille (2014).

[100] The earliest literary reference seems to be Seneca's *Epistulae ad Lucilium* in which he ascribes the invention of glass windowpanes to his own time (first half of the first century CE). Seneca, Epistles, XC.25. According to Baatz, the innovation of window glass was closely related to the development of the great Roman thermae in the early empire. In order to accommodate an abundance of visitors, he claims, that they needed to be appropriately lit. Dietwulf Baatz, 'Fensterglastypen, Glasfenster und Architektur', in *Bautechnik der Antike: Diskussionen zur Archäologischen Bauforschung, Vol. 5*, ed. Adolf Hoffman, E.L. Schwandner, W. Höpfner and G. Brands (Mainz: Verlag Philipp von Zabern, 1991). The appropriate illumination of an enclosed space consistent with the function and use of this space is repeatedly mentioned in Vitruvius' *On Architecture*.

glass for ecclesiastical and imperial/aristocratic buildings during the fifth and sixth centuries. Roughly contemporary window glass fragments have been recovered from archaeological sites as diverse as the late-antique market city of Sardis, an early Christian basilica in Philippi in Greece, the Petra church in Jordan, the fortifications at Butrint in Albania and a cemetery church in Sion, Sous-le-Scex, in the Swiss Rhône Valley.[101] At Constantinople, the earliest examples of window glass were excavated at Hagios Polyeuktos, dating to the sixth or seventh century.[102] As regards the church of Hagia Sophia, Paul the Silentiary describes how the windows of the main semi-dome in the east are 'sheathed in thin glass (*hyalos*), through which, brilliantly gleaming, enters rosy-ankled Dawn'.[103] Although the term *hyalos* is ambiguous, Paul's characterisation of the brilliant and rosy light at dawn suggests the use of relatively colourless and translucent window materials. Aesthetically, at least, translucent and only faintly coloured window glass would have been preferable to other window materials that would have considerably modified the natural light, due to their high absorption coefficient.[104]

The nature of the window materials obviously determines the amount and quality of light that is transmitted. Depending on the chemical composition and the crystal structure of the glass, light is reflected, scattered and absorbed while travelling through the material at different rates.[105] The surviving examples of Roman and medieval window glass are usually not of an entirely homogeneous quality and often contain air bubbles and some colouring.[106]

101 Dell'Acqua (2005); Nadine Schibille, Fatma Marii, and Thilo Rehren, 'Characterization and provenance of late antique window glass from the Petra Church in Jordan', *Archaeometry* 50 (2008); N. Schibille, 'Supply routes and the consumption of glass in first millennium CE Butrint (Albania)', *JAS* 38 (2011); Sophie Wolf *et al.*, 'The composition and manufacture of early medieval coloured window glass from Sion (Valais, Switzerland) – a Roman glass-making tradition or innovative craftsmanship?', *Archaeometry* 47 (2005). The sixth-century dating of a fragment of strongly coloured window glass from San Vitale in Ravenna seems somewhat questionable. Carlo Cecchelli, 'Vetri da finestra del S. Vitale di Ravenna', *Felix Ravenna* 35 (1930): 15–16, 19; Friedrich Wilhelm Deichmann, *Ravenna: Hauptstadt des spätantiken Abendlandes, Vol. II, Kommentar, 2. Teil* (Wiesbaden: Frank Steiner Verlag GmbH, 1976), 139–41.

102 R. Martin. Harrison, *Excavations at Saraçhane in Istanbul, Vol. 1: The Excavations, Structures, Architectural Decoration, Small Finds, Coins, Bones, And Molluscs*, vol. I (Princeton, NJ: Princeton University Press, 1986), 204–6. Some literary evidence indicates that glass production was established in Constantinople already in the sixth century or even earlier, but no archaeological evidence of primary or secondary production has yet been unearthed in Constantinople. Elpidio Mioni, 'Il Pratum Spirituale di Giovanni Mosco', *Orientalia Christiana Periodica* 17 (1951).

103 Silentiary verse 410: *λεπταλέαις ὕαλοις κεκαλυμμένα, τῶν διά μέσσης φαιδρὸν ἀπαστράπτουσα ῥοδόσφυρος ἔρχται ἠώς*; translated in Mango (1972, reprint 1986), 82.

104 Other early window materials include thinly cut marble or alabaster slabs, mica and slabs of crystalline gypsum, but also fish bladders, stomachs of cattle, horn and parchment. R. J. Forbes, *Studies in Ancient Technology: Glass*, Vol. V (Leiden: Brill, 1957), 181–2; Kleinbauer (1999), 43; Schöne (1954), 434–8.

105 Richard Tilley, *Colour and the Optical Properties of Materials* (Chichester: John Wiley and Sons, 2000), 18–19, 28–33.

106 The colours of late antique window glass fragments range from transparent almost colourless, faint yellowish green and bluish green to dark bottle green. Schibille, Marii, and Rehren (2008); Wolf *et al.* (2005).

As a result, the light that is filtered through these heterogeneous windowpanes is more diffuse than in a modern interior environment and not quite as bright and crisp. Nonetheless, the absorption spectra of the window glasses from the Petra Church in Jordan revealed that these late antique window panes absorb the light relatively equally across the visible part of the spectrum and generally exhibit the least absorption, hence the greatest amount of transmission, roughly at 555 nm wavelength.[107] These findings imply that the light that is transmitted by these fifth- to seventh-century window glass fragments is perceived as virtually colourless with a possibly yellowish tinge similar to that of the light of the sun. Intriguingly, it is at exactly this wavelength of 555 nm that human photopic vision (colour vision) is most effective. In addition to the wavelength (colour) of light, the efficacy of vision is also dependent on the amount (intensity) of light. As the light intensity decreases, photopic vision gives way to scotopic vision (monochromatic vision). Throughout this transition phase (mesopic vision) the relative brightness of red changes in favour of blue colours, due to the photosensitive pigment (rhodopsin) that predominantly absorbs light in the blue-green part of the visible spectrum.[108]

With these caveats in mind, the level of light within Hagia Sophia seems to be reciprocally related to the colours and materials of its interior decoration. It is notable that there is a tendency of more blues and silver in areas that receive less light (inner narthex, barrel vaults piercing through subsidiary piers) as opposed to gold and red in areas that are brightly lit. Taken together, it would appear that the architects' concern was to provide sufficient light to support human photopic (colour) vision, possibly for the benefit of the colourful interior decorations. This suggests the use of high quality translucent window materials. It has to be admitted, though, that the human visual system is exceptionally good at compensating for changes in the level of lighting, meaning that our visual system is able to identify colours under varying light conditions. This capacity of the visual brain is termed colour constancy.[109] Human vision can operate over a range of illuminations greater than 12 orders of magnitude (10^{12}), which is similar to the range of light variations in the

[107] Schibille, Marii, and Rehren (2008); Schibille *et al.* (2012).

[108] Robert W.G. Hunt, *Measuring Colour* (Kingston-upon-Thames: Fountain, 1987, 3rd edition, 1998), 20–23; Robert F. Schmidt and Gerhard Thews, eds, *Human Physiology* (Berlin and London: Springer Verlag, 1989, 2nd edition), 241. The spectral sensitivity of the cones is defined by the trichromatic theory of colour vision, meaning there are three cone types with three different photosensitive pigments, corresponding to varying spectral sensitivities. The three types of cones have been thus designated either according to the wavelengths such as Long, Medium and Short (L, M, S) or consistent with the part of the spectrum they are sensitive to, mainly Reddish, Greenish and Bluish (R, G, B). It is assumed that their relative abundance on the retina is in a ratio of 40 to 20 to 1 for the R (580 nm), G (540 nm) and B (440 nm) cones, respectively.

[109] Karl R. Gegenfurtner, 'Cortical mechanisms of colour vision', *Nature Reviews/ Neuroscience* 4 (2003).

natural human environment.[110] By light versus dark adaptation, the sensitivity of the eye alone changes by a factor of 10,000.[111] Human visual perception is, therefore, easily adjusted to the differences in the environmental luminance. However, to be able to distinguish subtle differences in shades and hues and to obtain a clear impression of the vast interior of Hagia Sophia, the highest possible level of luminance is required. That this was indeed provided in the sixth century is evident from Procopius' and Paul the Silentiary's vivid descriptions of the polychrome interior decoration and precious materials. These literary sources give great value to the luminosity of the various colours that dominate the visual experience of the interior, supporting the assumption that window glass of high quality was used in the sixth century. As a result, the sacred space must have been indeed bathed in a profusion of light that dominated the aesthetic and spiritual experience of the building's interior.

Some Nocturnal Sun

So far, it has been shown that the architects of Hagia Sophia had a notable interest in maximising the natural illumination, not just to satisfy purely functional requirements to provide the interior with an adequate level of light, but also to convey wider spiritual and intellectual meanings. They created a brightly and evenly lit interior space, whose individual spatial units and architectural features were visually assimilated into a homogeneous system through the agency of natural light. More evidence for the structural and aesthetic significance of light within the sacred interior of Hagia Sophia and for a conscious light management system comes from the elaborate artificial light installations in the church. In late antiquity, artificial lighting was generally of great importance in ecclesiastical environments.[112] Paul the Silentiary offers an extensive description of a great variety of lighting devices that were installed throughout Hagia Sophia at the time of the building's re-consecration. It can be assumed that the nature of the artificial illumination had not changed dramatically from before the collapse of the main dome in 558 CE. Paul marvels especially at the illumination of the central space beneath the dome:

---

110 Hunt (1987, 3rd edition, 1998), 26–7; Schmidt and Thews (1989, 2nd edition), 241. The mean luminance of the natural human environment varies by many orders of magnitude from about $10^{-6} \frac{cd}{m^2}$ (candela per square metre) under an overcast night sky to as much as $10^{7} \frac{cd}{m^2}$ in bright sunshine with brightly reflective surfaces.

111 R. Greger and U. Windhorst, eds, *Comprehensive Human Physiology: From Cellular Mechanisms to Integration* (Berlin and London: Springer Verlag, 1996), 769; Richard L. Gregory, *Eye and Brain: The Psychology of Seeing* (Oxford: Oxford University Press, 1998), 85.

112 One *Novalla* in the *Corpus Iuris Civilis* explicitly demands provisions for the maintenance of the light installations in the church (pref. 67). According to Onasch, the ecclesiastical laws of Justinian explicitly prescribed the installation of the lighting systems before the consecration of a building, thus turning lamps into sacred objects. Onasch (1993), 132.

> But no words are sufficient to describe the illumination in the evening … stretched from the projecting stone cornice, on whose back is planted the foot of the temple's lofty dome, long twisted chains of beaten brass, linked in alternating curves by many hooks … And to each chain he has attached silver discs (ἀργυρέους δίσκους), suspended circle-wise in the air around the central confines of the church. Thus, descending from their lofty course, they float in a circle above the heads of men. The cunning craftsman has pierced the discs all over with his iron tool so that they may receive shafts of fire-wrought glass (ὄφρα κεν ἐξ ὑάλοιο πυρικμήτοιο ταθέντας οὐριάχους δέξαιντο) and provide pendent sources of light for men at night … in the [same circle] you will see, next to the discs, the shape of the lofty cross with many eyes upon it, and in its pierced back it holds luminous vessels (ἄγγος ἐλαφρίζοντα σελασφόρον). Thus hangs the circling choir of bright lights (εὐσελάων δὲ κύκλιος ἐκ φαέων χορὸς ἵσταται) … And in a smaller, inner circle you will find a second crown bearing lights along its rim, while in the very centre another noble disc rises shining in the air, so that darkness is made to flee.[113]

According to Paul the Silentiary, at least two concentric circles of polycandela and one additional great disc of lamps were suspended from the main dome and the dome cornice, while a row of single lamps attached to bronze stakes was placed directly onto the cornice.[114] Remnants of the sixth-century suspension appliances are still visible today and confirm Paul the Silentiary's account. Van Nice and subsequently Lawrence Butler found a series of holes on the upper surface of the dome cornice, which had served as lamp beam placements. Originally 80 lamp beams were placed around the dome cornice, one below each rib and each window that projected over the nave and from where the polycandela were suspended. Two concentric circles of 20 holes each were furthermore found in the dome shell itself.[115] These findings suggest that there might even have been three concentric circles of polycandela floating above Hagia Sophia's central space, the impression of which must have been mesmerising.

Paul the Silentiary went on to describe a sequence of single lamps that was installed along the lateral arcades. A silver vessel resembling a balance pan was placed underneath each arcade and a cup of light-giving oil was at its centre. These lamps seem to have been suspended from the lower nave cornice by twisted chains to different levels so as to follow a curved path and distribute their light equally. Floor lamps were fastened on beams between two-horned supports of iron on the ground floor as well as on the gallery along the cornices.[116] Again, architectural evidence confirms Paul's account. Craters, for example, were found at regular intervals on the upper surface around the

---

113 Silentiary verses 806–838.

114 Silentiary verses 862–880.

115 Laskarina Bouras and Maria G. Parani, *Lighting in Early Byzantium* (Washington, DC: Dumbarton Oaks Research Library and Collection, 2008), 31–6; Lawrence E. Butler 'The Nave Cornices of Hagia Sophia in Istanbul' (PhD, University of Pennsylvania, 1989), 69–70; Butler (1992); van Nice (1986), plate 28.

116 Silentiary verses 839–861.

entire gallery cornice that were destined to hold about 200 lamp beams.[117] In van Nice's detailed architectural drawings, a series of main holes is recorded on the surface of the upper cornice and, as Butler has pointed out, the pattern of cruciform scars suggests their use for the anchoring of lamp beams. The purpose of another type of holes, though, must remain unclear, but they may be lamp placement scars as well. There seems to be no correspondence between the two cornices, but a pattern of one lamp beam per column and two per intercolumniation appears to be the standard arrangement.[118] Paul mentions numerous further lamps installed above the chancel screen and hanging on twisted chains, illuminating the aisles, the naos, the east and west ends of the church at the higher as well as at the lower levels.[119] Hagia Sophia's interior was thus turned into an ever-changing and luminous sacred space, exploiting the effects of the flickering light of the candles and oil lamps to create the impression of animated matter.

No sixth-century lighting devices survive from Hagia Sophia itself, but comparative examples are preserved from contemporary contexts. The largest recorded polycandelon is a brass specimen from the sixth or seventh century in the British Museum, which might have held 17 lamps.[120] Other extant sixth-century polycandela formed part of a large treasure of ecclesiastical silver recovered from a single church found near Antalya in southern Turkey (also known as the Sion treasure). To this treasure belong a large circular polycandelon (56 cm in diameter with 16 circular sockets) and a cruciform polycandelon (total width of 56 cm with 12 circular sockets), now in the Dumbarton Oaks Collection.[121] The interspaces of all polycandela are cut out so as to obtain a pattern of openwork. This openwork would create a vivid play of light and shadow, of various motifs such as crosses and christograms, monograms and dolphins against the flickering light of the oil flames, especially when seen from below.[122]

---

117 Butler (1989), 59–67. Butler distinguished between two series of holes according to the dimensions of the brass beams, the shape of their ends and their location. He assumed that series A represents the earlier lighting system, whereas the series B might have been a later supplement.

118 Butler (1989), 68–9; van Nice (1986).

119 Silentiary verses 871–884: νύξ δὲ φαεινὴ ἠμάτιον γελόωσα ῥοδόσφυρός ἐστι καὶ αὐτὴ.

120 Donald M. Bailey, ed. *A Catalogue of the Lamps in the British Museum IV: Lamps of Metal and Stone, and Lampstands* (London: British Museum Press, 1996), 108, plates 48, 49, Q 3936 MLA. A somewhat simpler version is the plain metal ring perforated with holes for the glass vessel from the sixth or seventh century also in the British Museum, plates 146, 147, Q 3935 MLA.

121 Bouras and Parani (2008), cat. no. 25 and 26.

122 Cup-shaped glass vessels, to which a stem of either solid or hollow glass was attached, were placed into the holders of the polycandela. If hollow, the wick was placed inside the stem and presumably held by a wick-holder. B. Yelda Olcay, 'Lighting methods in the Byzantine period and findings of glass lamps in Anatolia', *JGS* 43 (2001): 80–81. A greenish cup-shaped glass lamp with a hollow stem (fifth to seventh century) survived in the Christian Schmidt Collection in Munich. See Stiegemann (2001), 216, Figure II.10.

Other lighting devices that can be identified from Paul's description are the single lamps along the lateral arcades that were probably bowl-shaped hanging lamps, suspended from adjustable chains, as frequently depicted in manuscripts.[123] They were first mentioned in the fourth century CE and appear to have been widespread because they were easy to use.[124] Lamps in the form of ships were some of the earliest multi-nozzled lamps and were very popular in the later Roman period. An example of a possibly fifth-century bronze boat lamp with three wick nozzles projecting from either side is in the Dumbarton Oaks Collection.[125] The floor lamps along the lateral arcades might have been devices that are commonly called λαμναὶ and κοσμηταρίτζια, which were metal strips fitted with candleholders.[126] The lamps above the chancel screen that Paul describes in terms of trees with fiery branches might have resembled the Jewish menorah that was traditionally called the *tree of light* and the *tree of life*. A seven-branched lamp-stand with Greek inscription, for example, is depicted in the manuscript of Cosmas Indicopleustes. In place of candles, seven lamps in the form of birds issue the flames from their beaks (Figure 2.7).[127] There can be no doubt that Hagia Sophia was equipped with an extraordinary array and number of different lighting installations.

Despite a great variety and number of lighting devices distributed throughout the sixth-century building, the light produced by the flames of the oil lamps and candles would most certainly appear muted compared to modern day standards. Butler calculated the light intensity of three sizes of polycandela (16, 12 and 9 lamps) and the surface luminance produced by such lighting devices. He came to the conclusion that an ordinary 40W light bulb is over 30 times brighter than the largest Byzantine polycandelon with 16 lamps and that it is unlikely that these lamps could generate a strong brightness for a vast interior space.[128] Bouras likewise concluded that this type of artificial lighting could not have illuminated the whole of the vast, cavernous edifice.[129] Still, to Paul the Silentiary and his contemporaries, the nocturnal light impression with thousands of flickering flames was evidently highly impressive. It is the very nature of the artificial light of candles and oil lamps with their flickering flames, the play of light on the reflective surfaces and the animated shadows cast by polycandela and other lavishly decorated lighting devices that brought about the unique spatial and visual experience that defined Hagia Sophia in the sixth century. Paul explicitly notes the quality of movement and animation when he describes

123 Laskarina Bouras, 'Byzantine lighting devices', *JÖB* 32 (1982): 479.

124 Olcay (2001), 84. Two bell-shaped lamps are preserved in the Christian Schmidt Collection in Munich (fourth to seventh century). See Stiegemann (2001), 219–20, Figure II.14.1 and 2.

125 Bouras and Parani (2008), cat. no. 14.

126 Bouras (1982), 480.

127 Exhibition 'Lighting in Early Byzantium' (Dumbarton Oaks, Washington, 1984). Florence, Biblioteca Laurenziana, MS Plut. 9.28, fol.126v.

128 Butler (1989), 75–6.

129 Bouras and Parani (2008), 36.

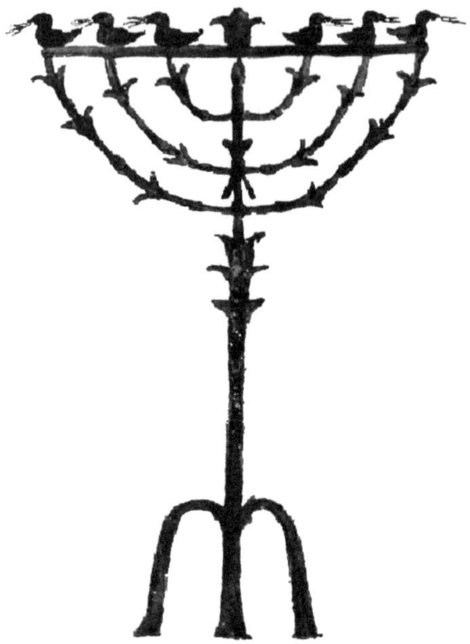

2.7 Lighting device in the shape of a menorah with birds with flames in their beaks (adapted from the manuscript of Cosmas Indicopleustes; Florence, Biblioteca Laurenziana, MS Plut. 9.28, fol.126v).

the light as brightly shining, glittering and luminous, recalling the scintillating effects he describes in context of the interior decoration. The numerous lighting devices were intentionally distributed throughout the building with no apparent emphasis on any spatial unit, even though a great quantity of lamps was gathered underneath the main dome. The result was a diffuse and non-directional illumination of the entire space, aided by the light effects of the polycandela with their openwork, creating a vibrant play of light and shadows. No sharply defined shadows were cast, even though the interior was rich in contrasts. Shadows and the light of neighbouring lamps merged, softening the edges of the contrasts. Light served as a unifier of the architectural structure and not, as has often been suggested, as a means of separation and differential articulation of individual spaces.

The pattern of illumination that emerges from both the natural and artificial lighting of Hagia Sophia in the sixth century is a homogeneous one, which sought to unify the interior spaces by flooding it with light throughout. The original architectural design and fenestration as well as the artificial lighting were co-opted to create an even, non-directional illumination, which is the principal aesthetic constituent of the original spatial and visual experience. The juxtaposition of light and dark elements in the configuration of the window openings and in the lateral arcades against the flood of light from the exterior walls recurs again in the open-cut polycandela and the deeply undercut capitals and arcade spandrels. The three-dimensional shaping of the interior is neutralised for the benefit of an overall impression of lavish glow and splendour, an impression Procopius and Paul the Silentiary tried to communicate in their sixth-century descriptions of Hagia Sophia. Light was no longer only functional and merely a means to an end in architectural terms, but light had become the very object of attention. In the sixth-century context of the Great Church, light had evolved into a constitutive as well as an aesthetic component of the building's design, and carried symbolic significance. The interior of Hagia Sophia was defined by the profusion of light, and it appears that it was the concern for an efficient illumination that motivated the peculiarly shallow dome profile, Hagia Sophia's specific orientation in relation to the sun's orbit and the building's extensive fenestration. It is, furthermore, very likely that high quality glass panes were used for the window closures and that these window sheets only slightly modified and diminished the quantity of light passing through. Yet, the advantage of ancient window glass was that it did not produce blinding hotspots of unobstructed sunlight, but a somewhat diffuse light quality. This in turn would have enhanced the glow of the colours of the mosaics and marble decoration. The interplay of architectural and decorative elements with an abundance of light established the dynamic atmosphere and visual consistency that underlies all well designed monumental architecture.[130] It was the function of light to preserve the harmony and unity of the architectural system that as an entity echoed the perfection and wisdom of the divine demiurge. At the most fundamental level, the sensation of light undoubtedly evokes a generic visual experience.[131] However, within the confines of the church of Hagia Sophia, the abundance of physical light also transmitted specific ideas about the conceptual and aesthetic properties of light in analogy to Neoplatonic theories on divine immanence and transcendence. Through light, Hagia Sophia excited an intense spiritual and epistemological experience. This interpretation is vindicated by the sixth-century descriptions of Hagia Sophia and the light management system reconstructed on structural and mathematical grounds. To what extent Hagia Sophia's treatment of light is unique, specifically created to convey the concepts of spiritual and epistemological enlightenment and by extension of divine wisdom, needs to be assessed in relation to the tradition of early Christian church architecture.

Tradition and Innovation

The innovative character of Anthemius' and Isodorus' design emerges more clearly when considering the local traditions and developments in church architecture preceding Hagia Sophia's construction in the sixth century. Although not much survives in Constantinople from the fourth and fifth centuries, the overall evidence suggests that prior to Justinian's foundations church buildings generally followed traditional plans and decorative forms.[132] The common type of church building throughout late antiquity was that of the basilica. The basilica had been adapted from the civil Roman assembly hall partly because of its suitability to house large congregations, but there is no standardised form of the early Christian basilica as such.[133] Late antique

130 Thomas (2007), Chapter 1.

131 Arnheim (1977), 208.

132 For an overview, see, for example, Krautheimer (1965, 4th edition, 1986).

133 Richard Krautheimer, 'The Constantinian basilica', *DOP* 21 (1967); Krautheimer (1965, 4th edition, 1986), 20–21; Cyril Mango, *Byzantine Architecture* (New York: H.N. Abrams,

basilicas could consist of a single nave like the Constantinian basilica in Trier (305–312), a nave flanked by one aisle on either side like Santa Sabina in Rome (422–432), Saint John Studios in Constantinople (c. 450) and the Panagia Acheiropoietos in Thessalonica (c. 470), or the basilica could be divided into a nave and four aisles such as San Giovanni in Laterano (c. 312–324), the Church of the Nativity in Bethlehem (c. 333) and the Holy Sepulchre in Jerusalem (dedicated in 335), Hagios Demetrios in Thessalonica (c. 470) and possibly the first building of Hagia Sophia in Constantinople (consecrated on 15 February 360).[134] Galleries surmounting the aisles are more commonly found in the eastern provinces as, for instance, in the Studios Basilica in Constantinople, the churches of Acheiropoietos and Hagios Demetrios in Thessalonica, the Holy Sepulchre in Jerusalem and, again, presumably in the first Hagia Sophia in Constantinople. Galleries are usually absent from western church buildings where the naves were instead fitted with clerestory windows as in the Lateran's Basilica or Santa Sabina in Rome. However, the presence of galleries did not always preclude clerestory windows (as in Hagios Demetrios).[135] What almost all the early Christian basilicas have in common, though, is that they are generally longitudinal and they are almost always timber-roofed with or without a coffered ceiling beneath.[136] Hence, the spatial quality of a basilica is very much determined by this lengthwise orientation, often heightened through the articulation of the apse space that traditionally terminated the nave.

St. John Studios

The only timber-roofed basilica in Constantinople from the fifth century still substantially preserved, albeit in ruins, is the church of St. John Studios near the Golden Gate (Figure 2.8). The construction of the church can safely be attributed to the middle of the fifth century, most certainly before 454 CE and possibly to the year 453 CE.[137] In principle following the arrangement of a basilica

1976), 58–75; Marlia Mundell-Mango, 'Building and architecture', in *The Cambridge Ancient History, Vol. XIV, Late Antiquity: Empire and Successors, A.D. 425–600*, ed. Averil Cameron, Bryan Ward-Perkins, and Michael Whitby (Cambridge: Cambridge University Press, 2000), 955–8.

[134] For the churches in Rome, see, for example, Hugo Brandenburg, *Die frühchristlichen Kirchen Roms vom 4. bis zum 7. Jahrhundert: Der Beginn der abendländischen Kirchenbaukunst* (Regensburg: Verlag Schnell and Steiner, 2004). For eastern churches, see, for example, Krautheimer (1965, 4th edition, 1986); Mango (1976); Thomas F. Mathews, *The Early Churches of Constantinople: Architecture and Liturgy* (London and University Park, PA: The Pennsylvania State University Press, 1971), 11–41. For specifically Constantinian basilicas see Krautheimer (1967).

[135] Unlike Mundell-Mango, I am therefore not convinced that the naves in eastern churches are necessarily dark in comparison, as the luminosity depends also on the configuration of the aisle and gallery and their windows as well as the fenestration of the apse and west walls. Mundell-Mango (2000), 957–8.

[136] Krautheimer (1965, 4th edition, 1986); Krautheimer (1967); Mango (1976), 61.

[137] Based on brickstamps, Bardill argued for a date between 448/9 and 451/2 CE. Jonathan Bardill, *Brickstamps of Constantinople* (Oxford: Oxford University Press, 2004),

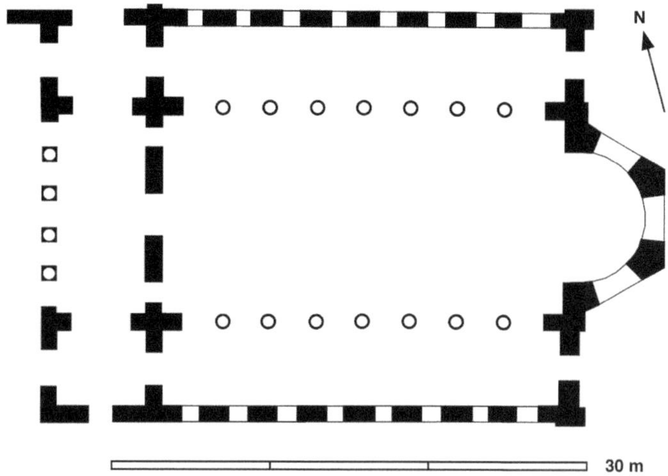

2.8 Ground plan of the Studios basilica in Istanbul (adapted from van Millingen 1912).

preceded by an atrium and narthex to the west, the outline of the main body of the church is almost square (about 25 m long excluding the apse and 24 m wide). Colonnades of seven green Thessalian marble columns on either side divided the interior into a nave and two aisles, while a gallery enveloped the central space on three sides, following in plan the aisles and narthex below.[138] The seven gallery columns on the northern and southern side were probably connected by arches rather than by a horizontal entablature like the one at ground level.[139] The main nave ended in a semi-circular apse with three large windows. There might not have been clerestory windows, but the aisles and galleries were extensively fenestrated with two ranges of eight large round-headed windows in the northern and southern walls, corresponding with the intercolumniations of the nave colonnades.[140] The interior must once have been sumptuously decorated with marble revetments and mosaics at least at the eastern end of the building in the apse and on the triumphal arch.[141] The capitals of the ground floor colonnades are of the so-called Theodosian composite type with acanthus leaves combined with diagonal corner volutes. Virtually identical ones have been found, for example, in the Acheiropoietos Church in Thessalonica.[142] The

60–61, 109. The Chronicle of Theophanes gives a date of 463 CE (Theophanes 1997, 175), followed by Mathews (1971), 19–27. Mango persuasively argues for a somewhat earlier date of 453 CE based on the text of an epigram recorded in the AP I, 4; Cyril Mango, 'The date of the Studius Basilica at Istanbul', *BMGS* 4 (1978).

138 Mango (1976), 61; Mathews (1971), 21–3; Alexander van Millingen, *Byzantine Churches in Constantinople: Their History and Architecture* (London: Macmillan and Co. Ltd., 1912), 35–61.

139 van Millingen (1912), 52.

140 While van Millingen does not commit to a decision as regards clerestory windows, Krautheimer merely assumes that the Studios basilica did not have any clerestory windows. van Millingen (1912), 53–4; Krautheimer (1965, 4th edition, 1986), 78–9; Mango (1976), 61.

141 The excavations conducted by the Russian Archaeological Institute in 1907–1909 yielded large quantities of mosaic tesserae and substantial traces of iron hooks for the fastening of the marble revetment. van Millingen (1912), 53; Mango (1976), 61.

142 W. Eugene Kleinbauer, 'Remarks on the building history of the Acheiropoietos church at Thessaloniki', *Actes du Xe Congrès International d'Archéologie* 2 (1980): 244–5.

entablature, on the other hand, is late Corinthian in nature, reminiscent of the propylaeum of Theodosius' Hagia Sophia. Unlike the Theodosian decoration, the acanthus frieze in the Studios basilica is more delicately carved and deeply undercut, thus increasing the contrast of the raised acanthus leaves against the dark background.[143] Judging from the uniformity of the interior decoration, it seems likely that the capitals and columns were made to order.[144]

Even though the church of St. John Studios, including the atrium and narthex, follows the elongated design of a traditional basilica, the almost square proportions of its main body weaken the longitudinal orientation and convey a more centralised impression. Given the large windows encircling the building at both the ground floor and gallery level, the interior must have been filled with plenty of light from all sides due to the openness of plan and the wide intercolumniations (about 3 m), regardless of the probable absence of clerestory windows. With its broad central nave, the use of colourful materials in the form of columns of green Thessalian marble, marble revetment and mosaic decoration combined with a profusion of light, the visual and spatial experience of the Studios basilica would not have been so dissimilar to that of Hagia Sophia in the sixth century, were it not for the horizontal entablature, the timber roof and the clear visual articulation of the apse and sanctuary. A timber-roofed edifice is generally much more connected to the ground than a domed structure. Whether St. John Studios featured an open truss roof or a coffered ceiling, either would have strongly impeded the vertical expansion and luminosity of the basilica. The emphasis lies, after all, on the horizontal plane enhanced by the continuous entablature of the nave colonnades. Despite (or possibly because) of the clear dominance of the horizontal plane and due to the widely spaced colonnades, the nave and aisles of the Studios basilica are not spatially distinguished. Instead, spatial boundaries are dissolved, the nave visually extends into the aisles aided by the unifying force of light, and the individual interior spaces are organically interlocked. Thus, the architectural structure of the Studios basilica, although fairly traditional in plan, already anticipates some fundamental visual and spatial features that were to become characteristic of Justinian's great foundations in the Byzantine capital and other urban and religious centres.

The Golden Octagon of Antioch and Santa Costanza in Rome

The openness of plan and the unified interior space is an essential quality of centralised church buildings. Centralised forms in the widest sense existed alongside the basilica type from the outset, most notably the *Anastasis Rotunda* in Jerusalem enclosing Christ's tomb (dedicated in 335 CE),[145] the

[143] Krautheimer (1965, 4th edition, 1986), 79; McKenzie (2007), 331.

[144] Mango (1976), 61.

[145] Martin Biddle, *The Tomb of Christ* (Gloucestershire: Sutton Publishing Ltd, 1999); Kenneth John Conant, 'The original buildings at the Holy Sepulchre in Jerusalem', *Speculum*

Megale Ekklesia (Great Church or *Golden Octagon*) of Antioch (dedicated in 341 CE),[146] the church of Santa Costanza in Rome built in the middle of the fourth century as a mausoleum for Constantine's elder daughter Constantina,[147] or San Stefano Rotondo in Rome (dedicated under Pope Simplicius between 468–483 CE).[148] These are all double shell structures where the central circular or octagonal core was surrounded by an ambulatory and in which the central space was covered with a dome made of timber or other lightweight material.

The Golden Octagon of Antioch is the earliest known centralised building specifically designed as a regular congregational church. Of considerable architectural and historical importance, this Great Church might have served as prototype not only of the aisled tetraconch churches in Syria and Mesopotamia (c. 460 to 550 CE), but also of related ecclesiastical structures.[149] It is known from Eusebius' literary evidence that the church was of enormous height, richly decorated with gold and other precious materials and designed in the form of an octagon (*octahedron*). This inner octagonal core was enveloped by many chambers (*oikoi*) and exedras on both the lower and upper levels. This structure in turn was surrounded by *periboloi* that may be translated as either a very high wall or vast enclosure or, in fact, as colonnades similar to the original exterior colonnade of Santa Costanza in Rome.[150] Given the absence

---

31 (1956); Virgilio C. Corbo, *Il Santo Sepolcro di Gerusalemme: aspetti archeologici dalle origini al periodo crociato* (Jerusalem: Franciscan Print Press, 1981–82); Charles Coüasnon, *The Church of the Holy Sepulchre in Jerusalem* (London: Oxford University Press, 1974); W. Eugene Kleinbauer, 'Antioch, Jerusalem, and Rome: The patronage of emperor Constantius II and architectural invention', *Gesta* 45 (2006); Robert Ousterhout, 'The temple, the sepulchre, and the martyrion of the Savior', *Gesta* 29 (1990).

146 Deichmann has persuasively demonstrated that the Great Church was not a palatine, i.e. imperial palace church as had been previously assumed, but it was built as a cathedral. Friedrich Wilhelm Deichmann, 'Das Oktogon von Antiocheia: Heroon-Martyrion, Palastkirche oder Kathedrale?', *Byzantinische Zeitschrift* 65 (1972); Glanville Downey, *A History of Antioch in Syria from Seleucus to the Arab Conquest* (Princeton, NJ: Princeton University Press, 1961), 342–50; Krautheimer (1965, 4th edition, 1986), 53–5. For an attribution to Constantius rather than Constantine, see Kleinbauer (2006). In an earlier article, Kleinbauer questioned whether the Great Church in Antioch must have necessarily been an octagon. W. Eugene Kleinbauer, 'The origin and functions of the aisled tetraconch churches in Syria and northern Mesopotamia', *DOP* 27 (1973).

147 Mark J. Johnson, *The Roman Imperial Mausoleum in Late Antiquity* (Cambridge and New York, NY: Cambridge University Press, 2009), 139–56; W. Eugene Kleinbauer, 'Santa Costanza at Rome and the house of Constantine', *Acta ad archaeologiam et artium historiam pertinentia* 18 (2004); Kleinbauer (2006); David J. Stanley, 'Santa Costanza: History, archaeology, function, patronage and dating', *Arte Medievale* 3 (2004).

148 Hugo Brandenburg, *Die Kirche S. Stafano Rotondo in Rom: Bautypologie und Architektursymbolik in der spätantiken und frühchristlichen Architektur*, ed. Christoph Markschies, Hans-Lietzmann-Vorlesungen (Berlin and New York, NY: Walter de Gruyter, 1998); Brandenburg (2004), 200–14 and references therein.

149 Deichmann (1972); Kleinbauer (1973); Kleinbauer (2006). The Justinianic church of Sts. Sergius and Bacchus in Constantinople and San Vitale in Ravenna have some characteristics in common with these early double-shell structures. Mundell-Mango (2000), 960–61.

150 Eusebius, *Vita Constantini*, III. 50; and *Speech on the Tricennalia of Constantine (Laus Constantini)* 9.15; for both Greek text and English translation, see Kleinbauer (1973), 111; Kleinbauer (2006).

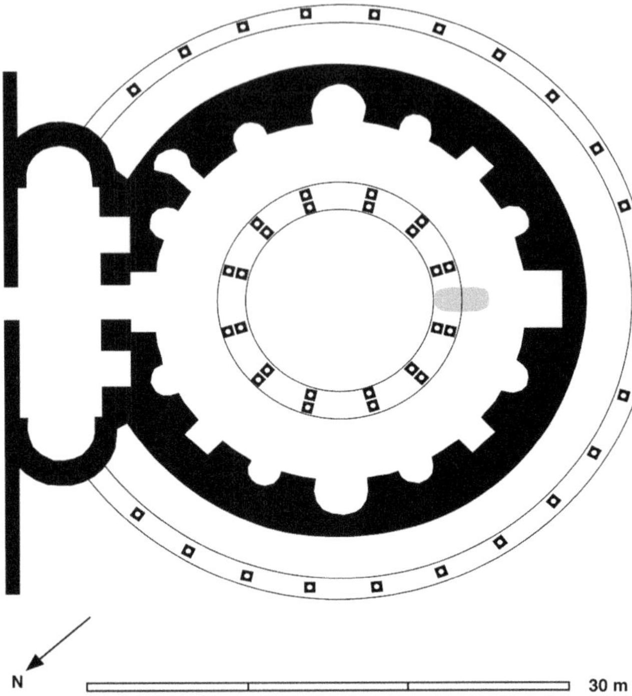

2.9 Ground plan of Santa Costanza in Rome (adapted from Brandenburg 2004).

of any archaeological or reliable pictorial evidence, the precise architectural arrangement of the Antiochian cathedral remains elusive.[151] However, if we assume that the mausoleum of Santa Costanza, attributed possibly to the patronage of Constantius II,[152] has close parallels with the Great Church in Antioch, then the smaller foundation in Rome should reflect some of the fundamental spatial and visual principles characteristic and common to both these double-shell buildings.

The church of Santa Costanza is the best-preserved architectural structure in Rome ascribed to the imperial patronage of the House of Constantine.[153]

---

[151] A seemingly octagonal building in the mid-fifth-century Megalopsychia mosaic in the Yakto complex of Daphne, a suburb of Antioch, is believed by many to be a representation of the Great Church. While this is indeed a possibility, the identification is ambiguous as no geographical names are preserved. Deichmann (1972); Kleinbauer (2006) and references therein.

[152] Kleinbauer (2006) has argued for Constantius II as patron of the fourth-century double-shell buildings, including Santa Costanza.

[153] David Stanley attributed Santa Costanza to the second quarter of the fifth century, based on archaeological and stylistic analysis and C14 dating of some concrete containing wood ash. Yet, the C14 testing allows equally for a date in the second half of the fourth century as it does for a date in the first half of the fifth century. David J. Stanley, 'New discoveries at Santa Costanza', *DOP* 48 (1994); Stanley (2004). Santa Costanza is more commonly dated to the mid-fourth century based on literary evidence and its brickwork.

In plan, the mausoleum originally consisted basically of three concentric circles (Figure 2.9). The cylindrical core structure (diameter of about 11.5 m) is separated by a circular colonnade of 12 pairs of columns from a wide ambulatory (internal diameter of about 23 m) that is enclosed by a massive wall (about 3.5 m thick). A now lost exterior colonnade used to surround the mausoleum (external diameter of about 38 m).[154] Rectangular and semicircular niches are cut out from the enclosure wall, of which four larger ones mark the main axes of the building (north/south and east/west). The southern rectangular niche opposite the entrance is clearly singled out by its size and structure: a low lantern tower lit by three windows rises above this niche, an oval slab of reddish Aswan granite was placed on the north-south axis directly beneath the tower between the two southernmost pairs of columns; these columns are imperceptibly higher and more widely spaced than the ones adjacent to the east and west, and the two reddish Aswan columns facing the ambulatory are paired only in this niche with two black and white *Mons Claudianus* marble columns facing the central space.[155] The ambulatory was initially not equipped with windows and presented a striking contrast to the bright central space. The high drum resting on the colonnade is heavily fenestrated with 12 huge clerestory windows, placed axially above the openings of the colonnades below.[156] The hemispherical dome surmounting the central space, as well as the niches and barrel vaults of the ambulatory were once decorated with mosaics, some of which survive. Virtually all the polychrome marble revetment on the inner face of the drum and ambulatory wall has been lost. In short, the double-shell structure of Santa Costanza once displayed a central space and main southern niche suffused with light against the backdrop of an unlit ambulatory, both spaces being extensively embellished with marble and mosaic decorations.

Through the sharp contrast in luminosity, the layering of the spatial units in Santa Costanza is much more defined than in the Studios basilica. The widely spaced columns (about 3 m) nonetheless allow for an integration of the spaces, drawing the visitors' gaze beyond the mesh of columns into the dimly lit outer shell. The light management of many other late antique ecclesiastical structures was similarly focused on the central nave and apse with the help of large clerestory windows in contrast to the side aisles that were devoid of windows.[157] Large clerestory windows and unlit aisles can be

Nick Henck, 'Constantius ὁ φιλοκτίστης', *DOP* 55 (2001); Johnson (2009), 139–56; Kleinbauer (2006).

154 Jürgen J. Rasch and Achim Arbeiter, *Das Mausoleum der Constantina in Rome (Spätantike Zentralbauten in Rom und Latium; Vol. 4)* (Mainz: Philipp von Zabern, 2007).

155 Johnson (2009), 144–6; Kleinbauer (2006), 137; Stanley (2004), 125–7.

156 The window openings of the outer wall of the ambulatory show clear signs that they are later additions and date certainly not earlier than the sixth century. Johnson (2009), 155–6.

157 While Stanley identifies parallels in the fourth-century churches of Santa Sabina and Santa Maria Maggiore in Rome, according to Krautheimer, 'the great Constantinian

found, for instance, in the contemporary church of Old St. Peter or the early fifth-century churches of Santa Sabina and Santa Maria Maggiore in Rome.[158] Unlike these early basilicas, though, the spatial experience of Santa Costanza's interior is defined by the high concentration of light beneath the central dome that radiates from its core outward. The luminous dome structure attracts the viewers' attention and emphasises the building's vertical dimension. The perceptual effect is fundamentally different from that of horizontally designed basilicas. From a psychological point of view, to rise is to be liberated from the ground and to come into being.[159] This psychological effect might well explain the increasing popularity of centralised dome structures analogous to the idea of anagoge and the commencement of a spiritual journey upon entering a sacred space. Through the agency of light concentrated in the upper part of its central space and the vertical thrust, centrally planned buildings like the mausoleum of Santa Costanza have the capacity to transcend being and thereby convey a sense of monumentality.[160]

Whether or not these spatial and visual principles can be extrapolated to the Golden Octagon in Antioch hinges to a certain extent on the patronage of both buildings, if, as Kleinbauer has recently argued, the double-shell structure was an innovation of the age of Constantius II and, more precisely, both edifices along with the Anastasis Rotunda of the Holy Sepulchre in Jerusalem could be attributed to the direct imperial patronage of Constantius.[161] Aside from the shared patronage, the typological consideration also argues for basic structural characteristics common to these three earliest known double-shell buildings. Although there is little that can be said with absolute certainty about the architectural form of the Antiochian church, its most decisive feature, according to the description of Eusebius, was the building's 'extraordinary height ... designed in the form of an octahedron' and enveloped by ambulatories on two levels.[162] Also, the church historian Philostorgius (c. 368–439) appears to be speaking of a

churches must have looked similar to S. Costanza'. Krautheimer (1965, 4th edition, 1986), 43–4; Stanley (2004), 133.

158 Brandenburg (2004), 22, 167–80 and references therein; Günter identified here a difference between ecclesiastical buildings in Italy that tend to have windowless aisles until the late fifth century CE, whereas the aisles of Byzantine churches in the Greek east were typically fenestrated early on. Günter (1965), 72–80.

159 According to Arnheim, 'Being is essentially experienced as verticality'. Arnheim (1977), 35.

160 Edmund Thomas has observed that funerary monuments in particular have the capacity to confront us with human mortality, while religious buildings serve to re-define the relationship between man and God. Thomas (2007), 11. Applied to Santa Costanza that is both a mausoleum and religious structure this means that it can be considered a 'monument' at these different levels.

161 Kleinbauer (2006).

162 Eusebius, *Vita Constantini*, III.50; Kleinbauer (1973), 111. For a reconstruction of the church based on Eusebius' account and particularly the meaning of *oikoi* and *exedrai* see Adalbert Birnbaum, 'Die Oktogone von Antiochia, Nazianz und Nyssa. Rekonstruktionsversuche', *Repertorium für Kunstwissenschaft* 36 (1913).

domed building when he describes the church as σφαιροειδής (globular, spherical).[163] Therefore, the distinguishing element of the Great Church in Antioch was, similar to Santa Costanza, its vertical dimension culminating in a domical structure. Despite the lack of archaeological evidence, it would be difficult to imagine that the central space of the Great Church had been devoid of windows. The extensive fenestration of the edifice is supported by the dedicatory inscription recorded in the sixth-century chronicle of John Malalas that explicitly describes the building as flooded with light similar to the vaults of heaven.[164] There is no evidence as regards the fenestration of the ambulatories, but Eusebius' comment that the church was enclosed by *periboloi*, whether this designates a wall of some kind or a colonnade, could be taken to mean that there were no unobstructed window openings at ground level. The ambulatory would then have received light only indirectly from the centre of the building as observed with respect to Santa Costanza. On the other hand, it has been noted that churches in the eastern provinces tended to have fenestrated aisles and galleries to generate a more even distribution of light within.[165] Maybe the Great Church in Antioch did follow this lighting system and was evenly illuminated throughout. In this case, it would have clearly foreshadowed the illumination of Hagia Sophia in Constantinople and related buildings. Taken together, the relatively scarce evidence suggests that the interior of the Great Church in Antioch was dominated by its height, luminosity and the perceptual impression that is associated with a centralised, tall and possibly domed building and reminiscent of the impression of Hagia Sophia in Constantinople.

Another commonality between the Golden Octagon and Hagia Sophia is their title as *Megale Ekklesia* (Great Church) and their dedications. Judging from the dedicatory epigram, the Antiochian cathedral was originally dedicated to Christ and commonly referred to as the *Megale Ekklesia*.[166] In the fifth century, the church came to be linked with the concept of harmony (homonoia, concordia), but the exact origin and date of this name remain in doubt.[167] Hagia Sophia had likewise been known originally merely as the

---

[163] Centuries later, Theophanes the Confessor likewise terms the church *sphairoeides*. Theophanes, *Chronographia*, translated in Theophanes (1997), 19.

[164] Malalas, *Chronographia*, 250: Χριστῷ Κωνστάντιος ἐπέραστον οἶκον ἔτευξεν; Οὐράνίαις ἁψῖσι πανείκελα, πανφανόωντα; Κωνσταντίου ἄνακτος ὑπόδρήσσοντος ἐφετμαῖς; Γοργόνιος δὲ κόμης θαλαμηπόλον ἔργον ὕφανε. Translated in Brian Croke, 'Malalas, the Man and His Work', in *Studies in John Malalas*, ed. Elizabeth Jeffreys, Brian Croke, and Roger Scott (Sydney: 1990), 173. The attribution of the inscription to the Great Church in Antioch has recently been challenged. Woods instead argued that it was the *praepositus sacri cubiculi* Gorgonius who had these verses inscribed, possibly on some gift to the bishop of Babylas. David Woods, '"Constantius", and a church-inscription from Antioch', *Vigiliae Christianae* 59 (2005). However, Kleinbauer has convincingly refuted this claim Kleinbauer (2006), 141, note 35.

[165] Günter (1965), 72–9; Krautheimer (1965, 4th edition, 1986), 129–39.

[166] Malalas, *The Chronicle*, 173.

[167] Deichmann expressed doubts about the authenticity of this appellation and argues that it is a later fabrication. Deichmann (1972), 50–52; Downey (1961), 345–6. Kleinbauer, on

Megale Ekklesia and the name Sophia came into use sometime in the early fifth century as indicated in Socrates' (c. 380–439) *Ecclesiastical History*.[168] This dedication refers to the Sophia of God, the second person of the Trinity that is Christ.[169] Hence, the two Great Churches of Antioch and Constantinople share their dedication to Christ and their association with a specific divine paradigm from the fifth century on. The Golden Octagon in Antioch served as the patriarchal church in one of the most important religious centres in the east and as such acted as a model for other churches at least in areas under Antioch's patriarchal jurisdiction.[170] It is feasible that it has also served as the prototype for other episcopal churches throughout the Byzantine realm. Some of the sixth-century foundations come to mind such as San Vitale in Ravenna, or in fact, the churches of Sts. Sergius and Bacchus and Hagia Sophia in Constantinople. In this context, it might be significant that the Golden Octagon in Antioch had to be restored after a devastating earthquake in 526 CE, hence during the reign of Justinian.[171]

In any case, fourth- and fifth-century ecclesiastical edifices had established some of the fundamental architectural principles that were to become characteristic of the sixth-century church of Hagia Sophia in Constantinople.[172] Since the fourth century, regular congregational churches were of two types: the longitudinal basilica and the centralised double-shell structure, the one emphasising the linear path, the other creating the psychological effect of a self-contained dwelling place with spatial depth.[173] Prior to the sixth century, no known monumental church building attempted to combine the qualities of the basilica and those of the centralised plan. Importantly, the two architectural types do not necessarily differ in their functional aspects or symbolic significance.[174] The choice is an aesthetic one. A centralised structure articulates the interior space much more than the oblong basilica and thus turns space into the very object of aesthetic experience. What is more, the space is decisively shaped through

---

the other hand, argues that the church was indeed dedicated to harmony by Constantius. Kleinbauer (2006), 128.

168 Socrates, *Ecclesiastical History*, II. 16 and 43; Deichmann (1972), 52–6; Glanville Downey, 'The Name of the Church of St. Sophia in Constantinople', *Harvard Theological Review* 52 (1959).

169 Downey (1959).

170 The mid-fourth-century church founded by Gregory of Nazianz, for example, is said to be modeled on the Golden Octagon in Antioch. Birnbaum (1913); Mango (1976), 87.

171 Birnbaum (1913), 188–90. Birnbaum seriously doubts any relationship between San Vitale and the Great Church in Antioch.

172 With respect to the four-corner support as one of the crucial structural principles in Hagia Sophia, Ćurčić has convincingly demonstrated that Hagia Sophia was the result of extensive architectural experimentation throughout the fifth century. Ćurčić (1992); Sedlmayr (1933).

173 Arnheim (1977), 89–91.

174 For example, Brandenburg (1998); Deichmann (1972); Kleinbauer (2006); in contrast, see, for example, André Grabar, *Martyrium: Recherches sur le culte des reliques et l'art chrétien antique, I* (Paris: Collège de France, 1946), 214.

the agency of light. Light and solar symbolism had long played a central role in Christianity, Christian iconography and architecture.[175] With the possible exception of the Great Church in Antioch, however, the light management system in these early churches is fundamentally different to that observed in the sixth-century church of Hagia Sophia. Light used to be more directed and concentrated typically in the main spaces, the central nave, the apse and the sanctuary. In the centralised double-shell structure of Santa Costanza, for example, light literally moulds the centrifugal space and radiates from the building's centre outward into the dimly lit ambulatory, drawing the viewer's attention to its source. An early form of a more homogeneous distribution of light is manifest in the fifth-century structure of the Studios basilica in Constantinople, but it has not yet come to full fruition due to its timber roof and the articulation of the apse area. Hagia Sophia is a mixture of both these concepts, as its interior becomes articulated through an even illumination and an architectural structure that emphasises the central space, horizontal plane as well as its verticality.

Sts. Sergius and Bacchus

Three other churches of the sixth century may be compared with Hagia Sophia in terms of their architectural structure and interior illumination: Hagios Polyeuktos, built immediately prior to the Justinianic foundations in Constantinople, San Vitale in Ravenna, built between about 526 and 547 CE, and Sts. Sergius and Bacchus, also built by Justinian. There has been some controversy about the date and function of the church of Sts. Sergius and Bacchus in Constantinople.[176] It was built alongside that of Sts. Peter and Paul within the precinct of the Palace of Hormisdas, the official residence of Justinian prior to his ascension to the imperial throne (518–527 CE).[177] An elaborate dedicatory inscription carved into the nave entablature explicitly credits the imperial couple, the 'sceptered Justinian (σκηπτοῦχος Ἰουστινιανὸς)' and 'God-crowned Theodora (θεοστεφέος Θεοδώρης)', suggesting that at the time of completion, Justinian had already been crowned emperor (in or after

[175] Jonathan Bardill, *Constantine, Divine Emperor of the Christian Golden Age* (Cambridge: Cambridge University Press, 2011), Chapter 8; Brandenburg (1998); Günter (1965); Krautheimer (1965, 4th edition,1986); Onasch (1993).

[176] Jonathan Bardill, 'The church of Sts. Sergius and Bacchus in Constantinople and the monophysite refugees', *DOP* 54 (2000); Brian Croke, 'Justinian, Theodora, and the church of Saints Sergius and Bacchus', *DOP*, 60 (2006); Richard Krautheimer, 'Again Saints Sergius and Bacchus at Constantinople', *Jahrbuch der österreichischen Byzantinistik* 23 (1974); Cyril Mango, 'The church of Saints Sergius and Bacchus at Constantinople and the alleged tradition of octogonal palatine churches', *JÖB* 21 (1972); Cyril Mango, 'The church of Sts. Sergius and Bacchus once again', *Byzantinische Zeitschrift* 67 (1975); Ifran Shahîd, 'The church of Sts. Sergios and Bakhos at Constantinople, some new perspectives', in *Byzantium State and Society: In Memory of Nikos Oikonomides* (Athens: Institute for Byzantine Studies, 2003).

[177] Procopius I.4.1–8; Mathews (1971), 42–51; van Millingen (1912), 62–83.

527 CE).[178] The church was certainly completed by 536 CE since the church is mentioned in the acts of the council held at Constantinople in May of the same year.[179] The stylistic characteristics of the monograms carved into the nave capitals might even provide a *terminus ante quem* of 533 CE.[180] The most plausible explanation is that the church was planned and built (at least commenced) while Justinian and Theodora were still resident in the Palace of Hormisdas (the mid-520s).[181] It is reasonably clear then that the church of Sts. Sergius and Bacchus predates the construction of Hagia Sophia by only a few years.

According to Procopius, Sts. Sergius and Bacchus shared its atrium with the neighbouring church of Sts. Peter and Paul. The two buildings were equal in size and beauty as 'each outshines the sun by the gleam of its stones, and each is equally adorned throughout with an abundance of gold'.[182] The distinguishing architectural feature of Sts. Sergius and Bacchus was its centralised shape and unusual irregular ground plan. The octagonal core (internal diameter of about 16 m) with four diagonal exedras is inscribed into a near-square outline (Figure 2.10). The octagon together with the protruding apse in the east and the east wall are laid out along a single axis, while the remaining walls of the enclosure do not conform to this axis. The skewed plan might be the result of different building campaigns and the fact that it was built against the earlier church of Sts. Peter and Paul to the south.[183] The core of the building is composed of eight wedge-shaped piers that mark the corners of the octagon and that are connected by eight broad arches, forming the sides of the octagon.[184] Above the exedras, the arches merge into spherical calottes similar to the exedras in Hagia Sophia. Upon the main arches rises a pumpkin dome divided into 16 alternating concave and flat segments, of which the latter are pierced by windows. Pairs of columns of alternately green Thessalian and red Synnade marble form two-story colonnades that envelop the octagon on all but the eastern side that is left open to accommodate the bema.[185] The lower colonnade has a richly carved horizontal entablature as opposed to the series of arches in the gallery arcades. These triple openings allow for the central space to communicate relatively unimpeded with the surrounding ambulatory and gallery. The church originally opened

178 The epigram was recently republished in Greek with an English translation and an extensive interpretation in Croke (2006). See also Bardill (2000), 2.

179 Mango (1972), 191; Mango (1975), 385–6.

180 The monograms are of the box or square type, rather than the cross-shaped that emerge first in the churches of Hagia Eirene and Hagia Sophia around the year 533 CE. Bardill (2000), 2–3.

181 As argued by Croke (2006).

182 Procopius I.4.4–5: ὁμοίως μὲν γὰρ ἑκάτερος τῇ αἴγλῃ τῶν λίθων ὑπεραστράπτει τὸν ἥλιον, ὁμοίως δὲ χρυσοῦ περιουσίᾳ πανταχόθι κατακορής ἐστι καὶ κατακομᾷ τοῖς ἀναθήμασιν.

183 Mathews (1971), 44–5.

184 The arch on the eastern side is significantly wider, articulating the bema.

185 van Millingen (1912), 73.

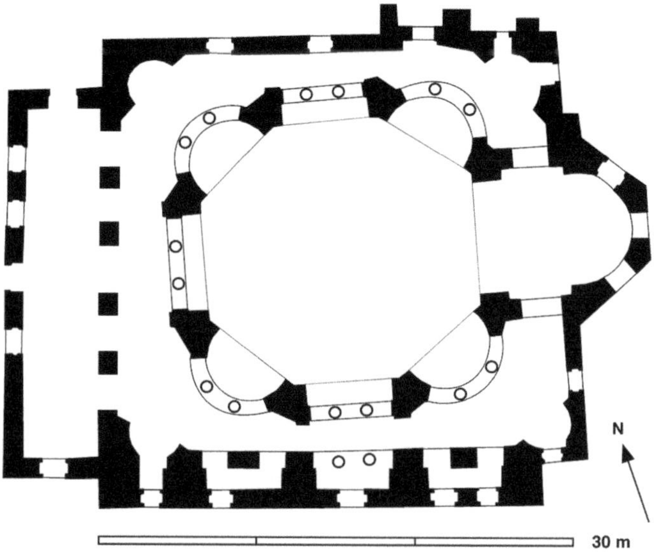

2.10 Ground plan of Sts. Sergios and Bacchus in Istanbul (adapted from Mathews 1971).

through many entrances on the north side into the palace of Hormisdas and on the south into the church of Sts. Peter and Paul.[186] Hence, the main light sources were those in the dome and in the semi-circular apse that protrudes beyond the east wall of the building and had two rows of three large round-headed windows. The contrast between the brightly lit centrepiece and the shaded ambulatory and galleries would have been even more pronounced in the sixth century because of the adjacent structures. As Alchermes noted, the skilful moulding of space through light and the interpenetration of the spatial units in the church of Sts. Sergius and Bacchus resonates in its delicately carved and shaped marble decoration.[187] The deeply undercut patterns on the entablature and capitals create rich contrasts, complemented at ground level by the bulging shape of the highly innovative fold or melon capitals that enhance the play of light and shade further.[188] From Procopius' description of the gleaming stones and gold decoration, it is clear that polychrome marble and gold mosaics once sheeted the sixth-century interior.[189] Many scholars have drawn attention to the architectural and decorative affinities between Sts. Sergius and Bacchus and

186 Mathews (1971), 42–51.

187 Joseph D. Alchermes, 'Art and architecture in the age of Justinian', in *The Cambridge Companion to the Age of Justinian*, ed. Michael Maas (Cambridge: Cambridge University Press, 2005), 362.

188 For a genealogy of these capitals, see McKenzie (2007), 342–3; van Millingen describes these capitals as cushion capitals, which seems fitting given their bulbous form. van Millingen (1912), 75.

189 Procopius I.4.5.

the slightly later church of Hagia Sophia: the domed core and exedras that open diagonally, extending into the ambulatory and galleries, and the style of the undercut marble decoration.[190] Moreover, both buildings present new solutions for a spatial design characterised by interpenetrating volumes and architectural shapes articulated through the use of the ever-changing effects of light and shade.[191] Some similarities have also been identified with San Vitale in Ravenna.[192]

San Vitale in Ravenna

Dedicated in 547 CE, the date of San Vitale's foundation is unknown.[193] Given the fact that bishop Ecclesius († 532 CE) is depicted in the apse mosaic of San Vitale offering a model of the church to Christ and is mentioned in the dedicatory epigram as the one who authorised the building's construction, it seems likely that the building had been planned and initiated already during Ecclesius' episcopate (522–532 CE).[194] It is even conceivable that Ecclesius had been inspired by the new church of Sts. Sergius and Bacchus, provided that construction of the latter had been well under way by 526 CE, when Ecclesius left Constantinople to return to Italy.[195] Like Sts. Sergius and Bacchus, the structure of San Vitale is a double-shell octagon, unique among the churches in Ravenna (Figure 2.11). Unlike the Constantinopolitan church, the enveloping shell of San Vitale is like its core octagonal in shape, only on an enlarged scale (about 33 m and 16 m).[196] Similar to Sts. Sergius and Bacchus, the inner octagon consists of eight wedge-shaped piers, but at Ravenna exedras with half domes open between all but the south-eastern bay. Here, a steep cross-vaulted presbytery extends eastwards into the lower semi-circular apse. The two octagons are skilfully woven together through a series of triple-arched semi-circular exedras on both levels, while the presbytery is accentuated through height, light and decoration. An octagonal drum with eight large

---

190 Alchermes (2005), 362; Mango (1976), 101–21; Mathews (1971), 42–3.

191 MacDonald argues that this spatial sculpturing is made possible through new solutions for the distribution of vault thrusts in later Roman architecture. William L. MacDonald, 'Some implications of later Roman construction', *The Journal of the Society of Architectural Historians* 17 (1958).

192 Deichmann (1976), 83–5; Krautheimer (1965, 4th edition, 1986), 162–70; McKenzie (2007), 341–3; Mundell-Mango (2000), 961; Eugenio Russo, *L'architettura di Ravenna paleocristiana* (Venezia: Instituto Veneto di Scienza, Lettere ed Arti Venezia, 2003).

193 Deichmann (1976), 48–9; Deborah Mauskopf Deliyannis, *Ravenna in Late Antiquity* (New York, NY: Cambridge University Press, 2010), 223–6.

194 Deichmann thinks this very unlikely, as this would give a construction period of 15 to 20 years on the basis of the monograms of the ground floor capitals that he attributes to Bishop Victor (537 – 544 CE). Mauskopf Deliyannis, on the other hand, notes that the letters of Victor Episcopus and those of Eclesius Episcopus would be identical apart from the T. Deichmann (1976), 484–9; Deliyannis (2010), 223–6 and note 109.

195 Ecclesius had accompanied Pope John (523 – 526 CE) to Constantinople. Deichmann (1976), 10.

196 The values derive from Deichmann's plate 27, measured between opposing octagonal sides.

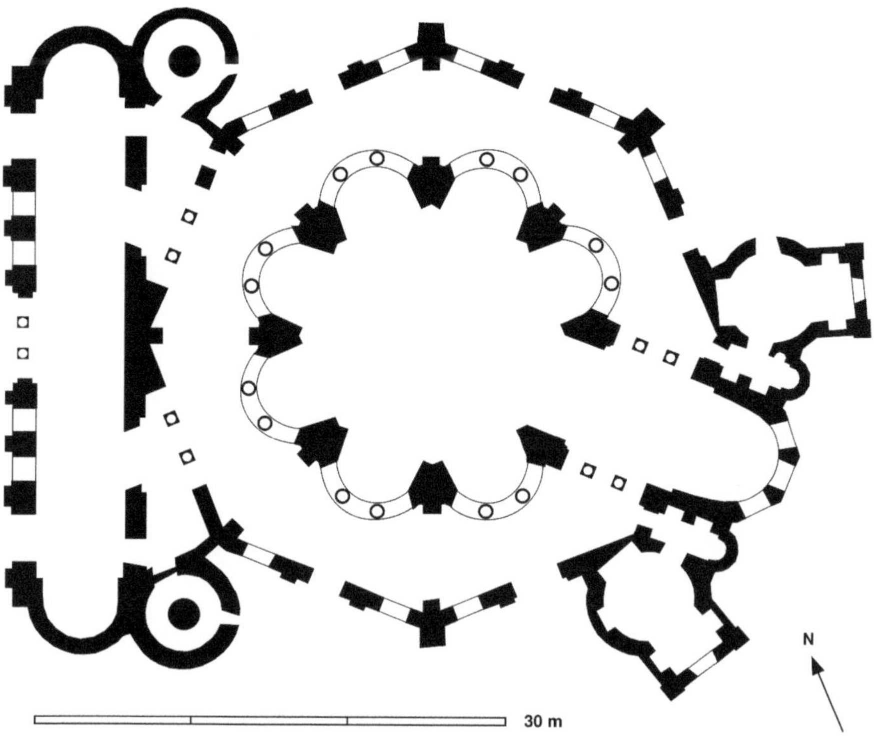

2.11 Ground plan of San Vitale in Ravenna (adapted from Deichmann 1976).

arched windows rises above the exedras and the presbytery arch to a height of close to 27 m and merges almost seamlessly into the circular dome (its apex is at 29 m above floor level) by means of spandrel like niches, for which no precursor has so far been identified.[197]

Through the substantial drum section, the interior of San Vitale appears much steeper than that of Sts. Sergius and Bacchus or, in fact, Hagia Sophia. The steepness of the drum also means that it is virtually impossible to obtain an unobstructed view of the entire architectural structure from any given angle. What is more, the windows are set vertically into the drum to create a light impression that enhances the sense of verticality in San Vitale further, in sharp contrast to the Constantinopolitan churches, where the windows are set into the curvature of the dome.[198] That light played a central role in the design of San Vitale is evident from the numerous windows that flood the sacred space with light from all directions. The centrepiece is lit through eight large dome windows, while the apse has three large windows in the lower semi-circular wall and a triple window in the tympanum above. The outer shell

[197] Deichmann (1976), 64.

[198] Deichmann (1976), 83–5; Russo (2003), 63–5.

of the edifice is highly fenestrated with axially aligned windows, three each at gallery and at ground level on each of the unobstructed octagonal sides. Even though there might be a gradation of brightness along the building's longitudinal axis from the main entrance in the west to the presbytery and apse in the east as Deichmann observed,[199] the openness of the architectural structure and the correspondence of inner and outer octagon allow the light to suffuse the interior completely, creating vibrant effects of light and shadow throughout the building.[200] The walls of the outer octagon appear as walls of light, against which the columns and piers of the interior cast a dark pattern.[201] The result is a relatively homogeneous interior space with intermingling bright and dark elements.

In this, San Vitale seems closer to Hagia Sophia than to the church of Sts. Sergius and Bacchus. In many ways, however, San Vitale and Sts. Sergius and Bacchus resemble each other in design and construction. Both edifices are true double-shell buildings (Hagia Sophia is not), and in both churches the lower colonnades are axially aligned with the triple openings at gallery level, even though in San Vitale the openings are arched at both levels. The bema and apse are architecturally articulated, stretching over the full height of the triumphal arch and flooded with light through large arched windows in the east. In the case of San Vitale, the bema and apse are further singled out by an elaborate decorative mosaic programme. A longitudinal orientation is thus adapted to the centralised structure, clearly defining a visual focus opposite the main entrance. The two contemporary church buildings are evidently aesthetically related to satisfy a sixth-century Byzantine taste. This is also reflected in the interior decoration of San Vitale for which the marble columns, capitals of Proconnesian marble and panelling, had been imported to Ravenna directly from the east.[202] Two fold capitals similar to the ones in the lower order of Sts. Sergius and Bacchus are found on the gallery of the presbytery in San Vitale. Almost identical examples of the impost capitals with lotus panels and the braided basketry frame worked in *à jour* from the lower arcades in San Vitale are part of the finds from the church of Hagios Polyeuktos in Constantinople.[203] There can be no doubt that the church of San Vitale drew inspiration from the architectural innovations and the new styles in the Byzantine capital. As an architectural example from the other end of the Byzantine Empire, San Vitale thus reflects the wider validity of the aesthetic of light that defined the development of ecclesiastical architecture in the sixth century.

---

199 This is due to the fact that at the western end, triple windows open into the space between the church, the narthex and the staircases. Deichmann (1976), 74–8; Friedrich Wilhelm Deichmann, *Ravenna: Hauptstadt des spätantiken Abendlandes, Vol. 1, Geschichte und Monumente* (Wiesbaden: Frank Steiner Verlag GmbH, 1969), 227–31.

200 Deliyannis (2010), 230; Russo (2003), 64–5.

201 Andrzej Piotrowski, 'Architecture and the Iconoclastic Controversy', in *Medieval Practices of Space*, ed. Barbara A. Hanawalt and Michal Kobialka (Minneapolis, MN: University of Minnesota Press, 2000), 116–19.

202 For a detailed survey of the marble decoration, see Deichmann (1976), 86–135.

203 Deichmann (1976), 96 and 99; McKenzie (2007), 339 and 43.

Hagios Polyeuktos

The architectural developments in Constantinople in the sixth century were decisively shaped by the construction of the church of Hagios Polyeuktos that may have been the largest and most sumptuous ecclesiastical building in the Byzantine capital before Justinian's Hagia Sophia. Commissioned by the distinguished noblewoman Anicia Juliana and completed presumably in the early to mid-520s CE,[204] the building is seen by many as a direct precursor of Justinian's churches of Sts. Sergius and Bacchus and Hagia Sophia. The three edifices appear to be stylistically and structurally closely connected.[205] The churches of Sts. Sergius and Bacchus and Hagia Sophia have often been seen as Justinian's response to the architectural and imperial challenge posed by Anicia Juliana's monumental building.[206] Of the main body of the church nothing remains apart from a massive foundation platform, but excavations in the 1960s yielded substantial fragments of architectural sculpture, including a monumental inscription whose text is preserved in full length in the *Palatine Greek Anthology* (AP, I.10).[207] All in all, some of the major architectural features can be recovered, albeit incompletely. Excluding the narthex and the projecting apse, the main body of the church roughly followed the outline of a square (51.5 × 52 m), internally divided into a central nave, aisles and a sanctuary in the east.[208] The nave was lined on either side with a series of exedras, three on either side, sustaining galleries above. These exedras were fitted with semi-domes, beautifully embellished with a peacock with its tail fanned out around the curvature of the semi-dome.[209] Although there is little that can be said with certainty about the type of the original roofing, there are a number of factors that warrant a masonry vault rather than a more traditional timber

[204] Hagios Polyeuktos is traditionally dated to the years 524–527 CE i.e. during the reign of Justin I. However, Bardill's re-evaluation of the brickstamps indicates that the bricks of the substructures date significantly earlier to between 508/09 and 511/512, while the bricks of the superstructure belong to the period between 517/518 and 520/521. Even if the bricks have not been stored for very long, this would still give a date of completion not earlier than 522 CE. Bardill (2004), 62–4, 111–16; Croke (2006), 55; Harrison (1986), 207–25; R. M. Harrison, *A Temple for Byzantium: The Discovery and Excavation of Anicia Juliana's Palace-Church in Istanbul* (London: Harvey Miller, 1989), 35; Jean-Pierre Sodini, 'La contribution de l'archéologie à la connaissance du monde byzantin (IVe-VIIe siècles)', *DOP* 47 (1993): 158; Cyril Mango and Ihor Ševčenko, 'Remains of the church of St. Polyeuktos at Constantinople', *DOP* 15 (1961); McKenzie (2007), 334.

[205] Carolyn L. Connor, 'The epigram in the church of Hagios Polyeuktos in Constantinople and its Byzantine response', *Byzantion* 69 (1999); Croke (2006); McKenzie (2007), Chapter 13.

[206] Connor (1999), 510–15; Croke (2006); Harrison (1989), 40; Shahîd (2003), 475–6; Mary Whitby, 'The St. Polyeuktos Epigram (*AP* 1.10): A literary perspective', in *Greek Literature in Late Antiquity: Dynamism, Didacticism, Classicism*, ed. Scott Fitzgerald Johnson (Aldershot: Ashgate, 2006), 167–8.

[207] Mango and Ševčenko (1961). For the text of the epigram and recent translations see Whitby (2006); Connor (1999).

[208] Harrison (1989), 52.

[209] Harrison (1986), 117–21, 414–6; Harrison (1989), 86–97; McKenzie (2007), 335. According to the epigram, 'columns standing upon sturdy columns' unmistakably suggests a two-story structure (*AP* 1.10 line 55).

roof.[210] Only a domed structure can explain the need for the massive, seven metre wide foundations running along either side of the nave. Furthermore, fragments of a range of thinner and lighter bricks were found that might have been used in vaults, while the arrangement of drainpipes appear to contradict the existence of a single pitched timber roof.[211] The existence of a dome crowning the central nave of Hagios Polyeuktos is also indicated in the inscription that was carved on the marble entablature around the wall inside the church, next to the entrance and around the four sides of the atrium.[212] The epigram describes how the edifice 'stands forth on deep-rooted foundations, springing up from below and pursuing the stars of heaven' and how the 'columns support the rays of the golden-roofed ceiling'.[213] Although the term κάλυπτρα simply means veil/cover, the building's pursuit of the stars of heaven may be taken as a reference to a spherical dome.[214] This configuration might well have been similar to Hagia Eirene, where the main arches carrying the dome open directly onto the galleries, or the naos might have been flanked to the north and south by tympana like in Hagia Sophia. The epigram defines the church as a 'shining house (οἶκον ἰδὼν λάμποντα)', a περίδρομος, which literally means 'encircled' and is translated with ambulatory.[215] All this appears to suggest an extensively fenestrated and centralised architectural structure, rather than an elongated traditional basilical design.[216]

There can be no doubt that the church of Hagios Polyeuktos was heavily fenestrated, given that about 2,500 fragments of marble transennae were recovered during the excavations. The tentative reconstruction of these window frames gives a sense of their original size and proportion. Out of 56 joining fragments a window frame could be rebuilt that was at least 1 m wide

---

210 Recently, Bardill argued in favour of a timber roof, emulating Solomon's famous temple, basing his argument mainly on Gregory of Tours' description of Hagios Polyeuktos' gilded ceiling as *camera* (*Patrologia Latina* 71, col. 793–795). Gregory speaks indeed in ambiguous terms, and *camera* could signify either a vaulted or a timber-roofed construction. Jonathan Bardill, 'A new temple for Byzantium: Anicia Juliana, King Solomon, and the gilded ceiling of the church of St. Polyeuktos in Constantinople', in *Social and Political Life in Late Antiquity*, ed. William Bowden, Adam Gutterridge, and Carlos Machado (Leiden and Boston, MA: Brill, 2006).

211 Sodini is quite explicit, saying that 'Elle est sans doute la première église à coupole de la capitale'. Connor (1999); Harrison (1986), 222–3, 408–14; Harrison (1989), 60, 127–36; Sodini (1993); Mango and Ihor Ševčenko (1961); McKenzie (2007), 334.

212 For the division and placement of the epigram, see Connor (1999); Liz James, '"And shall these mute stones speak?" Text as art', in *Art and Text in Byzantine Culture*, ed. Liz James (Cambridge: Cambridge University Press, 2007).

213 *AP* 1.10 lines 51–2 and 57: οἷος μὲν προβέβηκε βαθυρρίζοισι θεμέθλοις, νέρθεν ἀναθρώσκων καὶ αἰθέρος ἄστρα διώκων … κίοσιν ἑστηῶτες χρυσορόφου ἀκτῖνας ἀερτάζουσι καλύπτρης.

214 André Grabar, 'L'iconographie du ciel dans l'art chrétien de l'antiquité et du haut moyen age', *Cahiers Archéologiques* 30 (1982); Hautecoeur (1954).

215 LSJ; *AP* 1.10 line 69; translated in Whitby (2006); see also Connor (1999), 491–2.

216 I do think that part of Bardill's reconstruction is worth considering. For example, a regular arrangement of the three exedras on either side of the nave that rise into the upper story and that are topped with a semi-dome seems very likely and is in accord with the epigram. Whether or not such an internal structure could have supported a dome is not clear from the archaeological remains. Bardill (2006).

and approximately 2.5 m high. This frame most certainly formed the left part of a larger window made up of two or more such frames. The transennae formed a grid of 3 × 8 rectangular openings that measured on average 20 cm in width and approximately 25 cm in height.[217] These were destined to hold glass panes, evidenced by the large number of window glass fragments that have been retrieved from the site.[218] The range of window glass is by and large consistent with other late antique finds.[219] The shape and structure of the windows as well as the high quality and comparatively light colouration of the windowpanes with a thickness of as little as 1.5 mm to 3 mm allowed the transmission of plenty of near colourless light. The scarcity of evidence impedes a more detailed reconstruction of the window arrangement and distribution, but it seems safe to assume that the windows formed an integral part of the overall architectural system of Hagios Polyeuktos that was typical of the late antique building tradition and similar to that of Hagia Sophia.[220]

Parallels between Hagios Polyeuktos and Hagia Sophia are evident also from the exuberant decoration of the two churches. The interior decoration of Anicia Juliana's church included marble revetment, rich inlay panels and columns, mosaic decorations and an extraordinary variety of carved capitals and entablatures.[221] The carving of the capitals and entablatures is deeply undercut and rich in naturalistic and stylised floral and faunal motifs. The delicate latticework is virtually detached from the background that was originally painted with a bright blue pigment. It is likely that the remainder of the sculpture was also brightly coloured, even though no traces of paint have survived.[222] What emerges from the archaeological record is that Hagios Polyeuktos was decorated with a wide range of marbles and unusual architectural sculpture and motifs, the closest parallels of which were found in late antique Egypt.[223] The excavations also turned up a great wealth of

---

217 Harrison (1986), 140; Claire Nesbitt, 'Space, Light and Experience in Middle Byzantine Churches' (PhD, Newcastle University, 2007), 90.

218 R.M. Harrison and M.V. Gill, 'The Window Glass', in Harrison (1986), 204–6; The fragments from the seventh-century context came invariably from rectangular panes and were colourless, transparent bluish and greenish, from olive to dark bottle green, with some specimens of a pale yellowish brown. Nesbitt noted an interesting difference in the colour distribution of the early Byzantine compared to middle Byzantine finds. While notably more colourless and predominately pale shades were recovered from the seventh-century context, the middle Byzantine levels contained more of the bluish green glass and some dark brown samples. Nesbitt (2007), 89–92.

219 Compare, for example, Dell'Acqua (2005); Schibille, Marii, and Rehren (2008); Wolf *et al.* (2005).

220 Dell'Acqua (2005); Günter (1965); Loerke, Cutler, and Kazhdan (1991); Harrison (1986), 140.

221 Harrison (1989), 77–81; Harrison (1986), Chapter 5.

222 Hagios Polyeuktos was apparently decorated with the same diversity of marble stones as Hagia Sophia. Furthermore, similar opus sectile panes were found, combining mother of pearl with glass (yellow, gold leaf, pale green and dark blue) as well as red and green porphyry. Noteworthy are the remains of six opus sectile columns embellished with amethyst and opaque green glass that were presumably intended for the ciborium. Harrison (1989), 77–88; Harrison (1986), Chapter 6.

223 McKenzie (2007), 335–9.

mosaic fragments, consisting predominantly of glass of various shades of blues and greens, brownish black, red purple, brown and some rare yellow in addition to gold and silver tesserae.[224] The mosaic decoration appears to have been primarily non-figurative, predominantly consisting of abstract motifs of dark blues and shades of green. Figurative mosaics on gold ground appear to have existed in the area of the apse, making this the first set of figurative vault mosaics datable to the sixth century in Constantinople.[225]

To recapitulate, the church of Hagios Polyeuktos was probably a domed and to a certain extent a centralised structure, whose spatial experience was shaped by a lavishly polychrome decoration, the effect of which was enhanced by a profusion of natural light. Like Hagia Sophia, Anicia Juliana's church might have been similarly illuminated from all directions, and its architectural structure accentuated both the longitudinal axis towards the sanctuary and apse area as well as the vertical dimension owing to a gilded dome. An aesthetic appreciation of light and colours is obvious from both churches. Hagios Polyeuktos' interior seems to anticipate the spatial and visual effect of Hagia Sophia. Both edifices represent a novel architectural design, developed to appeal to the aesthetic expectations of sixth-century Constantinople. Whether this aesthetic appreciation of light and colours in Hagios Polyeuktos extended to the perception of the symbolic properties of light is not entirely clear. Bardill argued for an eschatological interpretation of Hagios Polyeuktos and its decoration. He demonstrated that the wealth of vegetable motifs, the superbly modelled peacocks and the internal architectural structure can be interpreted as a reference to the New Temple and to the New Jerusalem of the Book of Revelation.[226] In the context of a New Temple, it is perfectly plausible to interpret the light within as symbolically significant. If nothing else, the light could be seen as representing the promise of eternal life.

The stylistic and aesthetic similarities that link the churches of Hagios Polyeuktos and Hagia Sophia are not altogether unexpected given that church patronage in sixth-century Constantinople was politically and ideologically charged. The political rivalry between Justinian and Anicia Juliana is well documented and was proposed as the motivating factor underlying the construction of Sts. Sergius and Bacchus and the content of its epigram.[227] Anicia Juliana's unapologetic claim to imperial ancestry, her extraordinary piety and building activities are among the main themes of the inscription of Hagios Polyeuktos, composed within the tradition of the *basilikos logos*.[228] Juliana is named in line with Constantine the Great and

[224] R.M. Harrison and M.V. Gill, 'The Mosaics', in Harrison (1986), 182–96.

[225] Pieces of geometric marble pavement mosaics were also found. Harrison (1989), 78–80; Harrison (1986), 182–96.

[226] Bardill (2006).

[227] Croke (2006).

[228] Whitby (2006); James (2007); Schibille (2009). According to Menander Rhetor's instruction, the *basilikos logos* is a speech in praise of emperors, demonstrating mainly the emperor's virtues.

Theodosius I to corroborate her imperial credentials, and she is proclaimed to rival 'the wisdom of the celebrated Solomon' and his Temple in Jerusalem.[229] This comparison with Solomon is particularly believed to have provoked a Justinianic response in the form of the rebuilding of Hagia Sophia that too was acclaimed a *Templum novum Salomonis*.[230] The juxtaposition with Solomon and his wisdom is unmistakably political propaganda, reflecting the deep antagonism between Justinian and Anicia Juliana. Only a few years earlier, Juliana had been depicted on a dedication miniature (fol. 6v) of the *Vienna Dioscurides* (ca. 512 CE) where she is intimately associated with the imperial virtues of *megalopsychia, phronesis* and *sophia*. Imperial *Sophia* is a combination of virtues (*pietas, justitia*) that are needed for wise ruling, and not a divine or spiritual type of wisdom.[231] In focusing on Juliana's wisdom and ancestry, the epigram in Hagios Polyeuktos affirms her imperial legitimacy, rather than alluding to divine wisdom that is at the centre of Justinian's Great Church. Hagios Polyeuktos' luminosity is one of its defining aesthetic qualities, but unlike in Hagia Sophia, light is not interpreted in epistemological and theological terms, and light is not articulated as a divine paradigm. The imagery of light in the epigram represents merely an aesthetic value; it is seen as the source of beauty, but light is not assimilated to the Neoplatonic metaphysical aesthetics of light. By contrast, the mystical ideas of divine illumination and enlightenment (φωτισμός) are very much part of the interpretation of the light within the church of Hagia Sophia as evidenced in the textual descriptions of the Great Church.

Conclusion

In conclusion, it is the combination of shape, size and the specific aesthetics of light that are unprecedented and make Hagia Sophia unique. Its large fenestrated pendentive dome, flanked by two fenestrated semi-domes to the east and west, created the largest open vaulted interior in the ancient and medieval world with a free span of 31 by 67 m. The expanse of the vaulted space and the cascading arrangement of domes, semi-domes and diagonally opening exedra semi-domes distinguishes the Great Church from other buildings at the time. Also new is that the classical order of load and support is dissolved in Hagia Sophia. All late antique ecclesiastical buildings prior to Hagia Sophia conform to the classical system of supports and openings in vertical correspondence. In Hagia Sophia, the delicately carved latticework that covers the capitals, impost blocks and arches disguises the distinction

229 *AP* 10.1 lines 42–50.

230 As evidenced by a passage in Corripus, *In laudem Iustini Augusti minoris*, IV. 280–284; edited and translated in Averil Cameron, *Flavius Cresconius Corippus: In laudem Iustini Augusti minoris, Libri IV* (London: The Athlone Press, 1976), 81, 115, 204–5.

231 Bente Kiilerich, 'The image of Anicia Juliana and the Vienna Dioscurides: Flattery or appropriation of imperial imagery?', *Symbolae Osloenses* 76 (2001).

between supporting column and wall, while the gallery columns are literally placed over thin air.[232] The lack of vertical alignment of the lower and upper arcades in Hagia Sophia is a radically innovative design, contributing to the dynamic quality of its interior.

Hagia Sophia's dramatic design was not created *ex nihilo*; it borrowed many of its elements from the two-century old tradition of late antique church architecture. Pendentive domes had long been built and some possibly even on a monumental scale,[233] basilical and centralised buildings were equally frequent, while diagonal planning combined with interlocking spaces and overlapping views had their beginnings probably also in the fourth century.[234] Light had always played a central role in the design of ecclesiastical buildings. Unlike in Hagia Sophia, though, the lighting of late antique churches was usually directed, highlighting the central space and/or the sanctuary, as seen in Santa Costanza and early Christian basilicas in Rome and, to a lesser extent, in the Studios Basilica and the church of Sts. Sergius and Bacchus in Constantinople. In contrast, a more even distribution of light, more similar to that of Hagia Sophia, can be seen in San Vitale in Ravenna and can possibly be assumed for the church of Hagios Polyeuktos. Still, the apse area in both these churches is accentuated through elaborate figurative mosaics, providing the viewer with an unambiguous visual focus. Hagia Sophia's interior design is instead defined by a more holistic aesthetic experience of expanding and interconnected spaces that are homogeneously illuminated and with a strictly non-figurative monumental decoration (Plate 2). Hagia Sophia's sacred space, filled with an unprecedented play of light, shade and colours engaging with numerous curvilinear surfaces, has become the very object of its aesthetic experience. In its entirety, the architecture and interior decoration of Hagia Sophia epitomises an aesthetic concept of light and colour that is intimately linked with the idea of divine wisdom. Though Hagia Sophia is unique in many ways, the fact that related sixth-century churches display a similar taste for light and colour substantiates the hypothesis that the aesthetic appreciation of light was more universally valid in sixth-century Byzantium.

---

232 Silentiary (verses 392–394) commented on the audacity to place columns over empty air.

233 McKenzie argues that a floor mosaic in the church of St. John the Baptist in Jerash shows a major building with a pendentive dome in the city of Alexandria. Since the mosaic is firmly dated to 531 CE, this would mean that the depicted edifice predates Hagia Sophia. McKenzie (2007), 344–50; Ćurčić (1992).

234 MacDonald believes that the so-called Temple of Minerva Medica dating to the early fourth century may as well mark the beginnings of this artistic treatment of space and vistas. William L. MacDonald, 'Roman experimental design and the Great Church', in *The Hagia Sophia: From the Age of Justinian to the Present* ed. Robert Mark and Ahmet S. Çakmak (Cambridge: Cambridge University Press, 1992).

3

Clad in a Luminous Membrane: The Interior Decoration of Hagia Sophia

When Paul the Silentiary in his poem described 'the marble meadows gathered upon the mighty walls' of Hagia Sophia,[1] he expressed the late antique partiality for brilliant and polychromatic interior decorations. Paul particularly emphasises the iridescent, shining and glowing qualities of the material rather than its specific hue.[2] Colours nonetheless played a central role in the aesthetic experience of Hagia Sophia's interior as well.[3] The metaphor of the blossoming meadow, a poetic commonplace in late antiquity, conveys the sense of an aesthetic appreciation of a polychrome adornment.[4] This fascination with variety (ποικιλία), colour and the effects of light and contrasts found in late antique textual sources (poetry and ekphraseis) has a material equivalent in the marble and mosaic decoration of Hagia Sophia.[5] The

1 Silentiary verses 617–646.

2 Liz James has extensively discussed the concept that colour in Byzantium was less concerned with the hue than with the brightness and luminosity of the colour, which is also reflected in Byzantine colour terms. Liz James, *Light and Colour in Byzantine Art* (Oxford: Oxford University Press, 1996); Liz James, 'What colours were Byzantine mosaics?', in *Medieval Mosaics*, ed. Eve Borsook, Fiorella Gioffredi Superbi, and Giovanni Pagliarulo (Milan: Silvana Editoriale, 2000).

3 Elizabeth S. Bolman, 'Late antique aesthetics, chromophobia, and the Red Monastery, Sohag, Egypt', *Eastern Christian Art* 3 (2006); Elizabeth S. Bolman, 'Painted skins: The illusions and realities of architectural polychromy, Sinai and Egypt', in *Approaching the Holy Mountain: Art and Liturgy at St. Catherine's Monastery in the Sinai*, ed. Sharon E.J. Gerstel and Robert S. Nelson (Turnhout: Brepols, 2010).

4 As evidenced also in Procopius I.1.59–60: λειμῶνί τις ἂν ἐντετυχηκέναι δόξειεν ὡραίῳ τὸ ἄνθος. θαυμάσειε γὰρ ἂν εἰκότως τῶν μὲν τὸ ἁλουργόν, τῶν δὲ τὸ χλοάζον, καὶ οἷς τὸ φοινικοῦν ἐπανθεῖ καὶ ὧν τὸ λευκὸν ἀπαστράπτει, ἔτι μέντοι καὶ οὓς ταῖς ἐναντιωτάταις ποικίλλει χροιαῖς ὥσπερ τις ζωγράφος ἡ φύσις. See also Michael Roberts, *The Jeweled Style: Poetry and Poetics in Late Antiquity* (Ithaca, NY: Cornell University Press, 1989), 47–54.

5 Bolman (2010); Sandrine Dubel, 'Colour in Philostratus "Imagines"', in *Philostratus*, ed. E. Bowie and Jaś Elsner (Cambridge: Cambridge University Press, 2009); Roberts (1989); Thelma K. Thomas, 'The medium matters: Reading the remains of a late antique textile', in *Reading Medieval Images: The Art Historian and the Object*, ed. Elizabeth Sears and Thelma K. Thomas (Ann Arbor, MI: University of Michigan Press, 2002).

marble and mosaic surfaces are rich in brilliant colours, vibrant patterns and veining that interact with light and contribute substantially to the dynamic quality and overall luminosity of the ecclesiastical space. The distinctive taste for *poikilia*, polychromy and contrasts has been termed the *jewelled style* and was first defined in late antique Latin poetry but has since been applied to Greek ekphraseis as well as Byzantine ecclesiastical interiors.[6]

The choice of materials in Hagia Sophia clearly reflects and simultaneously shapes a jewelled style that is closely associated with an aesthetic of light.[7] The colour and texture of the decorative materials determine the optical appearance and the degree of the materials' interaction with light. Whereas a darkly coloured surface absorbs most of the light and reflects little, and therefore appears dark, a brightly coloured surface reflects most of the light. A perfectly smooth surface such as a mirror reflects light uniformly. By contrast, a textured, uneven surface reflects light in an incoherent way, at different angles.[8] When light strikes an opaque surface, some of its energy is absorbed and some of it is reflected. A close examination of the original marble revetment and mosaics in Hagia Sophia sheds light on the techniques employed by the craftsmen and designers to create texture and to manipulate or enhance the visual effects of the decoration. The treatment of light and colour that is intrinsic to these forms of interior adornments offers insights into visual and by extension aesthetic principles that guided their design. This chapter therefore examines the practical aspects of the interior decoration, exploring the individual materials, their colour, texture, and patterns as well as the compositional structure of the original sixth-century designs. It concentrates on configurations of colours and contrasts and on questions about the exploitation of optical effects and the aesthetic sensibilities of late antiquity.

Paul the Silentiary's ekphrasis of Hagia Sophia's marble decoration clearly advertises the late antique aesthetic taste for light and colour. What is striking is Paul's detailed knowledge of the different types of marble including their geographical provenance that promotes a 'material map' of the Byzantine Empire.[9] Some of the marble varieties used in Hagia Sophia travelled long distances, such as the black Celtic marble that was quarried in the French Pyrenees or the *giallo antico* from Chemtou in modern Tunisia, while others came from nearby quarries like the island of Proconnesos (modern-day

6 Bolman (2006); Bolman (2010); Bissera V. Pentcheva, 'Hagia Sophia and multisensory aesthetics', *Gesta* 50 (2011); Roberts (1989).

7 James (1996); James (2000); Gervase Mathew, *Byzantine Aesthetics* (London: J. Murray, 1963).

8 Vicki Bruce, Patrick R. Green, and Mark A. Georgeson, *Visual Perception: Physiology, Psychology, and Ecology* (Hove: Psychology Press, 1996, 3rd edition, 2000), 5.

9 Michael Greenhalgh, *Marble Past, Monumental Present: Building with Antiquities in the Mediaeval Mediterranean* (Leiden and Boston, MA: Brill, 2009), 35, 70; Jean-Pierre Sodini, 'Le goût du marbre à Byzance: sa signification pour les Byzantins et les non-Byzantins', *Études balkaniques* 1 (1994).

Marmara) in the Sea of Marmara (Appendix).[10] Coloured marble decorations had long been used in relation with imperial patronage. The use of marble from distant parts of the empire and the imperial connotation associated with certain marbles (for example red porphyry) undoubtedly helped to promulgate the material's prestige and aesthetic value.[11]

It appears that all the marble used in sixth-century Constantinople was newly quarried as opposed to re-used spolia, which means that marble was still extracted on an industrial scale during this period.[12] The final shaping and carving of the architectural sculpture seems to have taken place in Constantinople itself, given the lack of archaeological evidence for any secondary workshop activities at the Proconnesian quarries themselves. Raw or roughly shaped marble blocks must have been mass-produced and shipped from the island to Constantinople.[13] On the other hand, little is known about the provenance and production of Byzantine mosaic tesserae. Most of the raw glass probably originated from large primary glass production centres identified on the Levantine coast or in northern Egypt, as suggested by the analytical studies of some mosaic tesserae from Hagia Sophia and from the contemporary church of Hagios Polyeuktos.[14] However, how the secondary working of the tesserae was organised, where the glass was coloured and cut into tesserae or how and where the mosaicists procured their material is not known.[15]

Blossoming Marble Meadows

Although centuries of heavy use and several collapses of the dome and semi-domes have left their mark on the pavement of the nave, it is believed that

---

10 Silentiary verses 617–646; Nursin Asgari, 'The Proconnesian production of architectural elements in late antiquity, based on evidence from the marble quarries', in *Constantinople and its Hinterland: Papers from the Twenty-Seventh Spring Symposium of Byzantine Studies, Oxford, April 1993*, ed. Cyril Mango and Gilbert Dagron (Aldershot: Ashgate Publishing Ltd, 1995); Sodini (1994), 180.

11 The mid-fourth to mid-fifth century appears to have been a high point in *opus sectile* marble revetment for monumental buildings. Greenhalgh (2009); Federico Guidobaldi, 'La Lussuosa Aula presso Porta Marina a Ostia', in *Aurea Roma: dalla città pagana alla città Cristiana*, ed. Serena Ensoli and Eugenio La Rocca (Rome: Bretschneider, 2001); Annette Kleinert, 'Die Inkrustation der Hagia Sophia: Zur Entwicklung der Inkrustationsschemata im römischen Kaiserreich' (PhD, Westfälische Wilhelms-Universität, 1979), 45–71; Marina Sapelli, 'La Basilica di Giunio Basso', in *Aurea Roma: dalla città pagana alla città Cristiana*, ed. Serena Ensoli and Eugenio La Rocca (Rome: L'Erma di Bretschneider, 2001); Sodini (1994).

12 Asgari (1995); Greenhalgh (2009), 34, 69, 79.

13 Asgari (1995); Sodini (1994).

14 Robert H. Brill, *Chemical Analyses of Early Glasses* (New York, NY: Corning Museum of Glass, 1999); Nadine Schibille and Judith McKenzie, 'Glass tesserae from Hagios Polyeuktos, Constantinople: Their early Byzantine affiliations', in *Neighbours and Successors of Rome: Traditions of Glass Production and Use in Europe and the Middle East in the Later First Millennium AD*, ed. Daniel Keller, Caroline M. Jackson, and Jennifer Price (Oxford: Oxbow Books, 2014).

15 Liz James, 'Byzantine glass mosaic tesserae: Some material considerations', *BMGS* 30 (2006); Nadine Schibille *et al.*, 'Chemical characterisation of glass mosaic tesserae from sixth-century Sagalassos (south-west Turkey): Chronology and production techniques', *JAS* 39 (2012).

the original floor did not differ much from its present configuration.[16] The floor is paved with book-matched white and grey Proconnesian marble slabs, interrupted only by five parallel bands of green Thessalian marble. These green marble stripes vary in width (50–70 cm) and transverse the nave in a north-south direction thus dividing the length of the nave into segments of different size.[17] They seem to have been part of the original Justinianic flooring and might have served as liturgical demarcations.[18] A large square *opus sectile* panel (6 m side length) is located in the south-eastern part of the nave pavement (Figure 2.3A). Contrary to the traditional assumption that this panel post-dates Justinian's reign, it has recently been proposed that this *opus sectile* fits nicely into the overall design of Hagia Sophia and could therefore have been part of the original floor, albeit with a big central porphyry plaque instead of granite at its centre.[19] A smaller porphyry roundel (diameter of about 1 m) is inserted into the paving of the south-east exedra and is probably part of the original sixth-century floor.[20]

The remarkably plain sixth-century paving of Hagia Sophia (including the narthex, aisles and galleries) was enlivened mainly through the colour and veining of the Proconnesian marble flagstones. These had been sawn consecutively from the same marble block and unfolded so as to obtain a continuous pattern of different shades of grey veins. This simplicity is in stark contrast to the elaborate floor mosaics found in fourth- to sixth-century churches of Jordan, Palestine and Syria that often depict rich carpet-like patterns as well as nature imagery and personified natural forces (seasons, months, zodiac signs).[21] In context of this tradition of richly decorated floors, the use of large slabs of only one material for the pavement of Hagia Sophia may represent a conscious move toward 'puritanical

---

16 Fabio Barry, 'Walking on water: Cosmic floors in antiquity and the middle ages', *The Art Bulletin* 89 (2007); Rowland J. Mainstone, *Hagia Sophia: Architecture, Structure and Liturgy of Justinian's Great Church* (London: Thames and Hudson, 1988), 114–15; Rudolf H. W. Stichel, 'Die Hagia Sophia Justinians, ihre liturgische Einrichtung und der zeremonielle Auftritt des frühbyzantinischen Kaisers', in *Byzanz – das Römerreich im Mittelalter, Teil 2, 1 Schauplätze*, ed. Falko Daim and Jörg Drauschke (Mainz: RGZM, 2010), 28–35.

17 George P. Majeska, 'Notes on the archaeology of St. Sophia at Constantinople: The green marble bands on the floor', *DOP* 32 (1978).

18 Stichel (2010), 31–2.

19 Marcell Restle, 'Die Hagia Sophia Kaiser Justinians in Konstantinopel', in *Die Hagia Sophia in Istanbul. Bilder aus sechs Jahrhunderten und Gaspare Fossatis Restaurierung der Jahre 1847–1849*, ed. V. Hoffmann (Bern: O. Lange, 1999), 26; Stichel (2010), 33–5.

20 Stichel (2010); Christine Strube, *Die westliche Eingangsseite der Kirchen von Konstantinopel in justinianischer Zeit* (Wiesbaden: Harrossowitz, 1973).

21 For example Rachel Hachlili, *Ancient Mosaic Pavements: Themes, Issues, and Trends* (Leiden and Boston, MA: Brill, 2009); Ernst Kitzinger, 'Sylistic developments in pavement mosaics in the Greek East from the age of Constantine to the age of Justinian', in *The Art of Byzantium and the Medieval West: Selected Studies*, ed. W. Eugene Kleinbauer (Bloomington, IN: Indiana University Press, 1965, reprint 1976); Ernst Kitzinger, 'Mosaic Pavements in the Greek East and the Question of a "Renaissance" under Justinian', in *The Art of Byzantium and the Medieval West: Selected Studies by Ernst Kitzinger*, ed. W. Eugene Kleinbauer (Bloomington, IN: Indiana University Press, 1965, reprint 1976).

aniconism'.[22] It has recently been argued that the Proconnesian marble flooring with its wavy grey veining is evocative of the sea. The very term marble that is derived from the Greek verb μαρμάιρεῖν is associated with sparkle or gleam, while its Sanskrit root *mar* implies motion and was used in this double sense presumably by Homer when he describes the shimmering sea as ἅλα μαρμαρέην.[23] This tradition might have inspired Paul the Silentiary to liken the floor of Hagia Sophia to the 'waves of the sea' in his description of the ambo as a beacon of calm amidst the stormy sea.[24] In combination with the monumental golden dome above, the floor may then represent an image of the primordial sea of God's parting of the waters in Genesis.[25] The term *amarygma* (ἀμάρυγμα) also defines the animation of matter as it becomes alive (ἔμψυχος), and signifies the presence of *pneuma*.[26] Movement, animation and light are indeed qualities intrinsic to marble, and specifically to the wavy white and grey Proconnesian marble. The aesthetic appeal of the Proconnesian marble floor in Hagia Sophia lies in its beautiful veining of shades of grey, exhibiting a variegated surface rich in contrasts that is further enhanced through the marble's interaction with light. These visual characteristics thereby lend themselves to an aesthetic of light, while contributing significantly to the dynamic nature and luminosity of Hagia Sophia's interior.

Marble sheeting of various colours and provenance adorns the walls of Hagia Sophia up to the springing of the impost of the vaults and arches (Plate 3).[27] The entire revetment is set about 5 cm apart from the face of the bricks and fastened to the walls by iron spikes or hangers, thus concealing the stones and bricks underneath.[28] The marble slabs are again book matched, meaning that adjacent panels are successive slices from the same marble block and then unfolded, so that their natural veining forms a continuous, symmetrical pattern across the individual panels. Horizontal bands alternate with registers of a succession of upright rectangular marble panels. Simple white marble mouldings usually frame the rectangular slabs as well as all of the horizontal bands, while narrow bands of differently coloured marble frame the larger

22 Barry (2007), 627. For a sensual interpretation of the aniconic interior of Hagia Sophia see Bissera V. Pentcheva, *The Sensual Icon: Space, Ritual, and the Senses in Byzantium* (University Park, PA: Pennsylvania State University Press, 2010), 45–56.

23 *Iliad* 14 verse 273; Barry (2007), 631; Erkinger Schwarzenberg, 'Colour, Light and Transparency in the Greek World', in *Medieval Mosaics*, ed. Eve Borsook, Fiorella Gioffredi Superbi, and Giovanni Pagliarulo (Milan: Silvana Editoriale, 2000), 22.

24 Silentiary, *Ambonis*, verses 224–239.

25 For the tradition of associating marble with water see Barry (2007).

26 Pentcheva (2010), 137–8; Pentcheva (2011).

27 For a detailed description of the entire marble revetment of Hagia Sophia see Kleinert (1979), 7–44; for an extensive discussion on the marble balustrades and window panels, see Alessandra Guiglia Guidobaldi and Claudia Barasanti, *Santa Sofia di Costantinopoli: l'arredo marmoreo della grande chiesa Giustinianea*, Studi di Antichità Cristiana (Città del Vaticano: Pontificio istituto di Archaeologia Cristiana, 2004).

28 Emerson Howland Swift, *Hagia Sophia* (New York, NY: Columbia University Press, 1940), 74.

rectangular panels. The marble veneer became a sort of picture gallery, where the patterns and veining of the framed marble panels evoked latent images (Plate 4).[29] In fact, Paul the Silentiary explicitly points out the resemblance of the marble revetment with the art of painting, stating that 'the stones imitate the glories of painting'.[30] When looking at the marble incrustation of Hagia Sophia, Paul as well as Procopius saw blossoming meadows that nature itself had painted upon the mighty walls of the church.[31] A contemporary Syriac hymn describing the cathedral church of Hagia Sophia at Edessa likewise notes that the marble panels were like pictures not made by human hands.[32] The marble panels were divine creations or pictures, miraculous in a similar way to the *Mandylion* of Edessa, the alleged sacred image of the face of Christ not made by human hands. This reference to the divine creation substantiates the sanctity of the church interior and reiterates divine immanence. Aside from the image of the flowery meadow, the ekphraseis describe the marbles of Hagia Sophia as coming to life through the agency of light and their vivid patterns and contrasts. Especially Paul the Silentiary's enthusiasm for the sensuous properties of the marble, the impression of motion and scintillation bouncing off the polished surfaces establishes the marble as animated matter. The descriptions of Paul and Procopius clearly go beyond the purely visible and appeal to the mimetic faculty of the mind (φαντασία) of their audience to recognise the representational in what appears essentially abstract or, in other words, to recognise the divine in matter.[33] The ekphraseis thus closely control the perception of the sacred interior in terms of the aesthetics of light and animation and its theological meaning.[34]

Despite its highly rhetorical nature, Paul the Silentiary's description of the interior riches of Hagia Sophia is grounded in the material reality of the building. Paul certainly displays a surprisingly detailed knowledge of the nature and provenance of the different marbles. The individual types of marble that he mentions in his ekphrasis can indeed be identified and matched with Hagia Sophia's marble revetment *in situ* with the exception of the Lydian and Bosporus stones (Appendix). Many of the different types of marbles used in the decoration of Hagia Sophia exhibit prominent veins and markings. The

29 Barry (2007); Guidobaldi (2001); W. Eugene Kleinbauer, *Saint Sophia at Constantinople: Singulariter in Mundo* (Dublin and Peterborough, NH: William L. Bauhan, 1999), 41.

30 Silentiary verses 605–612.

31 Procopius I.1.60; Silentiary verses 617–618.

32 Strophe TETH translated in Andrew Palmer and Lyn Rodley, 'The inauguration anthem of Hagia Sophia in Edessa: A new edition and translation with historical and architectural notes and a comparison with a contemporary Constantinopolitan kontakion', *BMGS* 12 (1988): 132; John Onians, 'Abstraction and imagination in late antiquity', *Art History* 3 (1980).

33 Whereas Onians attributed abstraction for the increasing role of imagination, Pentcheva argued that the Byzantine viewer saw the presence of the spirit in the changing appearances. Onians (1980); Pentcheva (2011).

34 Patricia Cox-Miller, *The Corporeal Imagination: Signifying the Holy in Late Ancient Christianity* (University Park, PA: University of Pennsylvania Press, 2009), 10.

ever-changing pattern of forms is especially noticeable in the black and white Celtic marble or the green cipollino with extensive lighter veining in the naos of the church. The effect would have been stronger in the sixth century, when the marble surfaces were highly polished. Polish increases the contrasts between the dark and light elements within the individual stones and produces an even more pronounced play and flickering glow that dissolves the architectural form.[35] The interior of Hagia Sophia must originally have been much more vibrant, animated and luminous than at present, because the glow of the marble surfaces has since faded, clouded by a grey dusty layer (Plates 4–7). In the sixth century, in contrast, Hagia Sophia's sacred space must have been a composite of a great variety of different sparkling marbles and characterised by the juxtaposition of opposites and contrasts.[36]

Many of the contrasts and optical properties contained within the individual marble types are repeated on a grander scale in the overall configuration of the revetment. At ground level, substantial parts of the original marble surfaces remain and enable a reconstruction of the original arrangement and characteristics.[37] In the naos, the revetment is arranged in numerous layers, stretching across the entire height up to the springing of the gallery vaults, interrupted only by the gallery cornice and balustrade (Plates 3, 4). Vertical panels of green cipollino, Phrygian marble, porphyry and Celtic marble, and horizontal elements such as mouldings and bands of green Thessalian marble and Egyptian alabaster are well balanced. There is a constant change in size and colour. The warm colours of yellow and red coexist alongside fresh shades of green, grey and black.

The optical contrast of an object is determined by the difference in mean luminance of adjacent structures, and visual perception is primarily dependent on the detection of light-dark and colour contrasts.[38] As regards Hagia Sophia's marble revetment, the colour contrasts of neighbouring stones are enhanced by means of slightly projecting white marble mouldings that line the individual marble bands and panels. This technique serves to further intensify the perceived brightness of the individual colours, because

35 Günter observed a similar treatment of the marble revetment in Constantine's basilica in Trier. Roland Günter, 'Wand, Fenster und Licht in der spätantik-frühchristlichen Architektur' (PhD, Ludwig-Maximilians-Universität, 1965), 7–15.

36 Maria Fabricius Hansen, 'Meanings of style: On the "interiorization" of late antique architecture', *Acta Hyperborea* 8 (2001).

37 Eugenios Michael Antoniades, *Έκφρασις της Αγίας Σοφίας, ήτοι μελέτη συνθετική και αναλυτική υπό έποψιν αρχιτεκτονικήν, αρχαιολογικήν και ιστορικήν του πολυθρυλήτου τεμένους Κωνσταντινουπόλεως/Ευγενίου Μ. Αντωνιάδου τ. 2* (1908); Kleinert (1979), 7–44; Swift (1940), 73–5.

38 See, for example, Robert F. Schmidt and Gerhard Thews, eds, *Human Physiology* (Berlin and London: Springer Verlag, 1989, 2nd edition), 240–41; John L. Barbur and Karoline Spang, 'Colour constancy and conscious perception of changes of illuminant', *Neuropsychologia* 46 (2008); Karl R. Gegenfurtner, 'Cortical mechanisms of colour vision', *Nature Reviews/Neuroscience* 4 (2003); K. Moutoussis and Semir Zeki, 'A psychophysical dissection of the brain sites involved in color-generating comparisons', *Proceedings of the National Academy of Science of the United States of America* 97 (2000).

a colour seen against a white surrounding appears more brilliant than seen adjacent to another strongly coloured surface. The slight projection of the mouldings further articulates the contrast. The more precious marble plaques are additionally framed by either elaborately carved margins of white marble or bands of a paler stone, as for example on the main piers where alabaster bands run along plaques of Celtic marble and porphyry. The juxtaposition of yellow and bluish or dark purple colours also serves to enhance the inherent hues of the individual stones.

This is interesting in light of the effect of colour on the perceived luminosity of an enclosed space inasmuch as the degree of colourfulness influences the experienced (non-quantifiable) sensation of brightness. The perceived luminosity of an environment increases as its colour intensifies.[39] Additionally, light from the middle of the visible spectrum appears brighter than light at either end of the spectrum despite having the same intensity. Hence, the relationship between luminance (intensity of light) and luminosity (intrinsic brightness) is non-linear.[40] Taking into consideration these physiological phenomena, it is noteworthy that there is a crucial difference between the marble revetment in the naos and the auxiliary spaces of Hagia Sophia. The marble decoration of the aisle and galleries is characterised by a relative simplicity compared to that of the naos in terms of the types and colours of the marble. Some marbles feature extensively in the naos and apse but do not occur in the aisles or galleries, such as the black and white Celtic marble, the giallo antico and the yellow alabaster. Similarly, red porphyry hardly plays any role in the aisles and gallery revetment, while it is placed in prominent locations in the narthex (flanking the Imperial Door), the naos and in the apse. Green cipollino likewise seems to be restricted exclusively to the naos. This selective distribution of the marble suggests a conscious choice that is related to the visual appearance and luminosity of the material, although an element of prestige associated with certain marbles is apparent also. For example, Egyptian alabaster and giallo antico, Celtic marble and red porphyry rank among the more valuable materials in antiquity, and these types were mostly employed along the main axis of the church (narthex, naos and apse). Nonetheless, the allocation of the different marbles seems to have been also motivated by their visual properties. Most of the marble panels in the naos utilise intensely coloured and strongly animated stones. Once polished, the red of the porphyry, the yellow of the alabaster and the green of the cipollino generated a rich polychromatic surface, while alabaster, cipollino and the Celtic marble exhibit pronounced patterns and veining. The visual emphasis in the naos lies evidently on a proliferation of materials, colours, contrasts and

---

39 See, for example, Robert W.G. Hunt, *Measuring Colour* (Kingston-upon-Thames: Fountain, 1987, 3rd edition, 1998), 36.

40 Richard L. Gregory, *Eye and Brain: The Psychology of Seeing* (Oxford: Oxford University Press, 1998), 89; Hunt (1987, 3rd edition, 1998), 53.

textures. The strong colours and vibrant patterns of the marbles in the naos augmented the perceived luminosity and may have served to compensate for the lower level of luminance and to enhance and animate the relatively even illumination of the naos.[41]

The marble incrustation in the aisles and galleries differs in every point from that in the naos. In the auxiliary spaces, a minimal range of materials was employed that are generally more evenly and consistently patterned (Plates 5–7). Even though the loss of the entire revetment of the exterior walls impedes an accurate reconstruction of the decoration, it seems that the marble revetment in the aisles and galleries consisted mainly of Phrygian and Thessalian marble. The complementary colours of green Thessalian and red and white Phrygian marble and cipollino rosso were juxtaposed, thus enhancing their hues reciprocally (Plate 6). The veins and spots of these two marbles are arranged with some regularity and spread over the entire surface, creating a more homogeneous visual effect than was observed with respect to the marbles used in the naos. The decoration in the aisles and galleries thus generates a luminosity and visual impression that is more restrained than the animated and colourful brightness of the naos but still somewhat enlivened by bands and panels of the wavy cipollino rosso.[42]

Numerous scholars have suggested that the very nature of the marble revetment of Hagia Sophia contributed to a dematerialisation of its architectural structure.[43] However, the overall configuration of the materials and colours and the specific optical properties of the individual types of marble actually accentuate the surfaces as a canvas for the effects of light and colour. The degree of being full of light (*lichthaft*) as opposed to being substantial (*körperhaft*) depends on the entire range of the material's visual properties, including colours and texture of the surfaces and the varying combinations of these factors.[44] For example, while various colour order systems quote specific values of reflectivity for differently coloured marbles,[45] they do not account for the surface texture or the differences

41 Nadine Schibille, 'Light in Early Byzantium: The Church of Hagia Sophia in Constantinople' (PhD thesis, University of Sussex, 2004), 96–101; Nadine Schibille, 'Light as an aesthetic constituent in the architecture of Hagia Sophia in Constantinople', in *Manipulating Light in Pre-modern Times / Manipolare la luce in epoca premoderna*, ed. D. Mondini and V. Ivanovici (Mendrisio: Mendrisio Academy Press / Silvana Editoriale Cinisello Balsamo, 2014).

42 Compare, for example, the marble revetment of the Roman Pantheon. Günter (1965), 7–15.

43 Günter (1965); Heinz Kähler, *Die Hagia Sophia* (Berlin: Gebr. Mann, 1967), 3; Kleinbauer (1999), 41; Kleinert (1979), 7–44; Wladimir R. Zaloziecky, *Die Sophienkirche in Konstantinopel und ihre Stellung in der Geschichte der abendländischen Architektur* (Studie di Antichità Cristiana 12) (Rome and Freiburg: Pontificio istituto di archeologia cristiana, 1936), 54–6.

44 Günter (1965).

45 White marble has an average reflectivity of 80 per cent, raven black of about 6.7 per cent, red colours range from 12.6 per cent to 26.2 per cent and different green colours vary between 12.7 per cent and 59.7 per cent. See, for example, Hunt (1987, 3rd edition, 1998), 131–

that may occur due to the angle with which the light strikes the marble. Whereas dark surfaces generally absorb most incoming light, they may be highly reflective when polished, particularly when illuminated at an obtuse angle. In Hagia Sophia, the highly polished and multicoloured marbles cladding the surfaces created a luminosity that was at once vibrant as well as soft and diffuse. This effect was brought about by the consistency of the layering, an emphasis on horizontal components and the colourful nature of the marbles with their distinct veins and patterns. In this, Hagia Sophia differs from earlier traditions. The extant marble incrustations of the fourth and fifth centuries tend to use strongly coloured yet less patterned types of marble and to emphasise the structural aspects of the architecture through the use of, for instance, the application of marble pilasters.[46] The marble revetment in Hagia Sophia, on the other hand, while still following traditional schemata, displays an interest in the two-dimensional character of the surfaces, treating them as a canvas for the effects of colour and light. Hence, the marble revetment does not dematerialise the architectural structure of Hagia Sophia as such; it merely contributes to and highlights the effects of light and animation within the Great Church. This impression is echoed in the ekphrasis of Paul the Silentiary, who captures these optical properties when he describes the marbles as gleaming, bright, sparkling, glittering, shiny and shimmering, speckled, besprinkled, wavy, slanting and swirling.[47] The marble sheeting actively participates in the construction of Hagia Sophia's dynamic, polychromatic and luminous space.

The play of light and shadow is skilfully continued in the intricately carved marble capitals and arcade spandrels that are executed in white Proconnesian marble (Figure 3.1).[48] The entire architectural sculpture is deeply undercut, creating a complex relief-work of light and shade. The so-called 'kettle capitals' of the lower order are bowl shaped impost capitals capped by small Ionic volutes on either side and with characteristic imperial monograms on the face of the capital.[49] The acanthus and palm leaves as well as the

59; William M. C. Lam, *Sunlight as Formgiver for Architecture* (New York, NY: Van Nostrand Reinhold, 1986), appendix 13, 750–751.

46 For the tradition of marble revetments in the fourth to the sixth centuries, see Kleinert (1979), 45–87.

47 Silentiary, verses 617–646: Bright (λευκός), flash (στράπτω), silver-shining (ἀργύφεος), sparkle (ἀμάρυγμα), glowing (σελαγέω), shining through (διαυγάζω), flashing, sparkling, gleaming (μαρμαρυγή), spotted or speckled (δαίδαλος), winding or wavy (ἑλιγμός), slanting (λοξός), swirling (ἑλίσσω).

48 The main capitals used in the nave arcades and in the aisles are so-called bowl capitals capped by small Ionic volutes and bolster structures and decorated by various deeply undercut acanthus forms. Rudolf Kautzsch, *Beiträge zu einer Geschichte des spätantiken Kapitells im Osten vom vierten bis ins siebente Jahrhundert* (Berlin and Leipzig: W. de Gruyter, 1936), 194–7.

49 On late antique capitals see e.g. Kautzsch (1936). On Hagios Polyeuktos and Hagia Sophia, see Christine Strube, *Polyeuktoskirche und Hagia Sophia: Umbildung und Auflösung antiker Formen, Entstehung des Kämpferkapitells* (Munich: Verlag der Bayerischen Akademie der Wissenschaften, 1984).

3.1 Marble capital from the lateral arcades at ground level of Hagia Sophia.

monograms decorating the capitals are sharply undercut and so is the lacelike swirling leaf ornamentation on the archivolts and spandrels of the lower order arcades. This is topped with a richly carved marble cornice. The vertical surfaces and spandrels of the gallery arcades are decorated with *opus sectile* where white inlays form a pattern of scrolls and foliage on a dark background that is interrupted at regular intervals by discs of red porphyry. An *opus sectile* frieze also surrounds the walls of the aisles and inner narthex at the height of the imposts (Plate 28). The colour scheme here is again dominated by contrasts of light and dark. Cornices, which form the upper edges of the wall segments, consist of a console enclosed by egg and dart, an astragal and a frieze with patterns of foliage.[50] These delicately sculptured coatings and *opus sectile* surfaces add to the impression of weightlessness and contribute to a fluent transition between the wall, arcades and cornices. The entire carved ornament is worked in deeply cut *à jour*. Archivolts and cornices have the same relief character as the capitals and act as a unifying feature. These carved capitals and architectural sculpture might originally have been gilded, if

[50] Friedrich Wilhelm Deichmann, *Studien zur Architektur Konstantinopels im 5. und 6. Jahrhundert nach Christus* (Baden-Baden: B Grimm, 1956), 77–8.

Paul the Silentiary is to be believed. Traces of blue were indeed found in the background of some of the capitals of the gallery arcades,[51] and this colouring would have further detached and sculpted the foliage from its ground.

The deeply undercut and exquisitely worked architectural sculpture in Hagia Sophia exemplifies the late antique interest in high-quality three-dimensional relief, in texture and in the effects of light and dark that is apparent also in late antique miniatures such as ivories and cage-cups.[52] The concern for detail and skilled craftsmanship was adapted to Hagia Sophia's monumental scale. The carved Proconnesian marble elements (capitals, arcades, cornices) represent an integral part of the total architectural statement and function within the overall visuality of the ecclesiastical space. In fact, the entire carved ornamentation is subordinate to the whole architectural structure, but still to be enjoyed in its own right.[53] This is evident from Procopius' description of how the details are 'fitted together with incredible skill' and how 'each detail attracts the eye and draws it on irresistibly to itself'. Procopius emphasises here an aesthetic appreciation of the 'extraordinary harmony (ἁρμονίαν ἐκπρεπεστάτην)' of the building as a whole and the great variety of riches of which it is composed.[54] In this, Hagia Sophia and the ekphrastic account reflect the essential qualities of what has been termed the 'jewelled style' of late antiquity, the taste for extravagant variety and detail.[55]

The sharply undercut marble decoration has a double-shelled, diaphanous appearance that recapitulates the relationship between the nave and the aisles.[56] The three-dimensional shaping of the structural elements is dissolved, and the organic relation between load and support, evident in the classical order, has disappeared. The four main piers have been absorbed into the wall plane, and the archivolts of the arcades spring directly out of these walls to the right and left (as opposed to resting on pilasters). The capitals are equally equated with the wall plane, and a continuum of capital, archivolt and wall was thus achieved. The capitals were no longer treated as three-dimensional objects as such, but merely as support for the lattice of regular, rhythmic *chiaroscuro*.[57] This *chiaroscuro*, the dramatic contrast of light and dark elements,

---

51 Silentiary verses 376–377: καὶ τὰς μὲν χρυσέοισιν ἐλαφρίζουσι καρήνοις στικτοὶ πορφυρέοισιν ἀποστίλβοντες ἀώτοις κίονες. Kleinert (1979), 19–21; Strube (1984), 74, 95.

52 See, for instance, the central panel of the sixth-century Barberini ivory in the Musée du Louvre in Paris or most famously the fourth-century Lycurgus cup in the British Museum in London.

53 Jaś Elsner, 'Late antique art: The problem of the concept and the cumulative aesthetic', in *Approaching Late Antiquity: The Transformation from Early to Late Empire*, ed. Simon Swain and Mark Edwards (Oxford: Oxford University Press, 2004).

54 Procopius I.1.47.

55 Bolman (2006); Bolman (2010); Elsner (2004); Roberts (1989).

56 Hans Buchwald, 'Saint Sophia, turning point in the development of Byzantine architecture?', in *Die Hagia Sophia in Istanbul: Akten des Berner Kolloquiums vom 21. Oktober 1994*, ed. Volker Hoffmann (Bern and New York: P. Lange, 1997), 33.

57 Geometrical patterns were assimilated into the repertoire and merged with vegetable forms. Strube (1984), 106–7.

is reminiscent of the open-cut lighting devices with which the church was once equipped, and that is characteristic of Hagia Sophia's overall aesthetic appeal. The play of light and dark is an integral part of the building's visual totality and the prevailing theme of Hagia Sophia's aesthetics. The marble revetment and the deeply undercut capitals, archivolts and spandrels generate patterned and perforated surfaces from which light is unevenly reflected. This creates the appearance of an almost translucent light-permeated membrane that contributes to the overall impression of an at once vibrant yet consistent luminosity.

The Mosaic Decoration

Gleaming with gold, the mosaics that cover the vaults of Hagia Sophia mark a shift in medium, the luminosity and reflectivity of which could be carefully manipulated. The art of Byzantine mosaics is closely allied to light and participates actively in the creation of a luminous space.[58] Different techniques were employed to enhance the brightness and reflective properties of mosaics. For example, the interaction between adjacent materials and colours seems to have been taken into account.[59] In the following pages I will explore the designs, materials and colours of the sixth-century mosaics of Hagia Sophia and how the decoration exploited the effects of light and colour. My interest lies in the overall design and the principles governing its compositional structure and optical properties rather than in the individual motifs. Some of the pictorial *leitmotifs* of the mosaic decoration and their symbolic significance will be addressed in the subsequent chapter.

Despite the considerable transformation and loss of much of the sixth-century mosaics, particularly in the galleries, it is possible to reconstruct tentatively the overall design of the original mosaics of Hagia Sophia.[60] Most of the ornamental mosaics at ground level are believed to date to the sixth century. Here, glass mosaics cover the entire ceiling of the inner narthex, including the window soffits on the west and the lunettes on the east as well as the aisles. These

---

[58] James (1996); James (2000); Liz James, 'Color and meaning in Byzantium', *Journal of Early Christian Studies* 11 (2003); James (2006).

[59] James (1996), 4–8; Mathew (1963), 5.

[60] The mosaics are either completely lost due to numerous earthquakes, structural repairs and additions, or they have simply been changed to accommodate the needs or aesthetic tastes over a period of almost 1500 years. During Hagia Sophia's use as a mosque, the mosaics were gradually concealed with paint or plaster and a considerable fraction has still not been uncovered to this day (e.g. Plate 15). On the basis of the sparse archaeological findings and the drawings and watercolours by Cornelius Loos (around 1710) and the Fossati brothers (1847–1849), Karen Boston has attempted a reconstruction of the original mosaic decoration of Hagia Sophia. See Karen A. Boston, 'Imaging the Logos: Display and Discourse in Justinian's Hagia Sophia' (PhD, University of London, 1999), 175–217.

mosaics consist of geometric patterns and crosses on gold ground.[61] Typically, ornamental borders outline the individual architectonic surface units. In the narthex, the border is composed of interlocked dark blue and silver stepped patterns, decorated with red and green jewels (Plates 8–11), while in the aisles it is a band of interlocked red and gold stepped designs, flanking a sequence of alternating swastikas and quatrefoils that are inscribed into dark blue squares and roundels, respectively (Plates 12, 13). These ornamental borders enclose a large double cross in the apex of the vaults. The surface units between these decorative borders can basically be considered the picture spaces and are decorated with a limited repertoire of geometric shapes, stars and Latin crosses with jewelled cross arms. One motif that prevails in the groined vaults of both the narthex and the aisles are pointy multicoloured egg-shaped designs that have been identified as lotus buds or winged palmettes (Plates 10, 11, 14).[62] Other conspicuous elements are huge jewelled Latin crosses in the barrel vaults of the aisles (Plates 16, 17) and two continuous braided large-angled zigzag bands in the intrados of the transverse arches (Plates 12, 29). These bands are interwoven so as to form a chain of rhombi and their cross points are interlaced by circles, creating together an endless string of knots. The tunnel vaults in the passageways that pierce the western subsidiary piers and the southern buttress piers are homogeneously covered in different carpet-like patterns of grids, diamonds, quatrefoils, squares and roundels on a gold or silver background (Plates 18, 19). The principal colours of what are believed to be the original sixth-century mosaics were gold, silver, red, blue and green.

---

[61] Previous scholarly publications usually focus on the figural mosaics from later dates, but they frequently contain valuable information about the materials and techniques of the ornamental mosaics that are believed to date to the sixth century. Especially detailed sources are the numerous reports written during the course of the restoration undertaken by the Byzantine Institute and later Dumbarton Oaks over a period of 45 years (1933–1978). Robin Cormack, 'Interpreting the mosaics of S. Sophia at Istanbul', *Art History* 4 (1981); Ernest J. W. Hawkins, 'Further observations on the narthex mosaic in St. Sophia at Istanbul', *DOP* 22 (1968); Cyril Mango and Ernest J. W. Hawkins, 'The apse mosaics of St. Sophia at Istanbul: Report on work carried out in 1964', *DOP* 19 (1965); Cyril Mango and Ernest J. W. Hawkins, 'The Mosaics of St. Sophia: The church fathers in the north tympanum', *DOP* 26 (1972); Paul A. Underwood, 'A preliminary report on some unpublished mosaics in Hagia Sophia', *AJA* 55 (1951); Paul A. Underwood, 'Notes on the work of the Byzantine Institute in Istanbul: 1954', *DOP* 9–10 (1956); Paul A. Underwood and Ernest J. W. Hawkins, 'The mosaics of Hagia Sophia at Istanbul: The portrait of the emperor Alexander, a report on work done by the Byzantine Institute in 1959 and 1960', *DOP* 15 (1961); Thomas Whittemore, *The Mosaics of St. Sophia at Istanbul, Preliminary Report on the First Year's Work 1931–1932: The Mosaics of the Narthex* (Oxford: Oxford University Press, 1933); Thomas Whittemore, *The Mosaics of St. Sophia at Istanbul, Second Preliminary Report on the Work done in 1933–1934: The Mosaics of the Southern Vestibule* (Oxford: Oxford University Press, 1936); Thomas Whittemore, *The Mosaics of Haghia Sophia at Istanbul, Third Preliminary Report on Work done in 1935–1938: The Imperial Portraits of the South Gallery* (Oxford: Oxford University Press, 1942); Thomas Whittemore, *The Mosaics of Haghia Sophia at Istanbul, Fourth Preliminary Report on Work done in 1934–1938: The Deesis Panel of the South Gallery* (Oxford: Oxford University Press, 1952).

[62] Boston (1999), 179; Robin Cormack and Ernest J. W. Hawkins, 'The mosaics of St. Sophia at Istanbul: The rooms above the southwest vestibule and ramp', *DOP* 31 (1977): 203; Mango and Hawkins(1972), 34.

The lack of monumental figurative mosaics in the sixth-century design of Hagia Sophia has led to speculations about the underlying reasons. It has been suggested that the large scale of the building is not conducive to figural representations or, in fact, that time was too short to allow for a more elaborate decorative scheme.[63] However, I do not believe that the mosaic decoration was a choice of compromise. Rather, the visual effect of the ornamental mosaics provides at least part of the answer. The original design of the ground-floor mosaic displays an astonishing consistency in its repertoire, creating a unity that served as a vehicle of light rather than providing any exclusive visual focus. Procopius explicitly refers to the non-existence of a specific focal point,[64] which indicates that his description and the mosaic decoration both reflect and share an aesthetic of an all-encompassing visual experience.

The dating of the extant non-figurative mosaics at gallery level is problematic. Non-figurative mosaics are preserved in the soffits of the nave arcades, in the barrel or tunnel vaults alongside the lateral nave arcades and the adjacent intrados as well as in the upper niches on the subsidiary piers that terminate the exedras. However, not all of these non-figurative mosaics can be attributed to the original sixth-century ornamentation. While working on the mosaic portrait of the emperor Alexander (912–913 CE) on the north gallery, Underwood and Hawkins identified three distinct phases in the history of the ornamental mosaics at gallery level. To the first phase, dating shortly before 537 CE, belong the rinceau scrolls on a gold background in the intrados of the exedra arcades (Plate 20), and the adjacent decorative borders with eight-pointed gold stars (towards the nave) and eight-sided cusped forms (towards the gallery side) on a dark violet background. While the soffits of the lateral arcades form part of the second phase, they seem to follow the original design closely, albeit with slight differences in the type of foliage, techniques and colours (Plate 21).[65] Underwood and Hawkins attributed the mosaics of the tunnel vault alongside the lateral arcades (Plate 26) and the intrados of the adjacent arches (Plate 22) to a third campaign in which the

---

63 John Beckwith, 'Byzantium: Gold and light', in Thomas B. Hess and John Ashbery (eds), 'Light from Aten to Laser', *Art News Annual* 35 (1969): 51; Cormack (1981), 134; Robin Cormack 'The Visual Arts', in *The Cambridge Ancient History. Late Antiquity: Empire and Successors, A.D. 425–600*, ed. Averil Cameron, Bryan Ward-Perkins, and Michael Whitby (Cambridge: Cambridge University Press, 2000), 905; Kähler (1967), 47.

64 Procopius I.1.47–8.

65 This conclusion is based on a patch of mosaic in the lower part of the westernmost arch of the northern lateral arcade. Underwood and Hawkins (1961), 199–202, 212–14. The author's dating of the second phase to shortly before 562 CE is inconclusive. Underwood and Hawkins dated the rebuilding of the tympana to 558–562 CE. This, however, is at odds with Mainstone's findings that suggest a date probably around 869 CE during the reign of Basil I. Rowland J. Mainstone, 'The reconstruction of the tympana of St. Sophia at Istanbul', *DOP*, 23–4 (1969–1970); Mainstone (1988), 97–8. Accordingly, the mosaics of the lateral gallery arcade were to be dated to the second half of the ninth century. The existence of silver tesserae among the gold of the background supports this later date, since the admixture of silver in the gold background is found only since the eighth century. Mango and Hawkins (1965), 141.

portrait of the Emperor Alexander was added in the early years of the tenth century, probably around 912 CE.[66]

Pictorial representations of Hagia Sophia from the eighteenth and nineteenth century show further ornamental mosaics in the intrados of the transverse arches on the north gallery that seem identical to the mosaics in the arches parallel to the lateral arcades (Plate 22). Since these transverse arches were not affected by the rebuilding of the tympana in the ninth century, this could indicate that the design of medallions alternating with lobed diamonds on a gold ground form part of the original sixth-century mosaic programme.[67] This suggests that the mosaic patch with a spider's web in the eastern part of the central bay on the south gallery (Plate 25) is also associated with the sixth-century design. Fossati furthermore recorded circles interlaced with rhombi of silver and blue upon a gold ground in the soffit of the small arch in the northeast corner of the north gallery, running parallel to the exterior wall, as well as in the corresponding arch on the opposite site.[68] According to the drawings of Cornelius Loos, the pattern on the arches parallel to the tunnel vaults recurred in the transverse arches of the galleries.[69] It seems then that many of the mosaic motifs re-appear in variable compositions and in different places, indicating an overall consistent mosaic programme.

Further remnants of the sixth-century mosaics are almost certainly preserved in the soffits of the western gallery arcades (Plate 24) and in the window soffits of the apse windows adjacent to the window transennae, with alternating St. Andrew's crosses in gold and multicoloured diamonds on a field of dark blue glass (Plate 27). Some ornamental mosaics were unveiled in the soffit of the bema arch that can equally be attributed to the sixth century (Plate 30). This geometric band originally curved around the edge and onto the western voussoir of the bema arch.[70] Its design is similar to the geometric border in the window reveals of the apse windows. Above the east springing of the south tympanum arch, a stylised palmette and tree motif was uncovered, the tidy workmanship and materials of which are characteristic of the sixth-century decoration.[71] Paul the Silentiary mentioned a monumental mosaic cross in the apex of the main dome,[72] while the dome ribs were possibly embellished

66 Underwood and Hawkins (1961), 205–8.

67 For a detailed discussion of the Fossati watercolours and drawings by Cornelius Loos see Boston (1999), 175–217.

68 Boston (1999), 180–86.

69 For some examples, see Alfred Westholm, *Cornelius Loos: teckningar från en expedition till Främre Orienten 1710–1711*, Nationalmusei skriftserie; n.s. 6 (Stockholm: Nationalmuseum, 1985), 41–56.

70 Mango and Hawkins (1965), 127, 32–7.

71 Mango and Hawkins (1972), 7, 11.

72 Silentiary, verses 506–508: τύπος σταυροῖο μεσόμ[φα]λος ἔνδοθι κύκλου λεπταλέηι ψηφῖδι χαράσσεται; translated in Cyril Mango, *The Art of the Byzantine Empire 312–1453: Sources and Documents* (Toronto: University of Toronto Press, 1972, reprint 1986), 83. 'At the very navel the sign of the cross is depicted within a circle by means of minute mosaic …'.

with a band of geometric designs of alternating diamonds and St. Andrew's crosses. Similar to the mosaics at ground level, the prevalent colours in the gallery, semi-domes and tympana are also gold, silver, red, blue and green.

The material, pictorial and textual evidence indicates conclusively that the original sixth-century mosaic decoration of Hagia Sophia was aniconic (non-figurative), and there is no proof of any changes to the mosaics prior to Iconoclasm. The sixth-century mosaic programme relies on only few basic motifs. The geometric border of alternating diamonds and St. Andrew's crosses, for example, is found in the bema arch, the inner edge of the northeast exedra windows and the lower parts of the ribs of the dome.[73] A simpler version of this pattern decorates the reveals of the apse windows. Virtually the same composition reappears in the room above the southwest ramp of Hagia Sophia and in the barrel vault above the passage that pierces through the southern buttress piers at ground level (Plate 19). Here the motifs are spread in rows over the entire barrel vault on a silver background. The diamonds and St. Andrew's crosses were also used separately in combination with other designs. Lobed diamonds are to be found in the intrados of numerous arches of both the south and north galleries (Plate 22) and St. Andrew's crosses are inscribed into quatrefoils in the vault of the passage piercing through the southwest subsidiary pier at ground level (Plate 18). The motif is also found on the carved beam casings of the west gallery and on the bronze doors leading from the outer into the inner narthex.[74] The tree or spade-like motif and the stylised palm leaves from the south tympanum correspond to the multicoloured egg-shaped lotus buds in the cross vaults of the aisles and narthex. While in the narthex (Plates 10, 11) the lotus buds and palmettes appear individually, the two motifs merge into winged lotus buds crowned by a fleur-de-lis in the vault mosaics of the aisles (Plate 14).

In spite of the fact that some ornamental mosaics have been proven to be of a later date based on their technique and materials, it is plausible that they actually imitate Justinianic designs for the sake of unity.[75] It seems, then, that the original mosaic decoration of Hagia Sophia followed an aesthetically coherent repertoire, consisting predominantly of geometric patterns and heavily stylised floral motifs characteristic of floor mosaics in the fifth and sixth century.[76] These motifs and patterns are spread across the surface and in so doing emphasise its solidity and unity without distinguishing between separate strata. The extensive use of decorative borders accentuates the

---

73 For extensive discussions of the original remains and motifs, see Mango and Hawkins (1965), 148, figure 39; Mango and Hawkins (1972), 33.

74 Mango and Hawkins (1972), 33, figures 54, 61.

75 Mango and Hawkins (1965), 148; Mango and Hawkins (1972), 32–5.

76 Kitzinger (1965, reprint 1976). Kitzinger observed a gradual development from geometric patterns to organic motifs in the late fifth and first half of the sixth century. Although his evidence derives mainly from floor mosaics, he pointed out that the wall and vault mosaics followed a similar progress. He also discusses the visual effect of the continuous decoration.

surfaces further. This artistic principle of outlining discrete surface units with borders derives ultimately from Roman frescoes and can also be found in fourth- to sixth-century mosaics in Rome, Ravenna or Poreč.[77] This aesthetic strategy of breaking up a composition into individual units (*segmenta*) was identified as one of the essential features of the late antique jewelled style and was recognised in contemporary literature, in textiles as well as the monumental frescoes of the Red Monastery in Upper Egypt.[78] Just as late antique patterned textiles often imitated mosaic designs, the mosaics of Hagia Sophia imitate textiles in that their balanced structure and the regular repetition of a limited set of motifs are evocative of the basic qualities of textile or carpet patterns (Plate 23).[79] Through the use of decorative borders and the carpet-like repetition of geometric designs, the mosaic surfaces are deliberately articulated. This achieves a unification of the entire mosaic plane and in so doing augments the infinity of the building. The even and continuous spread of the mosaic patterns does not dictate a visual focus or a rigid notion of space, as narrative scenes would do. Rather, the mosaics serve as a polychromatic and luminous membrane in order to generate a more universal spatial experience. The mosaics of Hagia Sophia are truly an artistic medium of colour and light. Light bounces unevenly off the mosaic surfaces and creates a homogeneous effect of a vibrant and scintillating skin that lines the entire interior of the building. This effect extends from the marble revetment and the carved capitals and arcade spandrels to the mosaic surfaces of the vaults. It is the light-bearing quality and overall programme of the decoration that creates and defines the unique aesthetics of this ecclesiastical space.

Sixth-century Materials and Colours

The visual properties of a mosaic depend on the materials and colours of its tesserae, the preparation of the foundation and the specific arrangement of colours and tesserae. These are important variables that are subject to individual choices and are critical for the visual character of the mosaic, and therefore indicative of aesthetic considerations. The internal material evidence from the mosaics has thus great potential to yield significant insights into aesthetic preferences at the time.

---

77 Anne Terry and Henry Maguire, *Dynamic Splendor: The Wall Mosaics in the Cathedral of Eufrasius at Poreč* (University Park, PA: The Pennsylvania State University Press, 2007), 72.

78 Bolman (2006); Bolman (2010); Roberts (1989), 111–18; Thomas (2002).

79 Mango and Hawkins claimed that the ornamental designs of the mosaic decoration were reminiscent of motifs that could be found in Egyptian textiles and Sasanian art. Gonosová investigated the dependence of fifth-century ornamental mosaic decoration on textiles. She came to the conclusion that the appearance of certain designs in mosaic decorations coincided with a more frequent use of patterned silks. Anna Gonosová, 'The formation and sources of early Byzantine floral semis and floral diaper patterns reexamined', *DOP* 41 (1987): 228–9, 37; Mango and Hawkins (1972), 34; Thomas (2002).

The design and construction of mosaics involves a complex sequence of technological decisions that is determined by material, architectural, economic or cultural constraints, which in turn reveal patterns of technological development, social agency and cultural values.[80] The first task of the mosaicists was to assemble the materials. In the case of the sixth-century mosaics of Hagia Sophia, the material of choice was glass, including gold and silver leaf tesserae.[81] Very little is known about how the mosaicists in late antiquity obtained their raw materials. Were the tesserae produced on site or were they procured from one or different places? If so, how was trade organised to ascertain the constant supply of raw materials?[82] Recent archaeological research strongly suggests that glass making (primary production) was distinct from glass working (secondary production), and that the primary manufacture of base glass from its raw materials occurred in a relatively small number of locations.[83] Sites of primary glass production have been identified in the coastal region of Syro-Palestine and Egypt, where raw glass was produced on an industrial scale in so-called tank furnaces.[84] This raw glass was widely traded throughout the Mediterranean and into central and northern Europe in the form of cullet, re-melted, coloured if required,

80 Nicholas David and Carol Krammer, *Ethnoarchaeology in Action* (Cambridge: Cambridge University Press, 2001); Marcia-Anne Dobres, 'Technology's link and chaînes: The processual unfolding of technique and technician', in *The Social Dynamics of Technology: Practice, Politics, and World Views*, ed. M.A. Dobres and C.R. Hoffman (Washington, DC: Smithsonian Institute Press, 1999); Marcia-Anne Dobres, *Technology and Social Agency: Outlining a Practice Framework for Archaeology* (Oxford: Blackwell Publishers Ltd, 2000); Mark Edmonds, 'Description, understanding and chaîne opératoire', *Archaeological Review from Cambridge* 9 (1990); Bill Sillar and Michael S. Tite, 'The challenge of "technological choices" for materials science approaches in archaeology', *Archaeometry* 42 (2000).

81 Kähler (1967), 47; Mango and Hawkins (1965), 127, 32–6; Mango and Hawkins (1972), 8, 21; Underwood and Hawkins (1961), 201; Whittemore (1933), 11–13.

82 Katherine M. D. Dunabin, *Mosaics of the Greek and Roman World* (Cambridge: Cambridge University Press, 1999); James (2006).

83 See, for example, Cesare Fiori and Mariangela Vandini, 'Chemical composition of glass and its raw materials: Chronological and geographical development in the first millennium A.D', in *When Glass Matters*, ed. M. Beretta (Florence: Olschiki 2004); Ian C. Freestone, Yael Gorin Rosen, and Michael J. Hughes, 'Primary glass from Israel and the production of glass in Late Antiquity and the Early Islamic period', in *La Route du Verre: Ateliers primaires et secondaires du millénaire av. J.-C. au Moyen Âge*, ed. M.D. Nenna (Lyon: Maison de l'Orient Méditerranéen, 2000); Ian C. Freestone, Matthew Ponting, and Michael J. Hughes, 'Origins of Byzantine glass from Maroni Petrera, Cyprus', *Archaeometry* 44 (2002); Ian C. Freestone, 'Primary glass sources in the mid first millennium AD', *Annales du 15e Congrès de l'Association Internationale pour l'Histoire du Verre: AIHV, New York-Corning* (2003).

84 Yael Gorin Rosen, 'Hadera, Bet Elie'zer', *Excavations and Surveys in Israel* 13 (1995); Yael Gorin-Rosen, 'The ancient glass industry in Israel: Summary of the finds and new discoveries', in *La Route du Verre: Ateliers primaires et secondaires du millénaire av. J.-C. au Moyen Âge*, ed. M.-D. Nenna (Lyon: Maison de l'Orient Méditerranéen, 2000); Marie-Dominique Nenna, Maurice Picon, and Michéle Vichy, 'Ateliers primaires et secondaires en Égypte à lépoque Gréco-Romaine', in *La Route du Verre: Ateliers primaires et secondaires du millénaire av. J.-C. au Moyen Âge*, ed. M.-D. Nenna (Lyon: Maison de l'Orient Méditerranéen, 2000); Marie-Dominique Nenna, 'Primary glass workshops in Graeco-Roman Egypt: Preliminary report on the excavations of the site of Beni Salama, Wadi Natrun (2003, 2005–2009)', in *Glass in the Roman Empire in honour of Jennifer Price*, ed. I.C. Freestone, J. Bailey, and C. M. Jackson (forthcoming); Oren Tal, Ruth E. Jackson-Tal, and Ian C. Freestone, 'New evidence of the production of raw glass at late Byzantine Apollonia-Arsuf (Israel)' *JGS* 46 (2004).

and worked into artefacts in secondary workshops.[85] Only a handful of compositional glass groups have been identified among first millennium glass assemblages from consumer sites all around the Mediterranean and Europe.[86] This relative homogeneity of Roman and post-Roman glass strengthens the centralised production model and reflects very stable economic and political conditions in the eastern Mediterranean at least through the sixth century.[87]

---

85 Robert H. Brill, 'The great glass slab from ancient Galilee', *Archaeometry* 20 (1967); Patrick Degryse *et al.*, 'A geochemical study of Roman to early Byzantine Glass from Sagalassos, South-west Turkey', *JAS* 32 (2005); Odile Dussart, 'Quelques indices d'ateliers de verriers en Jordanie et en Syrie du Sud de la fin de l'époque Hellenistique à l'époque Islamique', in *La Route du Verre: Ateliers primaires et secondaires du millénaire av. J.-C. au Moyen Âge*, ed. M.-D. Nenna (Lyon: Maison de l'Orient Méditerranéen, 2000); Alysia Fischer and W. Patrick McCray, 'Glass production activities as practised at Sepphoris, Israel (37 BC–AD 1516)', *JAS* 26 (1999); Freestone, Gorin Rosen, and Hughes (2000); Freestone (2002); Ian C. Freestone, 'The provenance of ancient glass through compositional analysis' in *Materials Issues in Art and Archaeology VII*, ed. Pamela B. Vandiver, Jennifer, L. Mass, and Alison Murray, (Warrendale, PA: Materials Research Society, 2005); Souen Deva Fontaine and Danièle Foy, 'L'épave Ouest-Embiez 1, Var: Le commerce maritime du verre brut et manufacturé en Méditerranée occidentale dans l'Antiquité', *Revue archéologique de Narbonnaise* 40 (2007); Danièle Foy and Marie-Dominique Nenna, 'Et vogue le verre!', in *Tout feu tout sable: Mille ans de verre antique dans le Midi de la France, Exhibition Catalogue Musée d'Histoire de Marseille, Juin-Décembre 2001*, ed. D. Foy and M.-D. Nenna (Aix-en-Provence: Édisud, 2001); Danièle Foy, Maurice Picon, and Michèle Vichy, 'Verres Omeyyades et Abbasides d'origine Egyptienne: Les témoignages de l'archéologie et de l'archéometrie'., *Annales du 15e Congrès de l'Association Internationale pour l'Histoire du Verre: AIHV, New York-Corning* (2003); Danèle Foy *et al.*, 'Caractérisation des verres de la fin de l'Antiquité en Méditerranée occidentale: l'émergence de nouveaux courants commerciaux', in *Échanges et commerce du verre dans le monde antique: actes du colloque de l'Association française pour l'archéologie du verre, Aix-en-Provence et Marseille, 7–9 juin 2001*, ed. D. Foy and M.-D. Nenna (Montagnac: Éditions Monique Mergoil, 2003); Danèle Foy, Michèle Vichy, and Maurice Picon, 'Lingots de verre en Méditerranée occidentale', *Annales du 14e Congrès de l'Association Internationale pour l'Histoire du Verre: AIHV, Amsterdam* (2000).

86 Two types of European Roman glass (with or without antimony), so-called HIMT (high iron, manganese and titanium) glass, Levantine I and II, Egypt I and II, and a glass type that bears some resemblance with HIMT glass and that has been identified among medieval glass assemblages from Europe. Marvis Bimson and Ian C. Freestone, 'The discovery of an Islamic glass-making site in middle Egypt', *Annales du 10e Congrès de l'Association Internationale pour l'Historie du Verre: AIHV* (1987); Robert H. Brill, 'Scientific Investigations of the Jalame Glass and Related Finds', in *Excavations at Jalame Site of a Glass Factory in Late Roman Palestine*, ed. G. D. Weinberg (Columbia, MO: University of Missouri Press, 1988); Ian C. Freestone, 'Chemical Analysis of 'Raw' Glass Fragments', in *Excavations at Carthage, Vol. II, 1: The Circular Harbour, North Side*, ed. H. R. Hurst (Oxford: Oxford University Press, 1994); Freestone (2002); Freestone (2005); Ian C. Freestone, Michael J. Hughes, and Colleen P. Stapleton, 'The composition and production of Anglo-Saxon glass', in *Catalogue of Anglo-Saxon Glass in the British Museum*, ed. Vera I. Evison (London: British Museum Press, 2008); P. Mirti, A. Lepora, and L. Sagui, 'Scientific analysis of seventh-century glass fragments from the Crypta Balbi in Rome', *Archaeometry* 42 (2000); Nadine Schibille, 'Supply routes and the consumption of glass in first millennium CE Butrint (Albania)', *JAS* 38 (2011); Bernard Gratuze and Jean-Noël Barrandon, 'Islamic glass weights and stamps: Analysis using nuclear techniques', *Archaeometry* 32 (1990); Nenna, Picon, and Vichy (2000); Edward V. Sayre and Ray W. Smith, 'Analytical studies of ancient Egyptian glass', in *Recent Advances in the Science and Technology of Materials, Vol. 3*, ed. A. Bishay (New York, NY: Plenum Press, 1974); E. V. Sayre and R. W. Smith, 'Compositional categories of ancient glass', *Science* 133 (1961).

87 Cécile Morrisson and Jean-Pierre Sodini, 'The sixth-century economy', in *The Economic History of Byzantium: From the Seventh through the Fifteenth Century*, ed. Angeliki E. Laiou (Washington, DC: The Dumbarton Oaks Research Library and Collection, 2002).

To date, there is no clear archaeological evidence for the secondary manufacturing of glass mosaic tesserae during the Roman and late antique period. In his twelfth-century writings, Theophilus describes a process identical to the production of windowpanes, known as the 'muff technique'.[88] First, molten glass was blown and shaped into long cylinders, which were cut lengthwise and opened out into sheets of glass. These sheets were then reheated in the annealing chamber of the furnace so as to flatten them under their own weight and the help of a smoothing block. For the production of gold and silver tesserae, a foil of gold or silver was placed on the sheets of glass and coated with a film of very clear ground glass. Together they were again fired, resulting in the metal leaf being sandwiched between two protective layers of glass.[89] The glass sheets were then cut into the required shapes and sizes.[90] Analytical data of some sets of late antique mosaic tesserae suggest a certain colour-specialisation during the secondary working stage, probably a direct result of varying melting conditions and degrees of difficulty involved in the production of some colours (for example dark red or gold leaf tesserae).[91]

The lack of any significant analytical data from Hagia Sophia allows only tentative conclusions to be drawn on the state of the glass industry in Constantinople in the sixth century and the Byzantine Empire at large. The little data that are available suggest that the mosaic tesserae from Hagia Sophia are in line with the Roman tradition and correspond to the chemical composition of other sixth-century mosaic assemblages like San Vitale in Ravenna and Hagios Polyeuktos in Constantinople.[92] These similarities point to a certain centralisation of production and supply of mosaic tesserae at least as regards the cultural and political centres of the Byzantine Empire during the sixth century.[93] The chemical characteristics of tesserae from more rural early Byzantine sites such as Sagalassos have proven to be different, indicating alternative supply patterns,[94] while smaller church foundations such as the Eufrasiana in Poreč seem to have been seriously affected by shortages in glass supplies.[95]

88 See Nadine Schibille, Fatma Marii, and Thilo Rehren, 'Characterization and provenance of late antique window glass from the Petra Church in Jordan', *Archaeometry* 50 (2008).

89 Theophilus, *On Divers Arts*, 40–43.

90 Frank Sear, 'Roman wall and vault mosaics', *Mitteilungen des Deutschen Archäologischen Instituts, Römische Abteilung* 23 (1977); Catherine Harding, 'The production of medieval mosaics: The Orvieto evidence', *DOP* 43 (1989); Marco Verità, 'Glass tesserae and gold leaf in the mosaics of Aquileia', *Quaderni Friulani di Archeologia* 16 (2006). According to Harding, the production of tesserae varied considerably from place to place. In some cases, glass was cast into flat cakes and then cut into pieces.

91 Schibille *et al.* (2012); Schibille and McKenzie (2014).

92 For some chemical data of some mosaic tesserae from Hagia Sophia, see Brill (1999), section IX. For a comparison of these data with San Vitale and Hagios Polyeuktos, see Schibille and McKenzie (2014).

93 Schibille and McKenzie (2014).

94 Schibille *et al.* (2012).

95 Terry and Maguire (2007), 78–82.

There is certainly no sign of material shortages in the sixth-century mosaics of Hagia Sophia that are almost exclusively made of glass tesserae. This choice of material identifies a functional purpose of the mosaic that is quite different to floor mosaics and, in fact, fresco painting. Floor mosaics used glass only sporadically, because they primarily needed to be smooth and resistant.[96] The principal function of wall and vault mosaics, on the other hand, is display. Glass mosaics are highly reflective and were available in an almost infinite range of colours. The desired goal was no doubt to produce polychrome and luminous glass surfaces, and this objective determined the choice of the material and reflects a specific aesthetic appreciation of its optical properties.[97] It is surprising to find, then, that the original colour palette of Hagia Sophia's mosaics is limited to gold, silver, red, green and blue (very dark violet, almost black).[98] This restriction in colours in the sixth-century mosaics of Hagia Sophia is all the more striking in light of other fifth- and sixth-century mosaic decorations such as those at Ravenna, Poreč or Sinai that typically exhibit a much wider range of hues (Plates 32, 34–42). While the use of marble on the walls imposes a natural limitation on the variety of colours available (white/grey, black/blue, red, yellow and green; Appendix), the selection of a limited number of primary colours in the mosaic decoration of Hagia Sophia suggests that these colours were a deliberate choice and therefore symbolically and/or aesthetically significant.

The selection of colours in Hagia Sophia is evidently very specific. Upon closer inspection, these colours (gold, silver, red, blue and green) are essentially consistent with the classical antique palette of primary colours (white, black, red and yellow).[99] Aëtius, a first-century CE source, claims that the earliest proponent of this four-colour theory was Empedocles, for whom the primary colours were white (λευκός), black (μέλας), red (ἐρυθρός) and yellow (ὠχρός). The same four-colour spectrum can still be found in the Aristotelian writings as well as in Plato's *Timaeus*, albeit slightly modified.[100] Whether or not Empedocles was the first to associate these four colours with the four elements is unclear. Judging by the writings of Aëtius, Galen and Pseudo-Aristotle, it seems that by the early second century CE the relationship of the four primary colours with the four elements was a widely recurring theme

96 Sear (1977).

97 James (1996); James (2000).

98 Underwood and Hawkins observed that colours were used very selectively and that mixed colours were avoided. Underwood and Hawkins (1961), 201–2.

99 Nadine Schibille, 'A quest for wisdom: The sixth-century mosaics of Hagia Sophia in Constantinople and late antique aesthetics', in *New Light on Old Glass: Recent Research on Byzantine Glass and Mosaics*, ed. C. Entwistle and L. James (London: British Museum Press, 2013).

100 Vincent J. Bruno, *Form and Color in Greek Painting* (New York, NY: W.W. Norton, 1977), 56–8; Hermann Diels and Walther Kranz, *Die Fragmente der Vorsokratiker* (Berlin: Weidmannsche Buchhandlung, 1903), 31 A92; James (1996), 53–8; Schwarzenberg (2000), 17; Artistotle, *Minor Works*, 791a 1–4. For Plato, the fourth colour was shining (λαμπρός) instead of yellow (ὠχρός), which may refer to the same colour; Plato, *Timaeus*, 68A-D.

and that these primary colours were white, black, red and yellow.[101] The same four colours in addition to purple (πορφύρεος) are the colour terms most frequently used in Byzantine epigrams, demonstrating a certain continuity of the classical colour system into Byzantium.[102]

The question remains whether the colours of Hagia Sophia are indeed representative of this classical idea of primary that is pure and unmixed colours. The only obvious match is the colour red and does not require any further explanation. White and yellow could be identified with silver and gold, or the metallic tesserae could be taken out of the equation altogether and be considered precious metals that are in themselves evocative of divine light.[103] The issue of blue can also be resolved easily, because the deep blue/purple glass in the mosaic decoration of Hagia Sophia is so dark that it appears black anyhow. In fact, there is no such thing as truly black glass. Instead, black-appearing glass is produced simply by an excess of some of the colourants such as cobalt (bluish black), manganese (deep purplish black) or iron (greenish black). In this case it seems that green is the only mixed colour in the colour palette of Hagia Sophia and presents an additional facet of the Byzantine concept of colour that equally derives ultimately from classical antiquity. While for Plato, green is a mixture of flame-colour and black (πυρροῦ δὲ μέλανι πράσιον),[104] Aristotle's *De Coloribus* specifies that green (πράσινος) is the original colour in all plants.[105] It is telling then that in the mosaics of Hagia Sophia the colour green is primarily reserved for vegetable motifs. Green was evidently considered the appropriate colour of plants, whereby the mosaics document the quest for the right colour in order to satisfy the aesthetic expectation of a sixth-century audience.[106]

It follows that the sixth-century mosaics of Hagia Sophia used mostly primary colours in the ancient sense. This use of primary colours is in fact closely related to an aesthetic concern for simplicity and luminosity inasmuch

---

[101] For Empedocles, the colour of fire is white, while water is black without specifying the colour of the other two elements, earth and air. Katerina Ierodiakonou, 'Empedocles on colour and colour perception', *Oxford Studies in Ancient Philosophy* 29 (2005); John Gage, *Colour and Culture: Practice and Meaning from Antiquity to Abstraction* (London: Thames and Hudson, 1993), 29.

[102] James (1996), 78.

[103] Gage (1993), 58–9; Patrik Reuterswaerd, 'What colour is divine light?', in Thomas B. Hess and John Ashbery (eds), 'Light from Aten to Laser', *Art News Annual* 35 (1969): 120–121; James (1996), 103–7.

[104] Plato, *Timaeus*, 68c; the ambiguity of green as a mixture of flame-colour and black is discussed in Bruno (1977), 89–93.

[105] Aristotle, *De Coloribus*, 794B; cited in H. B. Gottschalk, 'The *De Coloribus* and its author', *Hermes* 92 (1964): 70; Georg Wöhrle, 'Ps-Aristoteles *De Coloribus* – A Theophrastean Opusculum?', in *On the Opuscula of Theophrastus: Akten der 3. Tagung der Karl-und-Gertrud-Abel-Stiftung vom 19.-23. Juli 1999 in Trier*, ed. William W. Fortenbaugh and George Wöhrle (Stuttgart: Steiner, 2002). The author of the work is still disputed, but it is generally accepted as part of the Peripatetic canon, with Theophrastus or Strato as possible authors.

[106] Schibille (2013).

as for the Byzantines, following ancient Greek tradition, the beauty of a colour was associated with its brightness, which in turn depended on the colour's purity.[107] A love for bright and pure colours emerges, for example, from Plato's *Phaedo*, in which Plato praises the colours of the upper world for their lustre and for being bright, clear and pure.[108] In the *Philebus* Plato explains that only unmixed colours (primary colours) are pure and intrinsically beautiful.[109] The reason for a preference for pure and simple (unmixed) colours lies in the fact that the mixing of colours was associated with a loss of luminosity.[110] That the Byzantines valued above all the brilliance and glitter of colours, becomes obvious also from the colour terms used in Procopius' and Paul the Silentiary's ekphraseis. Both authors employ only a limited selection of colour terms and these usually in combination with the sensation of dynamic splendour and brilliance. In his very brief mention of the interior decoration of Hagia Sophia, Procopius names only purple (ἁλουργός), green (χλωρός), red (φοῖνιξ) and white (λευκός),[111] while Paul the Silentiary's colour vocabulary is similarly limited to green (χλωρός, μορφή κύανεος – almost blue), various shades of red (ῥόδον, πορφύρεος φοῖνιξ), yellow (ὠχρός), white (λευκός) and black (μέλας).[112] The chosen colour terms are notoriously vague in matters of hue, while they are intimately connected with an interest in luminosity and movement.[113] It is plausible then that the colours used in the mosaics of Hagia Sophia correspond to the Byzantine (and Platonic) ideal of pure and luminous colours, testifying to an aesthetic of light and luminosity.

Colour in Byzantine thought was nonetheless tied to identity and meaning inasmuch as colour was recognised as the object of sight that ultimately constitutes matter and form.[114] Colour was not seen as a superficial or secondary attribute of the external world. Instead, colour was the element that gave meaning to an image, provided the true colours were applied.[115] Agathias Scholasticus, for example, remarked that 'art can convey by colours the prayers of the soul', indicating that colours were expressive and associated with the true being or innermost workings of the human soul.[116]

---

107 James (1996); James (2000).

108 Plato, *Phaedo*, 110e.

109 Plato, Philebus, 51b.

110 Eva Keuls, 'Skiagraphia once again', *AJA* 79 (1975); Eva Keuls, *Plato and Greek Painting* (Leiden: Brill, 1978). This belief is consistent with the so-called subtractive colour system, according to which any mixing of pigments tends to subtract part of the light from different parts of the spectrum by absorption. See Hunt (1987, 3rd edition, 1998), 38.

111 Procopius, I.1.60; for a glossary of Byzantine colour terms, see James (1996), 73–4.

112 Silentiary verses 620–646.

113 Jaś Elsner, 'Physiognomics: Art and text', in *Seeing the Face, Seeing the Soul: Polemon's Physiognomy from Classical Antiquity to Medieval Islam*, ed. Simon Swain (Oxford: Oxford University Press, 2007), 219–21; James (1996), 49–51, 73–4.

114 James (1996); Robert S. Nelson, 'To say and to see: Ekphrasis and vision in Byzantium', in *Visuality Before and Beyond the Renaissance*, ed. Robert S. Nelson (Cambridge: Cambridge University Press, 2000).

115 This aspect is elaborated in James (2003).

116 Agathias, *On another on the Island of Platé*, in AP I.34: οἶδε δὲ τέχνη χρώμασι πορθμεῦσαι τὴν φρεὸς ἱκεσίην; Hans Georg Thümmel, *Die Frühgeschichte der ostkirchlichen*

Colour evidently constituted the very nature of matter and was considered the defining characteristic of a substance, the expression of its true nature and spirit (πνεῦμα).[117] Realism was thus established by applying the correct colours.[118] This is certainly reflected in the use of green to identify plant motifs in the mosaic decoration of Hagia Sophia, and it is highly likely that the other colours also signify the right colour in the relation to the significance of the sacred space. Specifically, the colours of the mosaics all correspond to the Platonic ideal of pure and luminous colours and enhance the visual brilliance and brightness of Hagia Sophia's interior.

That visual considerations were indeed fundamental to the design and layout of the mosaic decoration of Hagia Sophia in the sixth century is evidenced, above all, in the overall configuration of patterns and combination of colours. The individual motifs are frequently accentuated by clear outlines, and the decorative borders are often separated from the gold ground by rows of silver as, for instance, in the aisles, gallery arcades and semi-dome windows (Plates 13, 27).[119] These outlines and silver trims augment the colour contrast between the gold background and the motifs, thus counteracting the effect of the optical fusion of neighbouring colours.[120] The repertoire of motifs used to adorn the gold grounds also include stretches of monochromatic geometric patterns (red or dark blue) that consist basically only of outlines. Examples for these can be found in the intrados of the transverse arches (Plate 29) and the winged lotus buds in the aisles (Plate 14). These line drawings and monochromatic designs emphasise once more the two-dimensionality of the surface. The mosaic decoration does not attempt to appear as something other than what it is. It is simply a polychrome, reflective surface that lines the vaults of the building and in so doing remains true to the solidity and unity of the architectural structure underneath. It is colour that bestows meaning inasmuch as it seems sufficient to adumbrate the form in colour to render it recognisable. The somewhat more elaborate modelling of form and the choice of colours in the narthex mosaics that stands in contrast to the simpler line drawings of the aisles may indicate a premeditated symbolic differentiation of the two spaces, which will be discussed in the next chapter.

Bilderlehre, Texte und Untersuchungen zur Geschichte der altchristlichen Literatur (Berlin: Academie Verlag, 1992), 114.

[117] James (1996), 45.

[118] During the iconoclastic controversy, colour took on a theological significance that proved crucial in the debate on the value of images. Gage (1993), 47–8; James (2003).

[119] Underwood and Hawkins noted a difference in the outline of the arcade soffit panels between the original mosaics and their later replacements. While in the original mosaic, the panel is surrounded by a single row of grey marble, two rows of red glass is found in its stead in the later mosaics. Underwood and Hawkins (1961), 201–2.

[120] For a discussion of the principles of colour fusion and reciprocal intensification of contrasting colours in ancient Greek times see, for example, Keuls (1975); Keuls (1978).

Sixth-century Techniques

An awareness of light and colour and physiological phenomena associated with the perception of colour are visible in the careful execution of the sixth-century mosaics and even in the setting patterns and techniques. A brief look at the plaster and underpainting illustrates the issue of colour further. Although practices varied from workshop to workshop, there seems to have been a consistency in the application of several layers of plaster.[121] The foundation underneath the mosaics of Hagia Sophia consists of a rendering bed, an intermediate layer and a setting bed.[122] The latter, into which the mosaic cubes were finally set, was applied in sections and then painted. In the case of the sixth-century gold background in Hagia Sophia, the setting bed was usually painted red.[123] Since the paint is sometimes exposed in the interstices between single tesserae, this lends an additional cast of colour to the mosaic.[124] The red underpaint enhances the brassy quality of gold, which was evidently appreciated in the sixth century. This stands in contrast to the later technique of using yellow ochre underpaint and the trend of mixing an appreciable proportion of silver tesserae into the gold background of monumental mosaics, with which the mosaicists tried to lighten the gold background in the eighth through to the tenth centuries.[125] The other colour found underneath the sixth-century mosaics of Hagia Sophia is a dark blue, almost black pigment that accentuates the rinceaux of the gallery arcades and the geometric borders in the apse and the windows of the exedras.[126]

Considerable differences in both materials and techniques enable a distinction of the original mosaics from later reproductions.[127] In contrast to later mosaics, the sixth-century mosaics are generally more tidily executed. The gold ground is set in very neat rows. In the groined vaults of the narthex and aisles, work evidently began in the apex with the circular asterisk, and then moved away in concentric circles until the gold background meets with the ornamental border (Plates 9, 13). This setting pattern is

121 Vitruvius specifies three separate layers of plaster for mosaic pavements, first a layer of rubble (*statumen*), followed by a layer of rubble and lime (*rudus*) and finally, the upper layer (*nucleus*), a finer mortar mixed with crushed tile or potsherds. Vitruvius 7.1.3–4; Dunabin (1999).

122 Natalia B. Teteriatnikov, *Mosaics of Hagia Sophia, Istanbul: The Fossati Restoration and the Work of the Byzantine Institute* (Washington, DC: The Dumbarton Oaks Research Library and Collection, 1998).

123 An exception seems to be the patches of original gold background on the vertical surface of the tympana on a yellow-ochre setting bed, which is typical for later mosaics. Underwood and Hawkins (1961), 201; Mango and Hawkins (1965), 136; Mango and Hawkins (1972), 8, 21–2.

124 Terry and Maguire (2007), 77.

125 Mango and Hawkins (1965), 141.

126 Underwood and Hawkins (1961), 201; Mango and Hawkins (1965), 135.

127 Cormack and Hawkins (1977); Mango and Hawkins (1965); Mango and Hawkins (1972); Underwood and Hawkins (1961).

followed also in between the winged lotus buds in the aisles. Within the individual ornaments, the rows of tesserae adapt to the individual shapes that are additionally outlined by a single line or at most two rows of gold tesserae (Plates 11, 15). This careful setting of the tesserae contributed to the visual detachment of the motif from its gold background. The tesserae of the decorative bands seem to be set along the length of the band, thus emphasising the impression of beams radiating from the double cross in the apex of the vaults. The coloured tesserae are slightly larger than the metallic ones, but they are generally carefully selected for size, shape and their precise colour. Some attempts at the modeling of light can be observed, involving the use of different shades of the same hue. This is visible, for example, in the teardrop serifs suspended from the cross arms of the large Latin crosses in the aisles,[128] in the lotus buds (Plate 11) and in the geometric shapes of the transverse arches in the narthex or highly formulaic in the leafy motif in the upper niches on the subsidiary piers that terminate the exedras or the rinceau scrolls in the gallery exedra soffits (Plate 20).[129] Apart from the shadings of the narthex mosaics that, to a certain degree, aim at a realistic rendering of light, the modulation of light and shadow is rather mechanical and does not really produce an illusory impression. Rather, it counteracts naturalism and accentuates the stylised character of the decoration. This tendency is most overt in the motif of leaves (Figure 3.2, Plate 20) and less in the geometric and geometric-like floral designs. It seems that every attempt was made to undermine any naturalistic portrayals for the benefit of a more universal decorative and visual quality.

While the directional arrangement of the tesserae and shades of colours serve to model animated form, a further technique was used to exploit the reflective properties of the mosaic surfaces. In many of the vertical backgrounds of the sixth-century mosaics, the gold tesserae are slightly inclined to face downward. This has been observed in the fields of the lunettes on the east wall of the narthex,[130] in the western tympanum of the west bay of the south aisle, including the gold cubes within the outline of the Latin cross,[131] as well as in the vertical surface of the tympana.[132] That this tilting of the tesserae was intentional is illustrated by the fact that the technique is practiced less consistently in mosaics of later periods,[133] and by a pattern of application that

---

[128] Paul A. Underwood and Lawrence J. Majewski, 'Notes on the work of the Byzantine Institute in Istanbul: 1957–1959: The conservation of a Byzantine fresco discovered at Etyemez, Istanbul', *DOP* 14 (1960): 209.

[129] There are possibly some colour gradations in the jewels that decorate the cross arms of the large Latin crosses in the aisle decoration.

[130] Whittemore (1933), 11–13. No regularity in the inclination was identified. Whereas the tesserae were most inclined in the two southernmost bays (A, B), they were less inclined in bay C and set even more vertically in lunette F.

[131] Underwood and Majewski (1960), 209.

[132] Mango and Hawkins (1972), 8.

[133] The tilting of gold tesserae can be seen in the tunnel vaults along the lateral gallery arcaded (Plate 26, 31). The wide spacing of the tesserae and the poor workmanship suggest

3.2 Motif of a leaf in the aisle of Hagia Sophia with mosaic tesserae of different shades (of green) to model the effect of light.

is apparent in the window soffits and reveals of the narthex windows. Here, the tesserae of the gold ground in the northern reveals of most windows are neatly set in slight inclination from top to bottom. No such setting pattern was recorded for the southern reveal of the same windows.[134] This shows that the mosaicists aimed at optimising the view from ground level and may have taken into account not only the spectator's viewpoint, but also the direction of the illumination. The northern reveal of the windows catches direct sunlight during afternoon hours, which the tilted cubes reflect downward to the beholder, making the mosaics appear more brilliant. The southern reveal, on the other hand, is never directly illuminated. As a result, the inclination of the tesserae does not make any difference for the luminosity of the surface and was thus evidently deemed superfluous. This differential application of the technique confirms that the tilting of the tesserae in the narthex of Hagia Sophia was not coincidental but that the technique was deliberately employed to secure a more vivid and sparkling surface that catches and reflects the light towards the spectator. The fact that the technique was used selectively furthermore suggests that it took more effort and was more time intensive to carefully angle the individual cubes rather than to simply set them flush

that these mosaics belong to a later restoration campaign consistent with the re-erection of the tympana walls in the later ninth CE. Still, the specific tilting of the gold (and not the coloured tesserae) maximizes the reflection of light.

134 Whittemore (1933), 11–13.

with the surface. This shows that the mosaicists adapted their technique to the architectural setting and natural light sources.

The purpose of this discussion of the materials and colours has been to demonstrate how deeply imbued the interior decoration of Hagia Sophia is with visual effects. It is the careful and deliberate use of colours and materials that testifies to an aesthetic of light. Mosaics are most effective when they are appropriately lit in terms of direction, intensity and spectral distribution of the light.[135] The mosaic decoration certainly benefited from the building's advantageous illumination described in the previous chapter, turning the surfaces into a vibrant pattern of colours and contrasts. The mosaics, together with the marble revetment, carved capitals and arcade spandrels, acted as a diaphanous skin, proclaiming solidity and unity, while simultaneously creating a vivid and brilliant impression. The interior decoration produced pervasive and mutable light effects that constituted the dynamic quality of Hagia Sophia's sacred space and its aesthetic experience.

The antique concept of architectural order had lost its significance and the plasticity of the architectural structures was dissolved in the process. Aided by the effects of light bouncing off the polished marble surfaces and the highly reflective glass mosaics, the interior decoration concealed the structural masonry, avoiding any exclusive focal point. Just as Hagia Sophia's space is permeated with light, so the endlessly repeating patterns, colours and motifs act as a visual unifier. As Procopius pointed out, the gaze is attracted by the various individual elements of the edifice, all of which are equally irresistible.[136] It is once again unity in multiplicity that distinguishes Hagia Sophia, mimicking the Neoplatonic notion that the instantaneous perception of all being in its multiplicity, not individually or sequentially, is the closest humans can get to a vision of God. It thus seems that a specific programme underlies the architectural and interior design of Hagia Sophia that aimed at creating a paradisiacal environment and to project divine immanence. This is, of course, part of the larger aesthetic of the late antique jewelled style that relished lavish details, the variety of materials and luminous colours, and above all, the play of light and shadow.

[135] Eva Zányi, Carla Schroer, Mark Mudge, and Alan Chalmers, 'Lighting and Byzantine glass tesserae', *EVA London Conference 11–13 July 2007* (2007).

[136] Procopius, I.1.47–8.

1 Study of Light in apse, 1948. Byzantine Institute. © Dumbarton Oaks, Image Collections and Fieldwork Archives, Washington, DC.

2 Virtual reconstruction of the interior of Hagia Sophia looking south-east. © Lars Grobe, Oliver Hauck, Andreas Noback, Rudolf H.W. Stichel and Helge Svenshon (Technische Universität Darmstadt); published in (Stichel, 2008).

3 Virtual reconstruction of the cross section of Hagia Sophia along its longitudinal axis as seen from south. © Lars Grobe, Oliver Hauck, Andreas Noback, Rudolf H.W. Stichel and Helge Svenshon (Technische Universität Darmstadt); published in Grobe *et al.* (2010).

4 Naos of Hagia Sophia looking from the west gallery towards the northern arcades and tympanon.

5 View of south aisle of Hagia Sophia looking east.

6 Marble revetment in the west bay of the south aisle of Hagia Sophia.

7 Marble revetment on the western gallery of Hagia Sophia.

8 Original sixth-century mosaic decoration in the cross vault of the inner narthex of Hagia Sophia.

9 Detail of the decorative borders enclosing a double cross in the apex of an inner narthex vault.

10 Silver stars design in the mosaic decoration of the inner narthex vault.

11 Stylised lotus bud motif with shading in the inner narthex vault.

12 Original sixth-century mosaics in the south aisle vaults of Hagia Sophia.

13 Detail of the cross vaults in the south aisle, showing the ornamental band and double cross in the apex.

14 Stylised winged lotus buds in the cross vaults of the south aisle.

15 Central design in the south aisle cross vault, where the sign of the cross has been 'whitewashed'.

16 Large Latin cross in the south aisle of Hagia Sophia.

17 Detail of the mosaic rendering of jewels and pearls of the *crux gemmata* in the south aisle (detail of plate 16).

18 Mosaic decoration in the barrel vault of the south-western subsidiary pier, connecting the aisle and the naos of Hagia Sophia.

19 Mosaics in the barrel vault of the south-western buttress pier.

20 Dual-coloured vines in the soffit of the north-eastern exedra arcades of Hagia Sophia at gallery level (possibly sixth century).

21 Similar plant motif in the soffits of the lateral arcades of the south gallery.

22 (*below*) Mosaic decoration in the soffits of the lateral arcades at gallery level parallel to the tunnel vault on the gallery side.

23 (*top right*) Central arch of the south gallery arcade parallel to the tunnel vault on the gallery side.

24 (*bottom right*) Mosaic decoration of the central arch of the west gallery arcades.

25 Remains of a spider web motif in the spandrel of the central cross vault in the south gallery of Hagia Sophia.

26 Mosaics in the tunnel vaults behind the south gallery arcade (probably not sixth century).

27 Apse window of Hagia Sophia with sixth-century transennae and mosaics.

28 Transition between marble revetment and mosaic decoration in the inner narthex of Hagia Sophia, including opus sectile and undercut cornice.

29 Detail of zigzag pattern on the transverse arches of the south aisle.

30 Patch of possibly sixth-century ornamental border on the western rim of the eastern barrel vault (adjacent to the apse semi-dome).

31 Detail of mosaic decoration in the tunnel vault alongside the lateral arcades on the gallery, showing the inclination of gold-leaf tesserae (probably not sixth-century).

32 Apse mosaic in the monastery of Saint Catherine at Sinai. Robert Sisson. © National Geographic Creative.

33 Schematic representation of the mosaic programme in the apse of Saint Catherine's monastery. On the left of the two central windows above the triumphal arch, Moses removes his sandals before the burning bush; on the right, he receives the law from the hand of God. The apse conch below shows the transfiguration of Christ, completing the cycle of theophanies.

34 Mosaic decoration of the apse semi-dome of San Vitale in Ravenna.

35 Presbytery cross vault of San Vitale in Ravenna.

36 Detail of presbytery cross vault with *Agnus Dei* in the apex.

37 Justinian panel on the northern wall of the apse in San Vitale.

38 Detail of emperor Justinian and bishop Maximian, in front of another figure that was added later.

39 Theodora panel on the southern wall of the apse.

40 Detail of the three Magi on Theodora's *chlamys*.

41 Lunette on the northern presbytery wall showing Abraham feeding the three men/angels and the sacrifice of Isaac.

42 St. Mark and his lion on the southern presbytery wall of San Vitale.

4

Building a House of Wisdom – A Question of Meaning

The lack of monumental figurative art in the original design of Hagia Sophia was not, as has previously been argued, a choice of compromise but very much a conscious aesthetic decision.[1] Combined with the abundance of light streaming in through the multitude of windows and augmented by extensive artificial lighting installations, the mosaics functioned perfectly within the visual totality of the building's interior. The mosaics lined the vaults with a continuous and reflective polychrome skin, dominated by the sign of the cross, some stylised floral motifs and endlessly repeating geometric patterns, thus contributing to a homogeneous and unified visual impression. Architectural structure, decoration and illumination are integrated into an encompassing entity. As Cormack fittingly observed, 'these mosaics offered a highly successful visual, mesmeric effect'.[2] It is this mesmeric effect that was the motivating feature underlying the design of Hagia Sophia in its entirety. The message contained in and conveyed by the mosaics can consequently be used to build up a framework for the wider interpretation of Hagia Sophia as a building and monument.

Material splendour, images of precious stones and pearls, of luminous colours and light represented sublime purity, and only a pure temple was considered a worthy dwelling place of the divine.[3] As Dominic Janes demonstrated, images of treasure (jewels, pearls, gold and silver) were particularly suitable for the material visualisation of the divine glory because

---

1 John Beckwith, 'Byzantium: Gold and light', in Thomas B. Hess and John Ashbery (eds), 'Light from Aten to Laser', *Art News Annual* 35 (1969): 51; Robin Cormack, 'Interpreting the mosaics of S. Sophia at Istanbul', *Art History* 4 (1981): 134; Robin Cormack, 'The visual arts', in *The Cambridge Ancient History. Late Antiquity: Empire and Successors, A.D. 425–600,* ed. Averil Cameron, Bryan Ward-Perkins, and Michael Whitby (Cambridge: Cambridge University Press, 2000), 903; Heinz Kähler, *Die Hagia Sophia* (Berlin: Gebr. Mann, 1967), 47.

2 Cormack (2000), 903.

3 Dominic Janes, *God and Gold in Late Antiquity* (Cambridge: Cambridge University Press, 1998), 94–5. Siverstev discusses the human body as a potential temple for God, which is a sort of deification and in turn is closely tied with the acquisition of wisdom. Alexei Siverstev, 'The "Gospel of Thomas" and early stages in the development of the Christian wisdom literature', *Journal of Early Christian Studies* 8 (2000).

they were associated not only with the heavenly Jerusalem and the Temple of Solomon but also with imperial excellence and power.[4] The sumptuous decorative features transformed the interior of Hagia Sophia into a space of symbolic significance that acted upon the viewer by making the divine presence palpable. Hence, while the interior of Hagia Sophia may indeed have conjured up associations with the Temple of Solomon, with visions of heaven and the Heavenly Jerusalem as well as with the abundance of paradise, it also symbolised the divine essence.[5] By filling Hagia Sophia's space with an aura of divine presence in the form of colour and light, the interior became a *house of wisdom* inasmuch as the quest for God was tightly bound to the quest for divine wisdom.[6]

By far the most important decorative feature in the sixth-century design was the sign of the cross, closely allied with the motif of precious materials (jewels, gems, pearls). These two leitmotifs basically constitute the visual rhetoric and symbolism of the Great Church and provide an excellent opportunity for a detailed study of the ideology underlying the design as well as the visual attraction (aesthetics) of the building. Connected to this is the selective use of colours. The original mosaics of Hagia Sophia sought to transmit a specific message through a visual medium and to provoke an aesthetic and spiritual response. This is in effect a reverse process to an ekphrasis that uses language to appeal to the mind of the audience to visualise an object.[7] Both processes aimed at communicating meaning and as such both were equally bound by the experiences and expectations of the late antique viewer or listener. In this sense, the visual brain and the neurobiological basis of human perception is of central importance to this discussion insofar as visual art is ultimately the product of the visual brain.[8] The function of art analogous to the brain can be considered in terms of distilling information from the external world in the quest for knowledge. This technique is particularly pertinent to the function of art in late antiquity in that it tries to represent ideas of the intelligible (as opposed to the visible) by reducing the effect of materialistic realism. Yet, even the art of the intelligible will always remain confined to the categories of the material world and the visual brain. The language of art is therefore necessarily limited by the activities and capacities of the visual brain and human perception. The visual brain is conditioned through individual

4 Janes (1998), especially Chapter 4.

5 Passages from the Old Testament and the Book of Revelation provided the textual basis and justification for the material riches within the ecclesiastical context. Exodus 25–27; Kings 6; Ezekiel 1:26; Revelation 21.

6 This is illustrated in context of the Gospel of Thomas in Siverstev (2000).

7 For example, Liz James and Ruth Webb, '"To understand ultimate things and enter secret places": Ekphrasis and art in Byzantium', *Art History* 14 (1991).

8 For an excellent and accessible discussion of some fundamental aspects of the visual brain in relation to visual art, see Semir Zeki, *Inner Vision: An Exploration of Art and the Brain* (Oxford: Oxford University Press, 1999); Hideaki Kawabata and Semir Zeki, 'Neural correlates of beauty', *Journal of Neurophysiology* 91 (2004).

experiences similar to an ekphrasis that is dependent on a stored repertoire of memory images. This is why symbolic art and ekphraseis that provoke an association between images and ideas can be effective only within their cultural constraints.

Given this cultural specificity of artistic expression, different late antique mosaics ought to share in a common visual understanding, grounded in heightened visual sensibilities and the capacity to respond to seemingly abstract art imaginatively.[9] The non-figurative mosaics of Hagia Sophia can thus be considered in comparison with other surviving sixth-century mosaics from ecclesiastical contexts. The extensive mosaic cycles in the monastic church of Saint Catherine at Sinai and those in San Vitale in Ravenna that make use of representational art and that exhibit their content more literally, can therefore shed further light on the possible thought-processes elicited by looking at sixth-century Byzantine mosaic programmes in general and that of Hagia Sophia in particular.

Crosses and Jewels

The glaring absence of monumental figurative mosaics in Hagia Sophia in the sixth century seems at odds with the purpose of the building that was to symbolise Justinian's reign and proclaim his imperial power.[10] For artistic parallels, one needs to look as far afield as, for example, the mosaics of the Jacobite monastery at Qartamin in the far eastern parts of the empire.[11] However, the designs of the mosaic decoration in Hagia Sophia are not of a merely decorative nature, but they have a significant impact on the aesthetic (visual) and spiritual experience of the sacred space and as such play an active part in cognitive processes.[12] The sixth-century ekphraseis and the inauguration hymn repeatedly concentrate on the otherworldliness of Hagia Sophia's ecclesiastical space. These contemporary commentaries thereby confirm that Hagia Sophia's interior acted as a symbol. Contrary to the modern definition, late antique symbols were anything but arbitrary or subjective; 'symbols were

[9] John Onians, 'Abstraction and imagination in late antiquity', *Art History* 3 (1980): 17.

[10] Cormack (2000), 903.

[11] Ernest J. W. Hawkins and Marlia C. Mundell, 'The mosaics of the monastery of Mar Samuel, Mar Simeon, and Mar Gabriel near Kartmin', *DOP* 27 (1973).

[12] A number of studies are concerned with the nature and function of ornament in art. Gombrich, for instance, ascribed the aesthetic delight of geometrical patterns to their regularity in contrast to the randomness of nature. Yet, more intricate patterns are preferred to simpler ones, 'which are not felt to be boringly obvious but which we can still understand as the application of underlying laws'. Alfred Gell, *Art and Agency: An Anthropological Theory* (Oxford: Clarendon Press, 1998); Ernst H. Gombrich, *The Sense of Order: A Study in the Psychology of Decorative Art* (New York, NY: Cornell University Press, 1979); Oleg Grabar, *The Mediation of Ornament* (Princeton, NJ: Princeton University Press, 1992); Henry Maguire, 'Magic and geometry in early Christian floor mosaics and textiles', *JÖB* 44 (1994); Patrik Reuterswaerd, 'The forgotten symbols of God', *Konsthistorisk Tidskrift* 51 (1982); Ellen Swift, *Style and Function in Roman Decoration* (Farnham: Ashgate, 2009).

believed to represent objectively and to express faithfully various aspects of a universe that was perceived as deeply meaningful'.[13] A *symbolon* in the late antique sense was a sign of something other than the perceptible object itself that instigated a mental experience reaching beyond the sense perception.[14] In this sense and judging from the literary commentaries outlined in Chapter 1, Hagia Sophia's interior can indeed be considered a symbolic space. Concomitant with this is the inference that the non-figurative designs of the mosaics were motivated by aesthetic as well as symbolic considerations.

The prominence of the motif of the cross in the original mosaic decoration of Hagia Sophia created a distinctly Christian atmosphere.[15] By the sixth century, the sign of the cross had acquired complex and multifaceted meanings that had come a long way from the Hellenistic-Jewish and Graeco-Roman traditions, in which the cross was viewed as a symbol of a shameful death, of weakness and failure, the very opposite of what was considered divine.[16] Artistically, the sign of the cross emerged in the decoration of churches in the late fourth or early fifth century in a great variety of artistic forms that reflected varied theological themes.[17] The large Latin crosses in the aisles of Hagia Sophia (Plate 16) represent a concoction of several types, including the Latin cross *pattée* with flaring arms, the cross with teardrops at the ends of the cross arms, the *crux gemmata* adorned with pearls and precious stones or the *crux radiata* that is the cross of light characterised by colour or by rays radiating from the cross point.[18] The jewelled style is suggestive of the biblical account of the heavenly Jerusalem that is described as being built of gold and precious stones.[19] Pictorial representations of holy cities typically make extensive use of pearls and jewels. Fifth- and sixth-century mosaic decorations in Rome and Ravenna regularly show the golden walls of the heavenly cities of Jerusalem and Bethlehem to be embellished with pearls and precious stones

---

13 Gerhart B. Ladner, 'Medieval and modern understanding of symbolism: A comparison', *Speculum* 54 (1979): 227. See also, for example, Janes (1998), introduction; Swift (2009), 2–10.

14 H. Flanders Dunbar, *Symbolism in Medieval Thought and Its Consummation in the Divine Comedy* (New Haven, CT: Yale University Press, 1929), 6–16; Ladner (1979), 224–7. The Greek noun σύμβολον indicates the principle of association. It is derived from the verb συμβάλλειν, meaning 'bring together, unite, accumulate, come together' and also 'contribute, compare, conclude, infer, and interpret'; LSJ.

15 Many of the crosses were removed or altered during the Islamic period; for example, the carvings of the gallery balustrades were disfigured and some of the mosaics were painted or plastered over (for example, Plates 12, 15).

16 Erich Dinkler, 'Kreuzzeichen und Kreuz', *Jahrbuch für Antike und Christentum* 5 (1962): 100–101; Erich Dinkler, 'Das Kreuz als Siegeszeichen', *Zeitschrift für Theologie und Kirche* 62 (1965): 71; Martin Hengel, *Crucifixion in the Ancient World and the Folly of the Message of the Cross* (Philadelphia, PA: Fortress Press, 1977).

17 Robin Margaret Jensen, *Understanding Early Christian Art* (London and New York, NY: Routledge, 2000), 68 and Chapter 4; Erich Dinkler and Erika Dinkler-von-Schubert, 'Kreuz I. Teil: K. vorikonoklastisch', in *Reallexikon zur Byzantinischen Kunst*, ed. Marcell Restle (Stuttgart: Anton Hiersemann Verlag, 1995).

18 Dinkler and Dinkler-von-Schubert (1995), 26–30.

19 Revelation 21:18–20

in blue and green (Plate 34). Treasure substances like these were employed to heighten the prestige and power of the object in question.[20] By extension, the *crux gemmata* (jewelled cross), the prototype of which had been erected at Golgotha, was a sign of divine power and the victory of Christianity.[21] The connotation of the jewelled crosses found throughout the mosaic decoration of Hagia Sophia is twofold: they were strongly evocative of an eschatological interpretation signifying the ultimate Christian victory and true salvation, and they simultaneously embody the transfigured divine light.[22]

In late antiquity, the jewelled and luminous cross had above all a markedly eschatological connotation. The Gospel of Matthew (24:30) is possibly the earliest allusion to the transfigured sign of the cross of the *Parousia* (Christ's Second Coming).[23] In line with Matthew, the Syrian *Didache* states that 'then there will appear the signs of truth: first the sign of stretched-out [hands] in heaven, then the sign of a trumpet's blast'.[24] The association of the cross with the *Parousia* is made even more explicit in the *Epistula Apostolorum* dating to the second century CE. Addressing his disciples in the sixteenth epistle, Jesus is said to have stated:

> Truly I say to you, I will come as the sun which bursts forth; thus will I, shining seven times brighter than it in glory, while I am carried on the wings of clouds in splendour with my cross going on before me, come to the earth to judge the living and the dead.[25]

The theme of a luminous cross that was to precede Christ in his Second Coming was further developed in the writings of the fourth-century church fathers. In his catechetical lectures Cyril of Jerusalem (c. 313–386), for example, claims that 'a sign of a luminous cross shall go before the king, plainly declaring him who was formerly crucified … the sign of the cross shall be a terror to his foes; but joy to his friends who have believed in him, or preached him, or suffered for his sake'.[26] For Cyril, the cross is the unequivocal symbol

---

20 On the use of gold and precious materials in late antiquity, see Janes (1998), particularly Chapter 4.

21 Janes (1998), 123.

22 Angelo Lipinsky 'La crux gemmata', *Felix Ravenna* 30 (1950).

23 Dinkler and Dinkler-von-Schubert (1995), 7; Franz Joseph Dölger, 'Beiträge zur Geschichte des Kreuzzeichens IX', *Jahrbuch für Antike und Christentum* 10 (1967): 12.

24 *Didache* 16.6: καὶ τότε φανήσεται τὰ σημεῖα τῆς ἀληθείας· πρῶτον σημεῖον ἐκπετάσεως ἐν οὐρανῷ, εἶτα σημεῖον φωνῆς σάπιγγος, καὶ τὸ τρίτον ἀνάστασις νεκρῶν. Kirsopp Lake, ed. *Apostolic Fathers: I Clement, II Clement, Ignatius, Polycarp, Didache, Barnabas, The Shepherd of Hermas, The Martyrdom of Polycarp, The Epistle of Dio* (London and Cambridge, MA: Harvard University Press, 1913), 16, 6.

25 *The Epistle of the Apostles* 1,16; translated in James Keith Elliott, *The Apocryphal New Testament: A Collection of Apocryphal Christian Literature in an English Translation* (Oxford: Clarendon Press, 1993).

26 Cyril of Jerusalem, *Catechese*, XV, 22: σημεῖον δὲ ἀληθὲ ἰδικὸν τοῦ Χριστοῦ ἐστιν ὁ σταυρός. φωτοειδοῦς σταυροῦ σημεῖον πράγει τὸν βασιλέα, δηλοῦν τὸν σταυρωθέντα πρότερον, ἵνα ἰδόντες … φόβος τοῖς ἐχθροῖς τοῦ σταυροῦ τὸ σημεῖον, καὶ χαρὰ τοῖς φίλοις τοῖς εἰς αὐτὸν πιστεύσασιν ἢ κηρύξασιν αὐτὸν ἢ ὑπὲρ αὐτοῦ παθοῦσιν; translated

of Christ's power, reflected also in John Chrysostom's *De cruce et latrone*, according to which Christ had taken the cross with him to heaven to bring it forth triumphantly in his Second Coming.[27] The luminous cross was thus the ultimate symbol of Christ's triumph as he approaches from the east during the *Parousia*. This is part of the reason why we find depictions of luminous crosses represented in mosaic and adorned with precious stones in prominent places throughout early church buildings, most notably in the apse decorations in the east. Examples of this can still be seen in Santa Pudenziana in Rome or Sant' Apollinare in Classe in Ravenna.[28]

Whether or not the apse semi-dome of Hagia Sophia originally bore the sign of the cross in accordance with this eschatological tradition is a question that may never be answered. Nonetheless, the cross was a vital motif and was found in different sizes and shapes not only throughout the mosaic decoration, but also in the form of numerous church fittings. Some of the lighting devices were cross-shaped polycandela and the ambo, too, was adorned with silver crosses that picked up and reflected the flickering lights of countless lamps.[29] Jewels and pearls embellish the cross arms of the large Latin crosses of the mosaic decoration (Plate 17). Gemstones were thought of as sources of light in their own right, embodying the Byzantine concept of illumination (φωτισμός) in aesthetic as well as in spiritual terms.[30] The mosaic crosses were thus transformed from the *crux gemmata* (jewelled cross) into a *crux radiata* (cross of light). These crosses of light symbolised the luminous cross of the *Parousia* and simultaneously accentuated the light-bearing quality of the mosaic as an artistic medium. Through its association with the heavenly Jerusalem as the city of light that 'had no need of the sun, neither of the moon to shine in it: for the glory of God did lighten it',[31] Hagia Sophia's interior had obtained the connotation of a space filled with divine light. Procopius might

in Cyril of Jerusalem, 'Catechetical Lectures', in *Nicene and Post-Nicene Fathers, Series II Vol. 7, The Writings of Cyril and Gregory*, ed. Philip Schaff and Henry Wace (Grand Rapids, MI: WM. B. Eerdmans Publishing Co., 1894), 111.

27 John Chrysostom, *De cruce et latrone*, 309–418; Michele Loconsole, 'Il simbolo della croce tra Giudeo-Cristianesimo e tarda antichità: un elemento translatio Hierosolymae', *Liber Annuus* 52 (2002).

28 Erich Dinkler, *Das Apsismosaik von S. Apollinare in Classe* (Cologne: Westdeutscher Verlag, 1964); Erik Peterson, *Frühkirche, Judentum und Gnosis* (Rome, Freiburg and Vienna: Wissenschaftliche Buchgesellschaft, 1959).

29 Silentiary verse 828 (μεγάλου σταυροῖο), *Ambonis*, verses 206–208 (σταυροὺς ἀργυρέους).

30 Anthony Cutler, 'Uses of luxury: On the functions of consumption and symbolic capital in Byzantine culture', in *Byzance et les images: Cycle de conférences organisé au Musée du Louvre par le service culturel du 5 octobre au 7 décembre 1992*, ed. André Guillou and Jannic Durand (Paris: La documentation Française, 1994), 307.

31 Revelation 20:23; Flood discussed the symbolic content of pearl-like motifs in context of the Great Mosque of Damascus and its relationship with the Judaeo-Christian iconography of the Heavenly Jerusalem. Finbarr Barry Flood, *The Great Mosque of Damascus: Studies on the Makings of an Umayyad Visual Culture* (Leiden, Cologne and Boston, MA: Brill, 2001), Chapter 2.

well have had this apocalyptic passage in mind when describing the Great Church as 'not illuminated from without by the sun, but the radiance comes into being within it'.[32] Judging from the textual and material evidence, the crosses in Hagia Sophia convey the idea of the *Parousia* and the transfigured light of the divine, especially in combination with the profusion of physical light that permeated the sacred space throughout.

Just as light suffused Hagia Sophia's interior, so too was the sign of the cross ubiquitous. In other words, light and the cross both seem to function in the same unifying and cosmological capacity as indicated in some early Christian sources. For Justin Martyr (c. 100–165 CE), for example, the shape of the cross constituted the universe and all things in it. The cross exemplified the combining element within the divine creation and was seen as proof of the hegemony of the logos.[33] This cosmological line of argument was adopted and further developed especially by Gregory of Nyssa (c. 330–395) and Saint Augustine (354–430).[34] According to Gregory, the figure of the cross illustrates the laws of existence, 'because He Who at the hour of His pre-arranged death was stretched upon it is He Who binds together all things into Himself, and by Himself brings to one harmonious agreement the diverse natures of actual existences'.[35] Nothing can exist outside this divine principle insofar as God pervades all things and because the divine is the very substance of existence itself. Crucial here is the divine omnipresence and omnipotence by which God ties together the individual elements of his creation to form a continuous and harmonious totality. In reference to the Pauline letter to the Ephesians (3:18), Gregory ascribed to 'the figure of the cross the power that controls and holds together the universe' through which one 'may be exalted to know the exceeding glory of this power' and whereby the great mystery is manifest.[36] For Gregory, the projections of the cross and especially the outstretched figure of Christ on the cross unify the created universe and illustrate the all-embracing divine power. The crucified figure of Christ exemplifies through the form of his death 'this unspeakable and mighty power'.[37] The overall

32 Procopius I. 1. 30–31: φαίης ἂν οὐκ ἔξωθεν καταλάμπεσθαι ἡλίῳ τὸν χῶρον, ἀλλὰ τὴν αἴγλην ἐν αὐτῷ φύεσθαι, τοσαύτη τις φωτὸς περιουσία ἐς τοῦτο δὴ τὸ ἱερὸν περικέχυται.

33 Justin Martyr, *Apologia Prima*, 55; translated in *Ante-Nicene Fathers: The Writings of the Fathers down to A.D. 325. Vol. 1: The Apostolic Fathers, Justin Martyr, Irenaeus*, ed. Alexander Roberts, James Donaldson, and Cleveland Coxe (New York, NY: Christian Literature Publishing Co., 1885). Dinkler and Dinkler-von-Schubert (1995), 7.

34 Gerhart B. Ladner, 'St. Gregory of Nyssa and St. Augustine on the Symbolism of the Cross', in *Late Classical and Medieval Studies in Honor of Albert Mathias Friend, Jr.*, ed. Kurt Weitzmann (Princeton, NJ: Princeton University Press, 1955).

35 Gregory of Nyssa, *Oratio Catechetica Magna*, chapter XXXII; translated in 'The Great Catechism', in *Nicene and Post-Nicene Fathers, Series II. Vol. 5. Gregory of Nyssa: Dogmatic Treatises, etc.*, ed. Philip Schaff and Henry Wace (Grand Rapids, MI: WM. B. Eerdmans Publishing Co., 1893), 500.

36 Gregory of Nyssa, *Contra Eunomium*, NPNF 5:177.

37 Gregory of Nyssa, *Contra Eunomium*, NPNF 5:177; Ladner (1955).

configuration of the mosaic decoration in Hagia Sophia visualises this cosmological interpretation of the cross. The jewelled double crosses in the apex of each of the groined vaults in the aisles and the narthex are inscribed into a circular, ornamental band that stretches along the groins and surrounds all individual surfaces of the vaults (Plates 9, 13).[38] In so doing, the bands tie together the individual surfaces to create a continuous and uniform entity with the double cross as its seeming source. The double crosses constitute the focal points, from which the all-embracing bands depart and to which they return; the cross is the beginning and the end of all things.

This is only part of the story. Gregory of Nyssa's commentaries represent a direct response to the status of the cross as a form of knowledge of the logos. To appreciate the intricacies of this interpretation, the discussion must begin with the redefinition of the cross into a Christian symbol during the first and second centuries CE.[39] The symbolic identification of the cross as an instrument of divine power, Christ's victory over death and the salvation of humankind, an association familiar to Christians today, was not so obvious in early Christianity. Christ's violent death on the cross appeared irreconcilable with his divine nature, and this paradox initiated a substantial theological debate on the meaning of the cross.[40] The Pauline letters, written in the 50s CE and as such the earliest extant documents of the New Testament, represent a crucial moment in this debate. Paul's writings were highly influential in the subsequent exegetical tradition and the interpretation of the cross.[41] Of particular interest is the first letter to the Corinthians, in which Paul develops the theme of the cross of Christ as a revelation of God's power and wisdom in stark contrast to worldly wisdom, offering a detailed explanation for the meaning of divine wisdom in the first century CE.

> [18]For the message about the cross (λόγος τοῦ σταυροῦ) is foolish to those who are perishing, but to us who are being saved it is the power of God (δυναμις τοῦ θεοῦ). [19]For it is written, 'I will destroy the wisdom of the wise, and the discernment of the discerning I will thwart'. [20]Where is the one who is wise? Where is the scribe? Where is the debater of this age? Has not God made foolish the wisdom of the world? [21]For since, in the wisdom of God, the world did not know God through the wisdom, God decided, through the foolishness of our proclamation, to save those who believe. [22]For Jews demand signs and Greeks desire wisdom, [23]but we proclaim Christ crucified, a stumbling block to the Jews and foolishness to Gentiles, [24]but to those who are the called, both Jews and Greeks, Christ the Power of God and the wisdom of God. [25]For God's

38 Dinkler maintained that this type of double cross is not a sign of the cross in the strictest sense, but rather a Christogram, referring to the name of Christ. Dinkler and Dinkler-von-Schubert (1995), 27.

39 Dinkler traced the history of the cross as a Christian symbol in art back to the middle of the fourth century CE. Dinkler (1965), 7–18.

40 Dinkler (1962), 100–110; Dinkler (1965), 7; Hengel (1977).

41 Judith L. Kovacs, *1 Corinthians: Interpreted by Early Christian Commentators* (Cambridge and Grand Rapids, MI: Wm.B. Eerdmans Publishing Co., 2005).

> foolishness is wiser than human wisdom, and God's weakness is stronger than human strength.[42]

In this passage, Paul promotes a 'new way of *being* in the world ... by eliciting a new way of *knowing*' that is grounded in the cross of the crucified Christ.[43] He presents the unexpected, by attributing the power of God to the cross, which in the ancient world was a symbol of shame and defeat. In so doing, Paul challenges traditional ancient logic by turning the argument around. The image of the cross now proclaims a new world order.[44] It is exactly through the paradoxical logic of the cross that the divine power and wisdom are revealed as being beyond human understanding. Divine wisdom is utterly different from the wisdom of this world. Human wisdom is of little value and it is completely annihilated through the superiority of God's wisdom, bringing to pass what the prophets had long foretold.[45] God has deconstructed human wisdom by means of the cross, because humans fail to truly know God through their worldly wisdom (verse 21). What Paul calls the 'foolishness of the cross' signals that divine wisdom is antithetical to the wisdom of this world because Christ crucified is a contradiction in terms. From the perspective of traditional conception 'one may have a Messiah, or one may have a crucifixion; but one may not have both',[46] yet it is precisely this paradox that ultimately manifests divine wisdom. What is more, Paul's letter suggests that God willed this human failure as part of the divine plan, so that He could himself initiate the salvation of 'those who believe'.[47] The cross therefore signifies the beginning of a new order in which all values are transformed and the folly of a crucified Christ is recognised as the wisdom and salvation of God by 'those who are called'.[48] The λόγος τοῦ σταυροῦ constitutes not only the operative power of God and the salvation of mankind, but also and above all an epistemological dimension in that the cross redefines reality.[49]

---

42 I Corinthians 1:18–25.

43 Alexandra R. Brown, *The Cross and Human Transformation: Paul's Apocalyptic Word in 1 Corinthians* (Minneapolis, MN: Fortress Press, 1995), 12 (Brown's italics).

44 Brown (1995), 75–80.

45 I Corinthians 1:19 is a quotation of Isaiah 29:14 with only a slight variation. Gordon Fee, *The First Epistle to the Corinthians* (The New International Commentary on the New Testament) (Grand Rapids, MI: WM. B. Eerdmans Publishing Co., 1987), 69–70; Victor Paul Furnish, *The Theology of the First Letter to the Corinthians* (Cambridge: Cambridge University Press, 1999), 40; Peter Lampe, 'Theological wisdom and the 'Word about the Cross': The rhetorical scheme in 1 Cor 1–4', *Interpretation* 44 (1990): 120; Anthony C. Thiselton, *The First Epistle to the Corinthians: A Commentary on the Greek Text* (Grand Rapids, MI: W.B. Eerdmans Publishing, 2000), 159–61.

46 Fee (1987), 75.

47 Fee (1987), 72–4; Brown (1995), 84–6; Furnish (1999), 40.

48 Thiselton (2000), 167–75.

49 Dinkler and Dinkler-von-Schubert (1995), 4–5; Brown (1995), 8–11, 89–104, 150–54; Raymond Pickett, *The Cross in Corinth: The Social Significance of the Death of Jesus* (Sheffield: Sheffield Academic Press, 1997), 37–84; Thiselton (2000), 157–8. For a redefinition of wisdom, see also I Corinthians, 2:6–16.

Paul's first letter to the Corinthians was groundbreaking and highly influential in early Christian thought as regards the concept of divine wisdom. The patristic commentaries and homilies of the second to fourth centuries CE invested substantial exegetical attention to the ideas expressed in the Pauline letter.[50] Clement of Alexandria refers numerous times to Paul's passage when discussing the difference between the wisdom of God and human wisdom, which he compares to the relationship between the sun and the light of a lamp that is outshined by the light of the sun.[51] For Athanasius the cross has become a sign of divine concession to human inadequacy, because God became human and suffered on the cross so humans could more easily comprehend him.[52] John Chrysostom similarly discusses the inability of humans to recognise the things that are good for them. He argues at length that even though a crucified Christ may appear foolish and weak to the uninitiated, in truth the cross was proof of God's unparalleled wisdom and power. The wisdom of God transcends human understanding, and where human wisdom and reasoning inevitably fail, a leap of faith would lead to salvation.[53] At the beginning of the sixth century, the Pseudo-Dionysian definition of divine wisdom is still deeply imbued with Pauline theology, declaring that 'the foolishness of God is wiser than men'. Pseudo-Dionysius unequivocally recognises an anagogical capacity in the apparent contradiction of Paul's passage. Attributing foolishness to God 'in itself seems absurd and strange, but uplifts [us] to the ineffable truth which is there before all reasoning'. In acknowledging that divine wisdom 'transcends all reason, all intelligence, and all wisdom', Pseudo-Dionysius emphasises the limitations of human understanding and the need to employ negative terms in order to express the inability to grasp the divine qualities in terms of human categories.[54] According to Pseudo-Dionysius' negative theology, it is necessary to abandon all human sense and to describe the divine as that which underlies all but cannot be explained by human reason. The 'divine foolishness' highlights the disparity between the wisdom of God and that which is considered the wisdom of this world.[55] The reference to the Pauline letters lends an apostolic authority to the Pseudo-Dionysian writings and demonstrates the sustained interest in Paul's works in the early Byzantine theological tradition.

The widespread and continuous popularity of the concepts of divine wisdom in Byzantine thought and the status of the cross as a sign of salvation

---

50 I Corinthians figured prominently in the writings of Clement of Alexandria (c. 150–211/215), Origen (c. 185–254), Athanasius (c. 293–373), Gregories of Nyssa (c. 330–395) and Nazianzus (329–389), John Chrysostom (c. 347–407), Cyril of Alexandria (c. 378–444) and Theodoret (c. 393–460). See, for example, Kovacs (2005); Thiselton (2000), 196–9.

51 Clement of Alexandria, *Stromata*, 1:3, 1:18, 5:1.

52 Athanasius, *On the Incarnation*, see especially § 1, 15, 19, 24, 25.

53 John Chrysostom, *Homilies on First Corinthians*, IV.

54 Pseudo-Dionysius, *DN*, 865B-C.

55 Pseudo-Dionysius, *DN*, 865D-868A.

and the true nature of the divine logos is evidenced by the iconoclastic elevation of the cult of the cross.[56] The image of a cross was set up at the Chalke Gate in Constantinople in 815 and accompanied by a series of five poems, some of which unequivocally herald the cross as the most suitable means to 'show a clear and more complete knowledge' of the logos.[57] This elevation of the cross as one of the most potent symbols of Christianity is not an exclusively iconoclastic sentiment, but it illustrates more generally the theological debates surrounding the use of the cross and of images in Byzantium. The sign of the cross had long been discussed in the patristic writings, and it had equally long formed part of the visual repertoire in early church decorations.[58] In view of its close affinity with the late antique theology of wisdom, it hardly comes as a surprise that the church dedicated to *Holy Wisdom* (Hagia Sophia) was extensively decorated with the symbol of the cross, while it was devoid of monumental figurative representations. The cross clearly served as a symbol of divine wisdom, the promise of salvation and God's providential care for the world as had been extolled in the Apostolic and Patristic writings, most ardently by John Chrysostom.[59] The non-figurative mosaic decoration of Hagia Sophia agrees with the general consensus that the divine contradictions are beyond human comprehension and that it cannot or should not be expressed in human terms (representational art). The cross represents the means through which divine wisdom and power become operative, and it constitutes active salvation by transforming and uplifting those who believe. Its inherent paradox makes the cross the ultimate symbol of divine contradictions, a concept that is propagated throughout the Pseudo-Dionysian writings. The cross is endowed with a considerable anagogical capacity, because it makes the principles of divine wisdom accessible to the human mind that is otherwise incapable of grasping the true essence of divinity.[60]

The rich profusion of jewelled crosses in the mosaic decoration of Hagia Sophia reflects two fundamental symbolic facets of the cross in late antiquity. On the one hand, the jewelled style communicated eschatological ideas, while the sign of the cross as such was associated with an epistemological dimension. Both interpretations are entwined with the imagery of light in the sense of divine illumination as well as divine enlightenment. The jewelled crosses represent the true source of illumination, sustained by scriptural and theological sources that identified the figure of Christ with

56 Charles Barber, *Figure and Likeness: On the Limits of Representation in Byzantine Iconoclasm* (Oxford and Princeton, NJ: Princeton University Press, 2002), 83–105; John Moorhead, 'Iconoclasms, the cross and the imperial image', *Byzantion* 55 (1985).

57 γνῶσίν τε τὴν σὴν ἐμφανῆ δείξης Sπλέον; quoted, translated and discussed in Barber (2002), 92–5.

58 Barber (2002), 85–6.

59 Peter Stockmeier, *Theologie und Kult des Kreuzes bei Johannes Chrysostomus* (Trier: Paulinus Verlag, 1966).

60 Moshe Barasch, *Icon: Studies in the History of an Idea* (London and New York, NY: New York University Press, 1992), 158–81.

the rising sun and that develop the theme of Christ as 'the light of the world',[61] 'the life [that] was the light of all people',[62] 'the sun of justice',[63] 'the sun of resurrection',[64] or the 'sun of righteousness'.[65] There is, however, a crucial difference between the sun (and the pagan sun god) and the light of the Christian God. Whereas the light of the sun is created light, the divine light of the cross is non-created, because the monotheistic Christian God is pre-existing, transcendental light. Accordingly, whereas the pagan sun god is virtually identical with the light of the sun, the sun is but a component of the Christian God insofar as it exists.

Pseudo-Athanasius, an anonymous Greek author of the fourth century, explained how the light of the cross is more powerful and comprehensive in its effects than that of the sun. He described the functioning of the cross thus: 'A man who could learn nothing from the created sun, lo, now the sunlight of the cross surrounds him with its rays and he is illuminated'.[66] This comparison reveals once more the duality of φωτισμός in the sense of illumination and enlightenment. The fact that the cross in late antiquity was often represented in gold or made of gold and decorated with pearls and precious stones may have contributed substantially to its association with light.[67] Light was perceived as an inherent quality of jewels and gems during the sixth century. This is illustrated by Corippus, who described the throne of Justin II as 'proud with gold and jewels, having its own light without the sun; the nature of the gems illuminated all the areas around them, changing the colours of everything and putting into the shade the rays of shining Phoebus'.[68] This passage is remarkably reminiscent of Procopius' observation that Hagia Sophia's luminosity arises from within its sacred space and is not due to any external source.[69] It follows that the perceived luminosity of Hagia Sophia was partly due to its mosaic decoration representing crosses and precious stones. In any case, the abundance of light, be it physical (natural and artificial light) or symbolic (crosses and precious materials), was interpreted as a vehicle towards the intelligible and immaterial light of the divine. As such, the

---

61 Matthew 5:14: φῶς τοῦ κόσμου.

62 John 1:4–5: ἡ ζωὴ ἦν τὸ φῶς τῶν ἀνθρώπων.

63 Malachi 3:20.

64 Clement of Alexandria, *Protrepticum ad Graecos*, IX; translated in *The Ante-Nicene Fathers: The Writings of the Fathers Down to A.D. 325, Vol. II, Fathers of the Second Century*, ed. Alexander Roberts, James Donaldson, and Cleveland Coxe (New York: Christian Literature Publishing Co., 1885),, 196.

65 Malachi 4:2; Clement of Alexandria, *Protrepticum ad Graecos*, XI; translated in Roberts, Donaldson, and Coxe (1885), 203; such references may have informed the third-century mosaic of the *Sol Invictus* (or Christ Helios) in the mausoleum of the Julii beneath the Vatican. Jensen (2000), 42–4.

66 Pseudo-Athanasius, *Sermo in Passionem Domini*, 1056B; translated in Hugo Rahner, *Greek Myths and Christian Mystery* (New York: Harper and Row, 1963), 57–8.

67 For numerous examples see, for example, Janes (1998), 12–16.

68 Corripus, *In laudem Iustini Augusti minoris*, IV. 114–18; edited and translated in Averil Cameron, *Flavius Cresconius Corippus: In laudem Iustini Augusti minoris, Libri IV* (London: The Athlone Press, 1976), 76, 112.

69 Procopius, I. 1. 30–31.

aesthetic splendour of Hagia Sophia's sacred space and its mosaic decoration made manifest the metaphysical idea of spiritual illumination (φωτισμός) in the eschatological and epistemological sense.[70]

The prevailing image of the jewelled cross in conjunction with the suffusion of light was understood as a self-revelation of God, alluding to divine light, wisdom and salvation. The continuous repetition of motifs and patterns served to increase the sense of divine immediacy and to induce the faithful to aspire to the divine.[71] The cross in particular proved the perfect symbol to convey the power and wisdom of God that escapes human comprehension, an aspect postulated in the Pauline letters and subsequently elaborated in the exegetical works of the church fathers. Hence, the interior space of Hagia Sophia, of which the mosaic decoration is an essential constituent, adheres to the definition of a symbol (σύμβολον) in terms of the principle of association. In late antiquity and in the medieval age, the symbol served as an initiation into the mysteries of the universe and helped overcome the impotence of the human mind to grasp the idea of God.[72] This notion is the underlying element of the early Byzantine intellectual tradition and perception of reality reflected in the ekphraseis of Hagia Sophia and by implication materialised in the interior decoration of the Great Church. The synthesis of design, the vastness of the architectural space and the abundance of light created a vision of divine reality and truth.[73] The ecclesiastical space of Hagia Sophia was thus instrumental in the construction of the viewer's relationship with and ascent to God.[74]

Colour and the Byzantine Brain

The symbolic nature of the mosaic decoration of Hagia Sophia, consisting of non-figurative basic shapes and colours and enhanced by an abundance of light, proved to be a highly sophisticated way to express a complex theological discourse related to light, illumination, divine wisdom and salvation. Hagia

---

70 Eve Borsook, 'Rhetoric of reality: Mosaics as expressions of a metaphysical idea', *Mitteilungen des Kunsthistorischen Institutes in Florenz* 44 (2000); Bissera V. Pentcheva, *The Sensual Icon: Space, Ritual, and the Senses in Byzantium* (University Park, PA: Pennsylvania State University Press, 2010), 122; Cutler (1994), 307.

71 Maguire has discussed the potency of repeating geometric patterns to function as magical agents in early Christian floor mosaics and textiles. Evidently, not all geometrical patterns were considered magical, but potent signs, such as crosses, ringed stars, knots and swastikas in the right context could intensify a magical intent. The continuous repetition was a means to enhance and extend protection. Maguire (1994), 265–74.

72 Dunbar (1929), 6–16.

73 The architecture of Hagia Sophia was an integral part of the liturgy, proclaiming divine presence. See Robert Taft, 'The liturgy of the Great Church: An initial synthesis of structure and interpretation on the eve of iconoclasm', *DOP* 34/35 (1980/81): 47–8.

74 Similar observations have been made with respect to the mosaic decoration of the mausoleum of Galla Placidia in Ravenna. Ellen Swift and Anne Alwis, 'The role of late antique art in early Christian worship: A reconsideration of the iconography of the 'starry sky' in the 'Mausoleum' of Galla Placidia', *Papers of the British School at Rome* 78 (2010).

Sophia's sacred space was designed to communicate a religious reality and divine truth through an aesthetic experience, and to thereby guide the congregation towards the recognition of this reality and truth. The church of Hagia Sophia as a work of art has, therefore, a functional role with a potentially significant impact on society and the order of things. However, works of art communicate their meaning in accordance to the social and cultural conventions of the beholder, meaning the social, historical, cultural, biological, educational and personal variables that shape the perception of the individual.[75] At the neurobiological level, the human brain is shaped through experiences.[76] This is why perception and aesthetic appreciation are a function of earlier experience and familiarity with an object. Aesthetic experience is inevitably culturally defined and mediated through cultural conventions, values and memory. As perception varies, so can the meaning and interpretation of works of art. Since visual art is fundamentally a product of the visual brain to the extent that visual art is conceived and perceived through the brain and must necessarily conform to the principles of the visual brain, a work of art may in theory offer insights into the properties of the visual brain and *vice versa*.[77] This implies that works of art are a reflection of the expectations, knowledge and interests of the artists and patrons as well as the audience for which it was designed. By studying the mosaics of Hagia Sophia as an expression of the visual brain, the perceptual capabilities of the 'early Byzantine brain' could in principle be revealed.[78]

When drawing on neuroscience to explain aesthetic sensibilities, it is imperative to distinguish clearly between what this approach contributes to our understanding of a specific aesthetic as opposed to a general understanding of the human brain.[79] In terms of the early Byzantine brain, it can be assumed that the artists and/or patrons as well as the audience were visually literate and adept at reading (perceiving) the imagery according to early Byzantine traditions. The evocation of stored memory images (*phantasiai*) of past visual inputs is strongly implicated in the recognition of meaningful and familiar content in works of art.[80] Critical for a meaningful interpretation

---

[75] Camilo J. Cela-Conde *et al.*, 'The neural foundations of aesthetic appreciation', *Progress in Neurobiology* 94 (2011).

[76] This capacity for learning is also referred to as plasticity and describes the potential to transform the neuronal connectivity and signal transmission as a result of experience. For a recent review, see Ami Citri and Robert C. Malenka, 'Synaptic plasticity: Multiple forms, functions and mechanisms', *Neuropsychopharmacology Reviews* 33 (2008).

[77] Anjan Chatterjee, 'Neuroaesthetics: A coming of age story', *Journal of Cognitive Neuroscience* 23 (2011); Zeki (1999), 1–7.

[78] Semir Zeki, 'Essays on science and society: Artistic creativity and the brain', *Science* 293 (2001). For an attempt at the subject of 'Neuroarthistory', see John Onians, *Neuroarthistory: From Aristotle and Pliny to Baxandall and Zeki* (London and New Haven, CT: Yale University Press, 2007).

[79] Chatterjee (2011).

[80] Giorgio Careri, 'Physicists and painters: The similar search for meaning', *Leonardo* 22 (1989); Scott L. Fairhall and Alumit Ishai, 'Neural correlates of object indeterminacy in

of the interior splendour of Hagia Sophia, therefore, is a prior familiarity with the subject matter. The multifaceted meaning of the cross, for instance, that modern beholders may not be accustomed to, is evidenced in the lively theological debates during the early Byzantine period. Its association with divine wisdom and light is sustained by scripture, exegetical work, homilies, dogmatic treatises of the church fathers or the spiritual writings of figures such as Dionysius the Areopagite. This suggests a widespread interest in and familiarity with these theological issues. From the textual sources we also know that the concepts of divine wisdom and illumination were critical to the aesthetic experience and, in fact, to the justification (apology) of works of sacred art during the early Byzantine period.[81] Concomitant with these textual sources was the attempt to capture the essence of divine wisdom in works of art and architecture. This quest for knowledge reflected in the church of Hagia Sophia and the psychological mechanisms underlying the aesthetic experience of its sacred space identify a central commonality between the edifice as a work of art and the function of the visual brain.

According to Zeki, the pre-eminent function of human vision is to acquire knowledge about the world around us. In order to make sense of the continually changing visual input, the brain needs to extract the essential, non-changing characteristic properties of the external world that enable us to categorise and interpret what we see.[82] Vision and the cognitive and neural processes involved in an aesthetic judgment are highly complex active operations of forming mental images, discarding unusable information, selecting the essential and analysing the selected information in relation to the memorised data.[83] In relation to artistic production, the artist needs to decide what to include and what is essential and sufficient to visualise the most fundamental qualities (constancies) of an object.[84] Zeki argues that the human brain (central nervous system) as well as the creative artist both seek to understand the essential visual attributes of reality, breaking the visual information down into its components of colour, luminance and motion.[85] Although Zeki focuses on modern, predominantly abstract, that is to say, non-representational art that is governed by other principles than art with a semantic content, his observations have an immediate bearing on the interpretation of the mosaics of Hagia Sophia.

---

art compositions', *Consciousness and Cognition* 17 (2008); Jean Piaget, *Biologie et connaissance* (Paris: Gallimard, 1967).

[81] For example, Agathias Scholastikos, Hypatios of Ephesos.

[82] Zeki (1999), Chapter 1.

[83] Cela-Conde *et al.* (2011); Chatterjee (2011); Eric R. Kandel, *The Age of Insight: The Quest to Understand the Unconscious in Art, Mind, and Brain, from Vienna 1900 to the Present* (New York: The Random House Publishing Group, 2012); Alumit Ishai and Dov Sagi, 'Common mechanisms of visual imagery and perception', *Science* 268 (1995); Zeki (1999), Chapter 3.

[84] Vilayanur S. Ramachandran and William Hirstein, 'The science of art: A neurological theory of aesthetic experience', *Journal of Consciousness Studies* 6 (1999); Zeki (1999), Chapter 2.

[85] Chatterjee (2011); Zeki (1999), 22.

Analogous to the distilling capacity of the human brain, the apparent simplicity of the mosaics reduces the intricate theological discourse about divine wisdom and epistemological potential to the most basic yet fundamental forms. Hagia Sophia is not about any particularities but about the unity of the divine creation, and the interior decoration distils from the multitude of the created world that which best represents the divine essence and that which is easily and instantaneously recognised. A distinctly eschatological element is evident from the specific design of the *crux gemmata*, linking the mosaic decoration with the other prominent constituent of the sacred interior, that is, light. Light, in turn, was understood to elicit cognitive processes and thereby adds to the splendour and representational functioning of the sacred space. The light-filled interior of Hagia Sophia with its opulent decoration evoked emotional (spiritual) and aesthetic responses that are recorded in contemporary descriptions and express the perception of beauty and the quest for wisdom. In a way, the architecture and decoration of Hagia Sophia parallel the principles of an ancient ekphrasis in that both depend on the retrieval of stored memory images (*phantasiai*) and try to articulate abstract ideas by concrete means (language or materiality). Just as an ekphrasis communicates that which is non-verbal, the visual art of Hagia Sophia not merely reproduces the visible, but it makes things visible.[86] This means that the church of Hagia Sophia transcends reality, trying to communicate the mysteries of the Christian faith, the essence of which cannot really be known or represented. The ultimate purpose of this art is to obtain and convey knowledge about the transcendent (divine) reality that lies beyond the ordinary reality of the human world.

The semantic qualities of the mosaic decoration of Hagia Sophia and the Byzantine concept and use of colours gain a whole new dimension in light of recent neurobiological research into colour perception and the visual brain. The perception of colour is closely linked to visual memory and object recognition. Nijboer and her colleagues suggested that colour enables a faster identification of an image when compared to grey scale representations.[87] The human brain differentially processes colours depending on whether they are viewed in an abstract or representational context.[88] When humans view colour in an abstract image (the so-called Mondrian stimuli), an increase in regional activity in the brain is measurable in areas that have been identified as important centres for colour vision (V1, V2 and V4). When viewing coloured objects or scenes, additional brain areas come into play with a pronounced difference in the activation pattern between naturally and unnaturally coloured objects/images. Images with natural colours (such as red strawberries or

86 Paul Klee, *La théorie de l'art moderne* (Paris: Gonthier, 1964).

87 Tanja C.W. Nijboer *et al.*, 'Recognising the forest, but not the trees: An effect of colour on scene perception and recognition', *Consciousness and Cognition* 17 (2008).

88 Semir Zeki and Ludovica Marini, 'Three cortical stages of colour processing in the human brain', *Brain* 121 (1998).

yellow bananas) amplify activity in the frontal and occipital lobes as well as in the hippocampus, which suggests that memory, learning and judgement are important additional factors in this type of paradigm. Intriguingly, however, stimuli of images dressed in unnatural colours (colours that are usually not associated with the object, for example, blue bananas) follow a different pathway and do not activate the same areas of the brain.[89] In short, these different patterns of activation show that colour in the abstract is computed automatically, whereas objects with the right colours activate specific brain regions that are associated with higher cognitive functions such as memory. Hence, there can be no right or wrong colour in abstract art. With respect to representational art, on the other hand, there is a perceived categorical right or wrong. Memory, learning and judgement are decisive additional faculties used in this case.

These findings are of great interest in terms of Hagia Sophia's original colour scheme and the Byzantine concept of colour. In Byzantium colours were considered diagnostic in that a colour identified an object and bestowed meaning to an image. Artistically this meant that applying the right colour contributed to the realism of the artefact. In the mosaics of Hagia Sophia, identifiable motifs were clearly assigned the right colours: the colour green, for example, was reserved for vegetable motifs (leaves, buds, vines). If the mosaics of Hagia Sophia are accepted to be representational as opposed to merely decorative, it can then be assumed that the mosaicists applied the 'right' colours to the other designs in the mosaics as well. In other words, right colours consistent with the expectations and the collective memory of the people of sixth-century Byzantium were used to render the individual motifs. The appropriate colours aided the viewer in identifying the inherent meaning of the mosaics without the need of extensive visual scrutiny, provided one understands the language of communication.

The context that emerges from this is one in which the colours of the original sixth-century mosaic decoration of Hagia Sophia were recognised as meaningful. The colours represented the classical ideal of pure and luminous colours, expressing the aesthetic appreciation of light and illumination in its various connotations. The selection and the specific allocation of colours within the building testify to a conscious aesthetic choice that reflects their symbolic meaning in the Neoplatonic sense. There is, for example, a distinct difference between the mosaics in the aisles and the narthex of Hagia Sophia. Whereas the dominant colours in the narthex are blue and silver (Plates 8–11), the designs in the aisles mainly consist of red and gold (Plates 12–15).[90] The most probable explanation for this discrepancy is that the decoration

---

89 Zeki and Marini (1998).

90 Nadine Schibille, 'A quest for wisdom: The sixth-century mosaics of Hagia Sophia in Constantinople and late antique aesthetics', in *New Light on Old Glass: Recent Research on Byzantine Glass and Mosaics*, ed. C. Entwistle and L. James (London: British Museum Press, 2013).

accentuated the purpose of the narthex as a transitional anteroom that mediates between the exterior (material) and the interior (spiritual) realm. The visual and spiritual experience culminates in the church proper. The narthex can thus be seen as an initiation before entering the sacred space that offers a vision of 'a kind of heaven on earth'.[91] The blue in the narthex is suggestive of human ignorance and evokes the Pseudo-Dionysian concept of divine darkness. The 'blue colour is a sign of hiddenness' and inaccessibility of the divine that is at once absolute darkness and absolute light.[92] This concept of divine darkness is expressed through a luminous blue that best reflects the divine paradox. Within the main body of Hagia Sophia, blue is largely replaced by the splendour of red and gold. Especially an exuberant reddish tint of the overall mosaic surfaces seems to have been a desired effect in the sixth century and was heightened by a red coloured setting bed and the frequent juxtaposition of red and gold. The decorative borders in the aisles, for instance, and the interwoven zigzag designs in the transverse arches are red on gold (Plates 13, 29). The outlines of many of the cross designs are red and so are the contours of the motifs in the groined vaults of the narthex and the lozenges and medallions in the transverse arches of the galleries (on the assumption that they follow sixth-century designs). The close affinity of the colour red with gold might derive from the association of both colours with light. According to the sixth-century lexicon of Hesychius, the two different terms for red (ἐρυθρός, φοῖνιξ) were closely allied with the word for fire and flame (πυρρός).[93] Gold, too, was appreciated for its radiance and light-bearing quality.[94] At the same time, gold as the most precious metal was understood as a paradigm of divine light.[95] Within the sacred space of Hagia Sophia the colours red and gold thus represent aspects of divine light and shape the meaning of the mosaic decoration. Entering the sacred space of Hagia Sophia initiates the process of divine illumination through the palpability of divine presence in the form of physical and symbolic light, conveyed artistically through the choice of colours and motifs. This iconography of light and wisdom is most overtly expressed in the symbolic functioning of the cross that is present throughout the mosaic decoration and particularly in the aisles of Hagia Sophia.

There may also be a more profane explanation for the non-figurative nature of the mosaic decoration of Hagia Sophia. The veneration of the

---

91 Constantine A. Trypanis, 'Fourteen early Byzantine cantica', *Wiener Byzantinische Studien* 5 (1968): 143. Translated in Andrew Palmer and Lyn Rodley, 'The inauguration anthem of Hagia Sophia in Edessa: A new edition and translation with historical and architectural notes and a comparison with a contemporary Constantinopolitan kontakion', *BMGS* 12 (1988): 141.

92 Pseudo-Dionysius, *Epistles*, 1073A; Pseudo-Dionysius, *CH*, 337A-B.

93 Hesychius of Alexandria, discussed in Liz James, *Light and Colour in Byzantine Art* (Oxford: Oxford University Press, 1996), 73. Pseudo-Dionysius also expressed the correspondence between the colour red and fire. Pseudo-Dionysius, *CH*, 337A-B.

94 Plato, *Phaedo*, 110e; Plotinus, *Enneads*, I.6.1.

95 Pseudo-Dionysius, *CH*, 141B.

emperor's portrait was an established tradition that had hitherto never been seriously challenged. Religious images acquired a similar function only in the later sixth century after the reign of Justinian. The cult of religious images basically meant an infringement of imperial privileges and a shift of emphasis in the emperor's role from supreme earthly sovereign towards a role as representative of and subject to God.[96] In this sense, the non-figurative mosaics could be understood as an affirmation of the emperor's supreme power on earth, rather than placing emphasis on his subordination to a heavenly sovereign.[97] Although there might have been an element of this in the decoration of Justinian's building, the focus lies, I believe, on the concept of imperial wisdom. Upon entering the new church of Hagia Sophia in December 537 CE, Justinian is said to have exclaimed (as a ninth century source declares) 'O Solomon, I have conquered / surpassed thee' (ἐνίκησά σε, Σολομών).[98] According to the *Patria,* Justinian even placed a statue of Solomon at the Basilica cistern opposite the new church of Hagia Sophia.[99] Solomon had long been considered the prototypical wise king and ideal ruler, builder of the first temple in Jerusalem and a role model for all subsequent 'wise' kings.[100] The allusion to Solomon and his temple, the archetypical house of God, implicates a political and dynastic statement that evoked Solomonic ideals, which meant above all the quality of having been endowed with divine wisdom.[101] Following the Solomonic ideal, the emperor's wisdom was

96 Jaś Elsner, *Art and the Roman Viewer: The Transformation of Art from the Pagan World to Christianity* (Cambridge and New York, NY: Cambridge University Press, 1995), 177–89; Ernst Kitzinger, 'The cult of images before iconoclasm', *DOP* 8 (1954).

97 According to Theophanes, it was Justinian's successor Justin II, who 'added to the adornment of the churches that had been built by Justinian, namely, the Great Church, that of the Apostles as well as other churches and monasteries'. Theophanes, *Chronographia;* translated in Cyril Mango, *The Art of the Byzantine Empire 312–1453: Sources and Documents* (Toronto: University of Toronto Press, 1972, reprint 1986), 124. Mango expresses doubts that this passage meant that Justin II added pictorial cycles to the churches that had been built by Justinian, since the wording is too indefinite.

98 Preger 1902, 1.27, 105; see also the discussion in Gilbert Dagron, *Constantinople Imaginaire: Etudes sur le recueil des Patria* (Paris: Presses Universitaires de France, 1984), 268–9, 303–6; Georg Scheja, 'Hagia Sophia and Templum Salomonis', *Istanbuler Mitteilungen* 12 (1962).

99 Preger 1902, 2.40, 171; this was more likely a statue of Theodosius I. Dagron (1984), 268; Raymond Janin, *Constantinople Byzantine: Développement urbain et répertoire topographique* (Paris: Institut Français d'Etudes Byzantines, 1964, 2nd edition), 209.

100 Cornelis Bennema, 'The strands of wisdom tradition in intertestamental Judaism: Origins, developments and characteristics', *Tyndale Bulletin* 52 (2001).

101 About the ambivalence of the early Byzantine attitude towards Solomon's temple, see e.g. Dagron (1984), 303–6; Christine Milner, 'The image of the rightful ruler: Anicia Juliana's Constantine mosaic in the church of Hagios Polyeuktos', in *New Constantines: The Rhythm of Imperial Renewal in Byzantium, 4th–13th Centuries. Papers from the Twenty-Sixth Spring Symposium of Byzantine Studies, St. Andrews, March 1992,* ed. Paul Magdalino (Aldershot: Ashgate, 1994). For the concept of imperial wisdom in the context of Leo the Wise in ninth and tenth century Byzantium, see Shaun F. Tougher, 'The wisdom of Leo VI', in *New Constantines: The Rhythm of Imperial Renewal in Byzantium, 4th–13th Centuries. Papers from the Twenty-Sixth Spring Symposium of Byzantine Studies, St. Andrews, March 1992,* ed. Paul Magdalino (Aldershot: Ashgate, 1994).

considered a gift from God and consisted of a combination of numerous virtues that included religious wisdom (*pietas*), literary knowledge, judicial wisdom and the practical wisdom such as leadership and the art of building.[102] The inauguration hymn (*kontakion*), composed for Hagia Sophia's re-consecration in 562/563 CE, unmistakably echoes this wisdom tradition. As stated in the *kontakion*, Justinian received divine wisdom in the art of architecture in order to build the 'divinely constructed temple' of Sophia, just as Yahweh himself had given wisdom to Solomon.[103] In 565 CE, when dwelling on Hagia Sophia's dedication to wisdom, Corippus asserts that 'Wisdom (*Sapientia*) certainly made it worthy of Sophia: it began a beautiful temple and made it solid and strong, it began it and completed it and ornamented and glorified it with gifts. Let the description of Solomon's temple now be stilled'.[104] Hagia Sophia may therefore be considered the materialistic expression of Justinian's Solomonic wisdom, which is a reflection of divine wisdom inasmuch as Justinian's wisdom just as Solomon's wisdom was given by God. The imperial patron as the true initiator of the architectural masterpiece thus rivals the 'creator mundi'.[105]

Pictorial Tradition and the Language of Communication

Hagios Polyeuktos and Anicia Juliana's Epigram

Justinian's attempt to appropriate Solomon's temple could have been a direct response to Anicia Juliana and the church of Hagios Polyeuktos. The deep rivalry between Justinian and Juliana is seen as a crucial motivating factor for the construction of Justinian's Hagia Sophia.[106] Only a few years earlier,

[102] Bente Kiilerich, 'The image of Anicia Juliana and the Vienna Dioscurides: Flattery or appropriation of imperial imagery?', *Symbolae Osloenses* 76 (2001); Tougher (1994). The concept of imperial wisdom in context of the Old Testament has been extensively discussed by Kalugila. Leonidas Kalugila, *The Wise King: Studies in Royal Wisdom as Divine Revelation in the Old Testament and its Environment*, Coniectanea Biblica, Old Testament Series 15 (Stockholm: LiberTryck, 1980).

[103] *Oikoi* 12–14; a similar sentiment is also implicit in the two *ekphraseis* by Procopius and Paul the Silentiary; compare 1 Kings 5:12.

[104] Corripus, *In laudem Iustini Augusti minoris*, IV. 2802–84; edited and translated in Cameron (1976), 81, 115, 204–5.

[105] Carola Jäggi, 'Das kontrollierte Bild. Auseinandersetzungen um Bedeutung und Gebrauch von Bildern in der christlichen Frühzeit und im Mittelalter', in *Alles Buch, Studien der Erlanger Buchwissenschaft XXXIII*, ed. Ursula Rautenberg and Volker Titel (Erlangen-Nürnberg: Buchwissenschaft, 2009); Nadine Schibille, 'The profession of the architect in late antique Byzantium', *Byzantion* 79 (2009).

[106] Carolyn L. Connor, 'The epigram in the church of Hagios Polyeuktos in Constantinople and its Byzantine response', *Byzantion*, 69 (1999): 510–515; Brian Croke, 'Justinian, Theodora, and the church of Saints Sergius and Bacchus', *DOP* 60 (2006); R. Martin Harrison, *A Temple for Byzantium: The Discovery and Excavation of Anicia Juliana's Palace-Church in Istanbul* (London: Harvey Miller, 1989), 40; Ifran Shahîd, 'The church of Sts. Sergios and Bakhos at Constantinople, some new perspectives', in *Byzantium State and Society: In Memory of Nikos Oikonomides* (Athens: Institute for Byzantine Studies, 2003), 475–

Anicia Juliana had similarly claimed in a monumental inscription carved on the walls of her church of Hagios Polyeuktos that she 'has overpowered time and surpassed the wisdom of the celebrated Solomon'.[107] Her claim to imperial ancestry is rather unapologetically exhibited in the monumental inscription. Forty-one lines out of the 76-line epigram (*Palatine Greek Anthology*, I.10) were carved on the marble entablature around the walls inside the church at a location that made it difficult or near impossible to be read from the ground floor.[108] This part of the poem is a panegyric within the traditions of the *basilikos logos*, proclaiming Anicia Juliana's imperial ancestry and her extraordinary piety, celebrating her building programme and concluding with a prayer for her and her children's protection so that her family's 'unutterable glory' may survive for eternity.[109] The remaining 35 lines of the epigram that contain the ekphrasis of the building were inscribed next to the entrance and around the four sides of the atrium. This text would have been read before entering the building proper and accordingly shaped the viewer's expectations of the spectacle that was to come.[110] At line 48, the inscription makes the reference to King Solomon and his temple quoted above.

Harrison argued that reference to the Solomonic temple is made even in the use of the ancient royal cubit as the unit of measurement in Hagios Polyeuktos, giving an overall dimension of 100 cubits square.[111] These measurements, as has been pointed out by Milner, corresponded to the description of the visionary temple of Ezekiel and not to those of Solomon's temple. A possible relationship with Ezekiel's temple conveys a very different political and in fact religious message concerned with orthodox practices and the rightful ruler.[112] Still, the decorative programme of Hagios Polyeuktos bore some semblance to Solomon's temple that, according to biblical descriptions, was adorned with 'carved cherubim and palm trees and open flowers' as well as with pomegranates and capitals with networks in the shape of lilies.[113] Bardill

---

6; Mary Whitby, 'The St. Polyeuktos Epigram (*AP* 1.10): A literary perspective', in *Greek Literature in Late Antiquity: Dynamism, Didacticism, Classicism*, ed. Scott Fitzgerald Johnson (Aldershot: Ashgate, 2006), 167–8.

107 *AP* I.10, lines 47–8: χρόνον δ' ἐβιήσατο μούνη, καὶ σοφίην παρέλασσεν ἀειδομένου Σολομῶνος, quoted and translated in Whitby (2006); Connor (1999); Cyril Mango and Ihor Ševčenko, 'Remains of the church of St. Polyeuktos at Constantinople', *DOP* 15 (1961).

108 Connor (1999); Liz James, '"And shall these mute stones speak?" Text as art', in *Art and Text in Byzantine Culture*, ed. Liz James (Cambridge: Cambridge University Press, 2007).

109 Whitby (2006); James (2007); Schibille (2009).

110 Connor (1999): 497–500.

111 R. M. Harrison, 'The church of St. Polyeuktos in Istanbul and the Temple of Solomon', *Harvard Ukrainian Studies = C. Mango and O. Pritsak (eds.), Okeanos: Essays Presented to Ihor Ševčenko on his Sixtieth Birthday by his Colleagues and Students* 7 (1983); Harrison (1989), 137–44.

112 Milner (1994).

113 1 Kings 6–7; Harrison (1983); R. Martin Harrison, *Excavations at Saraçhane in Istanbul, Vol. 1: The Excavations, Structures, Architectural Decoration, Small Finds, Coins, Bones, And Molluscs*, (Princeton, NJ: Princeton University Press, 1986), 410–11; Harrison (1989), 137–9; Judith McKenzie, *The Architecture of Alexandria and Egypt 300 BC–AD 700* (London and New Haven, CT: Yale University Press, 2007), 334–5.

recently claimed that Hagios Polyeuktos emulated the temple of Solomon to the extent that it had a panelled wooden ceiling overlaid with gold leaf similar to the description of Solomon's temple in the first book of Kings.[114] The archaeological evidence, however, is more consistent with a domed structure.[115] Despite the marked architectural differences between Hagios Polyeuktos and the temple of Solomon, Anicia Juliana's church may have been designed to evoke the Holy Temple (Solomon's and Ezekiel's) as the symbol of divine kingship, possibly more so than Justinian's Hagia Sophia. As such, Hagios Polyeuktos can be considered political propaganda and reflective of the deep antagonism between her and Justinian.[116] The stress is on Anicia Juliana's imperial credentials, her dynastic legitimacy and ancestry, rather than divine wisdom, which is a central statement of Justinian's Great Church.[117]

Numerous features of the epigram in Hagios Polyeuktos exhibit parallels with the two ekphraseis of Hagia Sophia, indicating certain similarities in the aesthetic responses to the two edifices. It has actually been suggested that Procopius and Paul the Silentiary have consciously evoked Anicia Juliana and her church, because Justinian sought to outdo Juliana's building and literary achievements.[118] Given Hagios Polyeuktos' architectural grandeur and importance, however, it is hardly astounding to find its influence on Justinian's early church foundations and ekphraseis.[119] The epigram of Hagios Polyeuktos praises the church in terms familiar from the descriptions of Hagia Sophia discussed in the first chapter. Like Procopius and Paul the Silentiary, the epigram emphasises the sense of dynamism as the church 'stands forth' (προβέβηκε), 'springs up' (ἀναθρώσκω) and 'pursues the stars of heaven' (αἰθέρος ἄστρα διώκων); it 'extends from the west' and 'stretches to the east' (οἷος δ' ἀντολίης μηκύνεται ἐς δύσιν ἕρπων). This imagery and type of language are used to the effect of vividness (*enargeia*), to transform a monument made of stone into an image that is very much alive. The epigram dwells furthermore extensively on the visual effects of light:

---

114 Jonathan Bardill, 'A new temple for Byzantium: Anicia Juliana, King Solomon, and the gilded ceiling of the church of St. Polyeuktos in Constantinople', in *Social and Political Life in Late Antiquity*, ed. William Bowden, Adam Gutterridge, and Carlos Machado (Boston, Leiden: Brill, 2006). Bardill bases his argument on Gregory of Tours' description of Hagios Polyeuktos and the fact that this is not a first-hand account. Gregory must have relied on reports from visitors to Constantinople and/or possibly even the text of the epigram that might have been copied and circulated.

115 Connor (1999); Harrison (1989); Jean-Pierre Sodini, 'La contribution de l'archéologie à la connaissance du monde byzantin (IVe-VIIe siècles)', *DOP* 47 (1993); Mango and Ihor Ševčenko (1961).

116 Anicia Juliana's portrait on the dedicatory page of the *Vienna Dioscorides* shows her with the attributes of (imperial) *Sophia*. Kiilerich (2001).

117 Connor (1999); Harrison (1983); Harrison (1986), 420; Kiilerich (2001), 181–5; Milner (1994).

118 Whitby (2006), 167–8; Harrison (1989), 40.

119 The question of Justinian's response to Anicia Juliana's Hagios Polyeuktos has recently been extensively explored in relation to the church of Sts. Sergios and Bacchus and its monumental inscription. Croke (2006); Shahîd (2003).

> … glittering with the indescribable brightness of the sun on this side and on that! On either side of the central nave, columns standing upon sturdy columns support the rays of the golden-roofed covering. On both sides recesses hollowed out in arches have given birth to the ever-revolving light of the moon. The walls, opposite each other in measureless paths, have put on marvellous meadows of marble, which nature caused to flower in the very depths of the rock, concealing their brightness and guarding Juliana's gift for the halls of God, so that she might accomplish divine works.[120]

As in Hagia Sophia, the brightness within Hagios Polyeuktos is defined as indescribable and otherworldly.[121] Both churches are said to have shining golden roofs[122] and mighty walls that appear like flowering marble meadows which also contribute to the luminosity of the sacred space.[123] The impression of Hagios Polyeuktos' sacred space is deeply imbued with the effects of light, specifically with the light of the sun and the moon, the golden roof and the luminosity of the marble revetment that results in a 'shining house' (line 69: οἶκον λάμποντα). Light seems to be as crucial to the aesthetic experience of Hagios Polyeuktos as it is to that of Hagia Sophia. In Hagios Polyeuktos, however, light has not obtained the epistemological and theological connotations. Light in Anicia Juliana's church is not identified as a divine paradigm. To be sure, the church is a divine work, a temple built and embellished 'to receive God' (line 49), but the divine presence is not made as tangible as in the ekphraseis of Hagia Sophia. Whereas the epigram repeatedly alludes to the theme of wisdom in one way or another, it is mainly concerned with human wisdom or its shortcomings. For example, according to the epigram, no 'singer of wisdom' is able to contemplate the edifice in its entirety, let alone talk about it (lines 42, 67). This comment does justice to the rhetorical topos of indescribability (*aporia*), but nowhere is there an explicit link between wisdom and the physical light pervading the sacred space. In offering a textual commentary to the visuality of Hagios Polyeuktos, the epigram highlights light as a fundamental object of aesthetic experience. Light and luminosity were the cause and source of the building's beauty, for it was light that made the church a 'gracious splendour' (line 50: χαρίτων αἴγλην). The epigrammatic imagery of light then expresses an aesthetic interest in light and brilliance, but light is not assimilated to the Neoplatonic notion of metaphysical light and epistemological enlightenment.

Not much is preserved of the mosaic decoration of Hagios Polyeuktos that would allow for a detailed reconstruction of its original design. Circumstantial evidence suggests predominantly non-figurative, abstract motifs with dark blues and shades of green prevailing.[124] Judging from the archaeological remains

---

[120] *AP* 1.10 Lines 54–64, translated in Whitby (2006), 164.

[121] Compare Procopius I.1.30–31.

[122] Compare Procopius I.1.54–5 and Paul the Silentiary verse 668.

[123] Compare Procopius I.1.59 and Paul the Silentiary verse 616.

[124] In addition, some figurative mosaics in the area of the apse are believed to form part of the original sixth-century decorative programme, making them the earliest known set of

that yielded substantial material riches (beautifully carved architectural sculpture, marbles, glass inlays and tesserae),[125] the decoration within Hagios Polyeuktos was concerned with creating a sumptuous polychrome space, adhering to the late antique aesthetic of adornment and its appreciation of colour and light effects. Its interior may thus be considered symbolic of the eschatological light of the New Jerusalem. The architectural design, carved marble decorations and above all the delicately modelled peacocks and the rich plant motifs have likewise been interpreted as reflecting the apocalyptic New Temple and New Jerusalem.[126] Hagios Polyeuktos just like Hagia Sophia represents a direct response to and possibly an instance that may have shaped the aesthetic principles of variety (ποικιλία) and luminosity in sixth-century Constantinople. Unlike Hagia Sophia, however, the significance of light and wisdom remain in the realm of aesthetics that is the materialistic claim to imperial and spiritual supremacy and has no further theological ramifications.

The Transfiguration in Saint Catherine at Sinai and the Vision of God

In contrast to Hagios Polyeuktos, the sixth-century mosaics of the monastic church of Saint Catherine at Mount Sinai represent a distinct theological position made manifest in the specific sequence and iconographic details of the decorative programme (Plate 32). More specifically, central to the interpretation of the Sinai mosaics is the quest for the mystical vision of God and the acquisition of divine wisdom.[127] As such, the mosaics expound the Neoplatonic concept of anagoge in a much more explicit and, to the modern beholder, more accessible way than the non-figurative designs of Hagia Sophia. The mosaic programme at Saint Catherine can thus provide evidence for the pervasiveness of the metaphysical aesthetics of light and spiritual illumination.

The fortress and monastery at the foot of Mount Sinai was built by the Emperor Justinian between the years 548 and 565 CE as indicated by two inscriptions on the beams of the basilica roof.[128] The monastic church is

figurative monumental mosaics in Constantinople. Harrison (1989), 78–80; Harrison (1986), 182–96.

125 Harrison (1986); Harrison (1989); McKenzie (2007), Chapter 13.

126 Bardill (2006); McKenzie (2007), 334–5. McKenzie furthermore pointed out that the split palmette motif framing an egg could indicate Cherubim, which is interesting also in light of the mosaic decoration of the aisles in Hagia Sophia.

127 Elsner has discussed the mosaic programme in relation to some Patristic and Neoplatonic writings in terms of contemporary religious ideology. The following discussion of the apse decoration owes much to his excellent treatment of the matter. Jaś Elsner, 'The Viewer and the vision: The case of the Sinai Apse', *Art History* 17 (1994); Elsner (1995), 97–124; Jerzy Miziolek, 'Transfiguratio Domini in the apse of Mount Sinai and the symbolism of light', *Journal of the Warburg and Courtauld Institutes* 53 (1990); Robert S. Nelson, 'Where God walked and monks pray', in *Holy Image – Hallowed Ground: Icons from Sinai*, ed. Robert S. Nelson and Kristen M. Collins (Los Angeles, CA: The J. Paul Getty Museum, 2006).

128 Procopius also tells us that Justinian erected a church for the monks at the base of the mountain 'which he dedicated to the Mother of God' (V.8.5). This dedication was changed

a standard basilica with aisles and a timber roof. Legend holds that the monastery is located at the site where Moses encountered the Burning Bush (Exodus 3.1–6), conversed with God for 40 days and 40 nights and received the stone tablets with the Ten Commandments (Exodus 24.12–16), and where God showed himself to Moses, his 'back parts' only and not his face (Exodus 33.17–23). These appearances of God are commemorated in the mosaic decoration on the east wall of the church above the triumphal arch. To the left of a double window, Moses is shown to remove his sandals before the burning bush, while on the right, he receives the tablets or rather a scroll of the law from the hand of God (Plate 33). Together with the Transfiguration at the centre of the apse conch below, these scenes represent a set of three theophanies (visible manifestations of God).

Attributed to the Justinianic era, the Sinai mosaics evidently centre on the Transfiguration in the apse, which is the earliest extant major representation of the transfigured Christ and the earliest known example where rays of light project from the figure of Christ (Plate 32).[129] The story of the Transfiguration is recorded in the three synoptic gospels and refers to the event in which the divine nature of Christ is revealed to his three disciples Peter, James and John.[130] The Gospel of Matthew states that when 'he [Christ] was transfigured before them, and his face shone like the sun and his garments became white as light' Moses and Elijah appeared and spoke with him.[131] This is the very moment that is depicted in the apse mosaic of Saint Catherine. The figure of Christ clad in radiant white and gold garments is set against a mandorla of graduated shades of blue that consists of four concentric ellipses with the darkest blue directly surrounding the figure of Christ.[132] Eight beams of light emanate from the figure of Christ and extend across and beyond the mandorla to strike each of the individuals in his company: upright and furthest removed from the mandorla to the left and right are the prophets Elijah and Moses, kneeling beside Elijah

to Saint Catherine in the ninth century. Two inscriptions on the beams of the basilica's roof name the years of construction and the builder, Stephen of Aila. Ihor Ševčenko, 'The early period of the Sinai monastery in light of its inscriptions', *DOP* 20 (1966); A. Andreopoulos, 'The mosaics of the transfiguration in St. Catherine's monastery on Mount Sinai: A discussion of its origins', *Byzantion* 72 (2002); Nelson (2006), 16.

129 The Sinai mosaics are among the best-preserved examples of Byzantine monumental mosaic decoration and certainly unique for the sixth century. Andreopoulos (2002); Andreas Andreopoulos, *Metamorphosis: The Transfiguration in Byzantine Theology and Iconography* (Crestwood, NY: St. Vladimir's Seminary Press, 2005), 127–44; George H. Forsyth and Kurt Weitzmann, *The Monastery of Saint Catherine at Mount Sinai: The Church and Fortress of Justinian* (Ann Arbor, MI: University of Michigan Press, 1965), 12–16; Miziolek (1990); Kurt Weitzmann, 'The mosaic in St. Catherine's Monastery on Mount Sinai', *Proceedings of the American Philosophical Society* 110 (1966).

130 Matthew 17:1–9, Mark 9:2–9, Luke 9:28–36.

131 Matthew 17:2–3.

132 Three concentric circles of blue are traditionally interpreted to represent the Godhead and/or the Trinity. Barber (2002), 66; Paul Friedländer, *Johannes von Gaza und Paulus Silentiarius: Kunstbeschreibungen justinianischer Zeit* (Leipzig and Berlin: Teubner, 1912), 137–8.

is the apostle John and next to Moses is James, while the recumbent Peter underneath the mandorla seemingly awakens from sleep.[133] A partially restored ray above Christ's head connects the Transfiguration with a golden Greek cross within a blue medallion of different shades of blue on the inside of the triumphal arch.[134] The light rays are skilfully created by using the colour of the adjacent, somewhat lighter shade of blue, up to the points at which the beams emerge from the mandorla in the form of luminous silver rays set against the gold background of the apse. The natural light of the sun, falling through a double window set into the east wall above the triumphal arch, complements the light emanating from the transfigured Christ and intensifies the experience of the divine light depicted in the mosaic during the morning hours.[135]

Various intricate layers of meaning have been identified to underlie the overall mosaic programme of the monastic church, including eschatological, dogmatic, liturgical, topographic, typological and imperial connotations.[136] For example, Elsner suggested that there is a hierarchy of theophanies read clockwise, starting with the burning bush as the summon to prophetic ascent, the reception of the law as the summit of mystic vision, while the Transfiguration could be considered the ultimate theophany and vision of God as Christ 'face to face'.[137] Westerkamp recognised an element of hiddenness in the Transfiguration inasmuch as the ultimate source of light is lost in the darkness of the mandorla behind the figure of Christ, possibly symbolising the dark cloud of the second book of Moses that covers up the *tetragrammaton* (JHVH).[138] There can be no doubt that these images form the visual focus of the religious life at Sinai and that they exemplify above all the spiritual ascent and an encounter with the divine.[139] In so doing, the mosaics visualise the Neoplatonic and patristic model of vision and mechanisms of contemplation elaborated in, for example, the writings of Philo of Alexandria, Gregory of Nyssa and above all Pseudo-Dionysius, and for which light played a fundamental role in aesthetic as well as in spiritual terms.

In the New Testament, the Transfiguration is the visual manifestation of God *par excellence*. It is the revelation of the divine in the form of light, elegantly solving the Christological problem of simultaneously representing the divine and human natures of Christ.[140] The mosaics visualise light

---

133 In accordance with the version in Luke 9:32.

134 For a discussion about the number of rays see Miziolek (1990).

135 Andreopoulos (2002).

136 Andreopoulos (2005), 127–44; Forsyth and Weitzmann (1965), 12–16; Weitzmann (1966).

137 Elsner (1994); Elsner (1995), 97–124.

138 Dirk Westerkamp, 'Der verklärte Körper. Kleine Ästhetik der Mandorla', in *Drehmomente. Philosophische Reflexionen für Sybille Krämer* (Berlin: Freie Universität Berlin, 2011).

139 Elsner (1994); Elsner (1995), 97–124; George H. Forsyth, 'The monastery of St. Catherine at Mount Sinai: The church and fortress of Justinian', *DOP* 22 (1968); Andreopoulos (2002); Westerkamp (2011).

140 Andreopoulos (2002).

in several ways (Plate 32): There is the body of Christ that appears more luminous than the other figures, because of the whiteness of his garments; then there is Christ's mandorla that essentially constitutes the glory and the light of his divine nature; finally, there are the eight beams of light that emanate from Christ's body and virtually illuminate the space and figures around him.[141] Artistically, the deep blue of the surrounding mandorla creates a strong contrast and intensifies the impression of the luminosity of Christ's garments. The different shadings of the layers appear to portray a spherical confined space permeated by the beams of light.[142] In his commentary on the Transfiguration, Basil the Great notes that the disciples 'saw his beauty on the mountain more radiant than the very radiance of the sun'.[143] The apse mosaic of Saint Catherine essentially offers a visual exegesis of this experience of the divine light, which is considered beautiful (aesthetic) but which is most of all a symbolic manifestation of the transcendental divine light. The image of the transfiguration therefore marks the ultimate goal of the mystic ascent, namely the confrontation with the vision of God 'face to face', while the inverse rendering of the mandorla represents the principles of negative theology found in late antique patristic writings.[144]

The divine being in its unity and simplicity exceeds all knowing and understanding. Although the Transfiguration is one of the most immediate manifestations of the divine, it is still a differentiated appearance of the divine in visible form. This is why even the Transfiguration can only be an imperfect theophany, a symbol of the divine, never the divine being in itself, due to the limitations set by the human cognitive faculties. In an attempt to visualise the inaccessibility of the divine being that is beyond the reach of human comprehension, the concentric ellipses of the mandorla increase in luminosity the further they are removed from the central light source. The divine essence, which is hidden behind the figure of Christ, is thus revealed in the form of the deepest blue that is suggestive of divine darkness in analogy to the mystical theology of Pseudo-Dionysius, where the 'blue colour is the sign of hiddenness' (κυανῶν δὲ ὄντων τὸ κρύφιον).[145] The transfigured Christ

141 While Elsner identifies the mandorla with the biblical bright cloud out of which God spoke 'This is my beloved son', Andreopoulos recognises in the omission of clouds a diversion from the biblical account and in the mandorla an unambiguous representation of divine light. Miziolek maintains that the transfiguration, with its eight rays, is modelled on the depiction of the sun. Andreopoulos (2002); Elsner (1994); Miziolek (1990).

142 Similarly, the graduated shades of green at the lower part of the apse conch illustrate the depth of the face of the earth, where lighter colours imply a greater distance (closer to the horizon).

143 Basil, *Homily in Psalmos*, 44.5; col. 400, D-C (79): εἶδον δὲ αὐτοῦ τὸ κάλλος Πέτρος καὶ οἱ υἱοὶ τῆς βροντῆς ἐν τῷ ὄρει, ὑπερλάπον τὴν τοῦ ἡλίου λαμπρότητα. Translated in John. A. McGuckin, *The Transfiguration of Christ in Scripture and Tradition* (Lewiston, NY: Edwin Mellen Press, 1986), 169.

144 Elsner (1994); Elsner (1995), 97–124; Westerkamp (2011). This interpretation is still valid if Weitzmann's eschatological reading is accepted, that is if the figure of Christ is associated with his Second Coming. Forsyth and Weitzmann (1965).

145 Pseudo-Dionysius, *CH*, 337A-B; see also Andreopoulos (2002).

acts at the same time as the visible medium through which humans may gain access to his transcendent divine nature, because Christ is 'the way, and the truth, and the life; no one comes to the Father, but by me'.[146]

Nowhere are the principles of the mystical vision of the divine that is manifest in the mosaic decoration at Sinai explained more clearly than in the *Corpus Areopagiticum*. For Pseudo-Dionysius the point of departure in the ascent to the divine was contemplation freed from earthly desires.

> We shall be fulfilled with his visible theophany in holy contemplations, and it shall shine round about us with radiant beams of glory just as of old it once shone round the disciples at the divine Transfiguration. And then, with our mind made free of passion and spiritual, we shall participate in a special illumination from him, and in a union that transcends our mental faculties. There, amidst the blinding, blissful impulses of his dazzling rays we shall be made like to the heavenly intelligences in a more divine manner than at present.[147]

The mosaic programme at Sinai illustrates this process of the spiritual ascent that culminates in the mystical vision of God in the shape of the Transfiguration.[148] The incident of the bush that burns without being consumed is the first in a series of God's appearances in the form of light before Moses, signifying the beginning of his spiritual journey. Moses' mystical ascent is thus intimately linked to light, more precisely to the light of truth (God) in the form of the burning bush that illuminates 'the eyes of the soul with its own rays'.[149] Gregory of Nyssa's commentary on the episode leaves no doubt that for the early Byzantine beholder, the vision of physical light (I.20) led to the enlightenment of the soul (II.20).[150] This vision of light has moreover a didactic and cognitive dimension insofar as 'light teaches us what we must do to stand within the rays of the true light … When we do this the knowledge of the truth will result and manifest itself' (II.22).[151] Gregory's exegesis unmistakably associates the visual experience of light not only with a spiritual but most of all with an epistemological progress, provided the Christian worshipper follows the prescriptions for 'this quiet and peaceful course' of a spiritual life (II.19). This indicates once more that in late antiquity aesthetic and spiritual values are closely entwined, and that visible light (the aesthetic experience

146 John 14:6.

147 Pseudo-Dionysius, *DN*, 592C: τῆς μὲν ὁρατῆς αὐτοῦ θεοφανείας ἐν πανάγνοις θεωρίαις ἀποπληρούμενοι φανοτάταις μαρμαρυγαῖς ἡμᾶς περιαυγαζούσης ὡς τοὺς μαθητὰς ἐν ἐκείνῃ τῇ θειοτάτῃ μεταμορφώσει, τῆς δὲ νοητῆς αὐτοῦ φωτοδοσίας ἐν ἀπαθεῖ καὶ ἀΰλῳ τῷ νῷ μετέχοντες καὶ τῆς ὑπὲρ νοῦν ἑνώσεως ἐν ταῖς τῶν ὑπερφανῶν ἀκτίνων ἀγνώστοις καὶ μακαρίαις ἐπιβολαῖς. Translated and discussed in Elsner (1994), 96.

148 Elsner (1994); Simon Coleman and Jaś Elsner, 'The pilgrim's progress: Art, architecture and ritual movement at Sinai', *World Archaeology* 26 (1994).

149 Gregory of Nyssa, *De vita Moysis*, II.19.

150 Elsner (1994).

151 That Gregory offers a highly relevant reading of the Moses panels at Sinai was discussed in great detail by Elsner (1994); Elsner (1995), 97–124.

of light) provides the basis for the ascent to the divine light and truth and thereby for the acquisition of divine wisdom.

The initial stage of the mystical ascent could be inspired by visible symbols such as the mosaics in the church or the actual burning bush, which in the sixth century was believed to have still existed in a court behind the apse.[152] However, to proceed further along the path of knowledge (II.154, 158) to the summit of mystic union, it was essential to undergo a kind of purification (*katharsis*), to withdraw from the symbolic knowledge and to 'plunge into the truly mysterious darkness of unknowing'.[153] It is 'a mountain steep indeed and difficult to climb' (II.158), and those who reach the summit will be rewarded with a divine vision, similar to Moses to whom God eventually revealed himself on Mount Sinai. This divine revelation was only partial during Moses' lifetime. When Moses received the second set of commandments, he was actually denied the full vision of God 'for man shall not see me [God] and live' (Exodus 33.20). This episode is depicted in the second Moses panel on the right side of the double windows.[154] Standing between rocks, Moses receives the tablets of the law from the hand of God in the top left corner, which Moses explicitly avoids looking at. The scenery is in accordance with the account in Exodus where God says to Moses: 'I will put you in a cleft of the rock, and I will cover you with my hand until I have passed by; then I will take away my hand, and you shall see my back; but my face shall not be seen'.[155] Accordingly, Moses is allowed but a glimpse of God. A full vision of the divine is granted to both Moses and Elijah only posthumously in the New Testament Transfiguration of Christ.

Following the patristic tradition, the mosaic decoration in Saint Catherine's depicts the stories of Moses, literally illustrating the quest for divine wisdom and the soul's ascent to the divine (Plate 33). The Moses scenes seem to set an example for the sixth-century Christian viewer, visualising in a literal way what the pilgrims or monks had to do in order to attain the divine vision.[156] The image of the Transfiguration of Christ is the solution to the problem of showing the two seemingly irreconcilable natures of Christ by representing the human figure of Christ enveloped in a glory of divine light or, as it happens, divine darkness.[157] Still, the figure of Christ appears more dematerialised and ethereal, less voluminous than the other figures in the apse mosaic, thus establishing varying degrees of abstraction that signify

152 Forsyth (1968), 5–6.

153 Pseudo-Dionysius, *MT*, I.3.1000D-1001A; it is a tripartite ascent consisting of purification followed by illumination and perfection. Pseudo-Dionysius, *DN*, 536d. Compare also Plato's and Plotinus' concepts of purification. Plato, *Phaedrus*, 249D; Plotinus, *Enneads*, IV.7.10.

154 Elsner (1994); Elsner (1995), 97–124.

155 Exodus 33:22–3.

156 Elsner (1994); Elsner (1995), 97–124.

157 Andreopoulos (2002).

the degree of humanness of the figures, with the apostles at one end and the figure of Christ at the other end of the spectrum.[158] This effect is enhanced through increasing levels of brightness, from the somewhat dull brownish garments of the apostles to the shining white and gold of the figure of Christ. The different modes of representation in the mosaic mirrors the Neoplatonic and early patristic discourse of how the material world relates to the divine reality and how the latter could be represented in visual form in degrees of similarity.

The Sinai mosaics serve a powerful anagogical purpose in providing a paradigm of the viewer's own spiritual journey. The theme of the theophany is very much grounded in the physical space of the monastic church insofar as this is the site of the burning bush and, as Elsner and Coleman have noted, the Christian viewer is virtually an extension of the apostolic vision of the Transfiguration. The sixth-century beholder basically partakes in the mystic experience of the divine vision by implication.[159] The light that emanates from the figure of Christ has the power to transfigure not only himself, but also those in his vicinity, including the Christian pilgrim.[160] The physical light within the church further enhances the experience of immediacy. Contextualised through the rendition of the light of the Transfiguration in the apse mosaic, the physical light manifests the potency of the divine light. In the apsidal space of the church of Saint Catherine, light guides the devout to the immaterial light of God, which is the principal message of the mosaic decoration.[161] The figure of Moses in the panels to the left and right of a pair of double windows on the east wall above the triumphal arch is directed towards this source of light. Similarly, the vertical axis of the mosaic decoration extends from the figure of Christ along the beam of light to the cross on the underside of the triumphal arch, further to the Lamb of God, until it culminates in the window openings. Clearly, natural light is as much the focus of attention as is the theme of divine illumination depicted in the mosaic decoration. The mosaics combine biblical and exegetical elements to make a powerful visual statement about the contemplative path to divine revelation, sustained through the patristic and

158 Andreopoulos (2002); Andreopoulos (2005), 127–44; Antony Eastmond, 'Consular diptychs, rhetoric and the language of art in sixth-century Constantinople', *Art History* 33 (2010); Elsner (1994); Forsyth and Weitzmann (1965), 12–16; Weitzmann (1966).

159 Elsner (1994); Coleman and Elsner (1994).

160 The power of the light is artistically rendered in the colour graduation of the garments of the prophets and apostles, where they are struck by the beams of light. William C. Loerke, 'Observations on the representation of doxa in the mosaics of S. Maria Maggiore, Rome, and St. Catherine's, Sinai', *Gesta* 20 (1981); Nelson (2006).

161 Miziolek related the image of Christ in a mandorla from which eight beams of light radiate to the representation of *Sol Dominus Imperii Romani*, symbolising Christ as the Sun of Justice. The sixth-century inscription on the lintel on the original entrance to the monastery and the main entrance to the church seems to support this idea with Psalm 118.20: 'This is the gate of the Lord; the righteous shall enter through it'. The adaptation of this iconography betrays the Greco-Roman heritage of early Christian imagery. Loerke (1981); Miziolek (1990); Nelson (2006), 16.

mystical writings of Gregory of Nyssa and Pseudo-Dionysius. This spiritual ascent starts with a visual symbol (theophany) of the divine and ends in the divine darkness that is symbolised in the dark blue centre of the mandorla. The juxtaposition of this divine darkness and the brilliance of the figure of Christ exemplifies the divine paradox of immanence and transcendence.[162]

The Neoplatonic notion of divine enlightenment through the vision of light, whether physical or figurative, provides the conceptual framework for the perception and interpretation of the Sinai mosaics, just as the concepts of light and wisdom underlie the design and mosaic decoration of Hagia Sophia in Constantinople. The two decorative programmes rely on markedly different visual languages. While the mosaics in the monastery of Saint Catherine present the viewer with a narrative that allows for a more or less literal reading of the theological message they contain, the visual language in Hagia Sophia, as we have seen, is decisively abstract and requires the beholder to 'decode rather than read' the signs.[163] This corresponds to what has been identified as the different levels of style in early Byzantine literature, where the grand (ἁδρός) style is defined as having pompous words but plain thought, and the plain (ταπεινός) style has elevated thought but plain words.[164] Applied to the visual arts, the narrative of the Sinai mosaics may be considered grand but straightforward, while the relative simplicity of the decorative programme of Hagia Sophia parallels the plain yet profound style.[165] It has long been assumed that the artists responsible for the Sinai mosaics as well as the target audience must have been familiar with ongoing theological discourses.[166] This must be equally true for the designers and the audience of the church of Hagia Sophia in Constantinople. The choice of different visual languages reflects differences in the specific theological and political needs of the communities for which each image was designed.[167] Whilst Hagia Sophia embodies and conveys the concept of divine wisdom in the face of human ignorance, the monastic church of Saint Catherine centres on the theme of divine revelation. The latter highlights much more the potential to achieve divine enlightenment, even though the path is a laborious one, appropriate to the monastic context

---

162 Eric. D. Perl, *Theophany: The Neoplatonic Philosophy of Dionysius the Areopagite* (New York, NY: State University of New York Press, 2007), 29–32.

163 About the different visual languages in late antique art and its implications see, for example, Eastmond (2010).

164 This is the definition of an anonymous prolegomenon that was added to the progymnasmata of Aphthonius the Sophist (second half of the fourth century CE) sometime after the fifth century CE. George A. Kennedy, *Progymnasmata: Greek Textbooks of Prose Composition and Rhetoric* (Atlanta, GA: Society of Biblical Literature, 2003), 90, 95; Ihor Ševčenko, 'Levels of style in Byzantine literature', in *Akten des XVI Internationalen Byzantinistenkongresses I.1* (Vienna: Verlag der Österreichischen Akademie der Wissenschaften, 1981).

165 Eastmond observed the different levels of style in early Byzantine ivory consular diptychs. Eastmond (2010), 754–6.

166 Andreopoulos (2002); Andreopoulos (2005), 127–44; Elsner (1994); Forsyth and Weitzmann (1965), 12–16.

167 Eastmond (2010), 756.

where monks and pilgrims strive for spiritual perfection. The church of Hagia Sophia, on the other hand, was designed in the name of Justinian to assert his supreme status, and as a celebration of the divine as it was conceived in the sixth century.

The Mosaics of San Vitale in Ravenna and the Order of Being

The mosaic cycle in the monastic church of Saint Catherine at Sinai is notable for the theme of spiritual illumination (φωτισμός) and the importance of light to convey the stages of the anagogical process, starting with the aesthetic experience of physical and symbolic light. The mosaic programme of the church of San Vitale in Ravenna, another great monument of Justinian's reign, offers yet another solution for structuring the aesthetic and spiritual experience of its sacred space. The mosaics exhibit a complex narrative that operates on several levels of representation and that can give further validity to an epistemic interpretation of aesthetic experiences in the sixth century.

The axial orientation of the otherwise centrally planned edifice is decisively shaped by three windows in the apse's semi-circular wall and a triple window on the eastern wall above the apse, flooding the presbytery with plenty of natural light (Figure 2.11). This impression is further enhanced by the brilliance of the elaborate mosaics in the presbytery and in the apse that directs the gaze of the beholder immediately towards the east end of the building. The mosaic programme leads up to the apse conch that is decorated with a representation of the young and beardless figure of Christ seated upon a blue globe (Plate 34).[168] Christ is shown clad in a purple, gold-bordered tunic and *chlamys* and with a halo into which is inscribed a jewelled cross. In his left hand, Christ holds a scroll with the apocalyptic seven seals (the Book of Life) and with his right hand he offers a jewelled wreath to the martyr and patron saint Vitalis, who is depicted on the far left of the apse semi-dome and who is identified by an inscription. Two winged angels dressed in brilliant white flank the figure of Christ; the one on the left presents the said Saint Vitalis, while the one to the right mediates between Christ and the bishop Ecclesius at the far right, who is likewise identified by an inscription. Ecclesius is shown in the act of offering a model of the (his) new church to Christ. The scene is set upon a green and rocky paradisiacal ground, from which flow, beneath Christ's globe, the four rivers of paradise, against a gold background with red and blue clouds hovering at the top. These paradisiacal elements unequivocally allude to the eschatological character of the scene.[169]

---

[168] For the development of this iconography, see, for example, Jean-Michel Spieser, 'The representation of Christ in the apses of Early Christian Churches', *Gesta* 37 (1998).

[169] For detailed descriptions and discussion of the iconography of the mosaic decoration in San Vitale, see Deichmann (1969), 234–56; Friedrich Wilhelm Deichmann, *Ravenna: Hauptstadt des spätantiken Abendlandes, Vol. II, Kommentar, 2. Teil* (Wiesbaden: Frank Steiner Verlag GmbH, 1976), 143–87; Deborah Mauskopf Deliyannis, *Ravenna in Late Antiquity* (New York: Cambridge University Press, 2010), 236–50; Ernst Kitzinger, *Byzantine Art in the Making:*

Immediately beneath the conch of the apse and next to the group of apse windows are the eminent imperial panels of Justinian on the left/north (Plate 37) and Theodora on the right /south (Plate 39). These mosaics have sparked lively scholarly debates, resulting in a substantial bibliography that focuses mainly on iconography and possible meanings of the two panels.[170] There have been numerous speculations about the nature of the ceremony that is depicted and the functioning and significance of the imperial panels within the overall mosaic programme of San Vitale. Scholars largely agree that the two panels represent some kind of liturgical procession, possibly the First (Little) Entrance at the start of the liturgy that was then followed by a Second (Great) Entrance and the celebration of the Eucharist.[171] On the northern wall, Justinian is shown in the midst of his entourage, consisting on the viewer's right of two deacons and the bishop Maximian, who is the only figure identified by inscription, and on the left of two dignitaries and a group of six guardsmen (Plate 37). Since the emperor is not unequivocally identified by inscription, the picture could in principle be understood as a generic representation of a Byzantine emperor. Material evidence suggests that Maximian's head and accompanying inscription are slightly later

Main Lines of Stylistic Development in Mediterranean Art, 3rd – 7th Century (Cambridge, MA: Harvard University Press, 1977), 81–92; Otto G. von Simson, *Sacred Fortress: Byzantine Art and Statecraft in Ravenna* (Princeton, NJ: Princeton University Press, 1948), 23–39.

170 For example, see Luise Abramowski, 'Die Mosaiken von S. Vitale und S. Apollinare in Classe und die Kirchenpolitik Kaiser Justinians', *Zeitschrift für Antikes Christentum* 5 (2001); Irina Andreescu-Treadgold and Warren Treadgold, 'Procopius and the imperial panels of S. Vitale', *The Art Bulletin* 79 (1997); Deichmann (1969), 241–3; Deichmann (1976), 180–187; Deliyannis (2010), 236–50; von Simson (1948), 23–39; Elsner (1995), 177–89; Cesare Fiori, Magiangela Vandini, and V. Mazzotti, 'Colore e tecnologia degli 'smalti' musivi dei riquadri di Giustiniano e Teodora nella basilica di San Vitale a Ravenna – Color and technology of mosaic 'glazes' in the Justinian and Theodora's panels of the basilica of San Vitale in Ravenna', *Ceramurgia* 33, no. 3–4 (2003); Charles Barber, 'The imperial panels at San Vitale: A reconsideration', *BMGS* 14 (1990); Sarah E. Bassett, 'Style and meaning in the imperial panels at San Vitale', *Artibus et Historiae* 29 (2008); Johannes G. Deckers, 'Der erste Diener Christi. Die Proskynese der Kaiser als Schlüsselmotiv der Mosaiken in S. Vitale (Ravenna) und in der Hagia Sophia (Istanbul)', in *Art, Cérémonial et Liturgie au Moyen Âge. Actes du colloque de 3e Cycle Romand de Lettres Lausanne-Fribourg, 24–25 mars, 14–15 avril, 12–13 mai 2000*, ed. Nicolas Bock *et al.* (Rome: Viella, 2002); André Grabar, 'Quel est le sens de l'offrande de Justinien et de Théodora sur les mosaiques de Saint-Vital?', *Felix Ravenna* 81 (1960); Sabine G. MacCormack, *Art and Ceremony in Late Antiquity* (Berkeley, CA: University of California Press, 1981), 259–66; Thomas F. Mathews, *The Early Churches of Constantinople: Architecture and Liturgy* (London and University Park, PA: The Pennsylvania State University Press, 1971), 146–7; Anne McClanan, *Representations of Early Byzantine Empresses* (Houndsmills and New York, NY: Palgrave Macmillan, 2002), 121–48; Kitzinger (1977), 87–8; Giorgio Stricevic, 'Iconografia dei mosaici impèriali a San Vitale', *Felix Ravenna* 80 (1959); Giorgio Stricevic, 'Sur le problème de l'iconographie des mosaiques imperiales de Saint-Vital', *Felix Ravenna* 85 (1962).

171 The First Entrance connotation has been established by Mathews, while von Simson and subsequently Stricevic argued that the scene corresponds to the Eucharistic liturgy. Grabar, on the other hand, proposed an Apokombion, an offering by the church donors and Deichmann likewise saw in the panels the donation of liturgical vessels by the imperial couple on the occasion of the dedication of San Vitale rather than a liturgical procession. Deichmann (1976), 180–81, Grabar (1960); Mathews (1971), 146–7; von Simson (1948), 29; Stricevic (1959); Stricevic (1962).

modifications to the panel, as is the figure of an additional dignitary who seems to be squeezed in the space between the bishop and the emperor (Plate 38).[172] This additional dignitary changes the dynamic of the panel significantly and when eliminated, the processional character of the scene and the division between the ecclesiastical representatives and the group of secular figures becomes more pronounced. The emperor, positioned exactly on the central axis of the image, wears a white tunic and purple *chlamys* with an elaborately embroidered *tablion* and a large brooch on his right shoulder. His jewelled crown had been somewhat altered and reduced in the twelfth century,[173] and he is depicted offering a golden paten in the direction of the apse. Further attributes of the imperial status of this central figure are the gold halo outlined in red and the famous purple shoes that were exclusively reserved for the emperor, who is identified as Justinian for the simple reason that San Vitale was built and decorated during his reign. The empress in the facing panel on the south wall of the apse is accordingly assumed to be Justinian's wife, Theodora, preceded by two beardless male figures to the left and followed by a group of seven women on the right (Plate 39). The empress is similarly dressed in a white under-garment with an embroidered and jewelled hem and a purple *chlamys* with a picture of the three Magi offering gifts imprinted on its hem (Plate 40). The figure of Theodora is adorned with a large collar consisting of jewels and pearls and a heavy jewelled crown with long pearl *pendilia* in addition to an emerald necklace and earrings. With both hands, she extends a gold chalice (*scyphus aureus*) encrusted with gems in a gesture of offering towards the apse.[174]

Scholars have repeatedly pointed out the compositional and conceptual differences between the two panels.[175] For example, whereas Justinian is positioned on the central axis of the image, Theodora is offset to the left off centre; Theodora is portrayed in an architectural setting, while the background in Justinian's panel is plain gold; Theodora is notably taller than her entourage, while in the Justinian panel it is the bishop Maximian who is articulated through size and inscription; Theodora's eye level is somewhat higher than that of the other figures in the image, running approximately at the height of Theodora's nose as opposed to Justinian, who shares the same eye level with the other figures. The figure of the empress clearly stands out and is further accentuated through the scalloped niche in the background that was seen to signify Theodora's imperial status.[176] Justinian, on the

---

172 Andreescu-Treadgold argued that this figure was included at the same time the head of bishop Maximian replaced an original head of his predecessor Victor. Andreescu-Treadgold and Treadgold (1997).

173 Andreescu-Treadgold and Treadgold (1997).

174 This is the chalice in which the Eucharistic wine was offered at the altar according to von Simson (1948), 29.

175 Barber (1990); Bassett (2008); Deichmann (1976), 180–86; MacCormack (1981), 260–64.

176 Deichmann (1976), 182. Sabine MacCormack argued that the use of the niche indicated that Theodora was dead by the time the mosaic was created, while for Charles

other hand, is emphasised by his position at the centre of the panel, even though he shares the space with the figure of bishop Maximian.[177] The spatial composition of this panel is highly ambiguous: judging from his size and the position of his feet, Maximian seems to stand in front of everybody else and to lead the procession as he should according to liturgical protocol. Yet, Justinian's veiled left hand and the paten he is carrying slightly overlap with Maximian's elbow, thus bringing the figure of the emperor virtually to the forefront, implying that it is he who actually leads the way.[178] No doubt, these spatial ambiguities are deliberate and are meant to create a dramatic visual tension, possibly in response to the ecclesiastical and political turmoil in mid-sixth century Ravenna.[179] The intricate construction of (spatial) relationships within the panel can therefore be seen as an affirmation of Justinian's imperial sovereignty (he did after all re-conquer Ravenna in 540 CE) without giving offence to strict liturgical traditions. The imperial couple was expected to abide by the ideological and socio-political conventions of Byzantium. So whilst the image makes some concessions to the emperor's supreme status, he is nonetheless appointed a very specific place and function within the order of being, defined by Orthodox religion and Byzantine societal structures.[180]

The imperial panels are part of San Vitale's wider programme of decoration, the themes of which centre on the Eucharistic rite and the redemption of mankind.[181] The presbytery that towers above the apse (Plate 35) is covered with sacrificial scenes from the Old Testament in the lunettes above the arcades to the north and south, while depictions of Old Testament prophets frame these lunettes. The four evangelists occupy the narrow strips of wall flanking the gallery arcades (Plate 42). The whole composition culminates in the *Agnus Dei* (Lamb of God) in the apex of the presbytery cross vault directly above the altar (Plate 36).

The lunette on the north contains two episodes from the life of Abraham, namely the feeding of three men/angels at Mambre (Gen 18:1–16) and the Sacrifice of Isaac (Gen 22:1–19) (Plate 41). The lunette to the south shows Abel offering a lamb (Gen 4:4) and Melchisedek presenting bread and wine (Gen 14:17–20); both figures are identified by inscription. The northern lunette is flanked by Jeremiah on the left (west) and Moses receiving the law from the

Barber the niche was one means among many to distinguish the empress from the emperor. Barber (1990); Deckers (2002), 23; MacCormack (1981), 263–4.

177 The significance of the bishop Maximian within the imperial panels of San Vitale and the ecclesiastical landscape of mid-sixth century Ravenna has been varyingly discussed. Abramowski (2001); Andreescu-Treadgold and Treadgold (1997); Deichmann (1976), 183–4; Deliyannis (2010), 239–43; Kitzinger (1977), 87–8; Mathews (1971), 139–48; von Simson (1948), 9–18.

178 As Andreescu-Treadgold and Treadgold observed, the emperor has been given here the greatest prominence possible within a liturgical scenario. Andreescu-Treadgold and Treadgold (1997), 711.

179 Deliyannis (2010), 209–12, 241; Kitzinger (1977), 81–92.

180 Elsner (1995), 177–89; MacCormack (1981), 265–6.

181 Deichmann (1976), 143–81; Deliyannis (2010), 248–50; Kitzinger (1977), 81–92; von Simson (1948), 24.

hand of God (Ex 24:12) on the right (east). The lunette on the southern side has the prophet Isaiah on the right (west) and two Moses scenes on the left (east). At the top, Moses is shown taking of his shoes before the burning bush while at the bottom, he shepherds a flock of sheep at the foot of Mount Horeb (2 Ex 3). The four evangelists in the upper register are seated in a mountainous landscape, John and Lucas on the north, Mark and Matthew on the south (west/east, respectively). All four hold an open gospel book on their knees with writing utensils placed at their sides and their symbols hovering above – Matthew actually appears to be writing in his open book.[182] The broad arch opening into the apse semi-dome is decorated with a jewelled Chi-Rho monogram at its apex framed by eagles and a continuous pattern of cornucopia (Plate 34). On the east tympanum of the presbytery in the haunches above this arch at the height of the evangelists are images of the holy cities of Jerusalem on the left (north) and Bethlehem on the right (south). Both cities are shown with their walls richly encrusted with precious stones and pearls and palm trees underneath. The upper part of all three presbytery tympana is adorned with grapevines and acanthus vines growing out of baskets and chalices on a dark blue background. These rich vegetable scrolls form a smooth transition to the vault above that itself is covered carpet-like by inhabited rinceaux.[183]

According to Deichmann and Kitzinger, the mosaic in the presbytery vault is key to the entire composition of San Vitale's decorative programme, both in terms of its stylistic characteristics as well as its meaning (Plate 35).[184] At the centre is the Lamb of God (*Agnus Dei*) with a gold halo against a dark blue background that is decorated with 26 gold and silver stars and surrounded by a wreath of fruits and flowers (Plate 36). Four winged angels standing on blue globes support this *Agnus Dei* medallion with upraised arms, while four diagonal decorative bands embellished with flowers, fruits and birds extend from the wreath along the four groins of the vault, expanding in width up to their termini in the corners of the vault. Peacocks with their tails fanned out and standing on blue globes occupy the ends of these ornate beams. The four triangular panels between the bands have alternating green (north/south) and gold (east/west) backgrounds and are filled with multicoloured rinceaux that are inhabited by a staggering variety of animals.[185] When viewed in connection with the mosaics in the apse conch, the mosaics in the presbytery illustrate an apocalyptic vision similar to the one described in chapter five of the Book of Revelation:[186]

---

182 For the iconography and symbolic significance of the evangelists, see von Simson (1948), 26–7.

183 For the stylistic implications and their relation to earlier decorative schemes, see Kitzinger (1977), 81–92.

184 Deichmann (1969), 240–41; Deichmann (1976), 163–5; Kitzinger (1977), 91–2.

185 The golden triangles are inhabited by birds, while a great variety of different animals populate the green panels. Henry Maguire, *Earth and Ocean: The Terrestrial World in Early Byzantine Art* (University Park, PA: Pennsylvania State University Press, 1987), 76–7.

186 Discussed in Deichmann (1969), 240–41; Deichmann (1976), 164–7.

> [1]Then I saw in the right hand of the one seated on the throne a scroll written on the inside, and sealed on the back with seven seals
> ...
> [6]Then I saw between the throne and the four living creatures and among the elders a Lamb standing as if it had been slaughtered, having seven horns and seven eyes, which are the seven spirits of God sent out into all the earth.
> ...
> [11]Then I looked, and I heard the voice of many angels surrounding the throne and the living creatures and the elders; they numbered myriads of myriads and thousands of thousands, [12]singing with full voice, 'Worthy is the Lamb that was slaughtered to receive power and wealth and wisdom and might and honour and glory and blessing!' [13]Then I heard every creature in heaven and on earth and under the earth and in the sea, and all that is in them, singing, 'To the one seated on the throne and to the Lamb be blessing and honour and glory and might forever and ever!'

The significance of the mosaic decoration of San Vitale has now become clear. In light of this apocalyptic text, the mosaics in San Vitale can be interpreted as having a distinctly eschatological connotation with the salvation of mankind at its core.[187] It is the young, beardless figure of Christ of the *Parousia* that is depicted in the apse mosaic and not so much Christ's human nature, even though his purple *chlamys* has often been seen as an imperial reference.[188] There can be no doubt about the eschatological character of this scene, with the four rivers of paradise emerging from under the globe and the conspicuous red and blue clouds filling the upper part of the apse conch. The luminous clouds symbolise the divine light and power, whose full force is filtered through the clouds so as to make it attainable to human perception.[189] Not to forget the images of the holy cities of Jerusalem and Bethlehem above, constructed of gold and precious stones as noted in the Book of Revelation (21:18–20), and the abundance of living creatures all around. The mosaics conflate apocalyptic and paradisiacal settings and Old and New Testament narratives into a universal Christian history that is headed towards Christ's Second Coming.[190] God and the biblical promise of salvation are ubiquitous. The hand of God frequently appears amidst the red and blue clouds, and the prophets Isaiah and Jeremiah are associated with prophecies about the Incarnation and the Passion of Christ, while Moses scenes are related to the idea of redemption.[191] Since apostolic times, the Moses episodes of Exodus were seen to be references to the *Parousia* of Christ. In the mid-sixth century CE, Cosmas Indicopleustes

---

187 Abramowski (2001); Deichmann (1976), 164–7; von Simson (1948), 35–6.

188 André Grabar was the first to develop the idea that representations of Christ borrowed from the imperial iconography, while Thomas Mathews opposed this view vehemently and Spieser embraces the latter's position. Deckers (2002); André Grabar, *L'empereur dans l'art byzantin* (Strasbourg: Les Belles lettres, 1936); Thomas F. Mathews, *The Clash of Gods: A Reinterpretation of Early Christian Art* (Princeton, NJ: Princeton University Press, 1995); Spieser (1998).

189 Loerke (1981).

190 Deliyannis (2010), 248–50; MacCormack (1981), 265–6.

191 Deichmann (1976), 161–2; von Simson (1948), 26.

explicitly states in his *Christian Topography* that the events of Exodus were really 'shadows' (σκιά) of the salvation, of 'the deliverance from tyrannical bondage, the renovation of the world, accomplished by the resurrection from the dead'.[192] Seen in this light, the diverse imagery and symbolism in the mosaics of San Vitale merge into a coherent programme of decoration that makes a promise of salvation at least to those who conform to orthodox religion.

This is how the imperial panels are interconnected with the overall theme of the mosaic decoration. Irrespective of later alterations and restorations, the mosaics were most certainly put in place after the Byzantine re-conquest of Ravenna from the Ostrogoths in 540 CE, and presumably prior to Theodora's death in 548 CE.[193] During this period, the war with the Ostrogothic kingdom was still in full swing. It would then be absolutely consistent if the mosaics made an implicit statement of orthodox religion and Byzantine socio-political structures. In light of what I believe to be a generic rendering of a common liturgical procession, a specific identification of the figures as has previously been attempted does not matter.[194] What matters is the iconic assertion of a universal (Byzantine) world order in imitation of the divine order that is displayed in the apse.[195] More specifically, the imperial protagonists in the images act as role models who exemplify the ideal behaviour of a devout Christian, and who fulfil the expectations of the sixth-century congregation.

Since the time of Constantine the Great, the Byzantine Empire was considered an earthly reflection (*mimesis*) of the Kingdom of Heaven, and as there is but one God so there can only be one emperor.[196] The emperor embodied the divine order, and it was his duty to adhere to and re-enact this order of being. Piety and sacrifice were necessary imperial functions and were exercised by the emperor on behalf of his subjects. He was the only layperson with the privilege to enter the sanctuary during liturgy, a prerogative that

---

192 Cosmas Indicopleustes, *Christian Topography*, Book V; col. 193: ἀφέσεως λέγω δουλείας τυραννικῆς, καὶ ἀνακτίσεως κόσμου ἐξ ἀναστάσεως νεκρῶν ἐκτελουμένῆς; translated in John Watson McCrindle, ed. *The Christian Topography of Cosmas, an Egyptian Monk* (London: Hakluyt Society, 1897), 138; noted by von Simson (1948), 26.

193 Andreescu-Treadgold and Treadgold (1997).

194 It has previously been argued that some of the figures must be portraits of real people on account of their distinctive features. Andreescu-Treadgold identified the bearded officer next to Justinian as his general Belisarius, and the older woman next to Theodora as Belisarius' wife Antonina. The younger woman to Antonina's left could then be her daughter Joannina, while the young man on Belisarius' right could be her fiancé Anastasius. Andreescu-Treadgold names John the Nephew of Vitalian as the most likely candidate for the additional character on Justinian's left. Andreescu-Treadgold and Treadgold (1997); Deichmann (1976), 184–6; Mathews (1971), 139–48.

195 Elsner has discussed this aspect in comparison to the Roman tradition that rather emphasised individuality. Elsner (1995), 177–89; Deckers (2002), 30–31.

196 Johannes Kollwitz, *Oströmische Plastik der Theodosianischen Zeit* (Berlin: Walter de Gruyter, 1941), 145–52; Donald M. Nicol, 'Byzantine political thought', in *The Cambridge History of Medieval Political Thought c. 350-c.1450*, ed. J.H. Burns (Cambridge: Cambridge University Press, 1988).

signified his closeness to the divine.[197] Because of his supreme status, the emperor was meant to represent his subjects before God and to mediate between the human and the divine. In San Vitale, this mediating role is visually articulated in the position of Justinian on the threshold between the secular and the ecclesiastical space defined through the architectural structure of the apse. Justinian is placed in the exact elongation of the rim of the apse conch that demarcates the sacred from the more secular realm. Each group of people in the panel occupies its appointed space – the clergy on the innermost side of the apse directly beneath the image of Christ, the secular figures outside the frame of the apse conch, Justinian in the middle.[198]

The imperial panels are indicative of the rigid hierarchic order that defined Byzantine society, in which even the imperial couple and the clergy are allocated a firm place, according to their specific responsibilities.[199] In line with this, the imperial couple is shown in a gesture of sacrifice meant to demonstrate the virtue of imperial piety.[200] In this context, the unusually conspicuous depiction on the hem of Theodora's *chlamys*, representing the three Magi as they stride energetically in the direction of the apse is telling (Plate 40). This highly unusual inclusion of the scene of the Magi on Theodora's *chlamys* forges a direct visual link between the current imperial couple and the three wise kings who had come to Bethlehem to offer gifts and pay their respect to Christ, and to whom Christ had revealed himself.[201] The imperial panels thus make tangible this very first theophany. What is depicted is an imperial couple fulfilling their imperial function and in so doing promoting appropriate behaviour that will eventually lead to a vision of God. Through adherence to the given (divine) order of things, it ultimately becomes possible to ascent and to assimilate to the divine. It is through this order (*taxis*) and hierarchy that the human world is connected with the divine and through which humans gain access to and knowledge of God.[202] The mosaics of San Vitale aim to encourage behavioural and ideological conformity from the point of view of history as it is represented in the Old Testament scenes, and

---

[197] Deckers (2002); Rudolf H. W. Stichel, 'Die Hagia Sophia Justinians, ihre liturgische Einrichtung und der zeremonielle Auftritt des frühbyzantinischen Kaisers', in *Byzanz – das Römerreich im Mittelalter, Teil 2, 1 Schauplätze*, ed. Falko Daim and Jörg Drauschke (Mainz: RGZM, 2010), 41–51.

[198] Elsner (1995), 177–89; von Simson (1948), 29–33.

[199] For a discussion of imperial involvement in artistic innovation, see e.g. Robin Cormack, 'The emperor at St. Sophia: Viewer and viewed', in *Byzance et les images: Cycle de conférences organisé au Musée du Louvre par le service culturel du 5 octobre au 7 décembre 1992*, ed. André Guillou and Jannic Durand (Paris: La documentation Française, 1994).

[200] As Deckers claimed, the act of offering can be considered a generic example of imperial piety. Deckers (2002).

[201] For Stricevic, the act of offering is the main theme of the Magi, while for Grabar and McClanan the Magi have an unequivocal imperial connotation. Deckers argues that the image of the Magi is an allusion to *proskynesis* or *adoratio* in reference to the description of the Magi in the Gospel of Matthew 2:1–2; Deckers (2002), 36–7; Grabar (1960), 68; MacCormack (1981), 262–3; McClanan (2002), 133–4; Stricevic (1959), 10.

[202] Pseudo-Dionysius, *CH*, 164D.

exemplified by the imperial couple, and which will ultimately culminate at the end of history in the salvation of mankind in connection with the *Parousia*.[203] The quest for salvation and the quest for divine knowledge are tantamount to appropriate (pious) behaviour and the observance of the given social (divine) order. In view of the image of Christ enthroned on the orb of the cosmos, the imperial panels are a prescription for *mimesis* (assimilation) in the Neoplatonic sense insofar as the scenes represent the potentiality of assimilation to the divine through the orders of being. In all this, the central issue is not one of individual but of universal values, because it is through the unity of the creation that humans can attain knowledge of God.

Several stylistic principles contribute to the impression of universal transcendental qualities instead of individuality. For example, even though there is an abundance of species from flora and fauna, these are spread carpet-like over the entire surfaces and create a two-dimensional pattern rather than autonomous motifs or plasticity of form. The landscapes in the biblical scenes and the apostle images no longer define receding spatial depth, but are two-dimensional curtains against which the figures are projected.[204] Similarly, the arrangement of the figures in the imperial panels renounces spatial or proportional naturalism and places the emphasis on the hierarchical relationship between the figures.[205] The treatment of light and shade exemplifies this spatial ambiguity further. Different to other late antique mosaics where figures frequently cast distinct shadows to the right,[206] at San Vitale the pictorial elements do not define any shadows, even where the light source is assumed to be on the left and the figures and objects themselves are modeled by means of light. Shading in the mosaics of San Vitale no longer creates spatial depth or naturalistic renderings, but light and shade produce abstract patterns and light-dark contrasts, highlighting certain elements.[207] This type of shading deliberately undermines naturalism, while the lack of a defined consistent light source conveys a sense of the transcendental, augmented by what Deichmann described as *Konturlicht* (contour/outline light).[208] This contour light is a certain radiance created by outlining the figures in a colour that is lighter than the surrounding background. This artistic device was employed, for instance, in Mark's lion and most conspicuously in the sacrifice of Isaac, where Abraham is enveloped on his right in a bright blue outline against the green background while an aureole of light surrounds his head (Plates 41, 42). The same modeling technique has been observed in the mosaics of the

203 Elsner (1995), 177–89; MacCormack (1981), 265–6.

204 For the landscape setting as scenic *emblemata* see Kitzinger (1977), 81–92.

205 Stuart Cristo, 'The art of Ravenna in late antiquity', *The Classical Journal* 70 (1975).

206 Observed by Deichmann (1969), 251. Compare, for instance, the mosaics from Sant' Apollinare Nuovo in Ravenna or Sts. Cosmas and Damiano and Santa Maria Maggiore in Rome.

207 Deichmann discussed some of the shading effects. Deichmann (1969), 250–53.

208 Deichmann (1969), 252.

cathedral church of Eufrasius at Poreč.[209] Here, it was found that the glowing outline was applied systematically to either represent divine light or merely as an aesthetic element. Terry and Maguire noted that in artistic terms, this technique animates the mosaics by increasing the colour contrasts and thus enhances the richness of the individual colours. This optical method points to the aesthetic appreciation of intense colour and light effects that are inherent in the reflective material of the mosaics.[210]

The chromatic spectrum of the mosaics in San Vitale is much greater than that of Hagia Sophia. Glass tesserae of an impressive range of hues were employed. What is interesting is that there is a pronounced shift in the mosaics of San Vitale from a more natural colouration in the narrative scenes of the presbytery to stronger, clearer colours in the apse.[211] This differentiation befits the function of the apse mosaics to exhibit the heavenly realm that transcends time and space, whereas the mosaics in the presbytery recount biblical (historical) events. The somewhat less naturalistic colouration of the apse mosaics adds to the sense of otherness and expresses the fact that the figures here belong to a different, heavenly sphere. These artistic touches are supplemented by the external illumination of the mosaics. The three apse windows allow plenty of light into the presbytery, where the reflective gold background of the apse conch acts like a concave mirror, directing and concentrating the incoming light to the apex of the semi-dome and the Chi-Rho in the transverse arch above. The light entering through the three windows on the east wall of the presbytery gathers mainly in the presbytery vault and the Lamb of God at its centre. As Deckers has noted, this conscious light management system articulates the two central motifs, the *Agnus Dei* and the figure of Christ of the *Parousia,* and underlines the eschatological meaning of the mosaic programme.[212]

Light evidently played an important part in conveying a sense of divine presence and/or divine qualities also in San Vitale, both in the form of natural illumination and the artistic references to light and radiance. The glowing red and blue clouds in many of the images, the shining white garments of the principle agents of the divine plan (prophets, evangelists, saints, emperor) and the overall multicoloured luminosity within the sanctuary all allude to the omnipresent and transcendent divine force. The human figure of Christ presiding over the entire cosmos is merely one example of the divine being made manifest in visible form. The depiction of Christ enthroned on a globe is a theophany, witnessed by the prophets, apostles, evangelists and saints as well as the figures in the imperial panels. As such, the mosaics of San Vitale are ideologically related to those in the monastic church of Saint Catherine

209 Anne Terry and Henry Maguire, *Dynamic Splendor: The Wall Mosaics in the Cathedral of Eufrasius at Poreč* (University Park, PA: The Pennsylvania State University Press, 2007), 96.

210 Terry and Maguire (2007), 95–7.

211 Fiori (2003).

212 Deckers (2002), 25–6.

at Sinai. In both, the figure of Christ is shown in a transcendental space that belongs to a world distinct from the earthly reality.[213] The illumination and reflective mosaic surfaces in San Vitale participate in the creation of a luminous and multicoloured ambience that attests to the late antique aesthetic interest in the effects of colour and light. The desired outcome is one of abundance, of polychrome patterns and contrasts, of dynamic impressions of light, as well as the affirmation of the surface and a unity of design. The function of the decoration is to manifest the power of God and to transcend the boundaries between the human and the divine. The presbytery and apsidal space of San Vitale have thereby become a portal to the heavenly dimension. Everything in the sanctuary of San Vitale is colour and light, and thus exemplifies the Neoplatonic notion of beauty that combines visual pleasure with spiritual and cognitive functions.[214]

Aesthetic of Light and Colour

The comparison of the various sixth-century programmes of decoration reveals that the aesthetics of light and colour embodied in the church of Hagia Sophia in Constantinople is manifest also in other late antique ecclesiastical contexts. The observed differences are a matter of modes of representation. The mosaics at Sinai and in San Vitale at Ravenna allow, to a certain extent at least, for a narrative reading of the scenes. Even though there may be various additional intricate layers of meaning wrought into the imagery, at first glance we can easily identify the main protagonists and the biblical narratives that are acted out as well as the main themes that in both cases relate to theophany and the vision of God. These figurative compositions make relatively unambiguous and direct statements and may be associated with the 'grand' style in literature, which is elaborate and literal. The sixth-century mosaics of Hagia Sophia, on the other hand, are characterised by an exceptional simplicity that relies on the use of symbolic visual language and corresponds to Aphthonius' 'plain' style to express elevated thought.[215] Ultimately, the desired effect was the same; the individual mosaic programmes sought to visualise the notion of divine illumination and the quest for divine wisdom, only that they used different modes of visual language.

An aesthetic of light is evident in all three comparative examples discussed, but its association with an epistemological and transcendental dimension in the Neoplatonic sense is explicit only in the mosaic programme of Saint Catherine at Sinai. Here, the programme of decoration centres unequivocally on the theme of divine illumination and revelation. It visualises the

---

213 Spieser (1998).

214 The interior of San Vitale thus corresponds to the Neoplatonic concept of intelligible beauty, according to, for example, Plotinus, *Enneads*, V.8.10.30.

215 Kennedy (2003), 90, 95; Eastmond (2010).

Neoplatonic concept of mimesis to such an extent that it actually depicts the process of the assimilation towards God in terms of the different stages in the vision of divine light. In so doing, the architectural and decorative design of the monastic church offers a paradigm for the spiritual development of the congregation. Prior to the erection of the iconostasis in the seventeenth century, the mosaics at the eastern end of Saint Catherine were the visual focus of the edifice. Upon entering the church, attention must have been inevitably drawn to the mosaics in the conch of the apse and the wall above the triumphal arch. This directed axial emphasis was further augmented through the longitudinal orientation of the building's basilical structure. The visual and spatial experience would have doubtlessly been very different to the one in Hagia Sophia, which was not dictated by any particular architectural or decorative feature. This difference may be explained through a difference in purpose. The church of Saint Catherine was destined for a secluded monastic audience at a major pilgrimage site on the Sinai Peninsula. It served to provide the topographical framework for the pilgrims' movements and behaviour, reinforcing the ideology of a spiritual life in God.[216] Hagia Sophia, on the other hand, aimed at a simplification and clarification of its content, which is the volatility of human knowledge in light of divine wisdom symbolised by the sign of the cross. The decorative principles of Hagia Sophia crystallise the human inability to grasp the divine essence. The paradox of divine immanence and transcendence is made manifest in the richness of its interior decoration, the complex architectural structure and, above all, in the abundance of light within. Light as an artistic medium represents the divine qualities of unity and simplicity.

The schematic nature and hierarchical organisation of the mosaics of San Vitale in Ravenna are consistent with the aesthetic concepts of unity and the divine order of being, through which the earthly world is connected to the heavenly realm. Artistically, this is realised through an increasingly abstract style and the selective use of colours. In the heavenly paradise, the particularities of this world are dissolved and luminous colours prevail. The enthroned Christ is set in a paradisiacal landscape against a gold background. The dominant colour in the lateral narrative scenes, on the other hand, is not gold but a verdant bluish green. The selective colour scheme serves to highlight the different spheres and the different degrees of reality. The purpose of the mosaics in San Vitale was to proclaim the heavenly kingdom as a promise of salvation, and in so doing inspire the faithful to abide to the divine order of being and to aspire to assimilate to the divine. The appropriate ideal behaviour is carefully delineated in the mosaics, the reward of which is a vision of God. The normative role of the decorative programme is exhibited in the imperial panels and the overarching theme of offerings to God. It is

[216] Coleman and Elsner (1994).

prescriptive decoration inasmuch as it serves to establish and reinforce socio-cultural conventions.

The mosaics of Saint Catherine and San Vitale are paradigms for the potential ascent of the faithful towards the divine, one aimed at a monastic community and pilgrims; the other was destined for the everyday context of a parish church in a newly regained Byzantine province. In contrast, the church of Hagia Sophia was all about the spectacle of marvellous beauty, an architectural structure that escapes human understanding, its overwhelming luminosity, as well as the deliberately non-figurative interior decoration where colour, light and the symbol of the cross prevail. The imperial (aesthetic) splendour of Hagia Sophia was seen as a reflection of the divine splendour. The Great Church was the visual manifestation of human ignorance in the face of divine wisdom to which it was dedicated. In this sense, the church of Hagia Sophia advocated the concept of divine wisdom, bringing it into the limelight of Byzantine religious consciousness and culture.[217]

[217] John Meyendorff, 'Wisdom – Sophia: Contrasting approaches to a complex theme', *DOP* 41 (1987).

5

Hagia Sophia and the Concept of Beauty in the Sixth Century

The preceding chapters explored how the sixth-century architectural structure and interior decoration of Hagia Sophia responded to the late antique aesthetic of light, colour and their ephemeral effects. The sensuous perception of the beauty and luminosity of early Byzantine church buildings more generally was seen as the starting point for the spiritual journey (*theoria*) and assimilation to the divine (*theurgy*). On account of being the most important Greek Orthodox Church, Hagia Sophia undoubtedly helped to shape and promulgate this aesthetic of light within the Byzantine Empire. Unlike a basilica, Hagia Sophia's architectural structure with its different spatial layers and cascading dome and semi-domes established a centralised, seemingly circular space (χορός/χορα), filled with light.[1] Light and its effects that created scintillating surface appearances, contributed to the sense of animation (ἔμψυχος) that in turn served to articulate the otherwise ineffable divine. These phenomenal effects of light evidently led to the intense aesthetic reactions that were expressed in the sixth-century rhetorical descriptions, highlighting light as a major component of the aesthetic experience. The ecclesiastical interior animated through the tangible presence of light imbued the architectural structure of Hagia Sophia with divine *pneuma* and thus engaged the viewers' aesthetic as well as spiritual response.[2] The church of Hagia Sophia was literally brought to life through the agency of (divine) light

[1] Nicoletta Isar discussed the concept of chora/choros in context of the circular architectural space of Hagia Sophia. Nicoletta Isar, 'The iconic Chôra: A kenotic space of presence and void', *Transfiguration: Nordisk Tidsskrift for kunst og kristendom* 2 (2000); Nicoletta Isar, '"Xopos of light": Vision of the sacred in Paulus the Silentiary's poem Descriptio S. Sophia', *Byzantinische Forschungen* 28 (2004).

[2] Bissera Pentcheva discussed the role of ποικιλία in Byzantine aesthetics and the concept of *empsychos* and its link with *pneuma*, emphasising the significance of the other senses, above all sound for the spiritual experience of the Great Church as an 'icon of sound'. Bissera V. Pentcheva, *The Sensual Icon: Space, Ritual, and the Senses in Byzantium* (University Park, PA: Pennsylvania State University Press, 2010).

and the architectural space was transformed into a 'living temple' (ἔμψυχος ναός).[3]

The profound aesthetic experience of light and animation within the Great Church was associated with a spiritual and epistemological development that reached into the foundational problems of the meaning and value of vision and art in late antiquity. This aesthetic of light and animation and the understanding of beauty derived ultimately from the substantial body of Neoplatonic metaphysical thought. Neoplatonism was the dominant philosophical tradition of the fifth and sixth centuries, and most philosophically educated young men would have been acquainted, to a certain extent at least, with its metaphysical and ontological systems.[4] The entire ontological and epistemological systems of the Platonic and Neoplatonic traditions were explained in terms of radiance and light. The significance of the Neoplatonism of Plotinus and his concept of beauty for medieval aesthetic theories and the visual culture of early Byzantium have been widely recognised.[5] Plotinian Neoplatonism exerted a significant influence on patristic writings about the nature and unknowability of God and the possibility of the ascent of the soul to the mystical union with the divine. These two opposing conceptual strands were synthesised into a Christian metaphysics of light by Pseudo-Dionysius in the late fifth or early sixth century CE.[6]

The concept of beauty in sixth-century Byzantium as it emerges from the Pseudo-Dionysian writings is unmistakably grounded in patristic writings as well as in the metaphysics and mysticism of the later Platonic tradition.[7] This

---

3 See, for example, *oikos* 3 of the inauguration hymn in Constantine A. Trypanis, 'Fourteen early Byzantine cantica', *Wiener Byzantinische Studien* 5 (1968): 142; translated in Andrew Palmer and Lyn Rodley, 'The inauguration anthem of Hagia Sophia in Edessa: A new edition and translation with historical and architectural notes and a comparison with a contemporary Constantinopolitan kontakion', *BMGS* 12 (1988): 140; Pentcheva (2010), 53–6.

4 Anne Sheppard, 'Philosophy and philosophical schools', in *The Cambridge Ancient History, Vol. XIV, Late Antiquity: Empire and Successors, A.D. 425–600*, ed. Averil Cameron, Bryan Ward-Perkins, and Michael Whitby (Cambridge: Cambridge University Press, 2000); Peter T. Struck, *Birth of the Symbol: Ancient Readers at the Limits of their Texts* (Princeton, NJ: Princeton University Press, 2004), 207.

5 André Grabar, 'Plotin et les origines de l'ésthétique médiévale', *Cahiers Archéologiques* 1 (1945); Gary M. Gurtler, 'Plotinus and Byzantine aesthetics', *The Modern Schoolman* 66 (1989); Gervase Mathew, *Byzantine Aesthetics* (London: J. Murray, 1963); Oiva Kuisma, *Art or Experience: A Study on Plotinus' Aesthetics*, Commentationes Humaniarum Litterarum (Helsinki: Societas Scientaiarum Fennica, 2003); Jerome Stolnitz, '"Beauty": Some stages in the history of an idea', *Journal of the History of Ideas* 22 (1961).

6 Hugo Koch, 'Pseudo-Dionysius Areopagita in seinen Beziehungen zum Neuplatonismus und Mysterienwesen', *Forschungen zur christlichen Literatur- und Dogmengeschichte* I, 2/3 (1900); Dimitrios N. Koutras, 'The beautiful according to Dionysius', in *Neoplatonism and Western Aesthetics*, ed. Aphrodite Alexandrakis and Nicholas J. Moutafakis (New York, NY: State University of New York Press, 2002).

7 See, for example, Jaś Elsner, *Art and the Roman Viewer: The Transformation of Art from the Pagan World to Christianity* (Cambridge and New York, NY: Cambridge University Press, 1995), Chapter 3; Filip Ivanovic, *Dionysius the Areopagite and the Iconoclastic Crisis* (Eugene, OR: Wipf and Stock, 2010), Introduction; Gerhart B. Ladner, 'The concept of the image in the Greek Fathers and the Byzantine iconoclastic controversy', *DOP* 7 (1953); Andrea Wilson Nightingale, *Spectacles of Truth in Classical Greek Philosophy: Theoria in its Cultural*

chapter focuses on the deeper theological and philosophical implications of beauty and light to which Hagia Sophia represented an artistic and aesthetic equivalent. It argues that the material beauty manifest in the ecclesiastical space of Hagia Sophia was understood as a symbol in the Neoplatonic sense, that is to say the building was a link in the ontological chain of being, forming a continuum between the divine and human realms. The artistic beauty of Hagia Sophia had therefore an epistemological status within the Neoplatonic system of ontology. To explore aesthetic questions in late antiquity thus means to attend to the ways in which early Christians perceived and grasped the nature of God and being, the world they lived in and the dualism between the divine and human spheres. It is important to stress that there is not a direct causal relationship between any philosophical school and the art of early Byzantium. How the one may have influenced the other remains an unsolved question. It is unreasonable to expect an ancient work of art to conform to a philosophical axiom in its formalistic details. However, it is plausible that a work of art is in one way or other a reflection of the intellectual and cultural climate in which it was produced.[8]

Pseudo-Dionysius

The historical identity of the Christian Neoplatonist who is known under the name of Pseudo-Dionysius the Areopagite is still very much in the dark. The author himself claims that he was the first Athenian convert of St. Paul, living in the later first century CE.[9] The earliest surviving and securely dated documentary evidence of the Pseudo-Dionysian writings stems from the records of a council (*Collatio cum Severianis*) that took place in Constantinople in 532 CE between Chalcedonian bishops, led by Hypatius of Ephesus, and a group of Monophysites, delegates of the patriarch of Antioch, Severus (465–538 CE).[10] The Severians appealed to the writings of various theological

---

Context (Cambridge and New York, NY: Cambridge University Press, 2004); John Rist, 'Plotinus and Christian philosophy', in *The Cambridge Companion to Plotinus*, ed. Lloyd P. Gerson (Cambridge: Cambridge University Press, 1996); Catherine P. Roth, 'Platonic and Pauline elements in the ascent of the soul in Gregory of Nyssa's dialogue on the soul and resurrection', *Vigiliae Christianae* 46 (1992).

8 See, for example, Asli Gocer, 'A hypothesis concerning the character of Islamic art', *Journal of the History of Ideas* 60 (1999).

9 Pseudo-Dionysius, *DN*, 681B.

10 The *Collatio* was an attempt by Justinian to reconcile the monophysites and Chalcedonians. Rorem assumed that the *Corpus Areopagiticum* must have been written shortly before it was quoted. Sarah Klitenic Wear and John Dillon, *Dionysius the Areopagite and the Neoplatonist Tradition – Despoiling the Hellenes*, (Aldershot: Ashgate, 2007), 2; Andrew Louth, 'The reception of Dionysius up to Maximus the Confessor', in *Re-thinking Dionysius the Areopagite*, ed. Sarah Coakley and Charles M. Stang (Chichester: Wiley-Blackwell, 2009); Paul Rorem and John C. Lamoreaux, *John of Scythopolis and the Dionysian Corpus: Annotating the Areopagite* (Oxford: Oxford University Press, 1998), 9–16.

authorities, amongst them Dionysius the Areopagite, in support of their position that there is only one nature of the incarnate *Logos*. Hypatius, however, doubted the apostolic authenticity of Pseudo-Dionysius on account of his work being 'unknown to the Blessed Cyril'.[11] Even though Hypatius condemned the writings as forgeries, the *Corpus Areopagiticum* was soon to become part of the canon of orthodox patristic writings and was tremendously influential on Byzantine theological and philosophical thought.[12] The success of the Pseudo-Dionysian corpus was partly due to the fact that it offered one of the earliest systematic expositions of Christian theology in Greek,[13] complemented by the commentaries of neo-Chalcedonian scholars such as John of Scythopolis, who composed the earliest annotations perhaps around 532 CE.[14] Maximus the Confessor (580–662 CE) also played a major role in the later orthodox reception of the Pseudo-Dionysian writings.[15] Doubts over Pseudo-Dionysius' apostolic origin resurfaced again in the fifteenth century, but it was not before the era of modern scholarship in the nineteenth century that this line of critical enquiry was further developed.[16] The close connection between the Pseudo-Dionysian corpus and the Neoplatonic philosophy of Proclus was eventually established.[17] Allowing for influences of the Syrian

---

11 *Innocentii Maronitae epistula de collatione cum Severianis habita*, reprinted in *Acta conciliorum oecumenicorum*; cited and discussed in Jaroslav Pelikan, 'The Odyssey of Dionysian Spirituality', in *Pseudo-Dionysius: The Complete Works* (New York, NY: Paulist Press, 1987), 13.

12 The entire corpus had been translated into Syriac by Sergius of Reshaina, probably already before 532 CE. Theresia Hainthaler, 'Bemerkungen zur Christologie des Ps.-Dionys und ihrer Nachwirkung im 6. Jahrhundert', in *Denys L'Aréopagite et sa postérité en orient et en occident. Actes du Colloque International Paris, 21–24 septembre 1994*, ed. Ysabel de Andia (Paris: Institut d'études augustiniennes, 1997), especially 284–90; Alexander Golitzin, 'Dionysius Areopagita: A Christian mysticism?', *Pro Ecclesia* 12, no. 2 (2003); Alexander Golitzin, 'The mysticism of Dionysius Areopagita: Platonist or Christian?', *Mystics Quarterly* 19 (1993); Andrew Louth, *Denys the Areopagite* (London and New York, NY: Continuum, 2002), 112; Louth (2009).

13 Robert Browning, 'Education in the Roman Empire', in *The Cambridge Ancient History, Vol. XIV, Late Antiquity: Empire and Successors, A.D. 425–600*, ed. Averil Cameron, Bryan Ward-Perkins, and Michael Whitby (Cambridge: Cambridge University Press, 2000), 881.

14 While Wear and Dillon argue for a date no later than 532 CE, Rorem assumed a date between 537 and 543 CE. Klitenic Wear and Dillon (2007), 3; Rorem and Lamoreaux (1998), 39; Pelikan (1987).

15 See, for example, George Charles Berthold, *Maximus the Confessor: Selected Writings* (New York, NY: Paulist Press, 1985); Andrew Louth, *Maximus the Confessor* (London and New York, NY: Routledge, 1996).

16 It was the humanist Lorenzo Valla in 1457, followed by the Dutch scholar Erasmus in 1505, who first called into question Pseudo-Dionysius' apostolic origin. Klitenic Wear and Dillon (2007), 3.

17 The influences of Neoplatonic philosophers like Porphyry (234–305 CE) and Proclus (412–485 CE) on Pseudo-Dionysius has been extensively documented. See, for example, Klitenic Wear and Dillon (2007); Eric. D. Perl, *Theophany: The Neoplatonic Philosophy of Dionysius the Areopagite* (New York, NY: State University of New York Press, 2007); Salvatore Lilla, 'Pseudo-Denys l'Aréopagite, Porphyre et Damascius', in *Denys L'Aréopagite et sa postérité en orient et en occident. Actes du Colloque International Paris, 21–24 septembre 1994*, ed. Ysabel de Andia (Paris: Institut d'études augustiniennes, 1997); Louth (2009); Hugo Koch,

Damascius (c. 460–540 CE),[18] the writings of Pseudo-Dionysius can be firmly placed in the late fifth, probably early sixth century CE.

It appears that Pseudo-Dionysius' choice of pseudonym was not coincidental. He chose the identity of a Christian convert who lived in Athens, the site of the principal philosophical school at least until Justinian forbade pagans to teach philosophy in 529 CE, and who was swayed to convert after Paul had remarked that 'we ought not to think that the deity is like gold, or silver, or stone, an image formed by the art and imagination of mortals'.[19] This might be significant insofar as Pseudo-Dionysius himself elaborated extensively on issues revolving around the conceptualisation and representations of the divine. The surviving Pseudo-Dionysian works comprise four treatises: *Divine Names, Mystical Theology, Celestial Hierarchy, Ecclesiastical Hierarchy* as well as 10 letters. The *Divine Names* is the longest piece consisting of 13 chapters on the affirmative (cataphatic) theology. It examines the most significant divine names or attributes that affirm the nature of God in its plurality and singularity as the first principle and productive cause of all being.[20] Among these appellatives, Pseudo-Dionysius includes traditional Neoplatonic categories such as the Good, Being, Beauty, Light and Wisdom. Given the divine transcendence, with its unknowable and ineffable nature, however, Pseudo-Dionysius simultaneously posits his negative (apophatic) theology that is the central theme of the *Mystical Theology*. The negative theology consists of depriving the divine of every possible attribute, both positive and negative, because the divine cannot be characterised in human terms.[21] The divine escapes every perceptible and intelligible object and remains hidden in a mystical cloud of unknowing (ignorance).[22] Underlying the whole of the Pseudo-Dionysian system of

---

'Der pseudo-epigraphische Charakter der dionysischen Schriften', *Theologische Quartalschrift* 77 (1895); Henri D. Saffrey, 'Le lien le plus objectif entre le Pseudo-Denys et Proclus', in *Roma, magistra mundi. Itineraria culturae medievalis. Mélanges offerts au Père L. E. Boyle à l'occasion de son 75e anniversaire*, ed. J. Harnesse (Louvain-la-Neuve: Fédération Internationale des Instituts d'Études Médiévales, 1998); Josef Stiglmayr, 'Der Neuplatoniker Proclus als Vorlage des sogenannten Dionysius Areopagita in der Lehre vom Übel', *Historisches Jahrbuch* 16 (1895).

18 Mazzucchi identified Pseudo-Dionysius with Damascius, based on stylistic comparison as well as on Damascius vita, including his Christianity and Neoplatonism. Griffith, however, rejects the suggestion of Damascius being the author of the *Corpus Areopagiticum*. Rosemary Griffith, 'Neo-Platonism and Christianity: Pseudo-Dionysius and Damascius', *Studia Patristica* 29 (1997); Lilla (1997); Carlo Maria Mazzucchi, 'Damascio, autore del Corpus Dionysiacum e il dialogo Peri Politikes Epistemes', *Aevum: Rassegna di scienze storiche linguistiche e filologiche* 80 (2006).

19 *Acts of the Apostles* 17.29 and 34; Struck (2004), 258.

20 Inglis P. Sheldon-Williams, 'The Greek Christian Platonist Tradition from the Cappadocians to Maximus and Eriugena', in *The Cambridge History of Later Greek and Early Medieval Philosophy*, ed. A. H. Armstrong (Cambridge: Cambridge University Press, 1967), 460–61; Naomi Janowitz, 'Theories of divine names in Origen and Pseudo-Dionysius', *History of Religion* 30 (1991).

21 Inglis P. Sheldon-Williams, 'The Ecclesiastical Hierarchy of Pseudo-Dionysius – Part I', *The Downside Review* 82 (1964); Sheldon-Williams (1967), 460.

22 Ivanovic (2010), 15.

thought is the theory that the celestial (angelic) as well as the ecclesiastical (worldly) realms are organised in rigid hierarchical systems subdivided into triadic ranks. The two hierarchies regulate and describe how the faithful can be uplifted from the lower sensible to the intelligible and finally to the super-intelligible sphere that is the transcendental God and final cause of all being. The ascent follows the triad of purification, illumination and perfection and commences in the lowest ecclesiastical order of the catechumens through perceptible symbols and liturgical practices. This is what can be considered Pseudo-Dionysius' *Symbolic Theology* inasmuch as it is the theory of man's ascent through the hierarchical system by means of sensible and intelligible symbols.[23] This ascent ultimately culminates in an ecstatic vision of and union with the One. The aesthetic level of the Pseudo-Dionysian *Symbolic Theology* is thus intimately entwined with an epistemological element similar to the Platonic and Neoplatonic concepts of beauty.

Pseudo-Dionysius' fundamental aesthetic principles were based on a relatively well-established set of metaphysical thought. The *Corpus Areopagiticum* stood at the end of a centuries old Neoplatonic tradition (both pagan and Christian) reaching back at least to the third century CE that shared in a common vocabulary of light to describe a transcendental entity (Platonic ideas or the Christian God) and to explain and structure their ontological systems. Since Pseudo-Dionysius appropriated the language and ideas of his Neoplatonic predecessors, both pagan and Christian, (like Plotinus, Proclus or the Cappadocian church fathers), it is necessary to lay out some of the most important features of the Platonic and Neoplatonic metaphysics and ontology. The dualism between an intelligible world, that is to say the realm of the ideas that is accessible only to the mind (νόησις), and the material world that is perceived through the senses (αἴσθησις), was the legacy of Plato.[24] This dualism applies also to late antique aesthetic theories and the notion of beauty. Accordingly, it is essential to distinguish between particular examples of beauty (sensible instances of beauty) and 'what the beautiful itself is' (the form or idea of beauty).[25] Pseudo-Dionysius identified, in line with the Platonic tradition, beauty with the good, both of which belonged to the realm of the divine (ideas).[26] Distinct from, yet closely connected to this divine reality was the material world and the beauty within it. Beauty's specific function was to raise people's minds from the material to the immaterial divine. It was Pseudo-Dionysius who developed most fully

23 Pseudo-Dionysius mentions a work entitled *The Symbolic Theology*, but it is no longer preserved. Pseudo-Dionysius, *DN*, 597B and footnote 89 in *Pseudo-Dionysius: The Complete Works*, trans. Colm Luibheid and Paul Rorem (1987), 57.

24 The differentiation between intelligible forms and sensible objects is not a difference between two kinds of reality, but between reality and appearance. For an excellent discussion of this, see Perl (2007), Chapter 1.

25 Plato, *Hippias Major*, 287d: τί ἐστι τοῦτο τὸ καλόν.

26 Wladyslaw Tatarkiewicz, *History of Aesthetics. Vol. I. Ancient Aesthetics*, ed. J. Harrell (The Hague and Paris: PWN-Polish Scientific Publisher, 1970), 27–35; Koutras (2002).

the Byzantine aesthetic categories of beauty, light and symbol, completing in a way the formulation of an utterly transcendental Christian aesthetics that was intimately linked with a Christian notion of episteme and truth.[27]

For Pseudo-Dionysius, light and its images and metaphors satisfied the two forms of aesthetic experience. On the one hand, light produced brilliance and splendour and was thus pleasing to the eye (αἴσθησις), while on the other hand, the phenomenon of light provoked associations with the divine (the source of beauty).[28] His metaphysical synthesis of light and darkness discloses a pattern of thought that underlay the early Byzantine intellectual tradition more generally, evidenced also in the earlier fourth-century works of Gregory of Nyssa. The Pseudo-Dionysian writings can therefore provide the philosophical framework for the concepts of beauty and art in sixth-century Byzantium and for the interpretation of the aesthetic exemplified in the art and architecture of Hagia Sophia. Pseudo-Dionysius' metaphysical aesthetics of light represents a commonality in which art and architecture, literature and philosophy equally partook.

Beauty, Light and Being

The Pseudo-Dionysian aesthetic of light and animation is reflective of the Neoplatonic idea that beauty is tightly linked to being through the affiliation of beauty with the good, the two most fundamental features of the One/ God. In chapter four of the *Divine Names*, Pseudo-Dionysius groups together beauty and light that describe facets of God and that can ultimately all be identified with God and by extension with being itself. In this, he follows the Platonic philosophies as well as biblical and patristic traditions. The close correspondence between the good and beauty is grounded in the ancient Greek term καλόν, a term that means 'beauty' in the sense of beautiful appearances (αἴσθησις), but one that has an ethical dimension, too. This is evident, for example, from the Greek phrase καλός κ'ἀγαθός that designates the ideal man who is 'noble and good'.[29] In Plato's dialogues, the distinction between the good and beauty is frequently obscured to the point of overlapping, even though they are not identical.[30] In the Old and New Testament, καλός is essentially used synonymously with ἀγαθός and means both beautiful and good as in the 'good (καλός) shepherd'.[31] Both connotations can equally

[27] Victor Bychkov, 'Byzantine aesthetics', in *Encyclopedia of Aesthetics*, ed. Michael Kelly (Oxford and New York, NY: Oxford University Press, 1998).

[28] Mathew (1963), 6.

[29] Drew A. Hyland, *Plato and the Question of Beauty* (Bloomington and Indianapolis, IA: Indiana University Press, 2008), 5; Kuisma (2003), 43–5.

[30] Plato, *Hippias Major*, 296d-297c; in Diotima's speech in the *Symposium*, the priestess substitutes the good for the beautiful, emphasising their close connection. Plato, *Symposium*, 204e.

[31] For example John 10:11–14; Hebr 5:14; Gen 3:5; Ex 3:14; Matthew 19:17, 20:15.

be found in the writings of the Cappadocian Fathers. For Gregory of Nyssa (c. 330–395 CE), only God is truly good and really beautiful. God is at once the supreme good and beauty, and goodness and beauty are the salient divine qualities.[32] The experience of beauty in late antiquity thus involves the evaluation of its ethical as well as aesthetic qualities. There is simply no distinction between the two.

The Pseudo-Dionysian description of beauty has its roots in the *Symposium* that contains one of Plato's major discourses on beauty. In the *Symposium* beauty itself (αὐτὸ τὸ καλὸν) is defined as the object of love's desire that has an existence of its own, '[it] neither comes to be nor perishes, neither waxes nor wanes … but exist[s] ever in singularity of form independent by itself, while all the multitude of beautiful things partake of it'.[33] Plato clearly elevated beauty to the level of the ideas, of being and reality, and as such beauty is a formative first principle and an aspect of truth. Pseudo-Dionysius similarly postulates a transcendental divine beauty that is the cause of all sensible beauty and even borrows, as it seems, Plato's exact wording:

> It [beauty] is forever so, unvaryingly, unchangeably so, beautiful and neither coming into being nor perishing, neither waxing nor waning, not lovely in one respect while ugly in some other way. It is not beautiful at one time and ugly at another, beautiful in relation to one thing but not to another … [but] in itself and by itself it is the uniquely and the eternally beautiful … From this beauty comes the existence of everything, each being exhibiting its own way of beauty.[34]

Although the Pseudo-Dionysian concept of beauty has fundamental points in common with that of Plato, there are also some major differences. While the Platonic form of beauty is merely one among many, Pseudo-Dionysius equates beauty with being itself. It follows that all beings are beautiful insofar as they exist, for 'there is nothing in the world without a share of the Beautiful and the Good'.[35] In this, Pseudo-Dionysius differs also from his Neoplatonic

32 Thomas Böhm, *Theoria, Unendlichkeit, Aufstieg: Philosophische Implikationen zu De Vita Moysis von Gregor von Nyssa* (Leiden and New York, NY: Brill, 1996), 54–7; Colin Macleod, 'The preface to Gergory of Nyssa's Life of Moses', *Journal of Theological Studies* 33 (1982): 189; Ilaria Ramelli, 'Good/Beauty', in *The Brill Dictionary of Gregory of Nyssa*, ed. Lucas Francisco Mateo-Seco and Giulio Maspero (Leiden and Boston, MA: Brill, 2010).

33 Plato, *Symposium*, 211a-b: ἀεὶ ὂν καὶ οὔτε γιγνόμενον οὔτε ἀπολλύμενον … ἀλλ᾽ αὐτὸ καθ᾽ αὑτὸ μεθ᾽ αὑτοῦ μονοειδὲς ἀεὶ ὄν, τὰ δὲ ἄλλα πάντα καλὰ ἐκείνου μετέχοντα τρόπον τινὰ τοιοῦτον …

34 The translation is adopted with slight changes from Pseudo-Dionysius (1987), 77. Pseudo-Dionysius, *DN*, 701D-704A: ἀεὶ ὂν κατὰ τὰ αὐτὰ καὶ ὡσαύτως καλὸν καὶ οὔτε γιγνόμενον οὔτε ἀπολλύμενον οὔτε αὐξανόμενον οὔτε φθίνον, οὐδὲ τῇ μὲν καλόν, τῇ δὲ αἰσχρὸν οὐδὲ τοτὲ μέν, τοτὲ δὲ οὔ, οὐδὲ πρὸς μὲν τὸ καλόν, πρὸς δὲ τὸ αἰσχρὸν οὔτε ἔνθα μέν, ἔνθα δὲ οὒ ὡς τισὶ μὲν ὂν καλόν, τισὶ δὲ οὐ καλόν, ἀλλ᾽ ὡς αὐτὸ καθ᾽ ἑαυτὸ μεθ᾽ ἑαυτοῦ μονοειδὲς ἀεὶ ὂν καλὸν καὶ ὡς παντὸς καλοῦ τὴν πηγαίαν καλλονὴν ὑπεροχικῶς ἐν ἑαυτῷ προέχον. See also Wladyslaw Tatarkiewicz, *History of Aesthetics. Vol. II. Medieval Aesthetics*, ed. C. Barrett (The Hague and Paris: PWN-Polish Scientific Publisher, 1970), 33.

35 Pseudo-Dionysius, *DN*, 704B: καὶ οὐκ ἔστι τι τῶν ὄντων, ὃ μὴ μετέχει τοῦ καλοῦ καὶ ἀγαθοῦ.

predecessors like Plotinus. Although Plotinus identified beauty with being, he subordinated beauty and being to the good that had been there long before.[36] To Pseudo-Dionysius in contrast, beauty is no longer secondary to the good; rather beauty is identical with the good.[37] Following Gregory of Nyssa, who had conceived of the divine as supreme beauty and the good and the source of everything that is good and beautiful,[38] Pseudo-Dionysius merged the two divine attributes into an all-embracing divine paradigm *the Good/Beauty*. The Good/Beauty is equated with being itself, because the good, according to Pseudo-Dionysius, is effectively the efficient cause and origin of all being as well as that to which all being aspires to return.[39] These processes are expressed in the form of light and illumination:

> Light comes from the Good, and light is an image of this archetypal Good. Thus the Good is also praised by the name 'Light', just as an archetype is revealed in its image ... It gives light to everything capable of receiving it, it creates them, keeps them alive, preserves and perfects them ... It is the power of which embraces the universe. It is the Cause of the universe and its end. The great, shining, ever-lighting sun is the apparent image of the divine goodness ...[40]

Pseudo-Dionysius explains that the good creates solely by virtue of its existence. It diffuses itself (*Bonum est diffusivum sui*)[41] out of sheer goodness, and its 'rays are responsible for all intelligible and intelligent beings, for every power and every activity'.[42] The Pseudo-Dionysian creation is a spontaneous emanation from the good as the unique cause and recalls the Plotinian notion of the One's emanation 'by necessity'.[43] The bottom line is that the good/God cannot not produce, because the good/God and the act of creation is one and

36 Plotinus, *Enneads*, V.5.12.

37 Pseudo-Dionysius, *DN*, 704B: Διὸ καὶ ταὐτόν ἐστι τἀγαθῷ τὸ καλόν.

38 Gregory of Nyssa, *On Virginity*, chapter XI; Ramelli (2010).

39 For an extensive treatment of the Good in Pseudo-Dionysius, see Ysabel De Andia, *Henosis: L'union à dieu chez Denys l'Aréopagite* (Leiden, Cologne and New York, NY: Brill, 1996), 123–44.

40 Pseudo-Dionysius, *DN*, 697C: Ἐκ τἀγαθοῦ γὰρ τὸ φῶς καὶ εἰκὼν τῆς ἀγαθότητος. Διὸ καὶ φωτωνυμικῶς ὑμνεῖται τἀγαθὸν ὡς ἐν εἰκόνι τὸ ἀρχέτυπον ἐκφαινόμενον ... ἀλλὰ καὶ φωτίζει τὰ δυνάμενα πάντα καὶ δημιουργεῖ καὶ ζωοῖ καὶ συνέχει καὶ τελεσιουργεῖ ... καὶ περιοχὴ καὶ αἰτία καὶ τέλος, οὕτω δὴ καὶ ἡ τῆς θείας ἀγαθότητος ἐμφανὴς εἰκών, ὁ μέγας οὗτος καὶ ὁλολαμπὴς καὶ ἀείφωτος ἥλιος ...

41 For the history of the phrase see, for instance, Klaus Kremer, 'Bonum est diffusivum sui: Ein Beitrag zum Verhältnis von Neuplatonismus und Christentum', in *Aufstieg und Niedergang der römischen Welt*, ed. Wolfgang Haase (Berlin and New York, NY: Walter de Gruyter 1987); Klaus Kremer, 'Dionysius Pseudo-Areopagita oder Gregor von Nazianz? Zur Herkunft der Formel: Bonum est diffusivum sui', *Theologie und Philosophie* 63 (1988).

42 Pseudo-Dionysius, *DN*, 693B-C: Διὰ ταύτας ὑπέστησαν αἱ νοηταὶ καὶ νοεραὶ πᾶσαι καὶ οὐσίαι καὶ δυνάμεις καὶ ἐνέργειαι.

43 Stephen Gersh, *From Iamblichus to Eriugena: an Investigation of the Prehistory and Evolution of the Pseudo-Dionysian Tradition* (Leiden: Brill, 1978), 21–2; René Roques, *L'univers dionysien: Structure hiérarchique du monde selon le Pseudo-Denys* (Paris: Aubier, 1954), 101–2; Kremer (1987). Semmelroth argued vehemently against the emanation by necessity interpretation, saying that creation is a divine choice and gift to humanity. Otto Semmelroth, 'Gottes ausstrahlendes Licht: Zur Schöpfungs- und Offenbahrungslehre des Ps.-Dionysius Areopagita', *Scholastik* 28 (1953).

the same thing, or in other words, the act of creation is the good's/God's very own nature.[44] Its success depends on the aptitude (ἀναλογία) of the created being to receive the divine light of the good, implying a certain freedom on the part of the created world, for God cannot create being without their active participation.[45]

Pseudo-Dionysius parallels the creative potentiality of the good with that of the sun, and it is for this reason that the sun is the most appropriate image (εἰκών) of the divine goodness. Pseudo-Dionysius nonetheless distinguishes strictly between the light of the good/God and the light of the sun. The latter is created light and thus a mere image of the former, while the divine is uncreated light. This is in line with patristic and biblical sources. The book of Genesis, when recounting the history of creation, clearly differentiates between the light on the first day of creation and the creation of the sun on the fourth day.[46] The light of the first three days, according to Pseudo-Dionysius, was without form (ἀσχημάτιστος) and limitless (ἄμετρος),[47] while Gregory of Nyssa points to the singularity of this light in contrast to the multiplicity of lights on the fourth day, thus highlighting God as the everlasting true source of light.[48]

This distinction finds its artistic parallel in the architecture and perception of Hagia Sophia. The true light within its sacred space is the one that is reflected, refracted and transmitted and thereby transformed through the mediation of the Great Church. This divine light is explicitly contrasted with the light of the sun. Procopius and Paul the Silentiary affirm that the building's luminosity outshines the light of the sun and surpasses even the beauty of heaven.[49] The effects of μαρμαρυγή, the spectacle of light on the marble and mosaic surfaces described by both authors is indicative of the Byzantine belief that lifeless matter cannot but reflect divine light.[50] The term μαρμαρυγή signifies matter truly animated through divine illumination. The concept that the 'transcendent rays prefer to give off the fullness of their splendour more purely and more luminously in mirrors made in their image',[51] identifies Hagia Sophia's interior saturated with radiance as the perfect image or mirror of the divine light. The

---

44 Lloyd P. Gerson, *Plotinus* (London and New York, NY: Routlege, 1994), 28; Perl (2007), 49–52.

45 Pseudo-Dionysius, *DN*, 697D; Vladimir Lossky and Henri-Charles Puech, 'La notion des "analogies" chez Denys le Pseudo-Aréopagite', *Archives d'histoire doctrinale et littéraire du Moyen-Âge* 5 (1930), 28; Perl (2007), 42.

46 Gen 1:3–4, 14–18.

47 Pseudo-Dionysius, *DN*, 700A.

48 Gregory of Nyssa, *Hexaemeron*, GNO IV/1 65; *Contra Eunomium*, NPNF 144, 243; GNO II 180.1-12; Adolf Martin Ritter, 'Light', in *The Brill Dictionary of Gregory of Nyssa*, ed. Lucas Francisco Mateo-Seco and Giulio Maspero (Leiden and Boston, MA: Brill, 2010).

49 Silentiary verses 286–300; Procopius I.1.27–30, 61–3.

50 Pentcheva (2010), 146–8.

51 Pseudo-Dionysius, EH III(3).10.440B: Φανοτέρας γὰρ οὕτω τὰς θεοφανείας περιαυγασθήσονται τῶν ὑπερκοσμίων μαρμαρυγῶν εἰς τὴν τῶν ὁμοειδῶν ἐσόπτρων ἀγλαΐαν ὁλικώτερον καὶ διαυγέστερον ἐφιέντων διϊέναι τὴν οἰκείαν αἴγλην.

building's sacred space suffused with light is a true symbol in the Neoplatonic sense that tightly links the divine and the human realms. The *kontakion* written for the re-inauguration in 562 CE clearly states that in Hagia Sophia the 'heavenly one shared a roof with those on earth' and that the divinely inspired architectural masterpiece literally contains the uncontainable (ἀχώρητος).[52] As part of a continuous chain of symbols, the splendour of Hagia Sophia thus enjoyed a relatively high ontological status. This can be explained on the basis of Proclus' interpretation of being as a system of vertical chains through which the material world was inherently connected with the divine reality. One of Proclus' most famous examples was the solar chain that emanated from the One and became manifest first as the Greek god Apollo, then continued down to the realm of the νοῦς where it generated the Platonic form of the sun. It subsequently became a sort of sun-soul and finally entered the material world in the form of the physical sun. On the level of plants the 'solar quality' was found in the heliotrope and further down the chain of symbols it appeared as gold.[53] Proclus' solar chain contains other plants and minerals, most notably the lotus that 'shows this kind of sympathy'.[54] The same pattern can be identified in the design of Hagia Sophia. Through its affinity with the sun, the church belongs to this solar chain. It stretches across the entire hierarchy from the highest levels of divine light reflected off its surfaces and the profusion of physical light from the sun to the lotus designs and gold tesserae in the mosaic decoration. Full of light, beauty and being, Hagia Sophia's interior is a symbol of divine light. As a symbol, it has the power to affect and transcend things and connect the human and divine spheres.[55] Light within Hagia Sophia thus comes as close as possible to the uncreated divine light, while it still reflects the multiplicity of the different ontological stages of light symbols.

It is through this ontological chain of being that the good, beauty and light simply represent different transcendent qualities that are identical with the good/God. As such, all three (good, beauty, light) can be considered the archetypal paradigms of all things good and beautiful.[56] What pagan and Christian Neoplatonism have in common is that all sensible beauty is grounded in an intelligible or transcendental divine beauty by way of participation (μέθεξις).[57] The share in beauty increases the closer something

---

52 *Oikos* 4: καὶ οὐ μόνον ὁμόστεγος τοῖς ἐν γῇ ἐστιν οὐράνιος; Trypanis (1968), 142; translated in Palmer and Rodley (1988), 140; Pentcheva (2010), 53–6.

53 Proclus, *On the Hieratic Art According to the Greeks*, 148.10–18; Eric R. Dodds, 'Theurgy and its relationship to Neoplatonism', *The Journal of Roman Studies* 37 (1947): 62; Anne Sheppard, 'Proclus' attitude to theurgy', *Classical Quarterly* 32 (1982): 220; Struck (2004), 231.

54 Proclus, *On the Hieratic Art According to the Greeks*, 149.12–25; Radek Chlup, *Proclus: An Introduction* (Cambridge: Cambridge University Press, 2012), 127–36.

55 Anne Sheppard, 'Studies on the 5th and 6th Essays of Proclus' Commentary on the Republic', *Hypomnemata: Untersuchungen zur Antike und zu ihrem Nachleben. Heft 61* (1980): 145–6; Struck (2004), 204.

56 Pseudo-Dionysius, *DN*, 701C-704C.

57 George M.A. Grube, 'Plato's theory of beauty', *The Monist* 37 (1927); Ramelli (2010); Tatarkiewicz (1970), 118.

is to its source, which is the highest principle of beauty (the One/God). Things have varying capacities of partaking in form, resulting in a hierarchy of beauty that correlates with the Neoplatonic hierarchical order of being. This implies that beauty and being are practically the same, and being more beautiful is the same as being more beingful.[58] What is more beautiful is that which has a greater share in Form (ἰδέα) or being (εἶναι). The beauty in sensible things is the share of being that shines through them. This means that even material beauty is not purely sensory but primarily noetic inasmuch as it includes the imperceptible element of the formative power (*logos*) conferred to an object through the agency of the soul.[59] The phenomenon of light plays once more a fundamental role, because it exemplifies the creative power of the soul.[60] Plotinus makes this analogy explicit, stating: 'As the rays of the sun light up a dark cloud, and make it shine and give it a golden look, so the soul entering into the body of heaven gives it life and gives it immortality and wakes what lies inert'.[61] Light (φῶς) is intimately associated with the life-giving quality of the soul and by extension the light of the One. Through the presence of the soul, bodies (matter), become living organisms that emanate the transcendental light, by which the living become more beautiful. This is why light constitutes an essential component of material beauty, because it makes visible the creative emanations of the One. This notion of beauty is also exemplified in a passage in which Plotinus states that statues that are more lifelike (ζωτικώτερα) are more beautiful just as 'an uglier living man [is] more beautiful than the beautiful man in a statue'.[62] That which transforms matter into a living, more beautiful being is the light of the good bestowed upon an object through the life-giving function of the soul.[63]

Like Plotinus, Pseudo-Dionysius defines beauty in relation to the degree of likeness to the One / God. As a result, material beauty is understood to contain something divine (divine light) and the visible and intelligible universe is really a world of symbols through which God reveals Himself. The beings closest to God receive the greatest amount of divine light and beauty, and

[58] Plotinus, *Enneads*, V.8.9.42: διὸ καὶ τὸ εἶναι ποθεινόν ἐστιν, ὅτι ταὐτὸν τῷ καλῷ, καὶ τὸ καλὸν ἐράσμιον, ὅτι τὸ εἶναι. For a recent discussion of the relationship between beauty and being, see Jens Halfwassen, 'Schönheit und Bild im Neuplatonismus', in *Neuplatonismus und Ästhetik: Zur Transformationsgeschichte des Schönen*, ed. Verena Olejniczak Lobsien and Claudia Olk (Berlin and New York, NY: Walter de Gruyter, 2007).

[59] Arthur H. Armstrong, 'Beauty and the discovery of divinity in the thought of Plotinus', in *Kephalaion: Studies in Greek Philosophy and Its Continuation Offered to Professor C. J. De Vogel*, ed. J. Mansfeld and L. M. de Rijk (Assen: Van Gorcum and Comp. B.V., 1975); Tatarkiewicz (1970), 318–20.

[60] Plotinus, *Enneads*, I.6.3.19: φωτὸς ἀσωμάτου καὶ λόγου καὶ εἴδους ὄντος.

[61] Plotinus, *Enneads*, V.1.2.202–3: οἷον σκοτεινὸν νέφος ἡλίου βολαὶ φωτίσασαι λάμπειν ποιοῦσι χρυσοειδῆ ὄψιν διδοῦσαι, οὕτω τοι καὶ ψυχὴ ἐλθοῦσα εἰς σῶμα οὐρανοῦ ἔδωκε μὲν ζωήν, ἔδωκε δὲ ἀθανασίαν, ἤγειρε δὲ κείμενον.

[62] Plotinus, *Enneads*, VI.7.22. 31–2: καὶ αἰσχίων ζῶν καλλίων τοῦ ἐν ἀγάλματι καλοῦ.

[63] Plotinus, *Enneads*, VI.7.22. 34; on the identification of beauty with that which is intelligible, see Perl (2007), 42–3.

they are the most similar to the divine.[64] To explain how the created universe relates to its creator, Pseudo-Dionysius introduces the concept of a hierarchy of being in Chapter 3 of the *Celestial Hierarchy* (CH):[65]

> In my opinion a hierarchy is a sacred order, a state of understanding and an activity approximating as closely as possible to the divine. And it is uplifted to the imitation of God in proportion to the enlightenments divinely given to it. The beauty of God – so simple, so good, so much the source of perfection – is completely uncontaminated by dissimilarity. It reaches out to grant every being, according to merit, a share of light and then through a divine sacrament, in harmony and in peace, it bestows on each of those being perfected its own form.[66]

The divine creation is illustrated on the basis of light, where the good is unchangeable and 'never loses the utter fullness of its light'.[67] All beings are assigned a share of the divine light and divine beauty according to merit and ability to partake in the divine light. The intelligible world will, as a result, always remain more beautiful than the material world because the intelligible realm is more luminous, where 'all is colour and beauty to its innermost part',[68] where the nature of beauty is 'simple, immaterial and formless'.[69] In the Platonised Christian late antiquity, light is thus not simply a metaphorical image of the good/beauty, but the good/beauty is light, it is 'the source of light and actually transcend[s] light' (ἀρχίφωτος καὶ ὑπέρφωτος).[70] This model of the good/beauty as light in the actual sense provides the framework for the Pseudo-Dionysian sensible as well as intelligible universe.[71] He inherited the Plotinian concept of light as the physical manifestation of the creative energy of the soul that anticipated the Pseudo-Dionysian understanding of light as an act (ἐνέργεια) of the first principle of being by virtue of its identity with the good/beauty.[72] Light is not merely a metaphor, rather, the One/God is light and light is ultimately the One/God.[73] Light is literally a manifestation and a revelation of the transcendental divine reality.

---

64 Roques provides an excellent discussion of symbolism in the *Corpus Areopagiticum*. René Roques, 'Symbolisme et théologie négative chez le Pseudo-Denys', *Bulletin de l'Association Guillaume Budé* 4 (1957).

65 For a discussion on *hierarchia* see Klitenic Wear and Dillon (2007), 51–73.

66 Pseudo-Dionysius, *CH*, 164D: Ἔστι μὲν ἱεραρχία κατ' ἐμὲ τάξις ἱερὰ καὶ ἐπιστήμη καὶ ἐνέργεια πρὸς τὸ θεοειδὲς ὡς ἐφικτὸν ἀφομοιουμένη καὶ πρὸς τὰς ἐνδιδομένας αὐτῇ θεόθεν ἐλλάμψεις ἀναλόγως ἐπὶ τὸ θεομίμητον ἀναγομένη, τὸ δὲ θεοπρεπὲς κάλλος ὡς ἁπλοῦν ὡς ἀγαθὸν ὡς τελεταρχικὸν ἀμιγὲς μέν ἐστι καθόλου πάσης ἀνομοιότητος, μεταδοτικὸν δὲ κατ' ἀξίαν ἑκάστῳ τοῦ οἰκείου φωτὸς καὶ τελειωτικὸν ἐν τελετῇ θειοτάτῃ κατὰ τὴν πρὸς ἑαυτὸ τῶν τελουμένων ἐναρμονίως ἀπαράλλακτον μόρφωσιν.

67 Pseudo-Dionysius, *DN*, 697D: καὶ ὑπερηπλωμένον ἔχει τὸ φῶς.

68 Plotinus, *Enneads*, V.8.10.30: πᾶν χρόας ἡ ἐπανθοῦσα κάλλος ἐστί.

69 Gregory of Nyssa, *On Virginity*, Chapter XI.

70 Pseudo-Dionysius, *DN*, 701B.

71 De Andia calls the Good the 'bien-soleil', illustrating that the sun is more than a simple metaphor of the Good. De Andia (1996), 127–8.

72 For Plotinus, see e.g. Arthur H. Armstrong, '"Emanation" in Plotinus', *Mind* 46 (1937); for Pseudo-Dionysius see Klitenic Wear and Dillon (2007), 17–18.

73 Beierwaltes has pointed this out for Plotinus, and he also recognized traces of this metaphysics of light in Plato's light metaphors. Werner Beierwaltes, 'Plotins Metaphysik

From the metaphysical concept of beauty as a divine attribute follow a series of implications for the interpretation of the church of Hagia Sophia. The most striking feature of the late antique concept of beauty is its identity with being and light, and the differential degree of beauty reliant on the object's capacity to partake in these divine paradigms. These features situate Hagia Sophia's sacred space that is all colour and light within the twilight zone between the material and the intelligible realms. The profusion of light and its reflections animated and transformed inert matter into a seemingly living organism, and in so doing, make the architectural structure more beingful and beautiful. Within the Neoplatonic hierarchical system of beauty and being, the building was evidently granted a considerable share in divine beauty and light, because it was an architectural masterpiece worthy of God.[74] The monumental decoration is decidedly simple and formless compared to, for instance, figurative art with images drawn by nature (marble meadows), and of the divine light made manifest in the sustained play of light on the reflective and undercut surfaces. It is particularly these phenomena of light and their effect on the animation of matter that confirm divine immanence. This also signifies an essentialist definition of the architectural structure in that the building's luminosity truly participates in that which it represents.[75] Hence Hagia Sophia's interior is genuinely a symbolic space.

Beauty, Light and Wisdom (Episteme)

Even more pertinent to the interpretation of Hagia Sophia, 'the House of Wisdom' (τῆς Σοφίας τὸ ἁγίασμα),[76] is the association of beauty and light with an epistemological dimension. The main sources to document the analogy between light and wisdom are once again the Bible and the Platonic tradition. According to Proverbs, wisdom was created at the beginning before the earth was made, and the Book of Wisdom describes wisdom as 'a reflection of eternal light, a spotless mirror … and an image of his goodness'.[77] In Plato's *Republic*, Socrates uses the analogy of the sun when defining the nature of the good and its epistemic potential.[78] Just as the light of the sun is the cause of vision and of the objects of vision, so too is the Platonic idea of good the source of reason and the objects of reason. While one requires physical light in order to see, the soul needs to dwell in 'the domain where truth and reality shine resplendent' in order to attain reason.[79] The source of illumination in

des Lichtes', in *Die Philosophie des Neuplatonismus*, ed. Clemens Zintzen (Darmstadt: Wissenschaftliche Buchgesellschaft, 1977).

74 Kontakion *oikos* 5; Trypanis (1968), 143; translated in Palmer and Rodley (1988), 141.

75 See also the discussion in Pentcheva (2010), 45–56.

76 Kontakion *oikos* 2; Trypanis (1968), 142; translated in Palmer and Rodley (1988), 140.

77 Proverbs 8:22–3; Book of Wisdom 7:24–6.

78 Plato, *Republic*, 508A–509B.

79 Plato, *Republic*, 508D: ὅταν μὲν οὗ καταλάμπει ἀλήθειά τε καὶ τὸ ὄν, εἰς τοῦτο ἀπερείσηται, ἐνόησέν τε καὶ ἔγνω αὐτὸ καὶ νοῦν ἔχειν φαίνεται.

the domain of truth and knowledge is the idea of good. Plato differentiates between the two sources (the idea of good and the sun), even though he likens the intellectual process (νόησις) to sense perception (αἴσθησις). For Plato, the image of light refers figuratively to how the good operates in the realm of the intellect to exemplify the illuminating capacity of the idea of good that generates the existence and essence of the objects of knowledge.[80]

In a similar sentiment, Gregory of Nyssa forges the link between light and wisdom, stating that the name light is applied to God, 'when he disperses the gloom of ignorance'.[81] Pseudo-Dionysius preserves the parallelism between light and cognitive functions, but he goes a step further, identifying God explicitly with light and wisdom.[82] In his *Celestial Hierarchy*, the members of the highest order of being that follow directly below God are 'full of a superior light beyond any knowledge'.[83] To this first hierarchy belong the seraphim, cherubim and thrones. Their names exemplify their likeness to God and the principles of creation. In other words, their names identify the specific powers that these highest orders receive directly from God. The uppermost rank, the 'fiery thrones' are the most perfect and dwell in the immediate vicinity of God, while the name cherubim, second in the hierarchy, signifies that the creative process is also associated with the 'outpouring of wisdom' that Pseudo-Dionysius considers the 'greatest gift of his light'.[84] The seraphim, 'fire-makers' or 'carriers of warmth', come third. They have the capacity to arouse and lift the lower orders and to purify by way of illumination through the divine light. Divine creation in the Pseudo-Dionysian sense then is above all the emission of light and wisdom, for these are the powers received and passed on by the first order of the celestial hierarchy. Wisdom is transmitted alongside light and beauty in ever diminishing degrees from the superior ranks of the thrones, cherubim and seraphim to the lowest creatures. The human hierarchy is modelled after the celestial hierarchy, but while the latter is purely incorporeal and conceptual, the human hierarchy manifests itself in numerous perceptible symbols. 'Out of necessity they made human what was divine. They put material on what was immaterial'.[85] The necessity arises

80 Plato, *Republic*, 509B.

81 Gregory of Nyssa, *Contra Eunomium*, NPNF 221.

82 Pseudo-Dionysius, *DN*, 700D: ὅτι φῶς νοητὸν ὁ ἀγαθὸς λέγεται διὰ τὸ πάντα μὲν ὑπερουράνιον νοῦν ἐμπιμπλάναι νοητοῦ φωτός, πᾶσαν δὲ ἄγνοιαν καὶ πλάνην ἐλαύνειν ἐκ πασῶν, αἷς ἂν ἐγγένηται ψυχαῖς, καὶ πάσαις αὐταῖς φωτὸς ἱεροῦ μεταδιδόναι καὶ τοὺς νοεροὺς αὐτῶν ὀφθαλμοὺς ἀποκαθαίρειν τῆς περικειμένης αὐταῖς ἐκ τῆς ἀγνοίας ἀχλύος καὶ ἀνακινεῖν καὶ ἀναπτύσσειν τῷ πολλῷ βάρει τοῦ σκότους συμμεμυκότας [The Good is described as the light of the mind because it illuminates the mind of every supra-celestial being with the light of the mind, and because it drives from souls the ignorance and the error squatting there. It gives them all a share of sacred light. It clears away the fog of ignorance from the eyes of the mind and it stirs and unwraps those covered over by the burden of darkness].

83 Pseudo-Dionysius, *CH*, 208C: πάσης ἀΰλου γνώσεως ὑψηλοτέρου φωτὸς.

84 Pseudo-Dionysius, *CH*, 205C: Χερουβὶμ τὸ γνωστικὸν αὐτῶν καὶ θεοπτικὸν καὶ τῆς ὑπερτάτης φωτοδοσίας δεκτικὸν.

85 Pseudo-Dionysius, *EH*, 376D: ἐν ἀνθρωπίνοις τε τὰ θεῖα καὶ ἐν ἐνύλοις τὰ ἄϋλα.

from the limited intellectual capacity of humans to grasp the idea of God, who is beyond all knowing and understanding. Physical light is once more defined as the image of the 'outpouring of an immaterial gift of light';[86] it is the material manifestation of divine light. The only difference is that the sensation of physical light is significantly weaker than that of divine light. Light is therefore the most appropriate symbol for the divine, because it is at once most similar to God and at the same time accessible to human comprehension. As such, light serves a spiritual and cognitive function in the *Corpus Areopagiticum*, while being quintessentially aesthetic in nature.

The significance of light and its close association with aesthetic and epistemological values are indebted to the Platonic and Plotinian perception of beauty. In Plato's *Phaedrus*, it is made perfectly clear that beauty is both a Platonic form as well as a sensory experience. In the reincarnation myth of the *Phaedrus*, Socrates explains that the human souls have once beheld true being and reality when dwelling with the gods, before they had lost their wings and had been plunged into a human body. Human beings are capable of recollection (ἀνάμνησις) of these things that really are (τὸ ὂν ὄντως) by gathering many sense perceptions into one coherent conception by means of reasoning (λογισμῷ).[87] While it may often be difficult to recollect the forms of more abstract concepts such as justice or *sophrosyne*, beauty possesses an extraordinary brilliance and immediacy on account of which it has a much stronger capacity to ensue memory and recognition of the essence of beauty within perceptible beauty. Unlike other forms 'beauty … shone in brilliance among the visions; and since we came to earth we have found it shining most clearly through the clearest of our senses … beauty alone has this privilege, and therefore it is most clearly seen and loveliest'.[88] This passage is central for understanding Plato's concept of aesthetic beauty in relation to cognition and its affinity with light. The very nature of beauty seems to make it a paradigm for the experience of being in general and ultimately for truth (ἀλήθεια).[89] This is because beauty, similar to light, has an immediate and powerful impact on the beholder due to its visibility and its capacity to motivate a strong reaction of love.[90]

Beauty's similarity with light derives from the shared property to reveal their being most clearly and most effectively, which makes them both vehicles of knowledge and truth.[91] Beauty and light bring about an intense

86 Pseudo-Dionysius, *CH*, 121D: τῆς ἀΰλου φωτοδοσίας εἰκόνα τὰ ὑλικὰ φῶτα.

87 Plato, *Phaedrus*, 249a–c.

88 Plato, *Phaedrus*, 250d–e: περὶ δὲ κάλλους, ὥσπερ εἴπομεν, μετ᾽ ἐκείνων τε ἔλαμπεν ὄν, δεῦρό τ᾽ἐλθόντες κατειλήφαμεν αὐτὸ διὰ τῆς ἐναργεστάτης αἰσθήσεως τῶν ἡμετέρων στίλβον ἐναργέστατα. ὄψις γὰρ ἡμῖν ὀξυτάτη τῶν διὰ τοῦ σώματος ἔρχεται αἰσθήσεων … νῦν δὲ κάλλος μόνον ταύτην ἔσχε μοῖραν, ὥστ᾽ ἐκφανέστατον εἶναι καὶ ἐρασμιώτατον.

89 Hyland (2008), 81–3; Nightingale (2004), 86–8.

90 Plato, *Phaedrus*, 251a–252c.

91 Martin Heidegger, *Vom Wesen der Wahrheit: Zu Platons Höhlengleichnis und Theätet* (Wintersemester 1931/32) (Frankfurt: Vittorio Klostermann, 1997, 2nd edition), 47–52.

visual sensation, and vision according to Plato's *Timaeus* is essential for the attainment of knowledge and philosophy.[92] In the passage from the *Phaedrus* quoted above, Plato defines vision to be the clearest of our senses, and in the *Republic* he identifies the eye as the 'organ of knowledge' that is far superior to the ear and to hearing.[93] Plato's model of sense-based vision provides a suitable analogy for the philosopher's metaphysical quest for wisdom and truth.[94] This philosophical *theoria*[95] is elaborated in Plato's *Analogy of the Cave*. Here, Plato recounts how after being released from the bondage of the cave, the philosopher literally journeys into the metaphysical realm of the Forms that is radiant with the light from the idea of good. The idea of good in the image of the sun is 'the cause for all things of all that is right and beautiful, giving birth in the visible world to light ... and itself in the intelligible world being the authentic source of truth (ἀλήθεια) and reason (νοῦς)'.[96] The final goal of the soul's ascent is the essence of truth (ἀλήθεια), which is 'unhiddenness'. The truth or unhiddenness of the Platonic forms is their intelligibility, their ability to be known, which is facilitated by the good.[97] On the level of sense perception, the experience of beauty seems to represent a kind of shortcut for the cognitive process, because beauty has its own special brilliance, unhiding the essence (being) of beauty most clearly. Through this the soul potentially attains true knowledge and wisdom.[98] The beauty represented in material beauty functions as a paradigm for truth by virtue of its close association with the idea of good.[99]

The process of epistemological enlightenment is redefined in the Neoplatonism of Plotinus. According to Plotinus, the soul delights in material beauty, because it recognises its own nature objectified in sensible matter. The experience of beauty is nothing else than an encounter with the soul's very own being and by extension with the archetype of beauty.[100] Hence, the soul's search for being and beauty is in essence an inner quest insofar as a successful pursuit of beauty requires the soul to turn away from sensible beauties that are

---

92 Plato, *Timaeus*, 47a–b.

93 Plato, *Republic*, 507c-508a, 518c: ὄργανον ᾧ καταμανθάνει.

94 Nightingale (2004), 10–12.

95 For the translation of the traditional practice of *theoria* defined as a pilgrimage to witness certain spectacles into the philosophical *theoria* of the fourth century BCE, see Nightingale (2004).

96 Plato, *Republic*, 517c: ἀγαθοῦ ἰδέα καὶ μόγις ὁρᾶσθαι, ὀφθεῖσα δὲ συλλογιστέα εἶναι ὡς ἄρα πᾶσι πάντων αὕτη ὀρθῶν τε καὶ καλῶν αἰτία, ἔν τε ὁρατῷ φῶς καὶ τὸν τούτου κύριον τεκοῦσα, ἔν τε νοητῷ αὐτὴ κυρία ἀλήθειαν καὶ νοῦν παρασχομένη.

97 Heidegger (1997), 8–19; Perl (2007), 8.

98 Plato, *Phaedrus*, 250d.

99 Hyland (2008), 83.

100 Arthur H. Armstrong, 'The divine enhancement of earthly beauties: The Hellenic and Platonic tradition', *Eranos Jahrbuch* 53 (1984); Kuisma (2003), 155–7; Jean-Marc Narbonne, 'Action, contemplation and interiority in the thinking of beauty of Plotinus', in *Neoplatonism and Western Aesthetics*, ed. Aphrodite Alexandrakis and Nicholas J. Moutafakis (New York, NY: State University of New York Press, 2002); Perl (2007), 21–2.

but images (εἰκόνες), traces (ἴχνη) and shadows (σκιαί), and to concentrate instead on the vision that awakens within.[101] The experience of beauty directs the soul's attention to its own being through likeness. In so doing, beauty triggers a stream of memories, reminding the soul of its very own nature and its implications. This principle of ἀνάμνησις recalls the epistemological ἀνάμνησις from Plato's *Phaedrus*, which refers to the recollection of forgotten knowledge from the time when the soul had not yet been corrupted by matter and had inhabited the realm of the gods.[102] In Plotinus' thought, ἀνάμνησις similarly implies the ability to remember, but it is the memory of one's own being that is stirred by beauty, for to know oneself is the same as to be beautiful.[103] To know oneself is to catch a glimpse of true being and beauty, a vision of the One, which resides inside every being.[104] In the experience of beauty, aesthetic and epistemological values evolve together, and jointly enable the cognitive and aesthetic development of an individual soul.[105]

Plotinus equates intellection (νόησις) with sense perception (αἴσθησις) in that they both are types of vision.[106] Perceptual and intelligible vision is expressed in terms of light, brightness, transparency and brilliance.[107] Light constitutes an essential component of aesthetic (material) and intelligible beauty. On the empirical level, the simple beauty of colour is said to be the result of 'the mastery of the darkness in matter by the presence of light which is incorporeal and formative power and form'.[108] Beauty, for Plotinus, exists primarily in the intelligible realm, while the beauties of this world are only weak reflections of this perfect beauty.[109] Intelligible 'beauty is just beauty' (καὶ τὸ καλὸν καλὸν); it is pure and not corrupted by something non-beautiful, that is to say matter.[110] The beauty of all being comes to life when illuminated with the light of the good.[111] True light is the creative activity of the One, while the νοῦς and the soul are 'light from light' and arranged in concentric circles

---

101 Plotinus, *Enneads*, I.6.8.7–8, I.6.8.24–8; Koutras (2002).

102 Plato, *Phaedrus*, 249a-c

103 Plotinus, *Enneads*, V.8.13.21–2

104 Plotinus, *Enneads*, I.4.10.

105 Kuisma (2003), 81–2.

106 See also Hadot's discussion on contemplation and vision. Pierre Hadot, *Plotinus or Simplicity of Vision* (London and Chicago, IL: The University of Chicago Press, 1993), 42–4, 61–3.

107 Beierwaltes discusses the implications of Plotinus' metaphysics of light, while Kuisma provides a brief overview on the aesthetics of light in Plotinus; Beierwaltes (1977); Kuisma (2003), especially 185–9.

108 Plotinus, *Enneads*, I.6.3.17–19: τὸ δὲ τῆς χρόας κάλλος ἁπλοῦν μορφῇ καὶ κρατήσει τοῦ ἐν ὕλῃ σκοτεινοῦ παρουσίᾳ φωτὸς ἀσωμάτου καὶ λόγου καὶ εἴδους ὄντοες.

109 Jean-Claude Fraisse, 'La simplicité du Beau selon Plotin', *Revue de Métaphysique et de Morale* 88 (1983); Kuisma (2003), 10–11; Paul Mathias, *Plotin du beau: Ennéades I,6 et V, 8* (Paris: Presses Pocket, 1991), Introduction; Tatarkiewicz (1970), 318.

110 Plotinus, *Enneads*, V.8.4.14–15; V.8.7.16–18.

111 Plotinus, *Enneads*, VI.7.22.11–12; see also Dominic J. O'Meara, 'Textes de Plotin sur la beauté: initiation et remarques', in *Art et vérité*, ed. I. Schüssler (Lausanne: Genos, 1996); Susanne Stern-Gillet, 'Le principe du beau chez Plotin: Réflexions sur Enneads VI.7.32 et 33', *Phronesis* 45 (2000).

around the One, illuminating the heaven and the world down to the human realm.[112] Light in the Plotinian sense is not imposed upon the form as different from it; rather, it is manifest within it. Light is 'the formative principle and form', the *logos*. Light is not only an attribute, but it is the very essence of being and beauty.[113] Sensible light is a genuine ἀνάλογον of intelligible light, because the material image is not different from the archetypal form. It is merely the differentiated manifestation of this form.[114] As such, physical light does indeed reflect true beauty and being and has epistemological value. Plotinus' recognition of the symbolic dimension of the material world, that is to say that the immaterial source is intrinsic to its material manifestation, is important for the subsequent, specifically Byzantine concept of beauty as well as the theory and practice of art.[115]

The epistemological value of the material world is fundamental to Gregory of Nyssa's conception of *theoria*, which in his thought means scientific knowledge, exegetical method and mystical contemplation.[116] Underlying Gregory's *theoria* is the belief that 'the knowledge of God through creation (τά ὄντα) leads to the knowledge of God himself (τὸ ὄντως ὂν)'.[117] This implies that because God is intrinsic to his creation, contemplating the unity of the created world can eventually lead to insights into the divine nature itself. Gregory's cognitive and spiritual path originates accordingly in the contemplation of the visible manifestations of God and strives for a return to the soul's original condition of divine likeness that is light and beauty inasmuch as God is true light, beauty and truth itself.[118] As such, the epistemological ascent towards a mystic vision of God is one of increasing light and beauty. Gregory's notion of *theoria* corresponds to the Platonic definition of philosophical *theoria* that aims for an understanding of the intelligible reality and which has the essence of truth/truth itself (ἀλήθεια) as its ultimate goal.[119] Fundamentally different is the definition of this essence of truth. For Plato, the essence of truth is complete unhiddenness under the bright light of the idea of the good. In the Christian tradition, the final encounter with God is in the form of a

112 Plotinus, *Enneads*, IV.3.17.

113 Being and beauty are identical in nature. Plotinus, Enneads, (V.8.9.42).

114 Beierwaltes ([1961] 1977); Perl (2007), 21–2.

115 Kuisma elaborates extensively on the implication of a symbolic approach to art. Grabar (1945); Kuisma (2003).

116 Daniélou explored Gregory's use of the term *theoria* in detail and distinguished 'connaisance scientifique, méthode exégétique, contemplation mystique'. J. Daniélou, *L'Être et le temps chez Grégoire de Nysse* (Leiden: Brill, 1970), 1; Böhm (1996), 69–70; Giulio Maspero, 'Theòria', in *The Brill Dictionary of Gregory of Nyssa*, ed. Lucas Francisco Mateo-Seco and Giulio Maspero (Leiden and Boston, MA: Brill, 2010).

117 Böhm (1996), 70–71; Daniélou (1970), 8; Maspero (2010).

118 Gregory of Nyssa, *De Vita Moysis*, 2.26; translated in Elsner (1995), 105; Gregory of Nyssa defines this process as φωταγωγία, which reflects its close association with light and illumination as well as enlightenment. Böhm (1996), 74–5, 240–42; Martin Laird, *Gregory of Nyssa and the Grasp of Faith: Union, Knowledge, and Divine Presence* (Oxford Early Christian Studies) (Oxford: Oxford University Press, 2004), 182.

119 Nightingale (2004), 5–6.

'luminous darkness' or, in the words of Pseudo-Dionysius, in the form of 'the mysterious darkness of unknowing'.[120] The theme of divine darkness asserts the inaccessibility and unknowability of God that can neither be experienced through seeing nor through discursive knowledge.[121] Gregory's mysticism of light and darkness clearly anticipates Pseudo-Dionysius in its language and imagery of light. However, whereas for Gregory of Nyssa the Christian God is necessarily beyond knowledge and remains unattainable, Pseudo-Dionysius in the sixth century allows for the possibility of a mystic union that transcends subject and object and annihilates any duality.[122]

The sacred space of Hagia Sophia is built on the paradox of divine transcendence and immanence and by extension the Christian concept of wisdom. The primary vehicle for the theme of wisdom was the profusion of light in combination with the aniconic the mosaic decoration. The sign of the cross that dominates the sixth-century mosaics makes reference to divine wisdom and to the limitations of the human intellect to grasp the idea of God. Through the simplicity of colour and light, the church of Hagia Sophia exhibits the concept of the divine *Logos* rather than the incarnate Christ as in Saint Catherine at Sinai or San Vitale in Ravenna. The inauguration hymn of Hagia Sophia substantiates the interpretation of the light within as instrumental in conveying the concept of divine wisdom by consistently emphasising the close connection between the physical light and the transcendent divine light that illuminates the human mind.[123] In equating light with the creative cause of being (divine light) and with cognition, the kontakion follows traditional philosophical lines of thought and evokes to a much greater extent than the ekphraseis the symbolic significance of the Great Church as the 'sanctuary of wisdom'. The kontakion implies that the building's magnificence derives not solely from its material splendours, but above all from the fact that it is God's chosen dwelling place. Light has proved to be the most appropriate visible medium that approximates the representation of the divine paradigms due to its own simplicity and unity. Light transforms the interior of Hagia Sophia into a divine dwelling place, enveloping all into a spiritual world.[124]

The mystical mode of viewing described in the two ekphraseis of Hagia Sophia is very much entwined with an aesthetic response to the edifice, which here refers to the appreciation of its beauty.[125] Paul the Silentiary remarks

---

[120] Gregory of Nyssa, *De Vita Moysis*, 2.163; Pseudo-Dionysius, *MT*, 1001A: τὸν γνόφον τῆς ἀγνωσίας εἰσδύνει τὸν ὄντως μυστικόν.

[121] Gregory of Nyssa, *De Vita Moysis*, 2.163; Böhm (1996), 252–5; Laird (2004), 179–80.

[122] Elsner (1995), 98 and ft. 36, 104, 116–17; Laird (2004), Chapter 7.

[123] Trypanis (1968); Palmer and Rodley (1988).

[124] Nelson calls this the ancient system of signification; see Robert S. Nelson, 'Byzantine Art vs Western Medieval Art', in *Byzance et le monde extérieur: contacts, relations, échanges : actes de trois séances du XXe Congrès international des études byzantines, Paris, 19–25 août 2001*, ed. Paule Pagès *et al.* (Paris: Publications de la Sorbonne, 2005).

[125] Jaś Elsner, *Roman Eyes: Visuality and Subjectivity in Art and Text* (Princeton, NJ: Princeton University Press, 2007), 30.

that Hagia Sophia is a 'love-inspiring sight',[126] which brings to mind Plato's *Phaedrus*, where the love-inspiring sight encourages the lover's soul to recall the memory of true beauty.[127] It is the material manifestation of beauty that stirs the emotions and occasions the experience of love, which in turn motivates the return to God.[128] In the ekphrastic vision of Hagia Sophia, the edifice itself is perceived as a work of beauty by way of which the divine is made accessible. The building's beauty consisted not in the material aspects alone, but in the formative principle that the artist bestowed on the material. In practical artistic terms, this would seem to imply that the darkness inherent in matter is conquered by means of colour and light. This Plotinian notion of beauty is reflected, I believe, in the luminous and polychromatic interior of Hagia Sophia. The architectural substance of the building is bereft of darkness; it is literally dematerialised in the metaphysical sense because everything within the Great Church is turned into colour and light.

Beauty, Light and Darkness

Recognising light as an intrinsic part of Hagia Sophia's fabric raises the question of divine darkness, a theme first developed by Gregory of Nyssa but that was ultimately rooted in the Bible.[129] The idea of divine darkness as a metaphor for the mystical knowledge of God is not found among pagan Platonists, because darkness contrasts with the Platonic theories on the nature of the absolute. Light is an integral part of the Platonic idea of good and is related to the epistemological process and truth.[130] Darkness is therefore irreconcilable with this idea of good, and for Plotinus darkness conflicts with the nature and activity of the νοῦς. Darkness in the *Enneads* is typically associated with unshaped matter and evil. The transcendent Christian God of Gregory of Nyssa and Pseudo-Dionysius, on the other hand, is the source of all being. God himself is beyond being and necessarily 'rises above the contradiction between finite and infinite'.[131] 'Intangible and invisible darkness', according to Pseudo-Dionysius, is for this reason a befitting attribute 'of that Light

126 Silentiary, verse 285: ἔπι πάσης θεῖος ἔρως ἀκτῖνας ἀνεπτοίηςεν ὀπωπῆς.

127 Plato, *Phaedrus*, 253e.

128 Pseudo-Dionysius, *DN*, 709D.

129 For differences between Pseudo-Dionysius and the Neoplatonic tradition, see Ivanovic (2010), 16–21; William Riordan, *Divine Light: The Theology of Denys the Areopagite* (San Francisco, CA: Ignatius Press, 2008), 71–112.; Lossky discusses the development of the theme of darkness in the patristic tradition, culminating in the writings of Pseudo-Dionysius. Vladimir Lossky, *In the Image and Likeness of God* (New York, NY: St. Vladimir's Seminary Press, 1985), 31–43.

130 As Heidegger has demonstrated, the idea is 'the look (Anblick) of something as something', thus revealing the very being of something (das Sein des Seienden). Light and idea are both related to seeing in the sense of perceiving and recognising things, which is the basis for a cognitive process. Heidegger (1997).

131 Pseudo-Dionysius, *DN*, 825B: πέρατος ὑπεροχικῶς τῶν ὡς ἀντικειμένων.

which is unapproachable because it so far exceeds the visible light'.[132] What is more, darkness is above light, and it is in fact light that is the unknowing.[133] Darkness and pure light become interchangeable, at least in reference to the unknowing of God.

The Pseudo-Dionysian concept of divine darkness is made explicit in his *Mystical Theology*, where he explains how the lower orders of the human hierarchy are gradually initiated into the mysteries of the communion in God. The union with God takes place only when all intellection is suspended, when 'everything perceived and understood, everything perceptible and understandable, all that is not and all that is' is left behind, because God is beyond being and knowledge.[134] Following Gregory of Nyssa's example, Pseudo-Dionysius grafted his notion of the mystical ascent on the biblical story of Moses climbing Mount Sinai:

> It is not for nothing that the blessed Moses is commanded to submit first to purification and then to depart from those who have not undergone this. When every purification is complete, he hears the many-voiced trumpets. He sees the many lights, pure and with rays streaming abundantly. Then, standing apart from the crowds and accompanied by chosen priests, he pushes ahead to the summit of the divine ascents … But then he [Moses] breaks free of them [perceptible and intelligible things], away from what sees and is seen, and he plunges into the truly mysterious darkness of unknowing.[135]

Purification constitutes the first stage of Moses' ascent, followed by illumination and perfection. Part of the purification process was the separation from the material universe, the shedding of any worldly concerns with the purpose of becoming more God-like.[136] The last stage is a plunge into darkness, which describes the ineffability of the divine nature. It is important to keep in mind that the image of darkness can have two opposing meanings. Darkness for Pseudo-Dionysius very often means simply blind human ignorance, being incapable of grasping the divine essence, which the spiritual ascent is meant to overcome. The mystical darkness occurs at the end of this ascent and is the darkness of unknowing.[137]

---

132 Pseudo-Dionysius, *DN*, 869A: ἀόρατον γνόφον τῷ φωτὶ τῷ ἀπροσίτῳ καθ' ὑπεροχὴν τοῦ ὁρατοῦ φωτός.

133 Pseudo-Dionysius, *MT*, 997A.

134 Pseudo-Dionysius, *MT*, 997B: καὶ τὰς αἰσθήσεις ἀπόλειπε καὶ τὰς νοερὰς ἐνεργείας καὶ πάντα αἰσθητὰ καὶ νοητὰ καὶ πάντα οὐκ ὄντα καὶ ὄντα.

135 Pseudo-Dionysius, *MT*, 1000C–1001A: Καὶ γὰρ οὐχ ἁπλῶς ὁ θεῖος Μωϋσῆς ἀποκαθαρθῆναι πρῶτον αὐτὸς κελεύεται καὶ αὖθις τῶν μὴ τοιούτων ἀφορισθῆναι καὶ μετὰ πᾶσαν ἀποκάθαρσιν ἀκούει τῶν πολυφώνων σαλπίγγων καὶ ὁρᾷ φῶτα πολλὰ καθαρὰς ἀπαστράπτοντα καὶ πολυχύτους ἀκτῖνας· εἶτα τῶν πολλῶν ἀφορίζεται καὶ μετὰ τῶν ἐκκρίτων ἱερέων ἐπὶ τὴν ἀκρότητα τῶν θείων ἀναβάσεων φθάνει … Καὶ τότε καὶ αὐτῶν ἀπολύεται τῶν ὁρωμένων καὶ τῶν ὁρώντων καὶ εἰς τὸν γνόφον τῆς ἀγνωσίας εἰσδύνει τὸν ὄντως μυστικόν …

136 Klitenic Wear and Dillon (2007), 119–20.

137 Lossky (1985), 31–43; Alasdair Charles Coles, 'The treatment of matter and divinisation language in the ecclesiastical hierarchy of Pseudo-Dionysius and his sources,

Leading up to this final stage of mystical union, the Pseudo-Dionysian spiritual path is essentially a path to knowledge that progresses from the level of rational discourse and with the help of perceptible images through the hierarchy of being to the contemplation of the divine. Given the absolute unknowability of the divine essence, though, Pseudo-Dionysius suggests the use of negative symbols, of 'dissimilar similarities', because they are more likely to inspire 'anagogical catharsis', which is the search for the immaterial content beyond the perceptible surface of the material object.[138] In his *Mystical Theology*, Pseudo-Dionysius rejects the seemingly more appropriate affirmations discussed in the *Divine Names* in favour of dissimilar names. The danger of similar symbols is that they are easily mistaken to be like God. Negations are meant to partially overcome the inability of the human intellect to grasp the true essence of the divine.[139] Since God is the cause of all things, he is known through all things; he reveals himself in the plurality of perceptible and conceptual symbols, both in the form of affirmative and negative symbols.[140] In the end, however, the divine is distinct from all things because he is 'beyond privations, beyond every denial, beyond every assertion'.[141] This is why all affirmations and negations fall short of any similarity and thus need to be denied and transcended.

Compared to most pagan Neoplatonists, Pseudo-Dionysius clearly forges a new and more positive attitude towards the sensible world by insisting that even the lowest creatures reflect a spark of the divine light and can thus assist the initiation into the realm of the divine. He refutes the connection between matter and evil, because even matter has some kind of being and 'must derive from the Good, since every being owes its origin to the Good'.[142] In this, Pseudo-Dionysius is close to Proclus, who argued that matter proceeds ultimately from the One and is therefore 'to a degree good and infinite, as well as that which is most obscure and formless'.[143] In the Proclian notion of reality, all things are bound together through the anagogic system of symbolic manifestations, where all members of the chains of being have an affinity with the highest One.[144] Pseudo-Dionysius similarly reverts time and again to the language of light to describe how the divine reaches down the hierarchical ladder to the lowest forms of being.[145] Hence, 'material lights are images of

as a basis for evaluating his sacramental theology' (PhD, University of London, 2003), 15–17; Laird (2004), 180.

138 Pseudo-Dionysius, *CH*, 144C; Roques (1957).

139 Pseudo-Dionysius, *DN*, 981B.

140 Pseudo-Dionysius, *DN*, 872A.

141 Pseudo-Dionysius, *MT*, 1000B.

142 Pseudo-Dionysius, *DN*, 729A: Εἰ δέ πως ὄν, τὰ δὲ ὄντα πάντα ἐκ τἀγαθοῦ, καὶ αὐτὴ ἐκ τοῦ ἀγαθοῦ ἂν εἴη.

143 Proclus, *Commentary on the Timaeus*, 117A.

144 James A. Coulter, *The Literary Microcosm: Theories of Interpretation of the Later Neoplatonists* (Leiden: Brill, 1976), 54–7; Struck (2004), 233–4.

145 Pseudo-Dionysius, *DN*, 697C.

the outpouring of an immaterial gift of light', and it is for this reason that for Pseudo-Dionysius, light is the most befitting of the divine names.

The language and imagery of light in the *Corpus Areopagiticum* reveal an intrinsically epistemological dimension of the Pseudo-Dionysian spiritual ascent. Even more important still is the theme of divine darkness that is the final goal of this spiritual ascent. No less than in the Platonic tradition, the Christian ascent culminates in some sort of truth, which in Pseudo-Dionysius is the darkness or the 'being of God in all its hiddenness'.[146] This suggests a very different notion of truth to that of the Platonic ἀλήθεια. The etymology of ἀλήθεια (unhiddenness) indicates that truth in the classical Greek sense is something that no longer possesses something else (hiddenness).[147] 'God in all its hiddenness' seems to be the inverse to this interpretation of ἀλήθεια. Even though the Platonic idea of good is a rather abstract concept, it enables the recognition of the essence of truth. Plato's dialectic journey towards ἀλήθεια narrated in the *Analogy of the Cave* is one from confinement to freedom and from darkness to light and involves the intellect as well as episteme.[148] By contrast, Pseudo-Dionysius, like Plotinus and Gregory of Nyssa reverse the process into a kind of soul-searching, where discursive reasoning needs to be abandoned in favour of contemplation.[149] Truth now is accessed through creative contemplation of one's very own being through the abandonment of sense perception and reason. This process requires the mystical transformation of the subject that obliterates the distinction between subject and object. To see the One, 'contemplation must be the same as the contemplated, and Intellect the same as the intelligible; for, if not the same, there will not be truth'.[150] Withdrawn from all external distractions and with the help of theurgic rites, one will ascent and eventually get a glance of the true being and the source of all being, which in the case of Pseudo-Dionysius is divine light or divine darkness.

Aesthetics of Light – A Tentative Conclusion

Based on the philosophical equation of beauty, light, being and wisdom, it is possible to establish a metaphysical aesthetics of light that is exemplified in the sixth-century architectural structure and design of Hagia Sophia. The concept of light as one of the central divine names in the *Corpus Areopagiticum*

146 Pseudo-Dionysius, *CH*, 180C: ἐστι τὸ τοῦ θεοῦ κρύφιον.

147 The Greek term indicates absence or negation, when compared to the German word *Wahrheit* and the Latin expression *veritas* that are positive in connotation. Heidegger (1997).

148 Laird (2004), 28; Nightingale (2004), 102–3, 114.

149 Sheppard discusses the increasing importance of theurgy and the concept of mystical experience that later Neoplatonists like Proclus understood to be the end of philosophy. John Bussanich, 'Plotinus' metaphysics of the One', in *The Cambridge Companion to Plotinus*, ed. Lloyd P. Gerson (Cambridge: Cambridge University Press, 1996); Hadot (1993), 41, 52–5; Sheppard (1980), 152–5.

150 Plotinus, *Enneads*, V.3.5.22–5.

takes the place that beauty occupies in the *Phaedrus*, where Plato discusses beauty's aptitude to illuminate and how this affects the cognition of truth. For Plotinus, too, it is beauty or being that inspires the search for its origin and the cognitive development of the soul. At the same time, beauty results from the light of the good, forming part of the Plotinian metaphysics of light. Still, it is beauty that Plotinus is interested in even though he accredits light with significant aesthetic value on the level of sense perception.[151] The development of a metaphysical aesthetic of light evidently reaches a new level in the Pseudo-Dionysian treatises in that he equates light with beauty and being.[152] The *Corpus Areopagiticum* exhibits a vivid sense for divine beauty that pervades the entire universe:[153]

> For beauty is the cause of harmony, of sympathy, of community. Beauty unites all things and is the source of all things. It is the great creating cause which bestirs the world and holds all things in existence by the longing inside them to have beauty. And there it is ahead of all as Goal, as the Beloved, as the Cause toward which all things move, since it is the longing for beauty which actually brings them into being. It is a model to which they conform.[154]

There is only one beauty, according to Pseudo-Dionysius, and this is divine beauty that bestows beauty and being upon the sensible universe through emanation.[155] All creation is beautiful because it originates in divine beauty, no matter how imperfect it may appear. Much more so than Plato or Plotinus, Pseudo-Dionysius emphasises the equation of beauty and being, typical of biblical and patristic writings such as those of Gregory of Nyssa. Beauty itself is identified with the other divine paradigms, first and foremost with the good, light and wisdom. The aesthetics of light formulated in the *Corpus Areopagiticum* is grounded not only in the simple identification of light as

---

151 Puigarnau differentiated between an aesthetic of light, resulting from the observation of visible light, and a metaphysic of light, which is the rationalisation of intelligible light. Alfonso Puigarnau, *Estética Neoplatónica: La representación pictórica de la luz en la Antigüedad* (Barcelona: Publicaciones Promociones Universitarias, 1995), 38.

152 Eco discussed different theories in medieval aesthetics, amongst which he noted the mathematical conception of beauty, a certain psychology of vision and the aesthetic metaphysics of light. Umberto Eco, *Art and Beauty in the Middle Ages* (London and New Haven, CT: Yale University Press, 1986), 17–27.

153 It was claimed that the concept of beauty began to lose its aesthetic significance and was eventually completely replaced by the concept of the sublime. Panayotis A. Michelis, 'Neo-Platonic philosophy and Byzantine art', *The Journal of Aesthetics and Art Criticism* 11 (1952); Panayotis A. Michelis, *An Aesthetic Approach to Byzantine Art* (London: Batsford, 1955); Tatarkiewicz (1970), 31.

154 Pseudo-Dionysius, *DN*, 704A: καὶ διὰ τὸ καλὸν αἱ πάντων ἐφαρμογαὶ καὶ φιλίαι καὶ κοινωνίαι, καὶ τῷ καλῷ τὰ πάντα ἥνωται, καὶ ἀρχὴ πάντων τὸ καλὸν ὡς ποιητικὸν αἴτιον καὶ κινοῦν τὰ ὅλα καὶ συνέχον τῷ τῆς οἰκείας καλλονῆς ἔρωτι καὶ πέρας πάντων καὶ ἀγαπητὸν ὡς τελικὸν αἴτιον, τοῦ καλοῦ γὰρ ἕνεκα πάντα γίγνεται, καὶ παραδειγματικόν, ὅτι κατ' αὐτὸ πάντα ἀφορίζεται.

155 As a divine paradigm, it is distinct from, but of the same essence (*homousios*) as God. All divine names can thus be identified with the essence of being. Hence, the Good, Light, the Beautiful and Wisdom are all somehow identical and yet distinct from one another.

a divine symbol, but in this equation of the different divine names. Within the metaphysical framework of Pseudo-Dionysian thought, light is at once aesthetically pleasing through its connection with beauty and the creative force of being with a distinctly epistemological dimension.

In Plato's *Republic,* light, and especially the light of the sun, serves as an analogy to the idea of good, from which derived the metaphorical link between existence, beauty and light. Plotinus and Pseudo-Dionysius developed the connection between light and being further, conceiving of light as a divine activity (ἐνέργεια), more precisely as the creative force that brings about being in everything that is, and whereby all other divine qualities are concomitantly passed on to all of creation. While Plato deals with metaphors of light, Plotinus and Pseudo-Dionysius develop a metaphysical aesthetics of light that underlies the perception of light in late antiquity and the associations it evoked. A fundamental difference between Pseudo-Dionysius and the Platonic and Neoplatonic tradition is the concept of divine darkness. Pseudo-Dionysius, no less than Gregory of Nyssa, dissolved the rigid polarity of light and darkness. Since everything that exists existed prior in God, the deity unites all contraries within himself. For this reason, the divine cannot be categorised by one thing and not by its negation. It follows that God is simultaneously absolute light and complete darkness. God is above all *Logos,* a term that is meant to convey the divine simplicity. 'Logos is simpler than any simplicity and, in its utter transcendence, is independent of everything … it is simple total truth'.[156]

How can these principles of contradictions and simplicity be translated into the perceptible world of plenty? It certainly does not allow for the conclusion that a church building, be it Gothic or Byzantine, planned according to the Pseudo-Dionysian system of thought, has to be suffused with light.[157] Neither would the edifice need to be a dark cave.[158] Instead, an ecclesiastical interior that reflects a similar pattern of thought and perception of light and beauty as the

156 Pseudo-Dionysius, *DN*, 872C: ὅτι πάσης ἁπλότητος ὁ θεῖος ὑπερήπλωται λόγος καὶ πάντων ἐστὶν ὑπὲρ πάντα κατὰ τὸ ὑπερούσιον ἀπολελυμένος.

157 Walter Haug, 'Gab es eine mittelalterliche Ästhetik aus platonischer Tradition?', in *Neuplatonismus und Ästhetik: Zur Transformationsgeschichte des Schönen*, ed. Verena Olejniczak Lobsien and Claudia Olk (Berlin and New York, NY: Walter de Gruyter, 2007); GA Andreades, *Die Sophienkathedrale von Konstantinopel* (Frankfurt: Frankfurter Verlags-Anstalt, 1931); Hubert Fänsen, 'Der "Lichtstil" in der mittelbyzantinischen Kreuzkuppelkirche', *Byzantinische Forschungen* 18 (1992); Heinz Kähler, *Die Hagia Sophia* (Berlin: Gebr. Mann, 1967); Konrad Onasch, *Lichthöhle und Sternenhaus: Licht und Materie im spätantik-christlichen und frühbyzantinischen Sakralbau* (Dresden and Basel: Verlag der Kunst, 1993); Lioba Theis, 'Lampen, Leuchten, Licht', in *Byzanz. Das Licht aus dem Osten. Kult und Alltag im byzantinischen Reich vom 4. bis 15. Jahrhundert. Katalog der Ausstellung im Erzbischöflichen Diözesanmuseum Paderborn*, ed. C. Stiegemann (Mainz: Verlag Philipp von Zabern, 2001); Wladimir R. Zaloziecky, *Die Sophienkirche in Konstantinopel und ihre Stellung in der Geschichte der abendländischen Architektur* (Studie di Antichita Cristiana 12) (Rome and Freiburg: Pontificio istituto di archeologia cristiana, 1936).

158 As suggested by Christoph Markschies, *Gibt es eine 'Theologie der gotischen Kathedrale'? Nochmals: Suger von Saint-Denis und Sankt Dionys vom Areopag* (Heidelberg: Universitätsverlag Carl Winter, 1995).

Corpus Areopagiticum would rather aim at an encompassing universal beauty that includes the opposing concepts of light and darkness and that reflects the quest for divine wisdom. Such a synthesis is indeed evident in the interior design and illumination of Hagia Sophia in Constantinople. Hagia Sophia is explicitly not a 'cave of cognition' in the Platonic sense, but a 'sanctuary of wisdom' with a distinctive Christian connotation as suggested by the anonymous inauguration hymn.[159] The wisdom of ancient philosophy (the wisdom of words)[160] had been replaced by the wisdom of the crucified Christ, the *Logos*, and incarnate light.[161]

Smooth reflective surfaces line the entire building, stretching from the highly polished marble revetments to the polychrome glass mosaic vaults.[162] The exterior walls of Hagia Sophia resemble screens of light rather than solid masonry and allow plenty of natural light to enter the building from all sides. The interior is thus unified through the agency of light, aided by filigree-like dark versus light patterns on a monumental (arcades and window transennae against walls of light) as well as on a minute scale (carved capitals and arcade spandrels). The artificial lighting aimed at a similar effect of an even non-directional illumination that is rich in contrast. Light and the play of shadows tie together the individual architectural spaces and elements, giving the interior of Hagia Sophia its own distinctive homogeneous character. The design of Hagia Sophia emphasises the richness and diversity of the created universe. The builders created a unified entity out of a multitude of individual components that are woven into a unique architectural space. It is this light-filled space as a whole that is the focus of attention more than any other architectural feature and that conveys the ineffable divine paradigms of beauty, the good and wisdom. Hagia Sophia is essentially an expression of the human quest for knowledge of an eternal truth amidst the perishable material reality of this world.

[159] Kontakion *oikos* 2; Trypanis (1968), translated in Palmer and Rodley (1988).

[160] I Corinthians 1:17–24.

[161] Zaga Gavrilović, 'Divine wisdom as part of Byzantine imperial ideology: Research into the artistic interpretations of the theme of medieval Serbia', *Zograf* 11 (1982); John Meyendorff, 'Wisdom – Sophia: Contrasting approaches to a complex theme', *DOP* 41 (1987).

[162] Piotrowski argued that the Pseudo-Dionysian notion of symbolic reality is much more explicit in post-iconoclastic church architecture such as Hosios Loukas as compared to San Vitale. Andrzej Piotrowski, 'Architecture and the Iconoclastic controversy', in *Medieval Practices of Space*, ed. Barbara A. Hanawalt and Michal Kobialka (Minneapolis, MN: University of Minnesota Press, 2000).

6

The Function of Art in the Sixth Century

The sacred interior of Hagia Sophia was seen as a symbol of divine light and beauty reflective of Pseudo-Dionysius' system of thought. Even though Pseudo-Dionysius was not concerned with artistic representations of the divine, his preoccupation with the basic question of how the invisible divine reality can be apprehended through the visible world makes the *Corpus Areopagiticum* an influential source for the theory and practice of art in the Byzantine Empire, particularly in the context of, and in response to, the iconoclastic controversy.[1] Pseudo-Dionysius' positive assessment of material objects and their use to initiate the ascent of the soul was not an *ex novo* development, but belongs to the theurgic tradition of earlier Neoplatonists such as Iamblichus and Proclus. Specifically, Proclus' metaphysics and ontology is an essential precursor. Proclus' continuous chain of σύμβολα / σύνθεματα that bind together the created universe and bridge the gap between the intelligible and the sensible realm, present an important step towards a more positive re-evaluation of the material world. This implies that works of art can potentially form an important link within these chains, too. The famous Zeus statue of Phidias, for example, was interpreted by Plotinus and Proclus alike as being divinely illuminated, reflecting qualities beyond the perceptible that had been mediated through the creative act of the sculptor.[2]

The model of artistic production as analogue to divine creation through the agency of the human mind, and the role of the artist analogous to the

---

1 Averil Cameron, 'The language of images: The rise of icons and Christian representation', in *The Church and the Arts: Papers Read at the 1990 Summer Meeting and the 1991 Winter Meeting of the Ecclesiastical History Society*, ed. Diana Wood (Oxford: Blackwell Publishers, 1992), especially 24–8; Filip Ivanovic, *Dionysius the Areopagite and the Iconoclastic Crisis* (Eugene, OR: Wipf and Stock, 2010), Chapter 4; Udo Reinhold Jeck, 'Philosophie der Kunst und Theorie des Schönen bei Ps.-Dionysios Areopagites', *Documenti e studi sulla tradizione filosofica medievale* 7 (1996), Andrzej Piotrowski, 'Architecture and the Iconoclastic Controversy', in *Medieval Practices of Space*, ed. Barbara A. Hanawalt and Michal Kobialka (Minneapolis, MN: University of Minnesota Press, 2000).

2 Plotinus, *Enneads*, V.8.1.39–40; Proclus, *Commentary on the Timaeus*, I, 265.18–26.

demiurge was an important Neoplatonic development, although it was based on the Platonic concept of participation (μέθεξις).[3] From the Neoplatonic perspective, works of art could offer insights into a higher reality, provided that the artist's mind was fixed on the conceptual and transcendent divine beauty. Similarly, Pseudo-Dionysius maintained that it was possible to reproduce 'an exact likeness of God (θεοειδέστατον ἴνδαλμα)' through the hierarchic principle and the persistent contemplation of divine beauty.[4] Works of art were therefore valued for their symbolic quality in the late antique sense of participation (μέθεξις), on account of which they could also instigate the process of reversion, from the visible to the invisible, from the sensible to the spiritual. The experience of beauty was accredited with a fundamental psychological and emotional effect that inspired not only aesthetic but above all, spiritual and epistemological progress. For Pseudo-Dionysius, it was 'the longing for beauty which actually brings them [everything] into being'.[5] This impelling force that guides man to the path of salvation is nothing else than divine love; it is the 'divine yearning for that immaterial reality which is beyond all reason and all intelligence … It is a hunger for an unending, conceptual, and true communion with the spotless and sublime light, of clear and splendid beauty'.[6] The ultimate object of this love is beauty, reminiscent of the Platonic and Plotinian ἔρος.[7]

Material splendour was meant to convey mystical ideas and present a possible path to God through an aesthetic experience. Hence, an anagogic function is intrinsic to beauty, and art had necessarily an aesthetic and moral value as well as an epistemological status.[8] Physical beauty in turn was closely associated with radiance and 'a certain living light (φῶς ζωτικὸν)' that shone through matter.[9] Light animated matter and thus turned matter

---

3 Aphrodite Alexandrakis, 'Neoplatonic influences on eastern iconography: A Greek-rooted tradition', in *Neoplatonism and Western Aesthetics*, ed. Aphrodite Alexandrakis and Nicholas J. Moutafakis (New York, NY: State University of New York Press, 2002); Moshe Barasch, *Icon: Studies in the History of an Idea* (London and New York, NY: New York University Press, 1992), 86.

4 Pseudo-Dionysius, *EH*, 473B-C; *CH*, 164D; Alexander Golitzin, 'Dionysius Areopagita: A Christian mysticism?', *Pro Ecclesia* 12, no. 2 (2003): 181–2.

5 Pseudo-Dionysius, *DN*, 704A: ἀγαπητὸν ὡς τελικὸν αἴτιον, τοῦ καλοῦ γὰρ ἕνεκα πάντα γίγνεται.

6 Pseudo-Dionysius, *CH*, 144A: ἔρωτα θεῖον αὐτὴν ἐννοῆσαι χρὴ τῆς ὑπὲρ λόγον καὶ νοῦν ἀϋλίας … τῆς πρὸς ἐκείνην τὴν καθαρὰν καὶ ἀκροτάτην διαύγειαν καὶ τὴν ἀφανῆ καὶ καλλοποιὸν εὐπρέπειαν αἰωνίας ὄντως καὶ νοητῆς κοινωνίας.

7 See, for example, Plotinus, *Enneads*, I.6.7.12–14; VI.7.15.1–3; VI.7.33.22–8; VI.9.4.16–18; Plato, *Symposium*, 210a–211d.

8 Alexandrakis (2002); Ivanovic (2010), 60; Carola Jäggi, 'Das kontrollierte Bild. Auseinandersetzungen um Bedeutung und Gebrauch von Bildern in der christlichen Frühzeit und im Mittelalter', in *Alles Buch, Studien der Erlanger Buchwissenschaft XXXIII*, ed. Ursula Rautenberg and Volker Titel (Erlangen-Nürnberg: Buchwissenschaft, 2009).

9 Marinus, a student of Proclus, described his master as exceedingly beautiful 'for not only did he possess the beauty of just proportions, but from his soul a certain living light (φῶς ζωτικὸν) bloomed upon his body, and shone so wondrously'. Quoted in Peter T. Struck, *Birth of the Symbol: Ancient Readers at the Limits of their Texts* (Princeton, NJ: Princeton University Press, 2004), 228.

into being. Within two or three generations of the *Corpus Areopagiticum*, the *kontakion* composed for the re-inauguration of Hagia Sophia in 562 CE celebrates the beauty and luminosity of the Great Church in language that is clearly evocative of the Neoplatonic and Pseudo-Dionysian notion of divine illumination as the cause and source of Hagia Sophia's beauty and epistemological dimension.

> This sacred church of Christ evidently outstrips in glory even the firmament above, for it does not offer a lamp of merely sensible light, but the shrine of it bears aloft the divine illumination of the Sun of Truth and it is splendidly illumined throughout by day and by night by the rays of the Word of the Spirit, through which the eyes of the mind are enlightened by him [who said] 'Let there be light!' God.[10]

This passage captures a vital aspect of the Byzantine aesthetic experience, one that was, as Gervase Mathew observed, not about 'beauty experienced only by the senses but Beauty apprehended through senses by Mind'.[11] The light of the *logos*, the Sun of Truth, is the source of Hagia Sophia's sensible beauty and of its epistemological and anagogic capacity. The edifice presents a gateway to the path that leads to an enlightened mind and eventually to God and true being. As such, the church of Hagia Sophia is one of those perceptible symbols that according to Pseudo-Dionysius fill the human hierarchy 'lifting us upward hierarchically until we are brought as far as we can be into unity of divinization'.[12] The spiritual ascent of Pseudo-Dionysius from material images and symbols 'toward the truth of the mind's vision' transcends knowledge and being itself through the creative force of the light from the good.[13] In the eye of the Byzantine beholder, Hagia Sophia's luminous beauty was reflective of this very transcendent divine light and, by extension, of the divine paradigms. Its sacred interior is thus located even higher up on the hierarchical ladder of perceptible images than the sun, for Hagia Sophia offers more than just sensible light as it 'outstrips in glory even the firmament'. This comparison recalls the primordial divine light on the first day of creation as opposed to the creation of the sun on the fourth day as well as the identification of Christ as the light of

10 Translated in Andrew Palmer and Lyn Rodley, 'The inauguration anthem of Hagia Sophia in Edessa: A new edition and translation with historical and architectural notes and a comparison with a contemporary Constantinopolitan kontakion', *BMGS* 12 (1988): 141. Oikos 6: καὶ αὐτὸ δὲ τὸ ἄνω στερεώμα ἡ σεπτὴ τοῦ χριστοῦ ἐκκλησία ἐμφανῶς ὑπερβάλλει ἐν δόξῃ. οὐ γὰρ διαίσθητὴν τοῦ φωτὸς λαμπηδόνα προϊσχεται, ἀλλὰ τὸν ἥλιον τῆς ἀληθείας θεϊκῶς λάμποντα φέρει ἄδυτον. καὶ τὸν λόγον τοῦ πνεύματος ταῖς ἀκτῖσι περιλάμπεται ἐν ἡμέρᾳ τε καὶ νυκτὶ εὐπρεπῶς, δι' ὧν τὰ ὄμματα καταυγάζει [τῆς] διανοίας ὁ εἰπῶν θεός. Γενηθήτω τὸ φῶς. Constantine A. Trypanis, 'Fourteen early Byzantine cantica', *Wiener Byzantinische Studien* 5 (1968): 143.

11 Gervase Mathew, *Byzantine Aesthetics* (London: J. Murray, 1963), 39.

12 Pseudo-Dionysius, *EH*, 373A-B: τὴν καθ' ἡμᾶς δὲ ὁρῶμεν ἀναλόγως ἡμῖν αὐτοῖς τῇ τῶν αἰσθητῶν συμβόλων ποικιλίᾳ πληθυνομένην, ὑφ' ὧν ἱεραρχικῶς ἐπὶ τὴν ἑνοειδῆ θέωσιν ἐν συμμετρίᾳ τῇ καθ' ἡμᾶς ἀναγόμεθα [θεόν τε καὶ θείαν ἀρετήν].

13 Pseudo-Dionysius, *DN*, 592D–593A.

God. Jesus himself proclaimed, 'I am the light of the world. Whoever follows me will never walk in darkness but will have the light of life'.[14]

In true Neoplatonic spirit, Pseudo-Dionysius assumed that there was a transcendent divine cause that was the model (παράδειγμα) for everything, including beauty that existed in the material world.[15] If aesthetic beauty depends on an archetypal and universal transcendental idea, then the central question must be how a work of art relates to that intelligible ideal. In addressing this issue, the status of art as a form of knowledge and truth in late antiquity can be re-assessed. Plato did not believe that a transcendental reality could ever be represented in perceptible form, or that an artist could ever have philosophical knowledge. In Plato's *Republic*, artistic representation (μίμησις) was defined as the production of likenesses (imitations) of sensible things, and as such they were inevitably thrice removed from the truth and reality of the forms that are the only things that really are.[16] From this follows Plato's generally critical attitude towards the mimetic arts in terms of their metaphysical status, because artistic representations were necessarily a medium of opinion and not of truth. What had since changed was that the Neoplatonists like Plotinus, Iamblichus and, above all, Proclus had developed the potentials of an allegorical interpretation of works of art.[17] This allowed for the symbolic representation of the intelligible world by indirect (artistic) means. To fully appreciate the aesthetic thought and the function of art in late antique Byzantium, the Platonic foundation on which it is based and from which it developed must be the point of departure.

Mimesis and the Symbol

One of the remarkable characteristics of Byzantine art is the shift in its representational mode, from the mimetic, rooted in the representation of the external material world, to the abstract and symbolic that is dependent on a

---

14 Genesis 1:3–4, 14–18; John 8:12; incidentally, the mosaic above the imperial door of Hagia Sophia, leading from the inner narthex into the church that is traditionally dated to the ninth century, depicts the enthroned figure of Christ presenting an open book with the inscription: εἰρήνη ὑμῖν. ἐγώ εἰμὶ τὸ φῶς τοῦ κόσμοῦ [Peace be with you. I am the Light of the World].

15 Pseudo-Dionysius, *DN*, 704A.

16 Plato, *Republic*, 597E, Myles F. Burnyeat, 'Culture and society in Plato's Republic', *The Tanner Lectures on Human Values* (1997): 29–6; Oiva Kuisma, *Art or Experience: A Study on Plotinus' Aesthetics*, Commentationes Humaniarum Litterarum (Helsinki: Societas Scientaiarum Fennica, 2003), 15–19; Stephen Halliwell, *The Aesthetics of Mimesis* (Princeton, NJ: Princeton University Press, 2002), 128–9; Eric D. Perl, *Theophany: The Neoplatonic Philosophy of Dionysius the Areopagite* (New York, NY: State University of New York Press, 2007), 5–7, 20–21, 83–4.

17 James A. Coulter, *The Literary Microcosm: Theories of Interpretation of the Later Neoplatonists* (Leiden: Brill, 1976), 32–41; Anne Sheppard, 'Studies on the 5th and 6th Essays of Proclus' Commentary on the Republic', *Hypomnemata: Untersuchungen zur Antike und zu ihrem Nachleben. Heft 61* (1980): 145–58.

transcendental reality and that tries to convey a hidden (divine) meaning.[18] The concept of mimesis is central to the understanding of art and its value within the Greco-Roman and Judeo-Christian cultures from Plato onwards.[19] The most elaborate treatment of mimesis in the visual arts occurs in Book Ten of the *Republic*, and it is commonly taken as proof of Plato's sustained and decisive condemnation of the arts.[20] Plato elaborates here on the tripartite ontological and epistemological hierarchy of (1) the forms or ideas made by God that belong in the realm of reality and truth, (2) material particulars made by humans that are copies of divine forms and (3) paintings (φαινομένα) made by imitators (μιμηταί).[21] This makes paintings by inclusive reckoning three times removed from truth. In contrast to the divine art of creation, mimetic art merely replicates appearances and can never grasp the essence of its model (idea). As regards its metaphysical status, mimetic art must therefore remain inferior to nature and is thus superfluous in epistemological terms. What is more, mimetic art is regarded by Plato as highly deceptive; it obscures truth, exploits basic emotional responses instead of appealing to reason, and is potentially dangerous inasmuch as it corrupts 'the mind of all listeners who do not possess as an antidote a knowledge of its real nature'.[22]

Plato's critique of the arts is grounded in the essential premise that art has the power to affect and shape the psyche of those exposed to it. It is exactly this psychological effect, however, that is the source for the pedagogical and anagogic potential of art developed in subsequent centuries.[23] Like Plato, Proclus was wary of the excessive emotional effect of tragedy and comedy, but in his commentary to the *Republic*, Proclus systematised the arts into a hierarchy of three types of poetry according to their metaphysical status and truth-value. The lowest category of poetry corresponds to the mimetic arts that are further

---

18 Jaś Elsner, *Art and the Roman Viewer: The Transformation of Art from the Pagan World to Christianity* (Cambridge and New York, NY: Cambridge University Press, 1995), Chapter 3; Michael Koortbojian, 'Mimesis or phantasia? Two representational modes in Roman commemorative art', *Classical Antiquity* 24 (2005); Mathew (1963), 38–47.

19 Mimetic art in the Platonic sense comprises a coherent group of artistic practices that are nowadays termed fine arts (i.e. poetry, music, visual arts and architecture) that can be differentiated from the wider category of techne of which art was merely a part. Christopher Janaway, *Images of Excellence: Plato's Critique of the Arts* (Oxford: Clarendon Press, 1995), 36–9; D. R. Grey, 'Art in the Republic', *Philosophy* 103 (1952); Halliwell (2002), 6–8; Joseph P. Maguire, 'The differentiation of art in Plato's aesthetics', *Harvard Studies in Classical Philology* 68 (1964).

20 Plato, *Republic*, 595c; Janaway (1995), Chapter 5; for an alternative view see Burnyeat (1997).

21 Plato, *Republic*, 596e-597e.

22 Plato, *Republic*, 595a-b, 598d-603b; λώβη ἔοικεν εἶναι πάντα τὰ τοιαῦτα τῆς τῶν ἀκουόντων διανοίας, ὅσοι μὴ ἔχουσι φάρμακον τὸ εἰδέναι αὐτὰ οἷα τυγχάνει ὄντα. Compare also 394d, 398a–b, 475d, 476b–c, 598d–603b.

23 There is no doubt that Plato bans mimetic art from his ideal state, while he advocates the pursuit of certain forms of mimesis that portray virtues and noble character, what is beautiful and graceful, noble, ideal or typical (what ought to be). See, for example, Plato, *Republic*, 377b, 378d–e, 391d–398a, 400e–401d, 604c–e; Burnyeat (1997), 217–22, 280–82; Grey (1952).

divided into eikastic and phantastic. Second in line comes didactic poetry, while the highest level of poetry is reserved for the inspired (ἐνθεαστικός) or symbolic kind that is able to mediate truth about the intelligible realities in allegorical form.[24] According to Proclus, these different types of art employed three different modes of representation. Inspired poetry uses symbols (συμβολα), didactic poetry employs *analogia* and likenesses (εἰκονες), while the lowest type of poetry, mimetic poetry, resorts to mimesis and εἴδωλα.[25] The difference is one of communication, whether the work of art exhibits its content clearly and directly (eiconic mimesis) or whether it hints at it secretly through a veil as it were (symbolic mimesis). To be sure, εἴδωλα refer to deceptive images with no relation to truth in line with his Platonic heritage. Proclus, however, was more interested in the highest form of poetry, and he clarified the workings of symbolism in context of the Homeric myths thus:

> For these symbols (i.e. the words and actions of Homeric myth) will clearly not resemble the divine substance. The myths, therefore, if they are not to fall short completely of the truth which is the divine beings, must somehow be made in the likeness of those realities the understanding of which they attempt to cover with the veil of visible reality.[26]

The image of symbolic mimesis no longer resembles its referent and is instead symbolically bound to it by the force of sympathy that connects the entire universe and that links the material with the spiritual world. Later on in his commentary to the *Republic*, Proclus explicitly states that 'symbols are not imitations (μιμητική)'.[27] Symbolic representation can thus make the divine accessible and convey metaphysical truths by way of ἀλληγορία that requires interpretation, because it hides what it hints at.[28] Symbolism may even represent things by their opposites and express 'the transcendent power of the models by those things most opposite to them and furthest removed from them'.[29] By pioneering the concept of artistic symbolism, Proclus redefined

---

[24] Proclus, *Commentary on the Republic*, I. 177.7–179.32; II, 107.14–108.16; Coulter (1976), 41–51; Sheppard (1980), 111, Chapter 5; Struck (2004), 241–2; Christos Terezis and Kalomoira Polychronopoulou, 'The sense of beauty (kallos) in Proclus the Neoplatonist', in *Neoplatonism and Western Aesthetics*, ed. Aphrodite Alexandrakis and Nicholas J. Moutafakis (New York, NY: State University of New York Press, 2002).

[25] Proclus, *Commentary on the Timaeus*, I. 30.11–18; cited and translated in Coulter (1976), 41, 140; Sheppard (1980), 200.

[26] Proclus, *Commentary on the Republic*, I. 73.11–16: οὐ γὰρ ἐοικότα φανεῖται τὰ σύμβολα ταῦτα ταῖς ὑπάρξεσι τῶν θεῶν. δεῖ δὲ ἄρα τοὺς μύθους, εἴπερ μὴ παντάπασιν ἀποπεπτωκότες ἔσονται τῆς ἐν τοῖς οὖσιν ἀληθείας ἀπεικάζεσθαί πως τοῖς πράγμασιν, ὧν ἀποκύπτειν τοῖς φαινομένοις παραπετάσμασιν τὴν θεωρίαν ἐπιχειροῦσιν. Cited and translated in Coulter (1976), 47, 135.

[27] Proclus, *Commentary on the Republic*, I. 198.14–15; cited and translated in Struck (2004), 239.

[28] Coulter (1976), 50–57; Sheppard (1980), 145–50, 197 ft. 97.

[29] Proclus, *Commentary on the Republic*, I. 77.22–24: τοῖς ἐναντιωτάτοις καὶ πλεῖστον ἀφεστηκόσιν τὴν ὑπέρχουσαν τῶν παραδειγμάτων ἀπομιμοῦνται δύναμιν. Sheppard (1980), 197; Struck (2004), 243–5. Sheppard argues for a clear distinction between analogia,

the metaphysical status of the mimetic arts, offering an innovative alternative to the Platonic mimesis, while this idea of opposite symbols clearly anticipates the Pseudo-Dionysian negative theology.

The Symbol and Anagoge

To understand how symbolic mimesis can function anagogically and why it was accredited with an epistemological dimension, we need to appreciate the role of symbolism within the Neoplatonic metaphysical and ontological system on which it was based. The idea that the human soul could potentially reach beyond the material to higher realities of truth is distinctly Neoplatonic and was the goal of philosophy since Plotinus, who was responsible for the most substantial and long-lasting modification of the notion of art as imitation.[30] Plotinus redefined the concept of mimesis as affinities between the different levels of his ontological hierarchy in analogy to the creative force of nature itself.[31] As such, mimesis pervaded all of creation and, by extension, reality. For Plotinus, the natural world itself is mimesis of the intelligible, and all embodied forms (the material universe) 'are already images (εἴδωλα) and imitations (μιμήματα)'.[32] Mimesis defines the likeness between comparable entities of different levels of being, for example, between human and divine logos (I.2.3.28), human and divine soul (II.1.5.8), soul and νοῦς (V.3.7.33) or between νοῦς and the One (II.9.2.3). In the *Enneads*, the language of mimesis recurs therefore primarily in the context of the hierarchy of being and the philosophical ascent towards a higher reality by way of assimilation (μίμησις) to an archetype.[33] Through mimesis, lower-order beings try to assimilate and ascend to higher levels of being and reality. The term mimesis refers to the process by which individual beings become more like their archetypes and thus approximate reality. This type of likeness is strictly non-reciprocal, meaning while the lower-level beings aspire to a likeness with their source, the higher orders of being never assimilate to anything lower.[34] The constant desire of every created being to return to its divine origin (first principle of being) is essential to Plotinus' worldview.[35] Mimesis is, for this reason, implicated in

where like is shown through like, and symbolism, where opposites are shown through opposites.

30 Stephen Halliwell, 'Aesthetics in antiquity', in *A Companion to Aesthetics*, ed. Stephen Davis *et al.* (New Malden, MA, Oxford: Wiley-Blackwell, 1992, 2nd edition, 2009); Paulina Remes, *Neoplatonism* (Stocksfield: Acumen Publishing Ltd, 2008).

31 Halliwell (2002), 313–23; Walter Haug, 'Gab es eine mittelalterliche Ästhetik aus platonischer Tradition?', in *Neuplatonismus und Ästhetik: Zur Transformationsgeschichte des Schönen*, ed. Verena Olejniczak Lobsien and Claudia Olk (Berlin and New York, NY: Walter de Gruyter, 2007).

32 Plotinus, *Enneads*, V.9.3.36–7.

33 Plotinus, *Enneads*, I.2.2.3, V.3.7.32, V.4.1.33, V.8.12.15; for a discussion of mimesis in the philosophy of Plotinus see, for example, Halliwell (2002), 313–23.

34 Plotinus, *Enneads*, I.2.2.41–0; Kuisma (2003), 48–51.

35 Remes (2008), 8–9.

the divine causation/creation, because creation and its reversal (participation) are inseparable. Artistic mimesis in turn is an imitation (μίμησις) of the divine creation and involves itself an original creative act.[36] It follows that mimetic art can potentially reach beyond the representation of the material world.[37]

In ontological terms, works of art necessarily rank lower than the models (παράδειγμα) after which they have been made. If material models are used and the work of art simply represents the visible forms and movements, it cannot have any particular cognitive function.[38] If, however, a work of art is modelled on the principles of nature in general, it could very well contribute to the process of noetic contemplation.[39] Plotinus ascribes some such potential to the art of music, architecture and carpentry, owing to their mathematical character, the principles of which belong to the intelligible world. Having said that, as soon as the mathematical paradigms are applied and made perceptible in architecture, carpentry or music they are no longer exclusively intelligible.[40] The difference is one between unity and multiplicity. The relative qualities of arrangement, order and proportion are characteristic of the multipartite nature of the material world, but they do not exist in the archetypal unity of the intelligible realm.[41] Since the pre-existing idea of the work of art in the artist's mind is essentially unified, it is considered more beautiful than the created artefact. Visual art may nonetheless still be expressive of the formative principle in the artist's soul by bypassing the obstacle of language and thus providing a more direct and intuitive access to the divine intellect.[42] For Plotinus, Egyptian hieroglyphs best exemplify this process, because they convey the intelligible reality through images (ἀγάλματα) instead of discursive language. In Egyptian hieroglyphs, 'every image is a kind of knowledge (ἐπιστήμη) and wisdom (σοφία) and is a subject of statements, all together in one, and not discourse (διανόησις) or deliberation (βούλευσις)'.[43] The strength of visual art is the simultaneity of perception, meaning it is perceived all at once in its entirety, in contrast to the temporal unfolding of language. Visual art is simply more unified than language and reasoning. This recalls Plotinus' view that '[pure] life is wisdom, wisdom not acquired by reasoning'.[44]

---

36 Plotinus, *Enneads*, IV.3.11.8–10; Anthony J. Close, 'Philosophical theories of art and nature in classical antiquity', *Journal of the History of Ideas* 32 (1971); Haug (2007).

37 André Grabar, 'Plotin et les origines de l'ésthétique médiévale', *Cahiers Archéologiques* 1 (1945); Halliwell (1992, 2nd edition, 2009), 20.

38 Plotinus, *Enneads*, V.9.11.1–6.

39 Plotinus, *Enneads*, V.9.11.7–10.

40 Plotinus, *Enneads*, V.9.11.10–17.

41 Plotinus, *Enneads*, I.2.1.42–5; I.6.3.6–9; he illustrates this point by means of a house and its intelligible model.

42 Jens Halfwassen, 'Schönheit und Bild im Neuplatonismus', in *Neuplatonismus und Ästhetik: Zur Transformationsgeschichte des Schönen*, ed. Verena Olejniczak Lobsien and Claudia Olk (Berlin and New York, NY: Walter de Gruyter, 2007).

43 Plotinus, *Enneads*, V.8.6.1–9.

44 Plotinus, *Enneads*, V.8.4.37: ἡ δὲ ζωὴ σοφία, σοφία δὲ οὐ πορισθεῖσα λογισοῖς.

In a way, Plotinus places works of art between the material, phenomenal world and the higher reality of the intellect, insofar as art represents things that are perceptible by the senses, while it also involves the idea in the artist's mind and possibly the intelligible principles of symmetry and order.[45] The ultimate experience is the 'recollection (ἀνάμνησις) of the truth' that follows upon the recognition that a work of art contains within it 'an imitation (μίμημα) on the level of the senses of something existing in νοῦς'.[46] This is not to say that the forms of the intellect can be imitated by sensible images or that the artist's idea can be translated one-to-one into a material object. To the question of how an intelligible idea can be made manifest or, in fact, how a work of art can be a μίμημα of the reality existing in νοῦς, the Neoplatonic answer would be through the symbolic relationship that permeates the Plotinian ontology. Within the Plotinian ontological system, everything is connected through a common source, which is the One, the efficient cause of all being and itself being beyond being (ἐπέκεινα ὄντος)[47] and beauty beyond beauty (κάλλος ὑπὲρ κάλλος).[48] The One is the principle from which everything derives its being as well as its beauty, and everything that is, is a sensible manifestation of the One.[49] What is crucial here is that the things of this world are beautiful because they participate in true beauty, and that material beauty, including works of art, are directly linked with the immaterial world of truth and reality.[50] The likeness between the material and the immaterial world is not one through imitation (mimesis in its narrow sense), but one through participation (μέθεξις). Material objects cannot represent intelligible ideas directly by imitation, but only indirectly by symbolism. By virtue of being an indirect representation, symbolic art can refer to virtually anything, including Platonic ideas, while still being grounded in the world of the senses. Good art is therefore always symbolic.[51]

With respect to artistic production, this means that the primary function of art is to redirect the attention of the viewer from the lower spheres of existence to the higher realm of reality and truth. In order to do so, works of art need to represent universal properties instead of individual features and to participate in form, because participating in form is what makes things

---

45 Halliwell (2002), 321–2; Remes (2008), 97–8; Wladyslaw Tatarkiewicz, *History of Aesthetics. Vol. I. Ancient Aesthetics*, ed. J. Harrell (The Hague and Paris: PWN-Polish Scientific Publisher, 1970), 321.

46 Plotinus, *Enneads*, II.9.16.44–7.

47 Plotinus, *Enneads*, V.5.6.11.

48 Plotinus, *Enneads*, VI.7.32.29.

49 Jean-Marc Narbonne, 'Action, contemplation and interiority in the thinking of beauty of Plotinus', in *Neoplatonism and Western Aesthetics*, ed. Aphrodite Alexandrakis and Nicholas J. Moutafakis (New York, NY: State University of New York Press, 2002); Perl (2007), 21–2.

50 Plotinus, *Enneads*, I.6.2.12–14; Audrey N. M. Rich, 'Plotinus and the theory of artistic imitation', *Mnemosyne* 13 (1960).

51 Bernard Bosanquet, *A History of Aesthetic* (London: George Allen & Unwin Ltd., 1892), 113–14; Kuisma (2003), 12, 24–31; Tatarkiewicz (1970), 321.

beautiful.[52] Beauty, according to Plotinus, is experienced on the level of the soul that acts as a mediator between the world of the senses and the realm of the intellect. Since they are of kindred nature, the soul recognises its own nature in the beauty of material things and becomes aware of the divine principle in which it participates. Material beauty thus initiates the ascent of the soul towards true beauty. By being purified and released from its material bonds through self-contemplation, the soul 'is raised to the levels of intellect [and] increases in beauty' and becomes more god-like.[53] In this sense, the return of the soul then was an inwardly directed contemplation, defined as a type of non-discursive experience of the intellect.

The intellectual contemplation advocated by Plotinus as a means to assimilate to the higher levels of reality was substituted by later Neoplatonists with the practice of theurgy and the ritual use of 'magic' symbols.[54] A succinct account of the theurgic use of material symbols is given by Iamblichus in the introduction to the Egyptian theology in his *De Mysteriis*:

> For these people, imitating the nature of the universe and the demiurgic power of the Gods, display certain signs of mystical, arcane and invisible intellections by means of symbols, just as nature copies the unseen principles in visible forms through some mode of symbolism, and the creative activity of the gods indicates the truth of the forms in visible signs.[55]

Mimesis here means the imitation of the demiurgic activity in a ritual practice that is called *theurgy* (god-work), creating visible symbols of the otherwise invisible principles that underlie the universe. Theurgic rituals formed an integral part of Iamblichus' Platonism and were supposed to assist the soul in its attempt to assimilate to the gods. The theurgic rituals served to overcome the rift between the soul's essence (οὐσία) and its activity (ἐνέργεια) that had been separated in the embodied soul. The ultimate purpose of theurgy was to unite the human ἐνέργεια with the ἐνέργεια of the gods and in so doing to initiate the soul's divinisation.[56] This idea of the divinisation of the human

52 Plotinus, *Enneads*, V.9.11.1–6.

53 Plotinus, *Enneads*, I.6.2.1–11, I.6.6.16–20: ψυχὴ οὖν ἀναχθεῖσα πρὸς νοῦν ἐπὶ τὸ μᾶλλόν ἐστι καλόν.

54 Remes (2008), 9–10; Sheppard (1980), 150; Anne Sheppard, 'Proclus' attitude to theurgy', *Classical Quarterly* 32 (1982): 220–21; Gregory Shaw, *Theurgy and the Soul: The Neoplatonism of Iamblichus* (University Park, PA: The Pennsylvania State University Press, 1995), 21–4, 162, 170.

55 Iamblichus, *De Mysteriis*, VII.1. 249,13–250, 7: οὗτοι γὰρ τὴν φύσιν τοῦ παντὸς καὶ τὴν δημιουργίαν τῶν θεῶν μιμούμενοι καὶ αὐτοὶ τῶν μυστικῶν καὶ ἀποκεκρυμμένων καὶ ἀφανῶν εἰκόνας τινὰς διὰ συμβόλων ἐκφαίνουσιν, ὥσπερ καὶ ἡ φύσις τοῖς ἐμφανέσιν εἴδεσι τοὺς ἀφανεῖς λόγους διὰ συμβόλων τρόπον τινὰ ἀπετυπώσατο, ἡ δὲ τῶν θεῶν δημιουργία τὴν ἀλήθειαν τῶν εἰδῶν διὰ τῶν φανερῶν εἰκόνων ὑπεγράψατο. Translated in 'Iamblichus, De Mysteriis', ed. E.C. Clarke, J.M. Dillon, and J.P. Hershbell (Atlanta, GA: Society of Biblical Literature, 2003), 291.

56 Martin Laird, *Gregory of Nyssa and the Grasp of Faith: Union, Knowledge, and Divine Presence* (Oxford Early Christian Studies) (Oxford: Oxford University Press, 2004), 9–11; Shaw (1995), 72–3.

soul rested upon the doctrine of the 'fallen soul'. According to this, the essence of the soul had completely descended in the body and could consequently not effect union with the divine of its own accord, for instance by mere contemplative introspection. Instead, the soul needed the help of the gods and relied on the theurgic activities, the works (ἔργα) of the gods.[57] Iamblichus leaves no doubt that 'it is not pure thought that unites theurgists to the gods ... for even when we are not engaged in intellection, the symbols (σύνθήματα) themselves, by themselves perform their appropriate work, and the ineffable power of the gods, to whom these symbols relate, itself recognises the proper images of itself, not through being aroused by our thought'.[58] In other words, intellectual contemplation alone is not sufficient, and the human soul needs sensible signs (symbols) that mediate the divine power and that actively help to divinise the soul.

The material basis of the process of divinisation required the physical world to be directly connected to the gods. For Iamblichus, material symbols (σύνθήματα, σύμβολα, σημεῖα) were indeed produced by the gods to serve simultaneously a cosmogonic and anagogic function.[59] The material world in its multiplicity was seen as a manifestation of the gods and their creative power, because the creative activity, the divine ἐνέργεια, revealed the divine οὐσία (essence).[60] The physical cosmos can therefore act as a guiding principle for the soul's return to the forms. The material symbols or images of the gods that Iamblichus invokes are things of nature, the stars and planets created by the gods, and not the artificial idols made by the image-makers (εἰδωλοποιός).[61] One of the most consistent symbols of the divine creation and theurgic divinisation of the soul was that of light and illumination. The creative act is described as one of illuminated matter, while the return and illumination of the soul 'might be called evoking the light (φωταγωγία)'.[62] The image of the sun that governed the whole world was accordingly granted a special status as symbol of the One itself in Iamblichus's system of thought.[63] The sun is no longer understood as only a conceptual analogue to the Good/One as in Plato's *Republic*, but it is now essentially and symbolically related to it.

---

57 Laird (2004), 9–11; Birger A. Pearson, 'Theurgic tendencies in Gnosticism and Iamblichus' conception of theurgy', in *Neoplatonism and Gnosticism*, ed. R. T. Wallis and Jay Bregman (Albany, NY: State University of New York Press, 1992), 255–63; Remes (2008), 115; Shaw (1995), 72–3, 85.

58 Iamblichus, *De Mysteriis*, II.11. 96, 13–97, 8: οὐδὲ γὰρ ἡ ἔννοια συνάπτει τοῖς θεοῖς τοὺς θεοουργούς ... καὶ γὰρ μὴ νοούντων ἡμῶν αὐτὰ τὰ σύνθήματα ἀφ' ἑυτῶν δρᾷ τὸ οἰκεῖον ἔργον, καὶ ἡ τῶν θεῶν, πρὸς οὓς ἀνήκει ταῦτα, ἄρρητος δύναμις αὐτὴ ἀφ' ἑυτῆς ἐπιγινώσκει τὰς οἰκείας εἰκόνας, ἀλλ' οὐ τῷ διεγείρεσθαι ὑπὸ τῆς ἡμετέρας νοήσεως. Translated in 'Iamblichus, De Mysteriis', 115.

59 Iamblichus, *De Mysteriis*, III.15. 135, 14–136, 6; Shaw (1995), 163–4.

60 Shaw (1995), 84, 219.

61 Iamblichus, *De Mysteriis*, III.28. 168–9.

62 Iamblichus, *De Mysteriis*, III.14. 132, 9–133, 5; V.23. 232, 14–16; translated in 'Iamblichus, De Mysteriis', 153–5.

63 Iamblichus, *De Mysteriis*, VII.2. 252, 8–11; translated in 'Iamblichus, De Mysteriis', 293. Shaw (1995), 173, 223–8.

An even more explicit statement about the relationship between symbols and their intelligible models is found in Proclus' *On the Hieratic Art*, where he explains that the individual levels of being are permanently bound together by the force of sympathy. Proclus postulated the divine henads (gods) that functioned as an extension of the supreme hypostasis, the One. Forming a continuous chain that binds all beings together and connected all beings to the One, the henads had a corresponding 'sympathetic' symbol (σύμβολα or σύνθήματα) in the material world.[64] These henads were partly transcendent and ineffable, and partly attainable and could be partaken of by entities of the lower ontological level, thus making a mystical union possible. Elemental to the connectedness of the different levels of Proclus' hierarchic universe is the idea that the higher levels of being generate or emanate all the lower substances by simple overflow, due to their superabundance and perfection. As a result of these continuous processions or emanations, all levels of being are ontologically linked and reflect the highest order of being, the One, in ever diminishing degrees.[65] Proclus explained this process in terms of light and illumination (ἔλλαμψις) from the transcendental light of the good that results in the soul's ascent through purification (κάθαρσις) and its subsequent likeness to the One.[66] As in Iamblichus, Proclus' reversion from the multiplicity of the material world to the singularity of the One needs the help of the divine light, because the soul is fully descended in the body and cannot save itself: 'for neither sense-perception, nor cognition based on opinion, nor pure reason, nor intellectual cognition of our type serves to connect the soul with those Forms, but only illumination from the intellectual gods renders us capable of joining ourselves to those intelligible and intellectual Forms'.[67] In Proclus' system, light acts as the unifying force, and light and the One are inseparably entwined. Participation in light is necessarily a participation in divinity, and illumination is identified with deification.[68]

---

64 Proclus, *On the Hieratic Art of the Greeks*, 148–9; Radek Chlup, *Proclus: An Introduction* (Cambridge: Cambridge University Press, 2012), 112–31; Eric R. Dodds, 'Theurgy and its relationship to Neoplatonism', *The Journal of Roman Studies* 37 (1947): 62; Pieter A. Meijer, 'Participation in Henads and Monads in Proclus' *Theologia Platonica* III, CHS. 1–6', in *On Proclus and his Influence in Medieval Philosophy*, ed. E.P. Bos and P.A. Meijer (Leiden, Cologne and New York, NY: Brill, 1992), 78; Remes (2008), 62, 70–74; Sheppard (1982), 220–21.

65 Lambertus M. de Rijk, 'Causation and participation in Proclus: The pivotal role of scope distinction in his methaphysics', in *On Proclus and His Influence in Medieval Philosophy*, ed. E. Bos and P.A. Meijer (Leiden, Cologne and New York, NY: Brill, 1992), 9–10; Remes (2008), 108; Christian Schäfer, 'μονή, πρόοδος und ἐπιστροφή in der Philosophie des Proklos und des Areopagiten Dionysius', in *Proklos Methode, Seelenlehre, Metaphysik: Akten der Konferenz in Jena am 18.-20. September 2003*, ed. Matthias Perkams and Rosa Maria Piccione (Leiden und Boston, MA: Brill, 2006), 356.

66 Werner Beierwaltes, *Proklos – Grundzüge seiner Metaphysik* (Frankfurt am Main: Vittorio Klostermann, 1965), 288–91.

67 Proclus, *Commentary on the Parmenides*, 949, 22–8; translated in Proclus, G.R. Morrow, and J.M. Dillon, *Proclus' Commentary on Plato's Parmenides* (Princeton, NJ: Princeton University Press, 1992), 300.

68 Proclus, *Théologie Platonicienne*, III 4, 16, 15 ff; Greek with French translation in Proclus, *Théologie Platonicienne, Livre III*, ed. Henri D. Saffrey and Leender G. Westerink (Paris: Les Belles Lettres, 1978), 16. Meijer (1992), 78.

There are different types and sources of light at the level of the henads, some more powerful than others and all having their own particularities.[69] However, the prototypical symbol of the transcendent light of the One in the physical world is the sun. Just as the sun illuminates and generates the things in the visible world, making everything sun-like (ἡλιοειδής), so, too, the good illuminates the things in the intelligible realm making them god-like through participation.[70] Evidently Proclus' view of the sun as a visible manifestation of the divine νοῦς is profoundly influenced by Plato's simile of the sun in the *Republic* (508a–509b), where Plato speaks of the sun primarily in terms of an analogy to the good that is not directly related. For Proclus, by contrast, the sun was a genuine symbol of the good that is immanent in and constitutive of the sun. The sun truly contains something of the divine radiance, which it reflects and communicates visibly to the material world. The connection is real. This is why in the Neoplatonic doctrines of Iamblichus and Proclus the light of the sun as the very real visible manifestation (symbol) of the first principle of being and its *energeia* enables the soul's ascent and contact with the supreme One.

It appears that Proclus endorsed much more than Iamblichus the Plotinian idea of inwardly directed contemplation that involves removing all bodily attachments and that leads to the ascent of the soul. The good, according to Proclus, is attained not by knowledge, but by surrender to the divine radiance, which in a way may be interpreted as self-contemplation that concentrates on the transcendent light reflected within each being. Proclus described this process as follows:

> If then, the divine is to be known at all, it remains only that it be graspable by the [corresponding] mode of existence of the soul … so that it is by the One [in us] that the most unitary realm is known, and by the ineffable element [in us], the ineffable. That is why Socrates in the Alcibiades was right to declare that it is by entering into itself that the soul can gain the vision not only of all other things but also of god; for it is through turning itself towards its own unity and the center of its whole life and shaking itself free of multiplicity and the variety of multifarious powers within it that the soul may raise itself to the highest 'vantage point' from which to view the whole of existence.[71]

The Proclean reversion of the soul is a progress from complexity to simplicity and from multiplicity to unity. The soul returns into itself and in so doing assimilates to the One that it will then be able to behold and to know. This is evidently reminiscent of the Plotinian mystical experience achieved by philosophical contemplation.[72] By the time of Proclus, however, the elevation

69 Proclus, *Commentary on the Parmenides*, 1044; Remes (2008), 73.
70 Beierwaltes (1965), 334–5.
71 Proclus, *Théologie Platonicienne*, I 3, 15, 15–24; translated in John M. Dillon and Lloyd P. Gerson, *Neoplatonic Philosophy: Introductory Readings* (Indianapolis, IA: Hackett Publishing Company, 2004), 290; Greek text with French translation in Proclus, *Théologie Platonicienne, Livre I*, ed. Henri D. Saffrey and Leender G. Westerink (Paris, 1968), 15.
72 Sheppard (1982), 224.

of the soul and its mystical union with the One had obtained a distinctly religious character, reflected in the increasing importance of theurgy and the use of magic symbols. The highest kind of cognition is attained only through mystical experience (μυστικὴ νόησις) and explicitly not through intellection.[73] Proclus specified that the cause of the ineffable initiation (μύησις) is faith 'for on the whole the initiation does not happen through intellection and judgment, but through the silence which is unifying and is superior to every cognitive activity'.[74] It seems then that faith has become a third, indispensable element in the reversion and anagogical ascent of the soul. Reaching the divine is now an epistemological, aesthetic as well as a religious endeavour that involves ritual practices and includes symbolic tokens.[75] This is how the highest form of art, divine symbols created by the inspired artist, can be directly related to Neoplatonic epistemology.

The Artist as Demiurge and the Highest Form of Art

Proclus grants works of art (specifically poetry) the capacity to convey the 'intellectual light of truth' and to initiate mystical union.[76] This quality derived ultimately from art's affinity with beauty through the mediation of the creative mind of the artist that is evident already in Plotinus' *Enneads*.[77] This idea of art as being able to express universal truths had come a long way from Plato for whom visual art by definition was always rooted in the world of the senses. Plato adamantly denied the possibility of the visual representation of the immaterial forms as these 'can be exhibited by reason (λόγος) only'.[78] Mimetic art was thus not grounded in knowledge nor could it embody any valuable insights or truths. For Plato, knowledge and truths were the exclusive prerogative of the philosopher, the lover of beauty (φιλόκαλος), whereas poets and other mimetic artists followed only in sixth place on the scale of knowledgeable souls.[79] The Neoplatonic inspired artist, in contrast,

---

73 Beierwaltes (1965), 313–29; Laird (2004), 11–12; Sheppard (1980), 149–50.

74 Proclus, *Théologie Platonicienne*, IV 9, 31, 10ff; quoted in Lucas Siorvanes, *Proclus: Neo-Platonic Philosophy and Science* (Edinburgh: Edinburgh University Press, 1996), 193; Greek text with French translation in Proclus, *Théologie Platonicienne, Livre IV*, ed. Henri D. Saffrey and Leender G. Westerink (Paris 1981), 31: οὐ γὰρ διὰ νοήσεως οὐδὲ διὰ κρίσεως ὅλως ἡ μύησις, ἀλλὰ διὰ τῆς ἑνιαίας καὶ πάσης γνωστικῆς ἐνεργείας κρείττονος σιγῆς.

75 Dodds (1947); Sheppard (1982).

76 Proclus, *Commentary on the Republic*, I.177.7–179.32; II, 107.14–108.16; Sheppard (1980), 171; Siorvanes (1996), 189; Terezis and Polychronopoulou (2002).

77 Halliwell (2002), 321–2; Kuisma (2003), 127–8; Gerhart B. Ladner, 'Bilderstreit und Kunst-Lehren der byzantinischen und abendländischen Theologie', *Zeitschrift für Kirchengeschichte* 50 (1931).

78 Plato, *The Statesman*, 285e–286a: λόγῳ μόνον ἄλλῳ δὲ οὐδενὶ σαφῶς δείκνυται; Burnyeat (1997).

79 Plato, *Phaedrus*, 248d–e; *Republic*, 476a–d; Whitney J. Oates, *Plato's View of Art* (New York, NY: Scribner, 1972), Chapter 4.

was fashioned after the Platonic demiurge in the *Timaeus*.[80] In the *Timaeus*, Plato sees the whole visible cosmos as a perfect image (εἰκών) of a unified intelligible model (παράδειγμα), for which the demiurge had fixed his gaze on the eternal that is 'apprehensible by reason and thought and is self-identical'.[81] The created cosmos is a perfect (τέλειος) living being (ζῷον), a true manifestation of the divine, characterised by oneness that neither lacks anything nor contains anything superfluous.[82] In short, the Platonic universe had been created so that it 'might be as similar as possible to the perfect and intelligible living creature for the purpose of representing its eternal nature'.[83] The Neoplatonic philosophers like Plotinus and Proclus grafted the concept of the inspired artists akin to the cosmic demiurge, who used intelligible paradigms as templates, producing works of art that convey deeper truths about the divine world in allegorical form. Analogous to the divine demiurge, the Neoplatonic inspired artist was capable of supra-rational cognition that enabled him to employ his metaphysical insights and embody them in works of art.[84]

In order to create the highest form of art, the artist needed to be metaphysically (divinely) inspired, which, in the Neoplatonic context, is naturally accomplished through the continuous chain of being that links the humblest to the highest divine being and that 'inspires' the return of every soul to its original source, the One. In response to a critic of art, Plotinus explained 'that the arts do not simply imitate what they see, but they run back up to the forming principles from which nature derives ... and since they possess beauty, they make up what is defective in things'.[85] By reaching beyond the outward appearances to the underlying principles (λόγοι) of nature, art could enhance and even improve on nature's imperfections and is consequently no further removed from reality than nature itself. According to this doctrine, an artist has access to knowledge of the formative principle and when engaging in creative activities, the artist imposes this conception of the form (εἶδος) onto matter, making it beautiful.[86] This is why a statue was considered more beautiful than a simple stone untouched by human creativity, but even more beautiful was the art (τέχνη) as it was in the mind of the artist.[87] The beauty

80 Coulter (1976), 30, 95–101; Gerhart B. Ladner, 'The concept of the image in the Greek Fathers and the Byzantine iconoclastic controversy', *DOP* 7 (1953); Sheppard (1980), 159; Struck (2004), 221–2.

81 Plato, *Timaeus*, 29a–b: οὕτω δὴ γεγενημένος πρὸς τὸ λόγῳ καὶ φρονήσει περιληπτὸν καὶ κατὰ ταὐτὰ ἔχον δεδημιούργηται.

82 Plato, *Timaeus*, 32b–34a.

83 Plato, *Timaeus*, 39d–e: ἵνα τόδε ὡς ὁμοιότατον ᾖ τῷ τελέῳ καὶ νοητῷ ζῴῳ πρὸς τὴν τῆς διαιωνίας μίμησιν φύσεως. Translation adapted from Coulter (1976), 97.

84 Coulter (1976), 98; Sheppard (1980), 172–4; Struck (2004), 243–5.

85 Plotinus, *Enneads*, V.8.1.35–8: ἔπειτα δεῖ εἰδέναι, ὡς οὐχ ἁπλῶς τὸ ὁρώμενον μιμοῦνται, ἀλλ' ἀνατρέχουσιν ἐπὶ τοὺς λόγους, ἐξ ὧν ἡ φύσις εἶτα καὶ ὅτι πολλὰ παρ αὑτῶν ποιοῦσι καὶ προστιθέασι δέ, ὅτῳ τι ἐλλείπει, ὡς ἔχουσαι τὸ κάλλος.

86 Plotinus, *Enneads*, V.8.1.10–18.

87 Plotinus, *Enneads*, V.8.1.18–26.

of a work of art was found in the pattern that the artist imposes onto the material. This pattern exists independently of its embodied form in the mind of the artist, where it is purer and more unified than when it is translated into a material object and therefore diffused and weakened. Plotinus' notion of representational art seems decidedly more positive than Plato's, and yet his comment that the unrealised conception of the art is more beautiful than the empirical work of art is an indication of his ambivalent attitude toward the material world. Plotinus argues in favour of an introspective contemplation of the form contained within the artist's mind instead of weakening its beauty by corrupting it with matter.[88]

If artistic mimesis is understood as simulation of the demiurgic act, the model of the mimetic arts must then be the cosmos itself. Olympiodorus (500–570 CE), head of the Alexandrian school in the sixth century, commented on the parallel between literature and the cosmos:

> A literary composition must resemble a living thing. Consequently, the best constructed composition must resemble the noblest of living things. And the noblest living thing is the cosmos. Accordingly, just as the cosmos is a meadow full of all kinds of living things, so, too, literary composition must be full of characters of every description.[89]

Olympiodorus clearly argues that good literature should follow the pattern of the cosmos and resemble a living creature. The most distinguishing features of the cosmos were the quality of a 'living thing' and variety, as well as unity and perfection if Plato's *Timaeus* is factored in. Similar claims had previously been made with respect to the other arts and, in fact, the art of architecture.[90] The Neoplatonists explained the mechanism of achieving cosmic similarity by way of symbols that translated the intelligible structure of the cosmos into visible form. Iamblichus, for example, in the passage on the Egyptian mastery of symbols quoted above, contrasts the demiurgic creation through the making of εἰκόνες with the signification of a higher meaning through these εἰκόνες, acting as συμβόλα of a higher reality and higher truth.[91] If applied to artistic production, works of art need to be primarily symbolic and imitate the qualities of the cosmos, mirroring the structure of the world of intelligible realities in symbolic form and thus producing a kind of mystic union with the One. This is what the Neoplatonic τελεστικὴ in context of

---

[88] Close (1971); Susanne Stern-Gillet, 'Neoplatonist aesthetics', in *A Companion to Art Theory*, ed. Paul Smith and Carolyn Wilde (Oxford and New Malden, MA: Wiley-Blackwell, 2002).

[89] Olympiodorus, *Commentary on the First Alcibiades of Plato*, 56.14–18: δεῖ τὸν λόγον ἐοικέναι ζῴῳ καὶ τὸν οὖν ἄριστα κατεσκευασμένον λόγον δεῖ τῷ ἀρίστῳ τῶν ζῴων ἐοικέναι. ἄριστον δὲ ζῷον ὁ κόσμος. ὥσπερ οὖν οὗτος λειμών ἐστι ποικίλων ζῴων, οὕτω δεῖ καὶ τὸν λόγον εἶναι πλήρη παντοδαπῶν προσώπων. Translated in Coulter (1976), 95.

[90] Vitruvius, *On architecture*, IX. 1.2; Nadine Schibille, 'The profession of the architect in late antique Byzantium', *Byzantion* 79 (2009). For a discussion of Olympiodorus' statement and its implications, see Coulter (1976), 95–101.

[91] Iamblichus, *De Mysteriis*, VII.1. 249, 13–250, 7; Struck (2004), 220–21.

theurgic rites might refer to, namely the magical theurgic practices where the use of συμβόλα transformed the statues of gods into receptacles for the transcendent presence of the divine, thus awakening the divine statue and making the divine presence tangible.[92]

The telestic art of animated statues of pagan Neoplatonism found a Byzantine equivalent in the telestic (performative) icon that initiated the transformative power of animation and spiritual perfection.[93] A similar cosmic interpretation and performative nature can be ascribed also to the church Hagia Sophia as evident from Procopius' and Paul the Silentiary's descriptions. Both sixth-century ekphraseis, in fact, recognised in the polychrome sacred space meadows in full bloom, while the animation of the interior under changing light conditions conveyed the sense of a living being or a dwelling place. Not only was Justinian as the patron of the church said to be divinely inspired,[94] the architectural structure followed strict mathematical principles that themselves are 'eternal and unchanging' divine qualities.[95] By Neoplatonic reckoning, Hagia Sophia is a true microcosmic entity, imitating the divine cosmos, striving for unity among multiplicity and containing the paradox of the divine immanence and transcendence. The Great Church seems to correspond to Proclus' highest form of art in that it manifests the divine in material form. The very function of the symbol is to reconcile the divine paradox and to negate the division between the intelligible and the material world.[96] In other words, it is the very act of concealing the divine in a perceptible symbol that has the potential to reveal the divine for what it really is, for the Christian God is known only 'through unknowing'.[97] The sacred space of Hagia Sophia that expressed the principles of divine intelligence provided access to higher realities and directed the human mind to divine truths. The medium of communication is the sensible beauty of Hagia Sophia's splendour and luminosity as well as the mathematical (divine) principles of symmetry, harmony and order to which the architects gave a visible form.

Art and Symbolism in the Early Christian Tradition

Artistic mimesis in the Neoplatonic sense was considered the simulation of the universe, and similarity means the degree of perfection measured in terms of the assimilation to the divine reality. These concepts recur in the early

92 Sheppard (1980), 151–6; Pierre Boyancé, 'Théurgie et télestique néoplatoniciennes', *Revue de l'histoire des religions* 147 (1955).

93 Bissera V. Pentcheva, *The Sensual Icon: Space, Ritual, and the Senses in Byzantium* (University Park, PA: Pennsylvania State University Press, 2010), 2–3, Chapter 1.

94 Procopius, I. 1. 27–30.

95 Ptolemy, I.1; Nadine Schibille, 'Astronomical and optical principles in the architecture of Hagia Sophia in Constantinople', *Science in Context* 22 (2009).

96 Ivanovic (2010), 51; Perl (2007), 29–32.

97 Pseudo-Dionysius, *DN*, 872A; Barasch (1992), 158–81; Perl (2007), Chapter 7.

Christian tradition, in which imitation (μίμημα) and likeness (ὁμοίωσις) play an important role in Christological debates and the doctrine of Christ as the image of God.[98] Humans were likewise made in the image or likeness of God, just as Christ was the image of his father. As a result, issues about images, likenesses, similarities and symbols were concerned with God himself, his incarnation in Christ and with the relationships between God and Christ, and God and humans.[99] Gregory of Nyssa asserts that because man was made in the image (ὁμοίωμα) of God and had since fallen from grace due to original sin, man's principal task was to trace back his steps to become again similar to the divine through imitation (μίμησις).[100] Gregory's very definition of Christianity is that it 'is the imitation of the divine nature'.[101] It is an imitation by way of participation in the divine goodness, which practically means to aspire to God by living a just and virtuous life in imitation of Christ.[102] In Gregory's *De Vita Moysis*, the life of Moses is presented as the prototypical example for an ideal mimetic Christian life that results in the assimilation and elevation of the soul to the divine.[103]

Like Gregory, Pseudo-Dionysius uses the term mimesis and its cognates exclusively in the context of the emulation of the divine (θεόμιμησιας) and the anagogical ascent.[104] God himself is inimitable (ἀμίμητος) and the human attempt at assimilation to the divine is defined as inimitable imitation (ἀμίμητος μίμημα).[105] This seeming contradiction in terms conveys the essence of the concept of mimesis that is fundamental to Gregory as well as Pseudo-Dionysius and that reflects a distinct Plotinian spirit, namely that likeness between entities belonging to hierarchically different levels is non-reciprocal. The created universe is the differentiation of God's unity into multiplicity, which basically means that God is nothing else than all forms of being rolled into one, but no particular being can ever be like God. In other words, the similarity between God and his creation is one-sided and there is inevitably a limit to the likeness between man and God that can never be complete.[106] In the end, God is complete dissimilarity (ἀνόμοισις) inasmuch

98 Ladner (1953).

99 Genesis 1:26; Ladner (1953).

100 Lucas Francisco Mateo-Seco, 'Imitation', in *The Brill Dictionary of Gregory of Nyssa*, ed. Lucas Francisco Mateo-Seco and Giulio Maspero (Leiden and Boston, MA: Brill, 2010); Torstein Theodor Tollefsen, *Activity and Participation in Late Antique and Early Christian Thought* (Oxford: Oxford University Press, 2012), 161–3.

101 Gregory of Nyssa, *De professione Christiana*, GNO VIII/1 136.7-8; quoted in Mateo-Seco (2010), 502.

102 Following St. Paul's designation of himself as μιμητής Χριστοῦ. I Corinthians 11:1; Ephesians 5:1; Ladner (1953), 13; Tollefsen (2012), 162–3.

103 Thomas Böhm, *Theoria, Unendlichkeit, Aufstieg: Philosophische Implikationen zu De Vita Moysis von Gregor von Nyssa* (Leiden and New York, NY: Brill, 1996), 267–8; Elsner (1995), 110–111.

104 For example, Pseudo-Dionysius, *CH*, 164D, 165B, 168B, 240A; *DN*, 913C; *EH*, 400B; *Epistle VIII*, 1085: 'he imitated the goodness of God'.

105 See, for instance, Pseudo-Dionysius, *Epistle II*, 1068A–1069A.

106 Pseudo-Dionysius, *DN*, 913D.

as he surpasses everything and 'he transcends all imitation and all grasping, as well as all who are imitated or participate'.[107]

In order to solve the perennial problem of how the One can be both absolute transcendent unity and the immanent cause of the multiplicity of all being, Pseudo-Dionysius adopted a theory of symbols not unlike that of Iamblichus and Proclus.[108] Grounded in the pagan Neoplatonic doctrine of participation, the Pseudo-Dionysian symbol is directly connected with the symbolised on an epistemological as well as a physical level.[109] This implies that the symbolised is actually intrinsic to the symbol, and that the symbol and its divine cause are intimately related. Symbols are not merely signs, but they are genuine manifestations of the divine paradigms in visible form. Pseudo-Dionysius specifies that after having been initiated into the divine order and rites with the help of sacred symbols and teachings, 'we shall recognise the stamps of which these things are impressions and the invisible things of which they are images'.[110] These perceptible images of conceptual things are divine gifts through which God reveals himself deliberately and actively.[111] For Pseudo-Dionysius, the created universe is ultimately *theophany*, the manifestation (visions) of God in the form of images or symbols. These symbols are God-given stepping-stones, through which man may contemplate the divine mysteries and thus be guided to a higher, spiritual reality. At the same time, these material symbols are 'veils' behind which God hides his true essence in order to protect the human mind from the full divine force.[112] The Pseudo-Dionysian symbols are a concession to the limitations of the human mind; they are vehicles of divine truths, which man would otherwise not have the ability to comprehend. Only in symbolic form is God knowable to the human mind as the underlying principle of being.[113]

In line with the idea of the 'fallen soul', man always relies on divine assistance in the imitation of and assimilation to God. The mechanism of divine assistance is best exemplified in Gregory of Nyssa's account of the irresistible attraction that beauty exerts over everything, drawing the soul up to its cause like a rope.[114] Since like attracts like and because man is made in the image of God, the human soul is drawn to God in what Gregory calls

---

107 Pseudo-Dionysius, *Epistle II*, 1069A: καθ' ὅσον ὁ ἀμίμητος καὶ ἄσχετος ὑπερέχει τῶν μιμήσεων καὶ σχέσεων καὶ τῶν μιμουμένων καὶ μετεχόντων.

108 Ivanovic (2010), 50–52.

109 de Rijk (1992); Perl (2007), 101–4; Meijer (1992); Otto Semmelroth, 'Gottes überwesentliche Einheit: Zur Gotteslehre des Ps.-Dionysius Areopagita', *Scholastik* 25 (1950).

110 Pseudo-Dionysius, *EH*, 397C: τίνων εἰσὶ χαρακτήρων τὰ ἐκτυπώματα καὶ τίνων ἀφανῶν αἱ εἰκόνες.

111 Pseudo-Dionysius, *CH*, 124A.

112 Pseudo-Dionysius, *CH*, 121b–c; Barasch (1992), 173–4; Lambros Couloubaritsis, 'Le sens de la notion "démonstration" chez le Pseudo-Denys', *Byzantinische Zeitschrift* 75 (1982).

113 Perl (2007), 104.

114 Gregory of Nyssa, *De anima et resurrectione*, PG 46: 89A-B; Catherine P. Roth, 'Platonic and Pauline elements in the ascent of the soul in Gregory of Nyssa's dialogue on the soul and resurrection', *Vigiliae Christianae* 46 (1992): 24.

ἐπέκτασις, the perpetual reaching out for more.[115] This persistent desire to approximate as closely as possible the divine underlies the Pseudo-Dionysian definition of hierarchy as 'a sacred order, knowledge and activity assimilated so far as possible to the form of God and leading up in due proportion to the illumination given by God'.[116] The purpose of this hierarchy clearly is to become an image of God. By being uplifted to the imitation of God (θεόμιμητον) through the ranks of the hierarchy of being, all things in this world can become 'images of God … clear and spotless mirrors reflecting the glow of primordial light and indeed God himself'.[117] Material symbols and ritual practices are instrumental in inciting people to contemplate the divine that is hidden within.[118] Yet, Pseudo-Dionysius was very much aware of the dangers associated with sensible beauty and its capacity to stir basic human emotions. He rejected analogies such as 'pictures of flaming wheels whirling in the skies … or multi-coloured horses' because these do not visualise the divine intelligences in an appropriate manner.[119] Like Proclus, Pseudo-Dionysius maintained that the transcendent God could not be represented through any kind of simple imitation, because the divine is invisible (ἀόρατος), ineffable (ἄρρητος), nameless (ἀνώνυμος), ungraspable (ἀκατάληπτος) and inscrutable (ἀνεξιχνίαστος).[120] Similar symbols that appear to represent divine properties based on the affirmative mode of designation are far from being similar to God, because the similarity between any symbol and the divine can never be complete. Ideally, the perceptible symbols must be stripped of all attributes and seen 'in their naked purity' in order to grasp the divine essence behind the material surface.[121] Following in the footsteps of Proclus and Gregory of Nyssa, Pseudo-Dionysius advocates therefore the principles of negative theology and dissimilar symbols.[122] The dissimilar symbols are those that are the most humble and basic manifestations and that seem far removed from any resemblance, while the similar ones are those that seem to be closely related to the divine paradigms, because they appear superficially noble and/or beautiful.[123] The similar symbols bear the danger

115 Mateo-Seco (2010); Tollefsen (2012), 164–6.

116 Pseudo-Dionysius, *CH*, 164D: Ἔστι μὲν ἱεραρχία κατ' ἐμὲ τάξις ἱερὰ καὶ ἐπιστήμη καὶ ἐνέργεια πρὸς τὸ θεοειδὲς ὡς ἐφικτὸν ἀφομοιουμένη καὶ πρὸς τὰς ἐνδιδομένας αὐτῇ θεόθεν ἐλλάμψεις ἀναλόγως ἐπὶ τὸ θεομίμητον ἀναγομένη. Translated in Golitzin (2003), 181.

117 Pseudo-Dionysius, *CH*, 165A: ἀγάλματα θεῖα τελῶν ἔσοπτρα διειδέστατα καὶ ἀκηλίδωτα, δεκτικὰ τῆς ἀρχιφώτου καὶ θεαρχικῆς ἀκτῖνος; Ladner (1953), 12, ft. 66; Perl (2007), 29–34.

118 Pseudo-Dionysius, *CH*, 476A–476B.

119 Pseudo-Dionysius, *CH*, 137A: τροχούς τινας πυρώδεις ὑπὲρ τὸν οὐρανὸν φανταζώμεθα … καὶ ἵππους τινὰς πολυχρωμάτους.

120 Pseudo-Dionysius, *DN*, 865C.

121 Pseudo-Dionysius, *Epistle IX*, 1104B: Δεῖ δὲ καὶ ἀποδύντας αὐτὰ ἐφ' ἑαυτῶν γυμνὰ καὶ καθαρὰ γενόμενα ἰδεῖν.

122 Pseudo-Dionysius, *CH*, 141A.

123 Pseudo-Dionysius, *CH*, 140B–C.

of misleading people into thinking that the symbols are what they represent, resulting in idolatry, because they overlook that a symbol, by definition, is different from that which it symbolises.[124] Negations or dissimilar symbols are hence more likely to elevate the soul beyond appearances to the immaterial archetypes by pronouncing the difference between the divine and its material manifestations. These types of symbols fulfil their essential function of cathartic anagoge better than any similar symbols ever could:[125]

> Sometimes the mysterious tradition of the scriptures represents the sacred blessedness of the transcendent Deity under the form of 'word', 'mind', and 'being'. It shows thereby that rationality and wisdom are, necessarily, attributes of God … he may also be represented as light and hailed as life. Now these sacred shapes certainly show more reverence and seem vastly superior to the making of images drawn from the world. Yet they are actually no less defective than this latter, for the Deity is far beyond every manifestation of being and of life; no reference to light can characterise it; every reason or intelligence falls short of similarity to it.[126]

Although Pseudo-Dionysius concedes that names and symbols like being, wisdom and light are manifestations of the divine, none of them do justice to the divine transcendence that by its very nature is not any being or object of thought. This is why all symbols, the divine names and positive affirmations no less than any material being or negations, are infinitely dissimilar and thus inadequate to define the divine being. In spite of this inadequacy, Pseudo-Dionysius is quick to remark that 'there is nothing which lacks its own share of beauty' and that everything is beautiful/good for the simple reason that all things exist only by participating in the divine paradigms.[127] This means that all symbols, whether intelligible (divine names) or sensible (worm), are at once similar and dissimilar, they are at once manifestations of God (similar) and finite beings (dissimilar).

Based on their simultaneously similar and dissimilar nature, all symbols, including artistic images, have a dual function: symbols reveal and conceal that which they symbolise. It is through perceptible symbols that the divine is made accessible and knowable. At the same time, symbols can

---

[124] Gerhart B. Ladner, 'Medieval and modern understanding of symbolism: A comparison', *Speculum* 54 (1979).

[125] For an excellent discussion of the various aspects of Pseudo-Dionysian symbolism, see René Roques, 'Symbolsime et théologie négative chez le Pseudo-Denys', *Bulletin de l'Association Guillaume Budé* 4 (1957); Haug (2007).

[126] Pseudo-Dionysius, *CH*, 140C: Ἀμέλει καὶ τὴν σεβασμίαν τῆς ὑπερουσίου θεαρχίας μακαριότητα τῶν ἐκφαντορικῶν λογίων αἱ μυστικαὶ παραδόσεις ποτὲ μὲν ὡς λόγον καὶ νοῦν καὶ οὐσίαν ὑμνοῦσι, τὴν θεοπρεπῆ λογιότητα καὶ σοφίαν αὐτῆς δηλοῦσαι … καὶ ὡς φῶς αὐτὴν ἀναπλάττουσι καὶ ζωὴν ἀποκαλοῦσι, τῶν τοιούτων ἱερῶν ἀναπλασμάτων σεμνοτέρων μὲν ὄντων καὶ τῶν προσύλων μορφώσεων ὑπερκεῖσθαί πως δοκούντων, ἀποδεόντων δὲ καὶ οὕτω τῆς θεαρχικῆς πρὸς ἀλήθειαν ἐμφερείας (ἔστι γὰρ ὑπὲρ πᾶσαν οὐσίαν καὶ ζωήν, οὐδενὸς μὲν αὐτὴν φωτὸς χαρακτηρίζοντος παντὸς δὲ λόγου καὶ νοῦ τῆς ὁμοιότητος αὐτῆς ἀσυγκρίτως ἀπολειπομένων).

[127] Pseudo-Dionysius, *CH*, 141C: τὸ μηδὲ ἓν τῶν ὄντων εἶναι καθόλου τῆς τοῦ καλοῦ μετουσίας ἐστερημένον … Πάντα καλὰ λίαν.

never be identical with God himself; they are but a weak reflection of the divine essence hidden in matter.[128] This apparent paradox can be resolved when looking at Pseudo-Dionysius' reflections on divine light and divine darkness. Pseudo-Dionysius states in the *Mystical Theology*, 'I pray we could come to this darkness so far above light! If only we lacked sight and knowledge so as to see, so as to know, unseeing and unknowing, that which lies beyond all vision and knowledge'.[129] This statement suggests Gregory of Nyssa's legacy, who had extensively discussed the theme of divine darkness in a positive, theological sense.[130] Gregory's ascent of the soul follows a pattern from the darkness of sin into the discursive light of knowledge and culminates in the non-discursive divine darkness of unknowing.[131] The concept of divine darkness in Pseudo-Dionysius and Gregory is dependent on the ineffability of the divine being that escapes all human categories and therefore cannot be experienced or grasped. The divine being is *ipso facto* known only 'through unknowing', meaning that the only knowledge humans can have is not to know God.[132] Since knowledge is traditionally associated with vision for which light is essential, not knowing is equivalent with not seeing and, by extension darkness, for not being able to see is the same as to see darkness.

The mysticism of darkness endorsed first by Gregory of Nyssa and then by Pseudo-Dionysius ultimately implies that the divine essence is revealed by way of being concealed. Darkness is best concealed by the presence of light.[133] The presence of light imparts knowledge of a discursive sort by enabling the apprehension of the multiple manifestations (symbols) of the divine being, through which God is revealed. In so doing, symbols facilitate the contemplation and participation in the divine being.[134] These cognitive processes grasp only the perceptible differentiation of the divine manifestations and not the divine simplicity and unity. Before the divine truth and mystical union can be experienced, all sense perception and intellection need to be abolished.[135] Pseudo-Dionysius illustrated this taking

128 Perl discusses these aspects extensively in his recent book. Perl (2007), 104–9; Dimitrios N. Koutras, 'The beautiful according to Dionysius', in *Neoplatonism and Western Aesthetics*, ed. Aphrodite Alexandrakis and Nicholas J. Moutafakis (New York, NY: State University of New York Press, 2002).

129 Pseudo-Dionysius, *MT*, 1025A: Κατὰ τοῦτον ἡμεῖς γενέσθαι τὸν ὑπέρφωτον εὐχόμεθα γνόφον καὶ δι' ἀβλεψίας καὶ ἀγνωσίας ἰδεῖν καὶ γνῶναι τὸν ὑπὲρ θέαν καὶ γνῶσιν αὐτῷ τῷ μὴ ἰδεῖν μηδὲ γνῶναι.

130 Martin Laird, 'Gregory of Nyssa and the mysticism of darkness: A reconsideration', *The Journal of Religion* 79 (1999).

131 Laird (1999), 178–91.

132 Pseudo-Dionysius, *DN*, 872A; Laird argues that this unknowing of God corresponds to the notion of faith. Barasch (1992), 161–2; Laird (2004), 12; Perl (2007), 104.

133 Pseudo-Dionysius, *Epistle I*, 1065A; compare Gregory of Nyssa, *In Canticum* XI, GNO VI:322.9–12.

134 Pseudo-Dionysius, *DN*, 588C-D.

135 Pseudo-Dionysius, *Epistle I*, 1065A; compare Gregory of Nyssa, *In Canticum* XI, GNO VI:322.13–323.9.

away of visible form and knowable content by means of a simile taken from a sculptor's workshop. The process is compared to the carving of a statue, for which the sculptors 'remove every obstacle to the pure view of the hidden image, and simply by this act of clearing aside they show up the beauty which is hidden'.[136] Similarly, the goal of the anagogic ascent is not any object of sight or knowledge; rather, the stripping of all symbols and the cessation of all intellectual activities leaves nothing but formless simplicity and the darkness of unknowing.[137]

In essence, Pseudo-Dionysius' negative theology implies that the divine being is known through unknowing. This divine contradiction implies that there can only be symbolic (indirect) knowledge of God, never knowledge of the divine cause in its hiddenness as such. The duality of transcendence and immanence also encompasses the concept of symbolism, for symbols reveal what is hidden by concealing it, and make accessible what is inaccessible by veiling it.[138] Pseudo-Dionysius valued the material manifestations of the divine source (symbols) not for their own sake as objects, but for the meaning they convey. The sensible form of the symbol stands only at the very beginning of the anagogic ascent and leads at first intuitively to the higher realities.[139] Only if the human mind is fixed on the conceptual and transcendent beauty that is concealed in sacred rites or images can it 'reproduce within itself an imitation of loveliness (κάλλιστον μίμημα)'.[140] Through the persistent contemplation of the divine beauty, it becomes possible to reproduce 'an exact likeness of God'. Holy men thus gain access to what lies hidden behind the mask of the visible universe, and they are then no longer attracted by the superficial beauty of dissimilar things (material symbols).[141] In order to penetrate the protective garb of the symbol, one needs to be familiar with the spiritual realities of that culture. In Pseudo-Dionysian terms, this means that one needs to be initiated first and undergo the sacrament of baptism or illumination (φωτίσματος) that bestows the gift of sight (ἰδεῖν ἐδωρήσατό) upon the faithful who can then gradually ascend towards a greater understanding and vision of the divine light.[142]

In line with his Neoplatonic predecessors, the Pseudo-Dionysian ascent is seen as a type of illumination, a progression from the initial darkness of ignorance to the divine darkness of unknowing via the epistemological light of truth. Pseudo-Dionysius clearly adopted the renowned Neoplatonic analogy of God and light. Nonetheless, the ultimate symbol of the divine being is

136 Pseudo-Dionysius, *MT*, 1025B: ὥσπερ οἱ αὐτοφυὲς ἄγαλμα ποιοῦντες ἐξαιροῦντες πάντα τὰ ἐπιπροσθοῦντα τῇ καθαρᾷ τοῦ κρυφίου θέᾳ κωλύματα καὶ αὐτὸ ἐφ' ἑαυτοῦ τῇ ἀφαιρέσει μόνῃ τὸ ἀποκεκρυμμένον ἀναφαίνοντες κάλλος.

137 Pseudo-Dionysius, *DN*, 592B.

138 Perl (2007), 107; Jeck (1996); Couloubaritsis (1982).

139 Pseudo-Dionysius, *CH*, 137B; Koutras (2002).

140 Pseudo-Dionysius, *EH*, 473B.

141 Pseudo-Dionysius, *EH*, 473C-476B.

142 Pseudo-Dionysius, *EH*, 392A, 425A-B.

darkness, which Pseudo-Dionysius defines also as the 'unapproachable light (ἀπρόσιτον φῶς)' that is 'invisible because of a superabundant clarity'.[143] Discursive cognition as a means to approach the divine is of little importance for Pseudo-Dionysius. Divine wisdom is beyond human comprehension and is therefore futile to seek by way of reasoning. This is why the mystical union with the divine is ultimately a leap of faith into the divine darkness of unknowing, aided by material symbols through which Christian wisdom and truth are made accessible to the feeble human mind. The classical Greek concepts of truth and wisdom have been redefined in religious terms.[144] The ultimate goal of *anagoge* in the *Corpus Areopagiticum* is the plunge into the 'brilliant darkness of a hidden silence' as opposed to the Platonic place in the sun.[145] Darkness still represents unknowing (negation of vision and knowledge), but unlike Plato and Plotinus, Pseudo-Dionysius does not consider this in 'terms of deprivation but rather in terms of transcendence'.[146] Darkness is no longer a bad thing.

Pseudo-Dionysius abandons the hitherto existing dualism of light and dark, material and spiritual.[147] For him these are merely different attributes and appearances of the supreme divine cause. In the Judeo-Christian tradition, God is necessarily the sole creator, and everything derives directly from the divine source.[148] The difference between intelligible forms and visible instances is not one of substance but one of varying degrees of similarity. The essence of the divine remains the same because as God generates and enlightens being, he emanates the same divine light albeit in ever diminishing degrees of power.[149] The transcendent, archetypal form at the highest levels of intelligibility is nothing else than the visible material form of being. The latter simply reflects the divine being in a lesser, more differentiated way.[150] Along this line of reasoning, the physical light of the sun is a perceptible token of the outpouring divine light and the process of enlightenment, thus providing

143 Pseudo-Dionysius, *Epistle V*, 1073A: ἀοράτῳ γε ὄντι διὰ τὴν ὑπερέχουσαν φανότητα. Ysabel De Andia, 'Transfiguration et théologie négative chez Maxime le Confesseur et Denys l'Aréopagite', in *Denys L'Aréopagite et sa postérité en orient et en occident. Actes du Colloque International Paris, 21–24 septembre 1994*, ed. Ysabel de Andia (Paris: Institut d'études augustiniennes, 1997).

144 Cameron (1992); Zaga Gavrilovic, 'Divine wisdom as part of Byzantine imperial ideology: Research into the artistic interpretations of the theme of medieval Serbia', *Zograf* 11 (1982); John Meyendorff, 'Wisdom – Sophia: Contrasting approaches to a complex theme', *DOP* 41 (1987).

145 Pseudo-Dionysius, *MT*, 997A–B: ὑπέρφωτον τῆς κρυφιομύστου σιγῆς γνόφον.

146 Pseudo-Dionysius, *Epistle I*, 1065A: Ταῦτα ὑπεροχικῶς, ἀλλὰ μὴ κατὰ στέρησιν.

147 Roques (1957), 107.

148 Schäfer (2006), 356–7.

149 Pseudo-Dionysius, *DN*, 644A; this is reminiscent of Plotinus' theory of the One's emanation in analogy to the radiation of the sun, where he shows that the One emanates without undergoing any alterations. Plotinus, *Enneads*, IV.3.17, V.3.12; Perl (2007), 202–3.

150 Sarah Klitenic Wear and John Dillon, *Dionysius the Areopagite and the Neoplatonist Tradition – Despoiling the Hellenes* (Aldershot: Ashgate, 2007), 91.

symbolic guidance to understanding the underlying divine principles.[151] The ultimate purpose of symbols in the Pseudo-Dionysian sense is to enlighten the beholder with the wisdom of God and to provide a glimpse of the eternal unity and simplicity that is the divine. The image of darkness, on the other hand, represents the mystical religious experience of unknowing.[152] Absolute darkness and absolute light are basically interchangeable insofar as they both reveal the hiddenness of the divine truth; they 'fill the eyes of our mind with the unifying and unveiled light'.[153] Darkness and light can be used to describe the divine remoteness.

A Metaphysical Aesthetic of Light and the Church of Hagia Sophia

The theme of light is constantly present in the *Corpus Areopagiticum*. Light exemplifies the act of creation (causation) as well as the reversion of every being through the ontological hierarchy towards God. In the thought of Pseudo-Dionysius, light is explicitly identified with the supreme good and beauty and thus provides an ideal paradigm of God.[154] Light has a mimetic effect in the sense of simulating divine presence. Light literally lays bare the intelligible realm of the divine by making visible and unifying the multiplicity of the physical world. In this sense, light can be considered one of the most powerful symbols, because it reveals the hidden layers of the cosmos. The anagogic capacity of light had been widely recognised, and in the context of art, light was performative in that it animated inert matter and transcended it into a 'living creature' analogous to the cosmos.

This is why the abundance of light within the church of Hagia Sophia transcends the building into a space of symbolic significance that provides the architectural framework for the spiritual and epistemological ascent of the faithful. The philosophical and theological doctrines of late antique Neoplatonism offer a rationale for a symbolic interpretation of Hagia Sophia, whose sacred space suggested a spiritual reality beyond the realm of sense perception for the sixth-century beholder. The medium of representation that established the relationship between the architectural structure and the divine presence was, above all, the phenomenon of light that pervaded the building's interior. The psychological impact and anagogic function of the splendour and luminosity of Hagia Sophia was acknowledged in the sixth century by Paul the Silentiary and Procopius alike. For Paul the Silentiary,

151 Pseudo-Dionysius, *EH*, 397C–400B; Andrzej Piotrowski, 'Architecture and the Iconoclastic Controversy', in *Medieval Practices of Space*, ed. Barbara A. Hanawalt and Michal Kobialka (Minneapolis, MN: University of Minnesota Press, 2000).

152 Pseudo-Dionysius, *MT*, 1001A.

153 Pseudo-Dionysius, *EH*, 428C: καὶ τὰς νοερὰς ἡμῶν ὄψεις ἑνιαίου καὶ ἀπερικαλύπτου φωτὸς ἀποπλήρωσον.

154 Pseudo-Dionysius, *DN*, 700D–701A.

light was truly part of the architectural fabric of the Great Church,[155] while Procopius attributes an anagogical function to the edifice when he states that the viewer's mind is 'lifted up toward God and exalted'.[156] The imagery of light in the two ekphraseis concerns both physical light and the spiritual light of divine immanence. It is clear that Hagia Sophia's exceptional luminosity determines the aesthetic experience of the ecclesiastical space and parallels a mystical experience that prepares the way for the spiritual ascent of the soul. By employing the rhetorical technique of *ekphrasis*, the two descriptions of Hagia Sophia reach beyond the mere surface appearance and turn the building's materiality into an object of intellection. The authors thereby bring Hagia Sophia literally to life for what it is, reflecting the constitutive Neoplatonic principle that to be is to be intelligible.[157]

The building's aesthetic beauty was the starting point for the assimilation and elevation of the soul to the heavenly sphere, culminating ultimately in the mystical union with the divine. The nature of the aesthetic experience of Hagia Sophia is consistent with the Neoplatonic concept of beauty as well as the anagogical function of art. The profundity of the aesthetic experience of light through which the divine is made manifest is reflected in the sixth-century anonymous inauguration hymn. For the author of the kontakion, there is something intrinsically luminous about Hagia Sophia's sacred space that originates from within and that presents a distinctly non-verbal and non-figurative means of access to the divine reality. As such, it is consistent with Pseudo-Dionysius' negative theology, according to which the divine cannot be adequately represented in verbal or, in fact, visual terms. Light is the only visible medium that approximates the representation of the divine paradigms due to its own simplicity and unity. The light-filled self-contained sacred space enables a virtually unmediated ascent to God in that light is at once agent as well as the object of vision and the boundaries between seeing and seen are broken down. The seen (light and by extension divine light) is directly experienced without mediation, providing access onto the spiritual path to the divine reality.

In addition to the mystical vision of light, the edifice itself was simply beyond human understanding and represented the principles of divine wisdom that 'has once more built herself a house'.[158] Pseudo-Dionysius defines divine wisdom as that which 'knows all things by knowing itself'.[159]

---

155 Nicoletta Isar recognised in Paul's consistent emphasis on the movement of light and his use of the term χορός distinctly Platonic and Neoplatonic influences. Additionally, she argued that Paul's ekphrasis was a kind of mystical vision that described an edifice reflective of the Pseudo-Dionysian notion of divine wisdom. Nicoletta Isar, '"Xopos of light": Vision of the sacred in Paulus the Silentiary's poem Descriptio S. Sophia', *Byzantinische Forschungen* 28 (2004).

156 Procopius, I.1.61–2.

157 Perl (2007), Chapter 1.

158 Proverbs 9:1.

159 Pseudo-Dionysius, *DN*, 869B.

Reflected in this definition is the Neoplatonic method of an inward-turned contemplation of one's very own being and its identification with the creative cause of all being.[160] This turn towards the inside is manifest in the design of Hagia Sophia, whose exterior is left bare so as to draw the attention to the meaning that is the intellectual and spiritual content of the architectural structure. It is above all the theme of wisdom and divine enlightenment that are the programmatic principles of the Great Church and its mosaic decoration. The dominance of the cross epitomises the notion of divine wisdom in contrast to the limitations of the human intellect to grasp the idea of God. It is through the divine foolishness of the cross, exceeding the wisdom of man that the faithful are uplifted 'to the ineffable truth which is there before all reasoning'.[161] The sacred space of Hagia Sophia is thus a material manifestation of the divine assistance needed to overcome the human limitations, lifting the soul to salvation. It does so by communicating the principles of the divine intellect through a combination of an extraordinary profusion of light, an unprecedented architectural structure and an interior decoration of exceptional beauty and symbolic significance. There can be no doubt that the building's aesthetic experience was intimately entwined with the metaphysical notion of divine illumination in the Neoplatonic and more specifically the Pseudo-Dionysian sense.

As was discussed in the previous chapter, the sacred space of Hagia Sophia was defined by colour, light and simplicity as well as mathematical principles, satisfying the Neoplatonic criteria of transcendental beauty. As a work of art and beauty, the building is an inspired agent of divine truth and reality, not through logical reasoning and understanding, but through aesthetic experience and contemplation. The light-suffused interior of Hagia Sophia thus constitutes the two aesthetic categories of beauty and art prevalent in late antiquity. It signifies the image of the divine light whereby it fulfils its anagogic function, while it also has a purely sensuous (aesthetic) quality that can be identified with the Neoplatonic notion of intelligible beauty. Consistent with the Platonic and Neoplatonic philosophies, the beauty and function of art are ultimately inseparable. Hagia Sophia's beauty depends as much on its anagogic purpose as its function is grounded in visual (aesthetic) qualities.

Late antique Neoplatonism offers a system of thought that reconciles the divine transcendence and immanence and that provides the conceptual framework for the interpretation of the church of Hagia Sophia in Constantinople and the contemporary literary commentaries to the edifice. The metaphysical interpretation of light in the *Corpus Areopagiticum* in particular helps to explain the notion of light as a symbol for absolute divine

[160] Isar recognised this self-reflexivity and self-containment in the structure of Paul the Silentiary's poem. Isar (2004).

[161] Pseudo-Dionysius, *DN*, 865C: μωρίαν θεοῦ τὸ φαινόμενον ἐν αὐτῇ παράλογον καὶ ἄτοπον εἰς τὴν ἄῤῥητον καὶ πρὸ λόγου παντὸς ἀναγαγὼν ἀλήθειαν.

values. Light, for Pseudo-Dionysius, is the visual appearance (theophany) of God *par excellence*, representative of the divine 'procession and return' and therefore the essence of being. As a symbol, light is capable of revealing divine truth by hiding its true nature in visible form. This is, for Pseudo-Dionysius, the very function of the material world but applies equally to works of art. The physical phenomena of light and darkness exemplify the divine simplicity and inaccessibility, but light was simultaneously equated with the first principles of beauty, the good and wisdom. Like Gregory of Nyssa, Pseudo-Dionysius recognises the metaphysical significance of divine light, and both attributed an aesthetic, moral as well as epistemological function to physical light. Judging from the extant literary sources, the ecclesiastical interior of Hagia Sophia gave rise to an aesthetic experience that reflects a similar pattern of thought. It is thus possible to postulate an early Byzantine metaphysical aesthetics of light. In the intellectual world of late antiquity, aesthetic experiences (experiences of beauty) cannot be separated from the cognitive and spiritual dimensions of art and beauty. It is for this reason that the post-Enlightenment definition of a pure (disinterested) aesthetic judgment that is divorced from any other kind of concerns such as moral or cognitive virtues does not apply to the late antique Byzantine world.[162] The aesthetic judgment in late antiquity carried evaluative implications that are moral as much as they are aesthetic. In the sixth century, the church of Hagia Sophia was accordingly perceived as a work of sublime beauty, and its interior was an expression of the Pseudo-Dionysian concept of symbolism in terms of the soul's assimilation and elevation to the divine. Hagia Sophia is a symbol in the Neoplatonic sense *par excellence*; it is an unmediated revelation of the divine paradigms and thus served to overcome the inability of the human intellect to grasp the idea of God by bridging the contrast between God's transcendence and immanence.

[162] Henry E. Allison, *Kant's Theory of Taste* (Cambridge: Cambridge University Press, 2001), 85–97; Janaway (1995), 192–3.

7

Hagia Sophia – Embodiment of an Early Byzantine Aesthetic

This study set out to define the aesthetic data contained in the architecture and decoration of Hagia Sophia in Constantinople as well as the aesthetic responses to the ecclesiastical space expressed in sixth-century literary sources. The semantic quality of the architecture of Hagia Sophia, and particularly the mosaic decoration and choice of motifs and colours, substantiates an aesthetic and ideology of light that is closely linked with the divine essence and with religious values. Light acted as a visual unifier and in combination with the mosaics exhibited a metaphysical idea of divine illumination. Whereas the reflective marble and mosaic surfaces served as vehicles of light, light in turn was an agent of divine revelation and salvation by way of divine illumination in the Neoplatonic sense. The prevalence of the cross in the decoration of the church, signifying the transcendental light of divine wisdom, corroborates this interpretation. The sacred space of Hagia Sophia was clearly meant to provide an environment that inspired the contemplation of the divine paradigms and to guide the faithful towards a spiritual reality and truth. The result was a universal and encompassing aesthetic and spiritual experience that becomes fully comprehensible only to those familiar with the visual culture and theological discourses of late antique Byzantium.

The close examination of the aesthetic experience in relation to Hagia Sophia in sixth-century Byzantium essentially meant to attend to the ways in which the material world in general and works of art in particular were perceived at the time. Perception and by extension aesthetic experiences are decisively shaped by cultural conventions and habits.[1] This can be partly explained from a physiological point of view, because perception is a function of the brain and as such it is an active process conditioned by experience and the visual environment. This provides a biological basis for the diversity of

1 James I. Porter, *The Origins of Aesthetic Thought in Ancient Greece: Matter, Sensation, and Experience* (Cambridge: Cambridge University Press, 2010), 491.

visual culture and by implication for the aesthetics of a particular time and place. Visual art is as much a product of the visual brain as it is part of a specific cultural context. In other words, the visual culture and the perception of aesthetic data are both expressions of the brain that can disclose the semantics of sixth-century art. The Byzantine concept of colour and the use of specific colours in the interior decoration of Hagia Sophia demonstrated that physiological aspects of vision indeed played a central role in the design of the mosaic and marble surfaces. Not only does the interior decoration of Hagia Sophia exhibit a concern for colour contrasts and the clarity of vision, but the choice of colours also illustrates that the mosaics are full of meaning. The result is visually compelling, both in terms of symbolic signification as well as regards the apparent beauty of Hagia Sophia.[2] The symbolic and aesthetic dimensions became manifest in the contemporary responses to the edifice, the ekphrastic descriptions of Procopius and Paul the Silentiary as well as the *kontakion* composed for the re-inauguration of the Great Church in 562 CE. Philosophical explanations of the aesthetic and ideology of light can be derived from the Neoplatonic identification of beauty, light and wisdom as paradigms of God. The philosophical concepts rationalise the physical and spiritual properties of light and thus provide the intellectual context within which the sixth-century decoration of Hagia Sophia has to be seen.

Drawing upon the philosophical and theological debates about the concept of beauty and the functioning of the sensible world in relation to a spiritual and epistemological process has proved a valuable framework for the interpretation of works of art in late antiquity. In the Platonic / Neoplatonic tradition, both pagan and Christian, the phenomenon of light played an essential role as the first principle of beauty. As such light was seen as the formative power and form that generates truth and reality and was closely affiliated with the concept of cognition and divine wisdom. At the same time, light had also a distinctly aesthetic appeal, due to its simplicity and purity. The phenomenon of light was evidently seen as powerful on the material (aesthetic) level as it was a fundamentally epistemological agent. These sentiments are clearly expressed in the ekphrastic tradition of late antiquity that uses the vocabulary of light and brightness to convey the aesthetic appreciation as well as the sublime quality and deeper spiritual and epistemological meaning of ecclesiastical interiors.

Together, the contemporary literary and philosophical sources as well as the material reality of Hagia Sophia in Constantinople present a convincing body of evidence for a metaphysical aesthetic of light in early Byzantium. Judging from the abundance and distribution of natural and artificial light inside the edifice as well as the nature of the interior decoration, light was found to be as

[2] In a recent study, it was found that the judgment of beauty correlates with the stimulation of the reward centre of the human brain. Hideaki Kawabata and Semir Zeki, 'Neural correlates of beauty', *Journal of Neurophysiology* 91 (2004).

much an aesthetic element as it had functional properties. The aesthetic value attached to light can be associated with the religious and epistemological ascent that Gregory of Nyssa and Pseudo-Dionysius discussed in the language of beauty, light and knowledge. Within the ecclesiastical space of Hagia Sophia, light and wisdom were programmatic elements that underlay the building's design and became symbols of Christian beauty and truth. The building corresponds to what Proclus would have defined as the highest form of art that was divinely inspired and that initiated a spiritual and epistemological transformation. The Great Church is certainly an exceptional edifice in many respects, not least due to its dedication to Holy Wisdom, one of the principal divine paradigms. Wisdom (σοφία) had increasingly substituted for intellect in the Neoplatonic understanding of reality in accordance with the Trinitarian doctrine and the equation of wisdom with Christ-Logos (the wisdom of the cross).[3]

Comparison with other sixth-century ecclesiastical structures, mosaic decorations and literary sources has demonstrated that the metaphysical aesthetic of light embodied in the church of Hagia Sophia reflected wider aesthetic theories and was shared across regions and different artistic media. No doubt, Hagia Sophia epitomises the conceptual maturity of the metaphysical aesthetic of light, but elements of this aesthetic are evident in other early Byzantine works of art and architecture in varying degrees. Light always occupied a central place in the architectural design of early Christian church buildings. Different types of church buildings, both centralised and basilical structures, exhibit a conscious light management system that implicates an aesthetic appreciation of light. Unlike the treatment of light in Hagia Sophia, however, in most early Christian ecclesiastical structures light was typically directed and localised, and served to highlight individual spatial units instead of unifying the interior space. As far as can be established, this artistic use of light is seldom linked to an epistemological and theological dimension in Neoplatonic terms in the way it was in the church of Hagia Sophia in Constantinople.

For example, light and wisdom are fundamental themes in the monumental epigram of the church of Hagios Polyeuktos in Constantinople, but the message seems less theological and more political in nature, while the transcendental connotation is barely developed.[4] The theme of wisdom recurs exclusively in comparison with Solomon and serves as a tool of political propaganda that is reflective of the deep antagonism between the church's patron, the imperial heiress Anicia Juliana, and the emperor Justinian. Nonetheless, the interior of Hagios Polyeuktos is defined in terms familiar from the descriptions of

[3] Stephen Gersh, *From Iamblichus to Eriugena: An Investigation of the Prehistory and Evolution of the Pseudo-Dionysian Tradition* (Leiden: Brill, 1978), 261–3; John Meyendorff, 'Wisdom – Sophia: Contrasting approaches to a complex theme', *DOP* 41 (1987).

[4] Markus Osterrieder, 'Das Land der Heiligen Sophia: das Auftauchen des Sophia-Motivs in der Kultur der Ostslaven', *Wiener Slawistischer Almanach* 50 (2002): 8.

Hagia Sophia, focusing on the building's brightness and luxurious interior decoration that also contributed to the perceived luminosity of the sacred space. Parallels between Hagios Polyeuktos and Hagia Sophia have also been observed with respect to the spatial structure and varied interior decorative features. The sixth-century interior of Anicia Juliana's church can be envisaged as an opulent polychrome space, which included marble revetment, rich inlay panels and columns, primarily non-figurative mosaic decorations and an extraordinary variety of carved capitals and entablatures.[5] The effect of the precious materials seems to have been further enhanced by a profusion of natural (and presumably artificial) light that interacted with the multi-coloured, reflective and sculptured surfaces. Judging from the epigram and the decorations, the aesthetic experience of Hagios Polyeuktos must have been decisively shaped by light and its effects, similar to Hagia Sophia. However, light was not directly linked to the divine paradigms of wisdom. Light in the epigram of Hagios Polyeuktos had not acquired the intricate Neoplatonic connotations of divine transcendence and divine immanence. The epigram simply expresses a love of light; light and luminosity are the sources of the aesthetic beauty of the edifice, for it is light that makes the church a gracious splendour (χαρίτων αἴγλην).[6] In both material and literary terms, the church of Hagios Polyeuktos unequivocally bears witness to the early Byzantine aesthetic appreciation of colours and light. What is missing are the mystical ideas about divine illumination and enlightenment as conveyed in the writings of Gregory of Nyssa and Pseudo-Dionysius.

The mosaic programme in the monastic church of Saint Catherine at Sinai, by contrast, centres on the theme of divine illumination and revelation. The mosaic decoration formed the visual focus of the edifice, inevitably drawing everybody's attention to the apse in the east of the building. This emphasis along the longitudinal axis was further augmented by the set of two windows above the triumphal arch that form an integral part of the decorative scheme. The mosaics visualise very explicitly the Neoplatonic understanding of mimesis. The depiction of Moses' ascent of Mount Sinai as the supreme symbol of the spiritual journey illustrates the spiritual path and process of emulation of the divine. The spiritual ascent to the mystical union with God consists of different degrees of visual manifestations of divine light. In so doing, the architectural and decorative scheme of the monastic church offers a paradigm for the spiritual development of the faithful. The aim of

[5] R. Martin Harrison, *A Temple for Byzantium: The Discovery and Excavation of Anicia Juliana's Palace-Church in Istanbul* (London: Harvey Miller, 1989), 77–81; R. Martin Harrison, *Excavations at Saraçhane in Istanbul, Vol. 1: The Excavations, Structures, Architectural Decoration, Small Finds, Coins, Bones, And Molluscs*, vol. I (Princeton, NJ: Princeton University Press, 1986), Chapter 5.

[6] *AP* I.10.50; Mary Whitby, 'The St. Polyeuktos Epigram (*AP* 1.10): A literary perspective', in *Greek Literature in Late Antiquity: Dynamism, Didacticism, Classicism*, ed. Scott Fitzgerald Johnson (Aldershot: Ashgate, 2006), 163–4.

this ascent was the 'mysterious darkness of unknowing'[7] made visible in the Transfiguration of Christ in the apse. The aesthetic and spatial experience of Saint Catherine is fundamentally different to that of Hagia Sophia, where the emphasis is on the unity and homogeneity of the interior space, aiming at a simplification and clarification of its content. The mosaic programme of Saint Catherine as a whole presents a much more elaborate visual exegesis of divine illumination and enlightenment as developed in the patristic and mystic writings of Gregory of Nyssa and Pseudo-Dionysius that starts at the level of material symbols and ends in divine darkness.[8] In this, the purpose of the mosaics of Saint Catherine at Sinai is the same as that of the church of Hagia Sophia in Constantinople. By simply using different modes of visual language, both monuments sought to create a specific aesthetic experience related to divine illumination and the volatility of human knowledge in light of divine wisdom. If the church of Hagia Sophia as a whole corresponds to the highest of the three types of art as defined by Proclus, the mosaic decoration of Saint Catherine at Sinai may be compared to the second rank that is didactic art.[9] While Hagia Sophia, as was shown, is concerned with conveying truths about Christian metaphysics and the divine reality in allegorical form, the mosaics at Sinai expound their meaning in a more straightforward and direct way in line with Proclus' definition of didactic art.[10] The difference is not so much a difference in content, but simply a difference in the mode of representation.

The Great Church of the city of Edessa in Mesopotamia, also dedicated to *Holy Wisdom*, represents yet another Justinianic ecclesiastical foundation with a similar emphasis on the notion of divine wisdom and illumination, for which the writings of Gregory of Nyssa and Pseudo-Dionysius can supply the theoretical framework. The church celebrated in a Syriac inauguration anthem seems to have replaced an older church that had fallen victim to a disastrous flood in 525 CE.[11] Construction on the Justinianic edifice appears to have been completed only in the 540s or the 550s CE, even though Procopius claims that the emperor Justinian immediately set about to restore the edifice. This sixth-

[7] Pseudo-Dionysius, *MT*, 1000A.

[8] Andreopoulos has noted that particularly the mandorla in the Sinai Transfiguration indicates that the divine darkness differs from the luminous circles that were commonly used until the eleventh century. Andreas Andreopoulos, 'The mosaics of the transfiguration in St. Catherine's monastery on Mount Sinai: A discussion of its origins', *Byzantion* 72 (2002).

[9] Anne Sheppard, 'Studies on the 5th and 6th Essays of Proclus' Commentary on the Republic', *Hypomnemata: Untersuchungen zur Antike und zu ihrem Nachleben. Heft 61* (1980): 162–202.

[10] This parallel needs to be qualified, because as Sheppard discussed, Proclus' didactic art is in theory not representational in any way. Sheppard (1980), 182–7.

[11] Kathleen E. McVey, 'The domed church as microcosm: Literary roots of an architectural symbol', *DOP* 37 (1983); Andrew Palmer and Lyn Rodley, 'The inauguration anthem of Hagia Sophia in Edessa: A new edition and translation with historical and architectural notes and a comparison with a contemporary Constantinopolitan kontakion', *BMGS* 12 (1988); Andrew Palmer, 'Procopius and Edessa', *AT* 8 (2000).

century church was again destroyed before the later twelfth century CE.[12] The symbolic thought encapsulated in the Syriac poem that was probably composed as an inauguration anthem for the consecration of the Justinianic church provides an interesting parallel to Hagia Sophia in Constantinople and the sapiential element in the interpretation of both buildings. The Edessa hymn predates the Greek *kontakion* composed for the re-inauguration of Hagia Sophia in Constantinople by about a decade and shares some of its central ideas with the Constantinopolitan poem.[13] A comparison of the two illustrates the formulation of the concept of divine wisdom into the ultimate symbol of Christian truth and beauty, and testifies to the ubiquity of this understanding of light and wisdom within Byzantine culture.

The Syriac hymn (*sôgîthâ*) comprises 22 strophes, each beginning with consecutive letters of the Syriac alphabet. Following Palmer's division of 3–7-9–3,[14] the first and the last groups constitute an exact mirror image, while the second section offers a cosmological interpretation of the building, and the third locates the church within the context of the history of salvation.[15] The three introductory strophes anticipate the main themes of the poem, which is the church as the visible manifestation of God,[16] who is 'Aleph and Tau, the beginning and the end',[17] and whose mysteries are revealed through this very temple. This is summarised in the third (Gimel) and again in the twentieth (Resh) strophe:

> GIMEL: Openly represented in the temple are the mysteries of thy Being and thy Dispensation; he who gazes at it intensely is filled with wonder at the sight.
>
> RESH: Sublime are the mysteries of this temple, which represents heaven and earth, the most high Trinity and the Dispensation of our Redeemer.[18]

---

12 Procopius, II.7.6; for a discussion of the date, see McVey (1983); Palmer and Rodley (1988). For reconstructions of the architectural structure of the church see Schneider's or Grabar's proposals. Heinrich Goussen, 'Über eine 'sugitha' auf die Kathedrale von Edessa', *Le Muséon* 38 (1925); André Grabar, 'Le témoignage d'une hymne Syriaque sur l'architecture de la cathédrale d'Édesse au VIe siècle et sur la symbolique de l'édifice chrétien', *Cahiers Archéologiques* 2 (1947): 44–54; Palmer and Rodley (1988); Alfons M. Schneider, 'Die Kathedrale von Edessa', *Oriens Christianus* 3/14 (1941).

13 McVey (1983); Palmer and Rodley (1988).

14 McVey assumes a division into strophes 1–4, 5–9 and 20–22; Palmer suggests a partition into strophes 1–3, 4–10, 11–19 and 20–22. McVey (1983); Palmer and Rodley (1988).

15 Palmer and Rodley (1988), 130–31.

16 The first word that is an address to God is variously translated as 'Being itself' or 'existence' or 'essence'. Dupont-Sommer argued that it comes closest to the Greek οὐσία and should be translated as essence rather than being. André Dupont-Sommer, 'Une hymne Syriaque sur la cathédrale d'Édesse', *Cahiers Archéologiques* 2 (1947); Cyril Mango, *The Art of the Byzantine Empire 312–1453: Sources and Documents* (Toronto: University of Toronto Press, 1972, reprint 1986), 57; McVey (1983), 96; Palmer and Rodley (1988), 131.

17 In analogy to Revelation 22:13; Palmer and Rodley (1988), 134.

18 I follow the translation given in Palmer and Rodley (1988), 131.

These two strophes establish the fundamental concepts of the poem: firstly, the divine being is mysterious and essentially unknowable; secondly, the divine can be known through his dispensation or creation; finally, the church of Hagia Sophia in Edessa is an exceptional example of this dispensation and can thus guide man to salvation. By contemplating the sacred edifice, the viewer will be filled with wonder and led onto the ascending path that leads to the mystical union with God. Kathleen McVey has demonstrated that the Edessa hymn itself is an architectural *theoria*, a contemplation of the church building, and that this contemplation proceeds from the material reality of the church to a higher level of divine truth.[19] The point of departure is the materiality of the edifice and the state of wonder that initiate the pursuit of *theoria* and the ascent toward the divine.[20] This basic principle echoes the Neoplatonic functionalist interpretation of the material world as a stepping-stone on the path to divine reality and truth. This is why the church of Hagia Sophia can at once represent heaven and earth. The building is grounded in the material world but attests to the heavenly realm through its bare existence and its allegorical interpretation in terms of Neoplatonic metaphysics. The Syriac hymn conceives of the church of Hagia Sophia in Edessa as the ultimate symbol of the divine being.

The second set of strophes of the Edessa hymn (Daleth to Jod) relates the architectural structure to the cosmos. The poem dwells on the dome being 'stretched out like the sky ... with gilded tesserae, like the shining stars of the firmament' (He), the conches that are 'gleaming and broad' (Zein) or 'the luminosity of its [the marble's] polished whiteness [that] forms a kind of reservoir of sunlight' (Teth).[21] The *sôgîthâ* unmistakably exhibits here close conceptual parallels with the Greek *kontakion* as well as the two ekphraseis of Hagia Sophia in Constantinople. Both edifices are said to be exceedingly luminous and to compete in beauty and luminosity with heaven itself. At the same time, the two hymns vary in some fundamental points. The church in Edessa is compared to a repository of sunlight, simply referring to an abundance of natural light that illumines the interior and brings to life the marble and mosaic decoration. Hagia Sophia in Constantinople, in contrast, is said to generate the light within,[22] implying that it is not the light of the sun, but the transcendental divine light that brightens and lights up its sacred space.

The Syriac hymn only briefly associates the light of the sun with a transcendent divine quality, when it recognises the light shining through the three windows in the sanctuary as symbolic of the Trinity (Mem). This symbolic

19 McVey (1983).

20 Andrea Wilson Nightingale, *Spectacles of Truth in Classical Greek Philosophy: Theoria in its Cultural Context* (Cambridge and New York, NY: Cambridge University Press, 2004), 253–4.

21 Translated in Palmer and Rodley (1988), 131–2.

22 Procopius, I.1.30.

interpretation evokes the Neoplatonic idea of light spreading out from its source, while its essence always remains unchanged and undiminished.[23] Likewise, the light coming through the numerous windows on all sides of the edifice 'stand for the Apostles and our Lord, for the Prophets, the Martyrs and the Confessors' (Nun). This statement is reminiscent of the Greek *kontakion*, where prophets, apostles and teachers are called 'spiritual luminaries' that enlighten 'with the lightning of their doctrines ... those drifting about on the ocean of sin'.[24] Although the function of light in the Syriac hymn is mostly implicit, it nonetheless makes a connection between light and cognition and by extension the concept of divine wisdom. The designation of the 'Cross of Light' (Ain), for example, that is fixed on the bema platform forges a close link between the concepts of light and wisdom. Not only can the cross be interpreted as a symbol of divine wisdom, but the incarnate Christ too, is identified with the wisdom of God insofar as wisdom had been engendered at the beginning of time 'the first of his acts of long ago' and then 'was beside him, like a master worker'.[25] Because of this, Christ the Son came to be known as the wisdom of God and as the light of men that too was conceived at the beginning of time or more precisely on the first day of creation.[26] Hence, the *Cross of Light* in the Syriac poem is equivalent with the *Cross of Christ* or the *Cross of Wisdom*, unambiguously identifying Christ with light and wisdom. The correlation between light and wisdom is further substantiated in the poem's allusion to the five wise virgins of Matthew (25:11–3), who had been granted access to the wedding feast, while the five foolish virgins were refused entry and were left in the 'outer darkness' (Mt 22:13).[27] Accordingly, those worthy and wise may enter the sacred space of Hagia Sophia that is like the 'Wedding-Chamber of Light' (Pe). In short, although the Syriac inauguration anthem never mentions divine wisdom by name, the prevailing imagery of light and the parallels with the Greek *kontakion* support the conclusion that divine wisdom in the form of light is the undeclared central theme of the poem.[28]

The cosmic and mystical dimensions of the poem have previously been recognised to reflect the Pseudo-Dionysian pattern of thought.[29] Notwithstanding the affinities between the Syriac poem and the *Corpus Areopagiticum*, a direct dependence of the inauguration hymn on the Pseudo-

23 Pseudo-Dionysius, *DN*, 697D; Plotinus, *Enneads*, IV.3.17, V.3.12; Grabar (1947), 56.

24 Translated in Palmer and Rodley (1988), 132–3, 142; *Oikos* 9: νοητοὺς καθορῶμεν φωστῆρας ... δόγμασιν ἀπαστράπτοντας ... καταυγάζτοντας ... τοὺς εἰς πέλαγος πλανωμένου ἁμαρτίας.

25 Proverbs 8:22, 30; John 1:4; Jonathan Bardill, *Constantine, Divine Emperor of the Christian Golden Age* (Cambridge: Cambridge University Press, 2011), 328; Palmer and Rodley (1988), 136–7.

26 Gen 1:3–4, 14–18.

27 McVey (1983), 10; Palmer and Rodley (1988), 136.

28 Palmer has argued that wisdom played a central role for the interpretation of the Syriac poem as it does for the Greek kontakion, but his analysis does not do justice to the extent of the analogies of light and wisdom. Palmer and Rodley (1988).

29 Goussen (1925); Grabar (1947); McVey (1983); Schneider (1941).

Dionysian corpus cannot be established. Instead, it is more plausible that the common intellectual and artistic environment of early Byzantium that was decisively shaped by an age-old Neoplatonic philosophical tradition resulted in similarities of visual perception and of spiritual and emotional responses to works of art. It is not at all surprising to find the same ideas expressed in literary commentaries and philosophical writings that are more or less contemporary and that are all concerned with the divine mysteries and the divine creation, for which light has always played a vital role. Already in the Old Testament, the divine nature was defined as intrinsically luminous; God was the sun, the light and salvation, the lamp that lightens up the darkness.[30] The association of light with cognition and episteme is similarly deeply ingrained in the Greco-Roman world, as reflected not least in the philosophies of Plato and Plotinus. It is because the two inauguration hymns as well as Pseudo-Dionysius' writings are grounded in these two traditions that they exhibit a common aesthetic appreciation of light, while recognising light as a divine paradigm and analogous to divine wisdom.

The emphasis of the Greek *kontakion* and the Syriac *sôgîthâ* on the unknowability of the divine that escapes human comprehension, but that can ultimately be grasped from the multitude of its creation through the concept of symbolism reflects fundamental Neoplatonic ideas.[31] Following the Neoplatonic system of thought, the Syriac poem suggests that the divine is made accessible to the human mind through the mediation of the created world and in this specific case through the church of Hagia Sophia in Edessa. The poem claims that the church 'openly represented' the divine mysteries and that the sight of the sacred building filled the viewer with wonder and amazement, which according to the Neoplatonic belief leads to the mystical vision of the divine. On a subliminal level, the luminosity of the ecclesiastical space can therefore be understood as mediator in this spiritual ascent and symbolic of divine wisdom. It is hardly a coincidence that the two churches dedicated to Holy Wisdom centred on the human inability to grasp the divine essence and that both buildings visualised the paradox of divine immanence and transcendence by means of an abundance of light within. Light as an artistic medium represents best the divine qualities of unity and simplicity. According to the Book of Wisdom, wisdom 'is a reflection of eternal light, a spotless mirror of the working of God, and an image of his goodness'.[32] Seen in this way, the dedication to Holy Wisdom is evidently more than a simple epithet and indeed the programmatic concept that informed the design and aesthetic interpretation of both buildings.

This interpretation is certainly illustrated in the Greek *kontakion* that celebrates the re-inauguration of Hagia Sophia in Constantinople and that

30 Psalms 27:1, 84:11; 2 Samuel 22:29.
31 Palmer and Rodley (1988), 137.
32 *Wisdom of Solomon* 7:26.

openly articulates the complex symbolic implications of light specific to the context of the Great Church and its dedication to Holy Wisdom. Hagia Sophia is unmistakably defined as a 'sanctuary of wisdom' as opposed to a 'rude cave', a comment made possibly in reference to Plato's analogy of the cave.[33] By means of a profusion of light, the ecclesiastical space proclaimed divine wisdom that is said to surpass the wisdom of ancient Greece as well as the Wisdom of Solomon and the Old Testament. This fundamental message is further reinforced by the prominence of the cross in the decoration of Hagia Sophia in Constantinople, recalling Paul's letter to the Corinthians in which he announced the wisdom of the cross.[34] The literary and architectural evidence thus show that the abundance of light within the church of Hagia Sophia symbolised the divine immanence and pointed to a transcendental (divine) reality and truth. In the late antique understanding of the *symbolon* this means that the divine essence is intrinsic to the visible light within the sanctuary. The physical light turned the building into a visible manifestation of divine wisdom that in the words of the Book of Proverbs 'has once more built herself a house'.[35]

Animated through the agency of light, the architecture and decoration literally come to life and thus become more beautiful and more 'beingful' in the Neoplatonic sense. The two Justinianic churches named Hagia Sophia are true sanctuaries of wisdom, equivalent to the Platonic place in the sun that is the realm of the ideas, or the Neoplatonic intelligible universe, where everything is colour and light. The distinctly Christian component in the architecture of Hagia Sophia in Constantinople is the emphasis on the effects of light and dark contrasts and the deliberate distribution of colours in line with the Christian Neoplatonism of Gregory of Nyssa and Pseudo-Dionysius, who denied the dualism of light and darkness for the simple reason that God naturally combines all contraries within himself. While light may have been a symbol of absolute divine values such as beauty, the good and wisdom, darkness was considered suitable to express (symbolise) the divine transcendence and inaccessibility. This paradox is what the Transfiguration in the mosaic decoration of the monastic church of Saint Catherine at Sinai tries to communicate and what in Hagia Sophia in Constantinople is visualised by means of contrast-rich architectural and decorative patterns and the selective use and distribution of pure and luminous colours. Both churches conceptualise vividly the multiplicity of the divine creation and the antithesis (or, indeed, synthesis) of divine light and divine darkness.

Although the nature of the mosaic decoration of the church of San Vitale in Ravenna is consistent with these aesthetic concepts, it reflects a different aspect of the Pseudo-Dionysian corpus. The specific design and arrangement

33 *Oikos 2:* οὐδὲ γὰρ ἄξιον τὸν βασιλέα εὐτελὲς σπήλαιον ὑποδύεσθαι διὰ ταῦτο προφθάσωμεν τῆς Σοφίας τὸ ἁγίασμα ὡς βασίλεια ἐμφανῶς θεϊκὰ ...

34 I Corinthians 1:18–25.

35 Proverbs 9:1.

of the mosaics in San Vitale illustrate the Pseudo-Dionysian idea of the divine order of being (hierarchy) and the relationship between heaven and earth. Artistically this was realised through a trend towards abstraction and the selective use of colours in the apse mosaics and the enthroned figure of Christ. In the heavenly realm of the apse, the particularities of this world are dissolved, and stronger and more luminous colours prevail. Not the specific identification of the figures matters, but the hierarchical order of being through which humans can gain access to the divine reality. The purpose of the San Vitale mosaics was to proclaim the heavenly kingdom as a promise of salvation, and in so doing inspire the faithful to abide to the divine order of being and to aspire to assimilate to the divine. Additionally, everything in the presbytery and apse of San Vitale is colour and light and obtains a transcendental quality free of the darkness of matter. The church of San Vitale thus exemplifies the Neoplatonic notion of beauty both in terms of visual pleasure in colours and light (aesthetics) as well as the spiritual and cognitive function (anagoge) of art. By transcending the boundaries between the human and the divine, the sanctuary of San Vitale provides a portal to the heavenly realm.

The close examination of the aesthetic data available for a number of early Christian ecclesiastical structures has identified common patterns in the visuality and concepts of art and beauty in late antique Byzantium. Many of the aesthetic principles are manifest across different art forms and media (literary, artistic and philosophical). These different artistic categories emphatically assert that the divine is beyond human comprehension, and that because of this, the main function of the material world and works of art in particular is normative and didactic. As we have seen in the case of Hagia Sophia in Constantinople, these ideas are forcefully conveyed in the form of an architectural masterpiece, its overwhelming luminosity and the deliberately non-figurative interior decoration where colour, light and the symbol of the cross are prevalent. In this way, the church of Hagia Sophia perpetuated the concept of divine light and divine wisdom and propelled these two divine paradigms into the limelight of Byzantine religious consciousness and culture.[36] The Pseudo-Dionysian notion of the divine names and the equation of the concepts of divine wisdom, beauty, light and the good provide the conceptual framework for the building's semantic quality and its aesthetic appeal in early Byzantium. The sacred space of Hagia Sophia suffused with light represents a symbol in the late antique Neoplatonic sense that requires interpretation and that forms a direct link with the divine reality. The experience of beauty was considered as one of the most powerful and immediate perceptual sensations. As such, the 'marvellous beauty' of Hagia Sophia can give unmediated access to the divine and initiate the ascent through the principle of association. Seeing the material splendour and light

36 Meyendorff (1987).

of Hagia Sophia literally implies seeing divine light and divine wisdom in significantly diminished and thus accessible form.

Late antique debates about light typically distinguish between uncreated and created light, between the uncreated light of the first day and the physical light of the fourth day of creation. This distinction is made explicit in a lengthy Latin inscription in the narthex of the *Capella Arcivescovile* in Ravenna:

> Either light was born here, or captured here it reigns free; it is the first light [light before light?], from which the current glory of heaven comes. The roofs, deprived [of light], have produced gleaming day, and the enclosed radiance gleams forth as if from secluded Olympus. See the marble flourishes with bright rays, and all the stones struck in starry purple shine in value, the gifts of the founder Peter. To him honor and merit are granted, thus to beautify small things, so that although confined in space, they surpass the large. Nothing is small to Christ; He, whose temples exist within the human heart, well occupies confining buildings.[37]

Although it was built during Theoderic's reign, the chapel and its decoration exhibit typical Orthodox elements,[38] and the emphasis on light may be a reference to ideologies popular in the Byzantine capital at the time. The epigram gives a remarkably condensed exegesis of the theology and aesthetics of light. The epigram's first two lines are an unequivocal allusion to the uncreated light from which everything else derives its luminosity,[39]

---

[37] Translated in Deborah Mauskopf Deliyannis, *Ravenna in Late Antiquity* (New York: Cambridge University Press, 2010), 192; I amended her translation of the second line that reads in the Latin 'Lux est ante, venit caeli decus unde modernum'.

Aut lux hic nata est, aut capta hic libera regnat.
Lux est ante, venit caeli decus unde modernum,
Aut privata diem pepererunt tecta nitentem,
Inclusumque iubar secluso fulget Olimpo.
Marmora cum radiis vernantur, cerne, serenis
Cunctaque sidereo percussa in murice saxa.
Auctoris pretio splendescunt munera Petri.
Huic honor, huic meritum tribuit, sic comere parva,
Ut valeant spatiis anplum superare coactis.
Nil modicum Christo est. Artas bene possidet aedes,
Cuius in humano consistunt pectore templa.
(Fundamen Petrus, Petrus fundator et aula.
Quod domus, hoc dominus, quod factum, factor et idem,
Moribus atque opere. Christus possessor habetur,
Qui duo consocians mediator reddit et unum.
Huc veniens fundat parituros gaudia fletus,
Contritam solidans percusso in pectore mentem.
Ne iaceat, se sternat humo morbosque latentes
Ante pedes medici, cura properante, recludat.
Saepe metus mortis vitae fit causa beatae.)

Quoted in Gillian Mackie, *Early Christian Chapels in the West: Decoration, Function, and Patronage* (Toronto: University of Toronto Press, 2003), 295, note 9.

[38] Deliyannis (2010), 196.

[39] Compare, for instance, Gregory of Nyssa, *Hexaemeron*, GNO IV/1 65; *Contra Eunomium*, NPNF 144, 243; GNO II 180.1-12; Adolf Martin Ritter, 'Light', in *The Brill Dictionary of Gregory*

while the description of the marbles and stones is an expression of the late antique aesthetic taste for the effects of light interacting with colours and reflective surfaces. The small chapel is transformed into an animated sublime monument through the intercession of colour and light so as to become a dwelling place for Christ. The aesthetic of movement, light and variety (*poikilia*) recalls the notion of art in imitation of the cosmos. In the end, there is nothing unworthy of the divine, because as we have seen in the negative theologies of Pseudo-Dionysius, even the lowest and smallest thing has its share in the divine beauty and can thus be sublimated into something higher up in the ontological hierarchy.[40] The inscription of the chapel leaves the reader with an impression of magnitude, very much in contrast to the diminutive size of the actual architectural structure (about 6 m in total length). The desired effect is monumentality, which is not a matter of size, but more a matter of meaning and content. Aesthetically, it is the concept of contrast that is fundamental:[41] the smallness of the chapel is contrasted with the transcendent Christ, the light may be captured but still reigns free, and the roofs are deprived of light but nonetheless turn everything into a luminous splendour. The spectator is caught in the bewildering contradictions of the decorative riches of the chapel but above all in the contradictions that make up the nature of the divine. It is the contrast between the effects of physical light within the confined space of the chapel and the boundless divine light that has no beginning and no end.

The aesthetic appreciation of light in early Byzantium is evidenced across the entire range of art forms and material categories; it is the foundation in which literature, architecture, mosaic art and philosophy equally shared. This commonality is an expression of how the world around us was perceived and interpreted in late antiquity. As Franses demonstrated, Byzantine vision could easily tolerate a degree of uncertainty and obscurity in the arts, because it was an accepted fact that there is much between heaven and earth that escapes human understanding.[42] This implies that late antique works of art and architecture leave room for or rather require the imaginative interpretation on the part of the beholder,[43] which in turn means that one needs to be familiar with the visual culture before gaining access to the meaning and value of a particular work of art. This is evocative of the need for initiation prior to the spiritual ascent through the Pseudo-Dionysian hierarchy.[44] It may have been for this reason that ekphrastic descriptions accompanying works of art

of Nyssa, ed. Lucas Francisco Mateo-Seco and Giulio Maspero (Leiden and Boston, MA: Brill, 2010).

40 Pseudo-Dionysius, *CH*, 141C, 144B; see also Porter (2010), 491.

41 Compare the discussion of Posidippus in Porter (2010), 483–7.

42 Rico Franses, 'When all that is gold does not glitter: on the strange history of looking at Byzantine art', in *Icon and Word: The Power of Images in Byzantium*, ed. Antony Eastmond and Liz James (Aldershot and Burlington, VT: Ashgate Publishing, 2003).

43 John Onians, 'Abstraction and imagination in late antiquity', *Art History* 3 (1980).

44 Pseudo-Dionysius, *CH*, 137B.

and architecture became increasingly important in the culture of the early Byzantine world as a guide to intelligent viewing. Aesthetics in late antiquity is more than the simple sensation of visual beauty and involves higher cognitive functions of memory and learning. Late antique aesthetics combines visual with intellectual, moral and religious/philosophical qualities and thus touches upon the core of cultural norms and values.

Appendix: The Marbles Found in the Interior Decoration of Hagia Sophia

Paul the Silentiary[1]	Modern designation[2]	Characteristics[3]	Application in Hagia Sophia
… the marble meadows gathered upon the mighty walls … cut from the green flanks of Carystus … (618–621).	Cipollino Carystian Marble Marmor Caristium	A light greenish or whitish stone with wavy bands of a dark green with a hint of blue; quarried along the southwest coast of Karystia in the southern part of the island of Euboea.	Mainly as rectangular plaques in the revetment of the main piers facing the naos.
… speckled Phrygian stone, sometimes rosy mixed with white, sometimes gleaming with purple and silver flowers … (622–625).	Pavonazzetto Marmor Phrygium	Nearly diaphanous white ground with coloured veins and markings, ranging from soft to deep shades of red, arranged in some regularity. This marble enjoyed some popularity in the early Byzantine Empire.	Rectangular plaques are for instance found flanking the double panels of cipollino on the main piers facing the naos.
… besprinkled with little bright stars that had laden the river-boat on the broad Nile … (625–627).	Egyptian red porphyry Porfido Rosso Porphyrites	Deep purple-red with generally minute flecks of white or sometimes clear rose colour. It had been associated with the figure of the emperor since Roman times. It is probably the most valuable marble in Hagia Sophia.	Used for the columns in the exedras; as narrow rectangular panels on the main piers and as circular medallions in the arcade spandrels.

Paul the Silentiary	Modern designation	Characteristics	Application in Hagia Sophia
… bright green stone of Laconia (628).	Serpentino Green Porphyry	Almost monochromatic of different shades of green with irregular marks varying in size and colour. The enclosures range from green to yellow, red and bluish.	Used in the opus sectile panels on the west wall of the naos, the bema and in the aisles.
… glittering marble with wavy veins found in the deep gullies of the Iasian peaks, exhibiting slanting streaks of blood red and livid white … (630–632).	Cipollino Rosso Jassic Marble Marmor Carium o Iassense	A blood-red stone of tiny crystals, with slanting veins and bands of bloodshot white; its stratified structure is reminiscent of an onion; commonly used for panels around openings, generally in small dimensions.	Predominantly employed in the aisles and galleries, typically alternating with the contrasting pavonazzetto.[4]
… pale yellow [stone] with swirling red from the Lydian headland … (632–633).	Possibly a Breccia Corallina[5]		Not clear.
The glittering crocus-like golden stone which the Libyan sun, warming it with its golden light, has produced on the steep flanks of the Moorish hills … (634–636).	Giallo Antico Libyan Marble Marmor Numidicum	This African marble can exhibit various shades of yellow. Monochromatic giallo antico is distinguished from a brecciate giallo antico. The first is uniformly coloured with occasional red veins running through; the second is similar to brecce with yellow or white marks on a background that has a tawny yellow to reddish shimmer. When exposed to fire, it modifies its colour scheme by emphasising its tonality. It was one of the more expensive marbles.	Used exclusively for narrow bands, as, for instance, in the revetment of the narthex, where it encloses upright rectangular panels of Celtic marble.
… of glittering black upon which the Celtic crags, deep in ice, have poured here and there an abundance of milk … (637–639).	Bianco e Nero Antico Celtic Marble Marmor Celticum	Deep black shiny marble with large irregular markings and veins of snow-white; quarried in the French Pyrenees; mining seems to have begun in the fourth century.	As upright rectangular plaques in the wall revetment of the main piers facing the naos.

Paul the Silentiary	Modern designation	Characteristics	Application in Hagia Sophia
… pale onyx with glint of precious metal … (640–641).	Egyptian Alabaster Lapis Onyx	Either pale yellow or honey coloured with broad opaque white zones in the form of winding waves and in some cases as concentric circles of various shades. In lesser quality, these zones can take on a grey or rose colour. It originates from the Nile valley, mainly along the eastern bank of the river.	Used for the horizontal bands encircling the naos or as slabs of small dimensions.
… [from] the land of Atrax … in parts vivid green not unlike emerald, in others of a darker green, almost blue, it has spots resembling snow next to flashes of black so that in one stone various beauties mingle … (640–645).	Thessalian Marble Molossian Marble Verde Antico	A vividly green stone of various shades, usually decorated with spots of various sizes, generally green and shades of blue, black and white, sometimes a yellowish ochre or tawny to red or rose coloured. This marble was commonly employed for columns, due to its resistant and compact texture.	Main columns of the side arcades as well as for some of the horizontal bands in the revetment and the pavement.
… the hills of Proconnesus have gladly offered their back to the life-giving Queen to cover the entire floor, while the polish of Bosporus stone shimmers gently, black with an admixture of white … (664–665).	Proconnesian Marble Marmo Cipolla	A milky-white stone with small crystals, often without any impurities. There are two variations, one in a uniform white with a hint of sky-blue in medium large crystals, mainly used for sculptures; the other has larger crystals and is interspersed with grey-bluish stripes, often applied in architecture on a larger scale. Its name derives from the place of its provenance on the Island of Marmara.	Used for the pavement and the eight square pillars in the aisles, the columns in the gallery, the capitals and archivolts and spandrels of the ground floor arcades as well as for door and window frames, balustrades and cornices.

1 Verse numbers are given in parenthesis. Paul Friedländer, *Johannes von Gaza und Paulus Silentiarius: Kunstbeschreibungen justinianischer Zeit* (Leipzig and Berlin: Teubner, 1912). Translated in Cyril Mango, *The Art of the Byzantine Empire 312–1453: Sources and Documents* (Toronto: University of Toronto Press, 1972, reprint 1986), 86–7.

2 Based on Raniero Gnoli, *Marmora Romana* (Rome: Edizioni dell'Elefante, 1971), 44–6.

3 Gabriele Borghini, ed., *Marmi Antichi* (Rome: Edizioni De Luca, 2001).

4 Annette Kleinert, 'Die Inkrustation der Hagia Sophia: Zur Entwicklung der Inkrustationsschemata im römischen Kaiserreich' (PhD, Westfälische Wilhelms-Universität, 1979), 4.

5 W. R. Lethaby and Harold Swainson, *The Church of Sancta Sophia Constantinople: A Study of Byzantine Building* (London and New York, NY: Kessinger Publishing, 1894, reprint 2004), 238–23; Gnoli (1971), 45.

Bibliography

Primary Sources

Agathias: *The Histories*, ed. J.D. Frendo, *CFHB IIA*, Berlin 1975.

———, *On Another on the Island of Platé*, ed. and trans. W.R. Paton, *The Greek Anthology*, Cambridge, MA and London: Harvard University Press, 1916.

Alexandria, Clement of: *Opera Omnia*, ed. J.P. Migne, *PG* 8, Paris 1857; trans. A. Roberts, J. Donaldson, and A.C. Coxe, *Ante-Nicene Fathers: The Writings of the Fathers down to A.D. 325. Vol. 2: Fathers of the Second Century: Hermas, Tatian, Athenagoras, Theophilus, and Clement of Alexandria*, New York, NY: Christian Literature Publishing Co., 1885.

Alexandria, Philo of: *De posteritate Caini*, ed. and trans. F.H. Colson and G.H. Whitaker, *Philo II*, Cambridge, MA and London: Harvard University Press, 1929.

Aristotle: *The Art of Rhetoric*, ed. and trans. J.H. Freese, Cambridge, MA and London: Harvard University Press, 1926.

———, *Minor Works*, ed. and trans. W.S. Hett. Cambridge, MA and London: Harvard University Press, 1936, reprint 1955.

Athanasius: *De incarnatione verbi*, ed. J.P. Migne, *PG* 28, Paris, 1887; trans. P. Schaff and H. Wace, *Nicene and Post-Nicene Fathers, Series II. Vol. 4: Athanasius: Selected Works and Letters*, Grand Rapids, MI: WM. B. Eerdmans Publishing Co., 1892.

Basilius Magnus: *Homiliae in Psalmos*, ed. J.P. Migne, *PG* 30, Paris, 1888.

Chrysostom, John: *In epistulam I ad Corinthios*, ed. J.P. Migne, *PG* 61, Paris, 1862; trans. P. Schaff, revised by T.W. Chambers, *Nicene and Post-Nicene Fathers, Vol. 12: Saint Chrysostom: Homilies on the Epistles of Paul to the Corinthians*, Grand Rapids, MI: WM. B. Eerdmans Publishing Co., 1889 .

———, *De cruce et latrone II*, ed. J.P. Migne, *PG* 49, Paris, 1862.

Corpus Iuris Civilis – Novellae, ed. R. Schöll and W. Kroll, Berlin: Weidmann, 1895.

Empiricus, Sextus: *Adversus Mathematics*, ed. I. Bekker, *Sextus Empiricus*, Berlin: Reimeri, 1842; A.A. Long and D.N. Sedley, *The Hellenistic Philosophers, 2 Vols*, Cambridge: Cambridge University Press, 1987.

Eusebius: *Vita Constantini*, ed. F. Winkelmann, *Über das Leben des Kaisers Konstantins*, Berlin: Walter de Gruyter, 1975, rev. 1991); trans. A. Cameron and S.G. Hall, *Eusebius Life of Constantine*, Oxford and New York: Oxford University Press, 1999.

Grammaticus, Leo: *Chronographia*, ed. I. Bekker, *CSHB*, Bonn: E. Weber 1842.

Gregoras, Nicephorus: *Byzantina Historia*, ed. L. Schopen and I. Bekker, *CSHB*, Bonn: E. Weber, 1829.

Iamblichus: *De Mysteriis*, ed. É. des Places, *Jamblique: Les mystères d'Égypte*, Paris: Les Belles Lettres, 1966; trans. E.C. Clarke, J.M. Dillon, and J.P. Hershbell, *Iamblichus On the Mysteries*, Atlanta, GA: Society of Biblical Literature, 2003.
Indicopleustes, Cosmas: *Christiana Topographia*, ed. J.P. Migne, *PG* 88, Paris, 1860.
Jerusalem, Cyril of: *Catecheses*, ed. J.P. Migne, *PG* 33, Paris, 1886; trans. P. Schaff and H. Wace, *Nicene and Post-Nicene Fathers, Series II, Vol. 7, The Writings of Cyril and Gregory*, Grand Rapids, MI: WM. B. Eerdmans Publishing Co., 1894.
Laertius, Diogenes: *Lives of Eminent Philosophers*, ed. and trans. R.D. Hicks, Cambridge, MA and London: Harvard University Press, 1925.
Longinus. *On the Sublime*, ed. and trans. W.H. Fyfe, revised by D.A. Russell, Cambridge, MA and London: Harvard University Press, 1995.
Malalas, John.: *Chronographia*, ed. B.G. Niebuhr, I. Bekker, L. Schopen and L. Dindorf, *CSHB*, Bonn: E. Weber, 1831; trans. E. Jeffreys, M. Jeffreys and R. Scott, *John Malalas: The Chronicle*, Melbourne: Australian Association for Byzantine Studies, 1986.
Martyr, Justin: *Apologia Prima*, ed. J.P. Migne, *PG* 6, Paris, 1857; trans. A. Roberts, J. Donaldson, and A.C. Coxe, *Ante-Nicene Fathers: The Writings of the Fathers down to A.D. 325. Vol. 1: The Apostolic Fathers, Justin Martyr, Irenaeus*, New York, NY: Christian Literature Publishing Co., 1885.
Nikolaos. *Progymnasmata*, ed. Joseph Felten. Leipzig: Teubner, 1913.
Nola, Paulinus of. *Carmina*, ed. W. de Hartel. Prague: F. Tempsky, 1894.
Nyssa, Gregory of: *Contra Eunomium libri duodecim*, ed. W. Jaeger, *Gregorii Nysseni Opera I*, Berlin: Weidmann, 1921; trans. P. Schaff and H. Wace, *Nicene and Post-Nicene Fathers, Series II, Vol. 5, Gregory of Nyssa: Dogmatic Treatises; Select Writings and Letters*, Grand Rapids, MI: WM. B. Eerdmans Publishing Co., 1893.
——, *De anima et resurrectione*, ed. J.P. Migne, *PG* 46, Paris, 1863.
——, *De professione Christiana*, ed. W. Jaeger Gregorii Nysseni Opera VIII, Part I, Leiden: Brill, 1952.
——, *In Hexaemeron*, ed. H.R. Drobner, *Gregorii Nysseni Opera IV, Part I*, Leiden: Brill, 2009.
——, *In Canticum Canticorum*, ed. H. Langerbeck, *Gregorii Nysseni Opera VI*, Leiden: Brill, 1960.
——, *De Vita Moysis*, ed. and trans. J. Daniélou, *La vie de Moïse out Traité de la perfection en matière de vertu*, Paris: Les éditions du cerf, 1968.
De Virginitate, ed. J.P. Migne, *PG* 46, Paris, 1863.
——, *Oratio Catechetica Magna*, ed. J.P. Migne, *PG* 45, Paris, 1863; trans. P. Schaff and H. Wace, *Nicene and Post-Nicene Fathers, Series II, Vol. 5, Gregory of Nyssa: Dogmatic Treatises, Select Writings and Letters*, Grand Rapids, MI: WM. B. Eerdmans Publishing Co., 1893.
Olympiodorus: *Commentary on the First Alcibiades of Plato*, ed. L.G. Westerink, Amsterdam: North-Holland Publishing Company, 1956.
Philostratus: *The Life of Apollonius of Tyana*, ed. and trans. C.P. Jones, Cambridge, MA and London: Harvard University Press, 2005.
Plato: *Hippias Major*, ed. and trans. W. R. M. Lamb, Cambridge, MA and London: Harvard University Press, 1925.
——, *Phaedo*, ed. and trans. H.N. Fowler, Cambridge, MA and London: Harvard University Press, 1966.
——, *Phaedrus*, ed. and trans. H.N. Fowler, Cambridge, MA and London: Harvard University Press, 1925.
——, *Philebus*, ed. and trans. W. R. M. Lamb, Cambridge, MA and London: Harvard University Press, 1925, reprint 2006.
——, *The Republic: Books I-V*, ed. and trans. P. Shorey, Cambridge, MA and London: Harvard University Press, 1930, reprint 1999.

——, *The Republic: Books VI-X*, ed. and trans. P. Shorey, Cambridge, MA and London: Harvard University Press, 1935, reprint 2000.

——, *Statesman*, ed. and trans. H.N. Fowler, Cambridge, MA and London: Harvard University Press, 1925, reprint 2006.

——, *Symposium*, ed. and trans. H.N. Fowler. Cambridge, MA and London: Harvard University Press, 1925.

——, *Timaeus*, ed. and trans. R.G. Bury, Cambridge, MA and London: Harvard University Press, 1929, reprint 2005.

Plotinus: *Porphyry on the Life of Plotinus and the Order of his Books: Enneads I*, ed. and trans. A.H. Armstrong, Cambridge, MA and London: Harvard University Press, 1966.

——, *Enneads II*, ed. and trans. A.H. Armstrong, Cambridge, MA and London: Harvard University Press, 1966.

——, *Enneads IV*, ed. and trans. A.H. Armstrong, Cambridge, MA and London: Harvard University Press, 1984.

——, *Enneads V*, ed. and trans. A.H. Armstrong, Cambridge, MA and London: Harvard University Press, 1984.

——, *Enneads VI. 1–5*, ed. and trans. A.H. Armstrong, Cambridge, MA and London: Harvard University Press, 1988.

——, *Enneads VI. 6–9*, ed. and trans. A.H. Armstrong, Cambridge, MA and London: Harvard University Press, 1988.

Preger, Theodor: *Scriptores originum Constantinopalitanarum*, Leipzig, Teubner, 1902.

Proclus. *Commentary on the Parmenides*, ed. V. Cousin, *Procli Philosophi Platonici. Opera Inedita*, Paris: A. Durand, 1864; trans. G.R. Morrow and J.M. Dillon, *Proclus' Commentary on Plato's Parmenides*, Princeton, NJ: Princeton University Press, 1987.

——, *Commentary on the Republic*, ed. W. Kroll, *Procli Diadochi in Platonis Rem publicam commentarii*, Leipzig: Teubner, 1899–1901.

——, *Commentary on the Timaeus*, ed. E. Diehl, *Procli Diadochi in Platonis Timaeum commentaria*, Leipzig: Teubner, 1903.

——, *On the Hieratic Art*, ed. J. Bidez, *Catalogue des manuscrits alchimiques grecs*, Bruxelles: M. Lamertin, 1928.

——, *Théologie Platonicienne, Livre I*, ed. and trans. H.D. Saffrey and L.G. Westerink, Paris: Les Belles Lettres, 1968.

——, *Théologie Platonicienne, Livre III*, ed. and trans. H.D. Saffrey and L.G. Westerink, Paris: Les Belles Lettres, 1978.

——, *Théologie Platonicienne, Livre IV*, ed. and trans. H.D. Saffrey and L.G. Westerink, Paris: Les Belles Lettres, 1981.

Procopius: *Buildings*, ed. and trans. H.B. Dewing, Cambridge, MA and London: Harvard University Press, 1940, reprint 2002.

Pseudo-Athanasius. *Sermo in Passionem Domini*, ed. J.P. Migne, *PG* 28, Paris, 1887.

Pseudo-Dionysius the Areopagite: *Opera Omnia*, ed. J.P. Migne, *PG* 3, Paris, 1857; trans. C. Luibheid and P. Rorem, *Pseudo-Dionysius: the Complete Works*, New York, NY: Paulist Press, 1987.

——, *De coelesti hierarchia; De ecclesiastica hierarchia; De mystica theologia; Epistulae*, ed. G. Heil and A.M. Ritter, Berlin: Walter de Gruyter, 1991.

——, *De Divinis Nominibus*, ed. B.R. Suchla, Berlin: Walter de Gruyter, 1990.

Quintilian: *Institutio Oratoria*, ed. and trans. H.E. Butler, Cambridge, MA and London: Harvard University Press, 1921.

Scholasticus, Socrates: *Historia ecclesiastica*, ed. J.P. Migne, *PG* 67, Paris, 1864; trans. P. Schaff and H. Wace, revised A.C. Zenos, *Nicene and Post-Nicene Fathers, Series II, Vol. 2, Socrates & Sozomenus: Ecclesiastical Histories*, Grand Rapids, MI: WM. B. Eerdmans Publishing Co., 1890.

Seneca: *Epistles, Vol. II*, ed. and trans. R.M. Gummere, Cambridge, MA and London: Harvard University Press, 1920.

Silentiarius, Paulus: *Ekphrasis toi naoi tes Hagias Sophias*, ed. P. Friedländer, *Johannes von Gaza und Paulus Silentiarius: Kunstbeschreibungen justinianischer Zeit*, Leipzig and Berlin: Teubner, 1912; trans. Cyril Mango, *The Art of the Byzantine Empire 312–1453: Sources and Documents*. Toronto: University of Toronto Press, 1972, reprint 1986; trans. P.N. Bell, *Three Political Voices from the Age of Justinian: Agapetus, Advice to the Emperor; Dialogue on Political Science; Paul the Silentiary, Description of Hagia Sophia*. Liverpool: Liverpool University Press, 2009.

Theon: *Progymnasmata*, ed. Michel Patillon. Paris: Les Belles Lettres, 1997.

Theophanes Confessor: *Chronographia*, ed. C. de Boor, 2 vols. Leipzig: Teubner, 1883–1885; trans. Cyril Mango and Roger Scott, *The Chronicle of Theophanes Confessor*, Oxford: Clarendon Press, 1997.

Theophilus. *De Diversis Artibus*, ed. and trans. C.R. Dodwell, *Theophilus: The Various Arts*, Oxford and New York: Oxford University Press, 1961, reprint 2004.

Vitruvius: *On Architecture*, ed. and trans. F. Granger, Cambridge, MA and London: Harvard University Press, 1934, reprint 1970.

Secondary Sources

Abramowski, Luise. 'Die Mosaiken von S. Vitale und S. Apollinare in Classe und die Kirchenpolitik Kaiser Justinians'. *Zeitschrift für Antikes Christentum* 5 (2001): 289–341.

Agosti, Gianfranco. 'Niveaux de style, littérarité, poétiques: pour une histoire du système de la poésie classicisante au VIe siècle'. In *Doux remède: Poésie et poétique à Byzance. Actes du IVe colloque international philologique Paris, 23–24–25 février 2006. Dossiers byzantines, 9*, edited by P. Odorico, P. Agapitos and M. Hinterberger. Paris: Centres d'études byzantines, néo-helleniques et sud-est européennes, École des hautes études en sciences sociales, 2009: 99–119.

Alchermes, Joseph D. 'Art and architecture in the age of Justinian'. In *The Cambridge Companion to the Age of Justinian*, edited by Michael Maas. Cambridge: Cambridge University Press, 2005: 343–75.

Alexander, Paul J. 'Hypatius of Ephesus: a note on image worship in the sixth century'. *The Harvard Theological Review* 45 (1952): 177–84.

Alexandrakis, Aphrodite. 'Neoplatonic influences on eastern iconography: A Greek-rooted tradition'. In *Neoplatonism and Western Aesthetics*, edited by Aphrodite Alexandrakis and Nicholas J. Moutafakis. New York, NY: State University of New York Press, 2002: 75–87.

Allison, Henry E. *Kant's Theory of Taste*. Cambridge: Cambridge University Press, 2001.

Andreades, G.A. 'Die Sophienkathedrale von Konstantinopel'. *Kunstwissenschaftliche Forschungen* 1. Frankfurt: Frankfurter Verlags-Anstalt, 1931.

Andreescu-Treadgold, Irina and Warren Treadgold. 'Procopius and the imperial panels of S. Vitale'. *The Art Bulletin* 79 (1997): 708–23.

Andreopoulos, Andreas. 'The mosaics of the transfiguration in St. Catherine's monastery on Mount Sinai: A discussion of its origins'. *Byzantion* 72 (2002): 9–41.

——, *Metamorphosis: The Transfiguration in Byzantine Theology and Iconography*. Crestwood, NY: St. Vladimir's Seminary Press, 2005.

Antoniades, Eugenios Michael. *Εκφρασις της Αγίας Σοφίας, ήτοι μελέτη συνθετική και αναλυτική υπό έποψιν αρχιτεκτονικήν, αρχαιολογικήν και ιστορικήν του πολυθρυλήτου τεμένους Κωνσταντινουπόλεως/Ευγενίου Μ. Αντωνιάδου τ.* 2. 1908.

Armstrong, Arthur H. '"Emanation" in Plotinus'. *Mind* 46 (1937): 61–6.

———, 'Beauty and the discovery of divinity in the thought of Plotinus'. In *Kephalaion: Studies in Greek Philosophy and Its Continuation Offered to Professor C. J. De Vogel*, edited by J. Mansfeld and L. M. de Rijk. Assen: Van Gorcum and Comp. B.V., 1975: 155–163.

———, 'The divine enhancement of earthly beauties: The Hellenic and Platonic tradition'. *Eranos Jahrbuch* 53 (1984): 49–81.

Arnheim, Rudolf. *The Dynamics of Architectural Form*. London, Berkeley and Los Angeles, CA: University of California Press, 1977.

Asgari, Nursin. 'The Proconnesian production of architectural elements in late antiquity, based on evidence from the marble quarries'. In *Constantinople and its Hinterland: Papers from the Twenty-Seventh Spring Symposium of Byzantine Studies, Oxford, April 1993*, edited by Cyril Mango and Gilbert Dagron. Aldershot: Ashgate, 1995: 263–88.

Baatz, Dietwulf. 'Fensterglastypen, Glasfenster und Architektur'. In *Bautechnik der Antike: Diskussionen zur Archäologischen Bauforschung, Vol. 5*, edited by Adolf Hoffman, Ernst-Ludwig Schwandner, Wolfram Höpfner and Gunnar Brands. Mainz: Verlag Philipp von Zabern, 1991: 4–13.

Bailey, Donald M., ed., *A Catalogue of the Lamps in the British Museum IV: Lamps of Metal and Stone, and Lampstands*. London: British Museum Press, 1996.

Barasch, Moshe. *Icon: Studies in the History of an Idea*. London and New York, NY: New York University Press, 1992.

Barber, Charles. 'The imperial panels at San Vitale: A reconsideration'. *BMGS* 14 (1990): 19–42.

———, *Figure and Likeness: On the Limits of Representation in Byzantine Iconoclasm*. Oxford and Princeton,NJ: Princeton University Press, 2002.

Barbur, John L., and Karoline Spang. 'Colour constancy and conscious perception of changes of illuminant'. *Neuropsychologia* 46 (2008): 853–63.

Bardill, Jonathan. 'The church of Sts. Sergius and Bacchus in Constantinople and the monophysite refugees'. *DOP* 54 (2000): 1–11.

———, *Brickstamps of Constantinople*. Oxford: Oxford University Press, 2004.

———, 'A new temple for Byzantium: Anicia Juliana, King Solomon, and the gilded ceiling of the church of St. Polyeuktos in Constantinople'. In *Social and Political Life in Late Antiquity*, edited by William Bowden, Adam Gutterridge and Carlos Machado. Leiden and Boston, MA: Brill, 2006: 339–70.

———, *Constantine, Divine Emperor of the Christian Golden Age*. Cambridge: Cambridge University Press, 2011.

Barnouw, Jeffrey. *Propositional Perception: Phantasia, Predication, and Sign in Plato, Aristotle, and the Stoics*. Lanham, MD.: University Press of America, 2002.

Barry, Fabio. 'Walking on water: Cosmic floors in antiquity and the middle ages'. *The Art Bulletin* 89 (2007): 627–56.

Bassett, Sarah E. 'Style and meaning in the imperial panels at San Vitale'. *Artibus et Historiae* 29 (2008): 49–57.

Beckwith, John. 'Byzantium: Gold and light', in Thomas B. Hess and John Ashbery (eds), 'Light from Aten to Laser'. *Art News Annual* 35 (1969): 45–57.

Beierwaltes, Werner. *Proklos – Grundzüge seiner Metaphysik*. Frankfurt am Main: Vittorio Klostermann, 1965.

———, 'Plotins Metaphysik des Lichtes'. In *Die Philosophie des Neuplatonismus*, edited by Clemens Zintzen. Darmstadt: Wissenschaftliche Buchgesellschaft, 1977: 75–117.

Beil, Ulrich J. 'Rhetorische "Phantasia": Ein Beitrag zur Archäologie des Erhabenen'. *Arcadia* 28 (1993): 225–55.

Bell, Peter N. *Three Political Voices from the Age of Justinian: Agapetus, Advice to the Emperor; Dialogue on Political Science; Paul the Silentiary, Description of Hagia Sophia.* Liverpool: Liverpool University Press, 2009.
Belting, Hans. *Bild und Kult: eine Geschichte des Bildes vor dem Zeitlalter der Kunst.* Munich: C.H. Beck, 1991.
Bennema, Cornelis. 'The strands of wisdom tradition in intertestamental Judaism: Origins, developments and characteristics'. *Tyndale Bulletin* 52 (2001): 61–82.
Berthold, George Charles. *Maximus Confessor: Selected Writings*. New York, NY: Paulist Press, 1985.
Biddle, Martin. *The Tomb of Christ*. Gloucestershire: Sutton Publishing Ltd, 1999.
Bimson, Marvis and Ian C. Freestone. 'The discovery of an Islamic glass-making site in middle Egypt'. *Annales du 10e Congrès de l'Association Internationale pour l'Histoire du Verre. AIHV* (1987): 237–43.
Bing, Peter. 'The politics and poetics of geography in the Milan Posidippus section one: On stones (AB 12–0)'. In *The New Posidippus: A Hellenistic Poetry Book*, edited by Kathryn Gutzwiller. Oxford: Oxford University Press, 2005: 119–140.
Birmelin, Ella. 'Die kunsttheoretischen Gedanken in Philostrats Appolonios'. *Philologus* 88 (1933): 149–80.
Birnbaum, Adalbert. 'Die Oktogone von Antiochia, Nazianz und Nyssa. Rekonstruktionsversuche'. *Repertorium für Kunstwissenschaft* 36 (1913): 181–209.
Böhm, Thomas. *Theoria, Unendlichkeit, Aufstieg: Philosophische Implikationen zu De Vita Moysis von Gregor von Nyssa*. Leiden and New York, NY: Brill, 1996.
Bolman, Elizabeth S. 'Late antique aesthetics, chromophobia, and the Red Monastery, Sohag, Egypt'. *Eastern Christian Art* 3 (2006): 12–4.
———, 'Painted skins: The illusions and realities of architectural polychromy, Sinai and Egypt'. In *Approaching the Holy Mountain: Art and Liturgy at St. Catherine's Monastery in the Sinai*, edited by Sharon E.J. Gerstel and Robert S. Nelson. Turnhout: Brepols, 2010: 119–40.
Borghini, Gabriele, ed., *Marmi Antichi*. Rome: Edizioni De Luca, 2001.
Borsook, Eve. 'Rhetoric of reality: Mosaics as expressions of a metaphysical idea'. *Mitteilungen des Kunsthistorischen Institutes in Florenz* 44 (2000): 31–8.
Bosanquet, Bernard. *A History of Aesthetic*. London: George Allen & Unwin Ltd., 1892.
Boston, Karen A. 'Imaging the Logos: Display and Discourse in Justinian's Hagia Sophia', PhD thesis, University of London, 1999.
Bouras, Laskarina. 'Byzantine lighting devices'. *JÖB* 32 (1982): 479–91.
Bouras, Laskarina and Maria G. Parani. *Lighting in Early Byzantium*. Washington, DC: Dumbarton Oaks Research Library and Collection, 2008.
Boyancé, Pierre. 'Théurgie et télestique néoplatoniciennes'. *Revue de l'histoire des religions* 147 (1955): 189–209.
Brandenburg, Hugo. *Die Kirche S. Stafano Rotondo in Rom: Bautypologie und Architektursymbolik in der spätantiken und frühchristlichen Architektur*. Hans-Lietzmann-Vorlesungen, edited by Christoph Markschies. Berlin and New York, NY: Walter de Gruyter, 1998.
———, *Die frühchristlichen Kirchen Roms vom 4. bis zum 7. Jahrhundert: Der Beginn der abendländischen Kirchenbaukunst*. Regensburg: Verlag Schnell and Steiner, 2004.
Brill, Robert H. 'The great glass slab from ancient Galilee'. *Archaeometry* 20 (1967): 88–95.
———, 'Scientific Investigations of the Jalame Glass and Related Finds'. In *Excavations at Jalame Site of a Glass Factory in Late Roman Palestine*, edited by G. D. Weinberg. Columbia, MT: University of Missouri Press, 1988: 257–91.
———, *Chemical Analyses of Early Glasses*. New York, NY: Corning Museum of Glass, 1999.

Brown, Alexandra R. *The Cross and Human Transformation: Paul's Apocalyptic Word in 1 Corinthians*. Minneapolis, MN: Fortress Press, 1995.

Browning, Robert. 'Education in the Roman Empire'. In *The Cambridge Ancient History. Late Antiquity: Empire and Successors, A.D. 425–600*, edited by Averil Cameron, Bryan Ward-Perkins and Michael Whitby. Cambridge: Cambridge University Press, 2000: 855–83.

Brubaker, Leslie. 'Perception and conception: Art, theory and culture in ninth-century Byzantium'. *Word and Image* 5 (1989): 19–32.

Bruce, Vicki, Patrick R. Green and Mark A. Georgeson. *Visual Perception: Physiology, Psychology, and Ecology*. Hove: Psychology Press, 3rd edition, 2000.

Bruno, Vincent J. *Form and Color in Greek Painting*. New York, NY: W.W. Norton, 1977.

Buchwald, Hans. 'Saint Sophia, turning point in the development of Byzantine architecture?'. In *Die Hagia Sophia in Istanbul: Akten des Berner Kolloquiums vom 21. Oktober 1994*, edited by Volker Hoffmann. Bern and New York, NY: P. Lange, 1997: 29–48.

Bultmann, Rudolf. 'Zur Geschichte der Lichtsymbolik im Altertum'. *Philologus* 97 (1948): 1–36.

Burnyeat, Myles F. 'Culture and society in Plato's Republic'. *The Tanner Lectures on Human Values* (1997): 217–324.

Bussanich, John. 'Plotinus' metaphysics of the One'. In *The Cambridge Companion to Plotinus*, edited by Lloyd P. Gerson. Cambridge: Cambridge University Press, 1996: 38–65.

Butler, Lawrence E. 'The Nave Cornices of Hagia Sophia in Istanbul'. PhD, University of Pennsylvania, 1989.

———, 'Hagia Sophia's nave cornices as elements of its design and structure'. In *Hagia Sophia from the Age of Justinian to the Present*, edited by Robert Mark and Ahmet S. Çakmak. Cambridge: Cambridge University Press, 1992: 57–77.

Bychkov, Victor. 'Byzantine aesthetics'. In *Encyclopedia of Aesthetics*, edited by Michael Kelly. Oxford and New York, NY: Oxford University Press, 1998: 321–323.

Çakmak, Ahmet S., Rabun M. Taylor, and Eser Durukal. 'The structural configuration of the first dome of Justinian's Hagia Sophia (A.D. 537–558): An investigation based on structural and literary analysis'. *Soil Dynamics and Earthquake Engineering* 29 (2009): 693–698.

Cameron, Averil. 'Procopius and the church of St. Sophia'. *Harvard Theological Review* 58 (1965, Variorum Reprints, 1981): 161–163.

———, *Flavius Cresconius Corippus: In laudem Iustini Augusti minoris, Libri IV*. London: The Athlone Press, 1976.

———, 'Images of authority: Elites and icons in late sixth-century Byzantium'. *Past and Present*, no. 84 (1979): 3–35.

———, *Procopius and the Sixth Century*. London: Duckworth, 1985.

———, 'The language of images: The rise of icons and Christian representation'. In *The Church and the Arts: Papers Read at the 1990 Summer Meeting and the 1991 Winter Meeting of the Ecclesiastical History Society*, edited by Diana Wood. Oxford: Blackwell Publishers, 1992: 1–42.

Cameron, Averil, and Alan Cameron. 'The Cycle of Agathias'. *The Journal of Hellenic Studies* 86 (1966): 6–25.

Careri, Giorgio. 'Physicists and painters: The similar search for meaning'. *Leonardo* 22 (1989): 113–115.

Cecchelli, Carlo. 'Vetri da finestra del S. Vitale di Ravenna'. *Felix Ravenna* 35 (1930): 1–20.

Cela-Conde, Camilo J., Luigi Agnati, Joseph P. Huston, Francisco Mora, and Marcos Nadal. 'The neural foundations of aesthetic appreciation'. *Progress in Neurobiology* 94 (2011): 39–48.
Chatterjee, Anjan. 'Neuroaesthetics: a coming of age story'. *Journal of Cognitive Neuroscience* 23 (2011): 53–62.
Chlup, Radek. *Proclus: An Introduction*. Cambridge: Cambridge University Press, 2012.
Citri, Ami, and Robert C. Malenka. 'Synaptic plasticity: Multiple forms, functions and mechanisms'. *Neuropsychopharmacology Reviews* 33 (2008): 18–41.
Close, Anthony J. 'Philosophical theories of art and nature in classical antiquity'. *Journal of the History of Ideas* 32 (1971): 163–84.
Coleman, Simon, and Jaś Elsner. 'The pilgrim's progress: Art, architecture and ritual movement at Sinai'. *World Archaeology* 26 (1994): 73–89.
Coles, Alasdair Charles. 'The treatment of matter and divinisation language in the ecclesiastical hierarchy of Pseudo-Dionysius and his sources, as a basis for evaluating his sacramental theology'. PhD, University of London, 2003.
Conant, Kenneth John. 'The first dome of St. Sophia and its rebuilding'. *The Bulletin of the Byzantine Institute* 1 (1946): 71–8.
———, 'The original buildings at the Holy Sepulchre in Jerusalem'. *Speculum* 31 (1956): 1–48.
Connor, Carolyn L. 'The epigram in the church of Hagios Polyeuktos in Constantinople and its Byzantine response'. *Byzantion* 69 (1999): 479–527.
Corbo, Virgilio C. *Il Santo Sepolcro di Gerusalemme: aspetti archeologici dalle origini al period crociato*. Jerusalem: Franciscan Print Press, 1981–82.
Cormack, Robin. 'Interpreting the mosaics of S. Sophia at Istanbul'. *Art History* 4 (1981): 1314–18.
———, 'The emperor at St. Sophia: Viewer and viewed'. In *Byzance et les images: Cycle de conférences organisé au Musée du Louvre par le service culturel du 5 octobre au 7 décembre 1992*, edited by André Guillou and Jannic Durand. Paris: La documentation Française, 1994: 225–253.
———, 'The Visual Arts'. In *The Cambridge Ancient History. Late Antiquity: Empire and Successors, A.D. 425–600*, edited by Averil Cameron, Bryan Ward-Perkins and Michael Whitby. Cambridge: Cambridge University Press, 2000: 884–913.
Cormack, Robin, and Ernest J. W. Hawkins. 'The mosaics of St. Sophia at Istanbul: The rooms above the southwest vestibule and ramp'. *DOP* 31 (1977): 175–251.
Corrigan, Kathleen. 'Iconography'. In *The Oxford Handbook of Byzantine Studies*, edited by Elizabeth Jeffreys, John Haldon and Robin Cormack. Oxford: Oxford University Press, 2008: 67–76.
Costelloe, Timothy M. *The Sublime: From Antiquity to the Present*. Cambridge: Cambridge University Press, 2012.
Coüasnon, Charles. *The Church of the Holy Sepulchre in Jerusalem*. London: Oxford University Press, 1974.
Couloubaritsis, Lambros. 'Le sens de la notion "démonstration" chez le Pseudo-Denys'. *Byzantinische Zeitschrift* 75 (1982): 317–35.
Coulter, James A. *The Literary Microcosm: Theories of Interpretation of the Later Neoplatonists*. Leiden: Brill, 1976.
Cox-Miller, Patricia. '"The little blue flower is red": relics and the poetizing of the body'. *Journal of Early Christian Studies* 8 (2000): 213–36.
———, *The Corporeal Imagination: Signifying the Holy in Late Ancient Christianity*. Philadelphia: University of Pennsylvania Press, 2009.
Cristo, Stuart. 'The art of Ravenna in late antiquity'. *The Classical Journal* 70 (1975): 17–29.

Croke, Brian. 'Malalas, the Man and His Work'. In *Studies in John Malalas*, edited by Elizabeth Jeffreys, Brian Croke and Roger Scott. Sydney: Australian Association for Byzantine Studies, 1990: 1–25.

——, 'Justinian, Theodora, and the church of Saints Sergius and Bacchus'. *DOP* 60 (2006): 25–63.

Ćurčić, Slobodan. 'Design and structural innovation in Byzantine architecture before Hagia Sophia'. In *Hagia Sophia from the Age of Justinian to the Present*, edited by Robert Mark and Ahmet S. Çakmak. Cambridge: Cambridge University Press, 1992: 16–38.

Cutler, Anthony. 'Structure and aesthetic at Hagia Sophia in Constantinople'. *The Journal of Aesthetics and Art Criticism* 25 (1966): 27–35.

——, 'Uses of luxury: On the functions of consumption and symbolic capital in Byzantine culture'. In *Byzance et les images : Cycle de conférences organisé au Musée du Louvre par le service culturel du 5 octobre au 7 décembre 1992*, edited by André Guillou and Jannic Durand. Paris: La documentation Française, 1994: 289–327.

Dagron, Gilbert. *Constantinople Imaginaire: Études sur le recueil des Patria*. Paris: Presses Universitaires de France, 1984.

Daniélou, Jean. *L'Être et le temps chez Grégoire de Nysse*. Leiden: Brill, 1970.

David, Nicholas, and Carol Krammer. *Ethnoarchaeology in Action*. Cambridge: Cambridge University Press, 2001.

De Andia, Ysabel. *Henosis: L'union à dieu chez Denys l'Aréopagite*. Leiden, Cologne and New York, NY: Brill, 1996).

——, 'Transfiguration et théologie négative chez Maxime le Confesseur et Denys l'Aréopagite'. In *Denys L'Aréopagite et sa postérité en orient et en occident. Actes du Colloque International Paris, 21–24 septembre 1994*, edited by Ysabel de Andia. Paris: Institut d'études augustiniennes, 1997: 293–328.

de Rijk, Lambertus M. 'Causation and participation in Proclus: the pivotal role of scope distinction in his methaphysics'. In *On Proclus and his Influence in Medieval Philosophy*, edited by E.P. Bos and P.A. Meijer. Leiden, New York and Cologne: Brill, 1992: 1–34.

Deckers, Johannes G. 'Der erste Diener Christi. Die Proskynese der Kaiser als Schlüsselmotiv der Mosaiken in S. Vitale (Ravenna) und in der Hagia Sophia (Istanbul)'. In *Art, Cérémonial et Liturgie au Moyan Âge. Actes du colloque de 3e Cycle Romand de Lettres Lausanne-Fribourg, 24–25 mars, 14–15 avril, 12–13 mai 2000*, edited by Nicolas Bock, Peter Kurmann, Serena Romano and J.-M. Spieser. Rome: Viella, 2002: 11–70.

Degryse, Patrick, J. Schneider, J. Poblome, M. Waelkens, U. Haack, and P. Muchez. 'A geochemical study of Roman to early Byzantine Glass from Sagalassos, South-west Turkey'. *JAS* 32 (2005): 287–99.

Deichmann, Friedrich Wilhelm. *Studien zur Architektur Konstantinopels im 5. und 6. Jahrhundert nach Christus*. Baden-Baden: B Grimm, 1956.

——, *Ravenna: Hauptstadt des spätantiken Abendlandes, Vol. 1, Geschichte und Monumente*. Wiesbaden: Frank Steiner Verlag GmbH, 1969.

——, 'Das Oktogon von Antiocheia: Heroon-Martyrion, Palastkirche oder Kathedrale?'. *Byzantinische Zeitschrift* 65 (1972): 40–56.

——, *Ravenna: Hauptstadt des spätantiken Abendlandes, Vol. II, Kommentar, 2. Teil*. Wiesbaden: Frank Steiner Verlag GmbH, 1976.

Deliyannis, Deborah Mauskopf. *Ravenna in Late Antiquity*. New York: Cambridge University Press, 2010.

Dell'Acqua, Francesca. 'Enhancing luxury through stained glass, from Asia Minor to Italy'. *DOP* 59 (2005): 193–211.

Diels, Hermann, and Walter Kranz. *Die Fragmente der Vorsokratiker*. Berlin: Weidmannsche Buchhandlung, 1903.
Dillon, John M., and Lloyd P. Gerson. *Neoplatonic Philosophy: Introductory Readings*. Indianapolis, IA: Hackett Publishing Company, 2004.
Dinkler, Erich. 'Kreuzzeichen und Kreuz'. *Jahrbuch für Antike und Christentum* 5 (1962): 93–112.
——, *Das Apsismosaik von S. Apollinare in Classe*. Cologne: Westdeutscher Verlag, 1964.
——, 'Das Kreuz als Siegeszeichen'. *Zeitschrift für Theologie und Kirche* 62 (1965): 1–20.
Dinkler, Erich, and Erika Dinkler-von-Schubert. 'Kreuz I. Teil: K. vorikonoklastisch'. In *Reallexikon zur Byzantinischen Kunst*, edited by Marcell Restle. Stuttgart: Anton Hiersemann Verlag, 1995: 12–19.
Dobres, Marcia-Anne. 'Technology's link and chaînes: the processual unfolding of technique and technician'. In *The Social Dynamics of Technology: Practice, Politics, and World Views*, edited by M. A. Dobres and C. R. Hoffman. Washington, DC: Smithsonian Institute Press, 1999: 124–146.
——, *Technology and Social Agency: Outlining a Practice Framework for Archaeology*. Oxford: Blackwell Publishers Ltd, 2000.
Dodds, Eric R. 'Theurgy and its relationship to Neoplatonism'. *The Journal of Roman Studies* 37 (1947): 55–69.
Dölger, Franz Joseph. 'Beiträge zur Geschichte des Kreuzzeichens IX'. *Jahrbuch für Antike und Christentum* 10 (1967): 7–29.
Downey, Glanville. 'Notes on Procopius' De Aedificiis Book 1'. In *Studies Presented to D. M. Robinson, vol. 2*, edited by G. Mylonas. St. Louis, MO: Washington University Press, 1953: 719–725.
——, 'The Name of the Church of St. Sophia in Constantinople'. *Harvard Theological Review* 52 (1959): 37–41.
——, *A History of Antioch in Syria from Seleucus to the Arab Conquest*. Princeton, NJ: Princeton University Press, 1961.
Dubel, Sandrine. '*Ekphrasis* et *enargeia*: la description antique comme parcours'. In *Dire l'évidence (philosophie et rhétorique antiques): actes du colloque de Créteil et de Paris (24–25 mars 1995)*, edited by Carlos Lévy and Laurent Pernot. Paris: L'Harmattan, 1997: 249–264.
——, 'Colour in Philostratus 'Imagines''. In *Philostratus*, edited by E. Bowie and Jaś Elsner. Cambridge: Cambridge University Press, 2009: 309–321.
Dubois, Page. 'Reading the writing on the wall'. *Classical Philology* 102 (2007): 45–56.
Dunabin, Katherine M. D. *Mosaics of the Greek and Roman World*. Cambridge: Cambridge University Press, 1999.
Dunbar, H. Flanders. *Symbolism in Medieval Thought and Its Consummation in the Divine Comedy*. New Haven, CT: Yale University Press, 1929.
Dupont-Sommer, André. 'Une hymne Syriaque sur la cathédrale d'Édesse'. *Cahiers Archéologiques* 2 (1947): 29–39.
Dussart, Odile. 'Quelques indices d'ateliers de verriers en Jordanie et en Syrie du Sud de la fin de l'époque Hellenistique à l'époque Islamique'. In *La Route du Verre: Ateliers primaires et secondaires du millénaire av. J.-C. au Moyen Âge*, edited by M.-D. Nenna. Lyon: Maison de l'Orient Méditerranéen, 2000: 91–93.
Eastmond, Antony. 'Consular diptychs, rhetoric and the language of art in sixth-century Constantinople'. *Art History* 33 (2010): 742–765.
Eco, Umberto. *Art and Beauty in the Middle Ages*. London and New Haven, CT: Yale University Press, 1986.
Edmonds, Mark. 'Description, understanding and chaîne opératoire'. *Archaeological Review from Cambridge* 9 (1990): 55–70.

Elliott, James Keith. *The Apocryphal New Testament: A Collection of Apocryphal Christian Literature in an English Translation*. Oxford: Clarendon Press, 1993.
Elsner, Jaś. 'The Viewer and the vision: The case of the Sinai Apse'. *Art History* 17 (1994): 81–102.
———, *Art and the Roman Viewer: The Transformation of Art from the Pagan World to Christianity*. Cambridge; New York: Cambridge University Press, 1995.
———, *Art and Text in Roman Culture*. Cambridge; New York: Cambridge University Press, 1996.
———, 'Structuring "Greece": Pausanias's Periegesis as a literary construct'. In *Pausanias: Travel and Memory in Roman Greece*, edited by Susan E. Alcock, John F. Cherry and Jaś Elsner. Oxford: Oxford University Press, 2001: 3–20.
———, 'Late antique art: the problem of the concept and the cumulative aesthetic'. In *Approaching Late Antiquity: The Transformation from Early to Late Empire*, edited by Simon Swain and Mark Edwards. Oxford: Oxford University Press, 2004: 271–309.
———, 'Physiognomics: Art and text'. In *Seeing the Face, Seeing the Soul: Polemon's Physignomy from Classical Antiquity to Medieval Islam*, edited by Simon Swain. Oxford: Oxford University Press, 2007: 203–224.
———, 'The rhetoric of buildings in the *De Aedificiis* of Procopius'. In *Art and Text in Byzantine Culture*, edited by Liz James. Cambridge: Cambridge University Press, 2007: 33–57.
———, *Roman Eyes: Visuality and Subjectivity in Art and Text*. Princeton, N.J.: Princeton University Press, 2007.
———, 'Art history as ekphrasis'. *Art History* 33 (2010): 10–27.
Evans, J. A. S. 'The dates of Procopius' Works: A recapitulation of the evidence'. *GRBS* 37 (1996): 301–313.
Fairhall, Scott L., and Alumit Ishai. 'Neural correlates of object indeterminacy in art compositions'. *Consciousness and Cognition* 17 (2008): 923–932.
Fänsen, Hubert. 'Der "Lichtstil" in der mittelbyzantinischen Kreuzkuppelkirche'. *Byzantinische Forschungen* 18 (1992): 185–196.
Fee, Gordon. *The First Epistle to the Corinthians* (The New International Commentary on the New Testament). Grand Rapids, MI: WM. B. Eerdmans Publishing Co., 1987.
Fiori, Cesare, and Mariangela Vandini. 'Chemical composition of glass and its raw materials: chronological and geographical development in the first millennium A.D'. In *When Glass Matters*, edited by M. Beretta. Florence: Olschiki, 2004: 107–50.
Fiori, Cesare, Mariangela Vandini, and V. Mazzotti. 'Colore e tecnologia degli 'smalti' musivi dei riquadri di Giustiniano e Teodora nella basilica di San Vitale a Ravenna – Color and technology of mosaic 'glazes' in the Justinian and Theodora's panels of the basilica of San Vitale in Ravenna'. *Ceramurgia* 33, no. 3–4 (2003): 135–154.
Fischer, Alysia, and W. Patrick McCray. 'Glass production activities as practised at Sepphoris, Israel (37 BC – AD 1516)'. *JAS* 26 (1999): 893–905.
Flood, Finbarr Barry. *The Great Mosque of Damascus: Studies on the Makings of an Umayyad Visual Culture*. Leiden, Cologne and Boston, MA: Brill, 2001.
Floros, Constantin. 'Das Kontakion. Mit 2 Abbildungen und einem Notenanhang'. *Deutsche Vierteljahrsschrift für Literaturwissenschaft und Geistesgeschichte* 34 (1960): 84–106.
Fobelli, Maria Luigia. *Un tempio per Giustiniano: Santa Sofia di Constantinopoli e la descrizione di Paolo Silenziario*. Rome: Viella, 2005.
Fontaine, Souen Deva, and Danièle Foy. 'L'épave Ouest-Embiez 1, Var: Le commerce maritime du verre brut et manufacturé en Méditerranée occidentale dans l'Antiquité'. *Revue archéologique de Narbonnaise* 40 (2007).
Forbes, Robert J. *Studies in Ancient Technology: Glass*. Vol. V, Leiden: Brill, 1957.

——, *Studies in Ancient Technology: Light*. Vol. VI, Leiden: Brill, 1966.
Forsyth, George H. 'The monastery of St. Catherine at Mount Sinai: the church and fortress of Justinian'. *DOP* 22 (1968): 1–19.
Forsyth, George H., and Kurt Weitzmann. *The Monastery of Saint Catherine at Mount Sinai: The Church and Fortress of Justinian*. Ann Arbor, MI: University of Michigan Press, 1965.
Foy, Danièle, and Marie-Dominique Nenna. 'Et vogue le verre!'. In *Tout feu tout sable: Mille ans de verre antique dans le Midi de la France, Exhibition Catalogue Musée d'Histoire de Marseille, Juin-Décembre 2001*, edited by D. Foy and M.-D. Nenna. Aix-en-Provence: Édisud, 2001: 100–112.
Foy, Danièle, Maurice Picon, and Michèle Vichy. 'Verres Omeyyades et Abbasides d'origine Egyptienne: Les témoignages de l'archéologie et de l'archéometrie'. *Annales du 15e Congrès de l'Association Internationale pour l'Histoire du Verre: AIHV, New York-Corning* (2003): 138–43.
Foy, Danièle, Maurice Picon, Michèle Vichy, and Valérie Thirion-Merle. 'Caractérisation des verres de la fin de l'Antiquité en Méditerranée occidentale: l'émergence de nouveaux courants commerciaux'. In *Échanges et commerce du verre dans le monde antique : actes du colloque de l'Association française pour l'archéologie du verre, Aix-en-Provence et Marseille, 7–9 juin 2001*, edited by D. Foy and M.-D. Nenna. Montagnac: Éditions Monique Mergoil, 2003: 41–85.
Foy, Danièle, Michèle Vichy, and Maurice Picon. 'Lingots de verre en Méditerranée occidental'. *Annales du 14e Congrès de l'Association Internationale pour l'Histoire du Verre: AIHV, Amsterdam* (2000): 51–57.
Fraisse, Jean-Claude. 'La simplicité du Beau selon Plotin'. *Revue de Métaphysique et de Morale* 88 (1983): 53–62.
Franses, Rico. 'When all that is gold does not glitter: On the strange history of looking at Byzantine art'. In *Icon and Word: The Power of Images in Byzantium*, edited by Antony Eastmond and Liz James. Aldershot and Burlington: Ashgate, 2003: 13–23.
Franz, Heinrich Gerhard. 'Transennae als Fensterverschluss: Ihre Entwicklung von der frühchristlichen bis zur islamischen Zeit'. *Istanbuler Mitteilungen* 8 (1958): 65–81.
Freestone, Ian C. 'Chemical analysis of 'raw' glass fragments'. In *Excavations at Carthage, Vol. II, 1: The Circular Harbour, North Side*, edited by H. R. Hurst. Oxford: Oxford University Press, 1994: 290.
——, 'Primary glass sources in the mid-first millennium AD'. *Annales du 15e Congrès de l'Association Internationale pour l'Histoire du Verre: AIHV, New York-Corning* (2003): 111–15.
——, 'The provenance of ancient glass through compositional analysis'. In *Materials Issues in Art and Archaeology VII*, edited by Pamela B. Vandiver, Jennifer L. Mass, and Alison Murray. Warrendale, PA: Materials Research Society, 2005.
Freestone, Ian C., Matthew Ponting, and Michael J. Hughes. 'Origins of Byzantine glass from Maroni Petrera, Cyprus'. *Archaeometry* 44 (2002): 257–72.
Freestone, Ian C., Yael Gorin Rosen, and Michael J. Hughes. 'Primary glass from Israel and the production of glass in Late Antiquity and the Early Islamic period'. In *La Route du Verre: Ateliers primaires et secondaires du millénaire av. J.-C. au Moyen Âge*, edited by M.D. Nenna. Lyon: Maison de l'Orient Méditerranéen, 2000: 65–83.
Freestone, Ian C., Michael J. Hughes, and Colleen P. Stapleton. 'The composition and production of Anglo-Saxon glass'. In *Catalogue of Anglo-Saxon Glass in the British Museum*, edited by V.I. Evison. London: British Museum Press, 2008: 29–46.
Friedländer, Paul. *Johannes von Gaza und Paulus Silentiarius: Kunstbeschreibungen justinianischer Zeit*. Leipzig and Berlin: Teubner, 1912.
Furnish, Victor Paul. *The Theology of the First Letter to the Corinthians*. Cambridge: Cambridge University Press, 1999.

Gage, John. *Colour and Culture: Practice and Meaning from Antiquity to Abstraction.* London: Thames and Hudson, 1993.

Gavrilović, Zaga. 'Divine wisdom as part of Byzantine imperial ideology: research into the artistic interpretations of the theme of medieval Serbia'. *Zograf* 11 (1982): 45–53.

Gegenfurtner, Karl R. 'Cortical mechanisms of colour vision'. *Nature Reviews / Neuroscience* 4 (2003): 563–572.

Gell, Alfred. *Art and Agency: An Anthropological Theory*. Oxford: Clarendon Press, 1998.

Gero, Stephen. 'Hypatius of Ephesus on the cult of images'. In *Christianity, Judaism and Other Greco-Roman Cults. Part II. Christianity*, edited by Jacob Neusner. Leiden: Brill, 1975: 208–16.

Gersh, Stephen. *From Iamblichus to Eriugena: An Investigation of the Prehistory and Evolution of the Pseudo-Dionysian Tradition*. Leiden: Brill, 1978.

Gnoli, Raniero. *Marmora Romana*. Rome: Edizioni dell'Elefante, 1971.

Gocer, Asli. 'A hypothesis concerning the character of Islamic art'. *Journal of the History of Ideas* 60 (1999): 683–92.

Goldhill, Simon. 'What is ekphrasis for?'. *Classical Philology* 102 (2007): 1–19.

Golitzin, Alexander. 'The mysticism of Dionysius Areopagita: Platonist or Christian?'. *Mystics Quarterly* 19 (1993): 98–114.

——, 'Dionysius Areopagita: a Christian mysticism?'. *Pro Ecclesia* 12, no. 2 (2003): 161–212.

Gombrich, Ernst H. *The Sense of Order: A Study in the Psychology of Decorative Art*. New York: Cornell University Press, 1979.

Gonosová, Anna. 'The formation and sources of early Byzantine floral semis and floral diaper patterns reexamined'. *DOP* 41 (1987): 227–37.

Gorin Rosen, Yael. 'Hadera, Bet Elie'zer'. *Excavations and Surveys in Israel* 13 (1995): 42–3.

——, 'The ancient glass industry in Israel: Summary of the finds and new discoveries'. In *La Route du Verre: Ateliers primaires et secondaires du millénaire av. J.-C. au Moyen Âge*, edited by M.-D. Nenna. Lyon: Maison de l'Orient Méditerranée, 2000: 49–63.

Gottschalk, H. B. 'The *De Coloribus* and its author'. *Hermes* 92 (1964): 59–85.

Gouillard, Jean. 'Hypathios d'Ephèse ou du Pseudo-Denys à Théodore Studite'. *Revue des études byzantines* 19 (1961): 63–75.

Goussen, Heinrich. 'Über eine 'sugitha' auf die Kathedrale von Edessa'. *Le Muséon* 38 (1925): 1–20.

Grabar, André. *L'empereur dans l'art byzantin*. Strasbourg: Les Belles lettres, 1936.

——, 'Plotin et les origines de l'ésthétique médiévale'. *Cahiers Archéologiques* 1 (1945): 15–33.

——, *Martyrium: recherches sur le culte des reliques et l'art chrétien antique, I*. Paris: Collège de France, 1946.

——, 'Le témoignage d'une hymn Syriaque sur l'architecture de la cathédrale d'Édesse au VIe siècle et sur la symbolique de l'édifice chrétien'. *Cahiers Archéologiques* 2 (1947): 41–67.

——, 'Quel est le sens de l'offrande de Justinien et de Théodora sur les mosaiques de Saint-Vital?'. *Felix Ravenna* 81 (1960): 63–77.

——, 'L'iconographie du ciel dans l'art chrétien de l'anqituité et du haut moyen age'. *Cahiers Archéologiques* 30 (1982): 5–24.

Grabar, Oleg. *The Mediation of Ornament*. Princeton: Princeton University Press, 1992.

Gratuze, Bernard, and Jean-Noël Barrandon. 'Islamic glass weights and stamps: analysis using nuclear techniques'. *Archaeometry* 32 (1990): 155–62.

Greatrex, Geoffrey. 'The dates of Procopius' works'. *BMGS* 18 (1994): 101–14.

Greenhalgh, Michael. *Marble Past, Monumental Present: Building with Antiquities in the Mediaeval Mediterranean*. Leiden and Boston: Brill, 2009.

Greger, Rainer, and Uwe Windhorst, eds. *Comprehensive Human Physiology: From Cellular Mechanisms to Integration*. Berlin and London: Springer Verlag, 1996.

Gregory, Richard L. *Eye and Brain: The Psychology of Seeing*. Oxford: Oxford University Press, 1998.

Grey, D. R. 'Art in the *Republic*'. *Philosophy* 103 (1952): 291–310.

Griffith, Rosemary. 'Neo-Platonism and Christianity: Pseudo-Dionysius and Damascius'. *Studia Patristica* 29 (1997): 238–43.

Grobe, Lars O., Oliver Hauck, and Andreas Noback. 'Das Licht in der Hagia Sophia – eine Computersimulation'. In *Byzanz – das Römerreich im Mittelalter, Teil 2, 1 Schauplätze*, edited by Falko Daim and Jörg Drauschke. Mainz: Römisch-Germanisches Zentralmuseum, 2010: 97–111.

Grube, George M. A. 'Plato's theory of beauty'. *The Monist* 37 (1927): 269–288.

Gürkan, Onur, Serhat Camlidere, and Mustafa Erdik. 'Photogrammetric studies of the dome of Hagia Sophia'. In *Hagia Sophia from the Age of Justinian to the Present*, edited by Robert Mark and Ahmet S. Çakmak. Cambridge: Cambridge University Press, 1992: 78–82.

Guidobaldi, Alessandra Guiglia, and Claudia Barasanti. *Santa Sofia di Costantinopoli: l'arredo marmoreo della grande chiesa Giustinianea* (Studi di Antichità Cristiana). Città del Vaticano: Pontificio istituto di Archaeologia Cristiana, 2004.

Guidobaldi, Federico. 'La Lussuosa Aula presso Porta Marina a Ostia'. In *Aurea Roma: dalla città pagana alla città Cristiana*, edited by Serena Ensoli and Eugenio La Rocca. Rome: Bretschneider, 2001: 251–62.

Günter, Roland. 'Wand, Fenster und Licht in der spätantik-frühchristlichen Architektur'. PhD, Ludwig-Maximilians-Universität, 1965.

Gurtler, Gary M. 'Plotinus and Byzantine aesthetics'. *The Modern Schoolman* 66 (1989): 275–84.

Guyer, Paul. *Values of Beauty: Historical Essays in Aesthetics*. Cambridge: Cambridge University Press, 2005.

Hachlili, Rachel. *Ancient Mosaic Pavements: Themes, Issues, and Trends*. Leiden and Boston: Brill, 2009.

Hadot, Pierre. *Plotinus or the Simplicity of Vision*. Chicago and London: The University of Chicago Press, 1993.

Hainthaler, Theresia. 'Bemerkungen zur Christologie des Ps.-Dionys und ihrer Nachwirkung im 6. Jahrhundeert'. In *Denys L'Aréopagite et sa postérité en orient et en occident. Actes du Colloque International Paris, 21–24 septembre 1994*, edited by Ysabel de Andia. Paris: Institut d'études augustiniennes, 1997: 269–92.

Halfwassen, Jens. 'Schönheit und Bild im Neuplatonismus'. In *Neuplatonismus und Ästhetik: Zur Transformationsgeschichte des Schönen*, edited by Verena Olejniczak Lobsien and Claudia Olk. Berlin and New York: Walter de Gruyter, 2007: 43–57.

Halliwell, Stephen. 'Aesthetics in antiquity'. In *A Companion to Aesthetics*, edited by Stephen Davis, Kathleen Marie Higgins, Robert Hopkins, Robert Stecker and David E. Cooper. Malden, MA and Oxford: Wiley-Blackwell, 1992, 2nd ed. 2009: 10–21.

———, *The Aesthetics of Mimesis*. Princeton: Princeton University Press, 2002.

Hammermeister, Kai. *The German Aesthetic Tradition*. Cambridge: Cambridge University Press, 2002.

Hansen, Maria Fabricius. 'Meanings of style: On the "interiorization" of late antique architecture'. *Acta Hyperborea* 8 (2001): 71–83.

Harding, Catherine. 'The production of medieval mosaics: The Orvieto evidence'. *DOP* 43 (1989): 73–93.

Harrison, R. Martin. 'The church of St. Polyeuktos in Istanbul and the Temple of Solomon'. *Harvard Ukrainian Studies = C. Mango and O. Pritsak (eds.), Okeanos: Essays*

Presented to Ihor Ševčenko on his Sixtieth Birthday by his Colleagues and Students 7 (1983): 276–9.

———, *Excavations at Saraçhane in Istanbul, Vol. 1: The Excavations, Structures, Architectural Decoration, Small Finds, Coins, Bones, And Molluscs*. Princeton, NJ: Princeton University Press, 1986.

———, *A Temple for Byzantium: The Discovery and Excavation of Anicia Juliana's Palace-Church in Istanbul*. London: Harvey Miller, 1989.

Haug, Walter. 'Gab es eine mittelalterliche Ästhetik aus platonischer Tradition?'. In *Neuplatonismus und Ästhetik: Zur Transformationsgeschichte des Schönen*, edited by Verena Olejniczak Lobsien and Claudia Olk. Berlin and New York: Walter de Gruyter, 2007: 19–42.

Hautecoeur, Louis. *Mystique et architecture: Symbolisme du cercle et de la coupole*. Paris: A. et J. Picard, 1954.

Hawkins, Ernest J. W. 'Further observations on the narthex mosaic in St. Sophia at Istanbul'. *DOP* 22 (1968): 151–66.

Hawkins, Ernest J. W., and Marlia C. Mundell. 'The mosaics of the monastery of Mar Samuel, Mar Simeon, and Mar Gabriel near Kartmin'. *DOP* 27 (1973): 279–296.

Heidegger, Martin. *Vom Wesen der Wahrheit: Zu Platons Höhlengleichnis und Theätet*. (Wintersemester 1931/32). Frankfurt: Vittorio Klostermann, 1997, 2nd edition.

Henck, Nick. 'Constantius ὁ φιλοκτίστης'. *DOP* 55 (2001): 279–304.

Hengel, Martin. *Crucifixion in the Ancient World and the Folly of the Message of the Cross*. Philadelphia, PA: Fortress Press, 1977.

Herrin, Judith. 'The Byzantine secrets of Procopius'. *History Today* 38 (1988): 36–42.

Hills, Paul. *Venetian Colour: Marble, Mosaic, Painting and Glass 1250–1550*. New Haven, CT and London: Yale University Press, 1999.

Hoffmann, Volker, and Nikolaos Theocharis. 'Der geometrische Entwurf der Hagia Sophia in Istanbul: Erster Teil'. *Istanbuler Mitteilungen* 52 (2002): 393–428.

Hohlweg, A. 'Ekphrasis'. In *Reallexikon zur byzantinischen Kunst*, edited by Marcell Restle. Stuttgart: Anton Hiersemann Verlag, 1971: 33–75.

Howard-Johnston, James. 'The education and expertise of Procopius'. *AT* 8 (2000): 19–30.

Hunt, Robert W.G. *Measuring Colour*. Kingston-upon-Thames: Fountain, 1987, 3rd ed. 1998.

Hyland, Drew A. *Plato and the Question of Beauty*. Bloomington, IN: Indiana University Press, 2008.

Ierodiakonou, Katerina. 'Empedocles on colour and colour perception'. *Oxford Studies in Ancient Philosophy* 29 (2005): 1–37.

Immerwahr, Henry R. 'Ergon: History as a monument in Herodotus and Thucydides'. *The American Journal of Philology* 81 (1960): 261–290.

Ioppolo, Anna-Maria. 'Presentation and assent: A physical and cognitive problem in early Stoicism'. *The Classical Quarterly* 40 (1990): 433–449.

Irwin, Eleanor. *Colour Terms in Greek Poetry*. Toronto: Hakkert, 1974.

Isar, Nicoletta. 'The iconic Chôra: A kenotic space of presence and void'. *Transfiguration: Nordisk Tidsskrift for kunst og kristendom* 2 (2000): 65–80.

———, '"Xopos of light": Vision of the sacred in Paulus the Silentiary's poem Descriptio S. Sophia'. *Byzantinische Forschungen* 28 (2004): 215–242.

Ishai, Alumit, and Dov Sagi. 'Common mechanisms of visual imagery and perception'. *Science* 268 (1995): 177–274.

Ivanovic, Filip. *Dionysius the Areopagite and the Iconoclastic Crisis*. Eugene, OR: Wipf and Stock, 2010.

Jäggi, Carola. 'Das kontrollierte Bild. Auseinandersetzungen um Bedeutung und Gebrauch von Bildern in der christlichen Frühzeit und im Mittelalter'. In *Alles Buch, Studien der Erlanger Buchwissenschaft XXXIII*, edited by Ursula Rautenberg and Volker Titel. Erlangen-Nürnberg: Buchwissenschaft, 2009: 18–31.

James, Liz. *Light and Colour in Byzantine Art*. Oxford: Oxford University Press, 1996.

———, 'What colours were Byzantine mosaics?'. In *Medieval Mosaics*, edited by Eve Borsook, Fiorella Gioffredi Superbi and Giovanni Pagliarulo. Milan: Silvana Editoriale, 2000: 35–46.

———, 'Art and lies: Text, image and imagination in the medieval world'. In *Icon and Word: The Power of Images in Byzantium. Studies Presented to Robin Cormack*, edited by Antony Eastmond and Liz James. Aldershot: Ashgate, 2003: 59–71.

———, 'Color and meaning in Byzantium'. *Journal of Early Christian Studies* 11 (2003): 223–33.

———, 'Byzantine glass mosaic tesserae: Some material considerations'. *BMGS* 30 (2006): 29–47.

———, '"And shall these mute stones speak?" Text as art'. In *Art and Text in Byzantine Culture*, edited by Liz James. Cambridge: Cambridge University Press, 2007: 188–206.

James, Liz, and Ruth Webb. '"To understand ultimate things and enter secret places": Ekphrasis and art in Byzantium'. *Art History* 14 (1991): 1–17.

Janaway, Christopher. *Images of Excellence: Plato's Critique of the Arts*. Oxford: Clarendon Press, 1995.

Janes, Dominic. *God and Gold in Late Antiquity*. Cambridge: Cambridge University Press, 1998.

Janin, Raymond. *Constantinople Byzantine: Développement urbain et répertoire topographique*. Paris: Institut Français d'Études Byzantines, 1964 (2ème édition).

Janowitz, Naomi. 'Theories of divine names in Origen and Pseudo-Dionysius'. *History of Religion* 30 (1991): 359–72.

Jeck, Udo Reinhold. 'Philosophie der Kunst und Theorie des Schönen bei Ps.-Dionysios Areopagites'. *Documenti e studi sulla tradizione filosofica medievale* 7 (1996): 1–38.

Jenkins, Romilly J.H. 'The Hellenistic origins of Byzantine literature'. *DOP* 17 (1963): 37–52.

Jensen, Robin Margaret. *Understanding Early Christian Art*. London and New York: Routledge, 2000.

Jessup, Bertram. 'The data of aesthetics'. *Proceedings and Addresses of the American Philosophical Association* 29 (1955–1956): 26–41.

Johnson, Mark J. *The Roman Imperial Mausoleum in Late Antiquity*. Cambridge and New York: Cambridge University Press, 2009.

Kähler, Heinz. *Die Hagia Sophia*. Berlin: Gebr. Mann, 1967.

Kalugila, Leonidas. *The Wise King: Studies in Royal Wisdom as Divine Revelation in the Old Testament and its Environment* (Coniectanea Biblica, Old Testament Series 15). Stockholm: LiberTryck, 1980.

Kandel, Eric. R. *The Age of Insight: The Quest to Understand the Unconscious in Art, Mind and Brain, from Vienna 1900 to the Present*. New York: The Random House Publishing Group, 2012.

Kapstein, Matthew T. 'Rethinking religious experience: Seeing the light in the history of religions'. In *The Presence of Light: Divine Radiance and Religious Experience*, edited by Matthew T. Kapstein. Chicago and London: University of Chicago Press, 2004: 265–99.

Kautzsch, Rudolf. *Beiträge zu einer Geschichte des spätantiken Kapitells im Osten vom vierten bis in siebente Jahrhundert*. Berlin and Leipzig: Walter de Gruyter, 1936.

Kawabata, Hideaki, and Semir Zeki. 'Neural correlates of beauty'. *Journal of Neurophysiology* 91 (2004): 1699–705.
Kelly, Michael. *A Hunger for Aesthetics: Enacting the Demands of Art*. New York: Columbia University Press, 2012.
Kennedy, George A. *Progymnasmata: Greek Textbooks of Prose Composition and Rhetoric*. Atlanta: Society of Biblical Literature, 2003.
Keuls, Eva. 'Skiagraphia once again'. *AJA* 79 (1975): 1–16.
——, *Plato and Greek Painting*. Leiden: Brill, 1978.
Kiilerich, Bente. 'The image of Anicia Juliana and the Vienna Dioscurides: Flattery or appropriation of imperial imagery?'. *Symbolae Osloenses* 76 (2001): 169–90.
Kitzinger, Ernst. 'The cult of images before iconoclasm'. *DOP* 8 (1954): 83–150.
——, 'Sylistic developments in pavement mosaics in the Greek East from the age of Constantine to the age of Justinian'. In *The Art of Byzantium and the Medieval West: Selected Studies*, edited by W. Eugene Kleinbauer. Bloomington: Indiana University Press, 1965, reprint 1976: 341–50.
——, 'Mosaic Pavements in the Greek East and the Question of a "Renaissance" under Justinian'. In *The Art of Byzantium and the Medieval West: Selected Studies by Ernst Kitzinger*, edited by W. Eugene Kleinbauer. Bloomington: Indiana University Press, 1965, reprint 1976: 49–63.
——, *Byzantine Art in the Making: Main Lines of Stylistic Development in Mediterranean Art, 3rd – 7th Century*. Cambridge, Mass: Harvard Universtiy Press, 1977.
Klee, Paul. *La théorie de l'art moderne*. Paris: Gonthier, 1964.
Kleinbauer, W. Eugene. 'The origin and functions of the aisled tetraconch churches in Syria and northern Mesopotamia'. *DOP* 27 (1973): 89–114.
——, 'Remarks on the building history of the Acheiropoietos church at Thessaloniki'. *Actes du Xe Congrès International d'Archéologie* 2 (1980): 241–257.
——, *Saint Sophia at Constantinople: Singulariter in Mundo*. Dublin and Peterborough, NH: William L. Bauhan, 1999.
——, 'Santa Costanza at Rome and the house of Constantine'. *Acta ad archaeologiam et artium historiam pertinentia* 18 (2004): 55–70.
——, 'Antioch, Jerusalem, and Rome: the patronage of emperor Constantius II and architectural invention'. *Gesta* 45 (2006): 125–45.
Kleinert, Annette. 'Die Inkrustation der Hagia Sophia: Zur Entwicklung der Inkrustationsschemata im römischen Kaiserreich'. PhD, Westfälische Wilhelms-Universität, 1979.
Klitenic Wear, Sarah, and John Dillon. *Dionysius the Areopagite and the Neoplatonist Tradition – Despoiling the Hellenes* (Ashgate Studies in Philosophy and Theology in Late Antiquity). Aldershot: Ashgate, 2007.
Koch, Hugo. 'Der pseudo-epigraphische Charakter der dionysischen Schriften'. *Theologische Quartalschrift* 77 (1895): 353–421.
——, 'Pseudo-Dionysius Areopagita in seinen Beziehungen zum Neuplatonismus und Mysterienwesen'. *Forschungen zur christlichen Literatur- und Dogmengeschichte* I, 2/3 (1900): 1–276.
Kollwitz, Johannes. *Oströmische Plastik der Theodosianischen Zeit*. Berlin: Walter de Gruyter, 1941.
Koortbojian, Michael. 'Mimesis or phantasia? Two representational modes in Roman commemorative art'. *Classical Antiquity* 24 (2005): 285–306.
Kostenec, Jan, and Ken Dark. 'Paul the Silentiary's description of Hagia Sophia in light of new archaeological evidence'. *Byzantinoslavica – Revue internationale des Études Byzantines* 69 (2011): 88–105.
Koutras, Dimitrios N. 'The beautiful according to Dionysius'. In *Neoplatonism and Western Aesthetics*, edited by Aphrodite Alexandrakis and Nicholas J. Moutafakis. New York: State University of New York Press, 2002: 31–40.

Kovacs, Judith L. *1 Corinthians: Interpreted by Early Christian Commentators*. Grand Rapids, MI and Cambridge: Wm.B. Eerdmans Publishing Co., 2005.

Krautheimer, Richard. *Early Christian and Byzantine Architecture*. New Haven, CT: Yale University Press, 1965, 4th ed. 1986.

———, 'The Constantinian basilica'. *DOP* 21 (1967): 115–40.

———, 'Again Saints Sergius and Bacchus at Constantinople'. *Jahrbuch der österreichischen Byzantinistik* 23 (1974): 251–3.

Kremer, Klaus. 'Bonum est diffusivum sui: Ein Beitrag zum Verhältnis von Neuplatonismus und Christentum'. In *Aufstieg und Niedergang der römischen Welt*, edited by Wolfgang Haase. Berlin and New York: Walter de Gruyter, 1987: 994–1032.

———, 'Dionysius Pseudo-Areopagita oder Gregory von Nazianz? Zur Herkunft der Formel: "Bonum est diffusivum sui"'. *Theologie und Philosophie* 63 (1988): 579–85.

Kuisma, Oiva. *Art or Experience: A Study on Plotinus' Aesthetics* (Commentationes Humaniarum Litterarum). Helsinki: Societas Scientaiarum Fennica, 2003.

Ladner, Gerhart B. 'Bilderstreit und Kunst-Lehren der byzantinischen und abendländischen Theologie'. *Zeitschrift für Kirchengeschichte* 50 (1931): 1–23.

———, 'The concept of the image in the Greek Fathers and the Byzantine iconoclastic controversy'. *DOP* 7 (1953): 1–34.

———, 'St. Gregory of Nyssa and St. Augustine on the Symbolism of the Cross'. In *Late Classical and Medieval Studies in Honor of Albert Mathias Friend, Jr.*, edited by Kurt Weitzmann. Princeton, NJ: Princeton University Press, 1955: 88–95.

———, 'Medieval and modern understanding of symbolism: A comparison'. *Speculum* 54 (1979): 223–56.

Laird, Martin. 'Gregory of Nyssa and the mysticism of darkness: A reconsideration'. *The Journal of Religion* 79 (1999): 592–616.

———, *Gregory of Nyssa and the Grasp of Faith: Union, Knowledge, and Divine Presence* (Oxford Early Christian Studies). Oxford: Oxford University Press, 2004.

Lam, William M. C. *Sunlight as Formgiver for Architecture*. New York: Van Nostrand Reinhold, 1986.

Lampe, Peter. 'Theological wisdom and the 'Word about the Cross': The rhetorical scheme in 1 Cor 1–4'. *Interpretation* 44 (1990): 117–31.

Leach, Edmund R. 'The gatekeepers of heaven: anthropological aspects of grandiose architecture'. *Journal of Anthropological Research* 39 (1983): 243–64.

Lehmann, Karl. 'The dome of heaven'. *The Art Bulletin* 27 (1945): 1–27.

Lethaby, William R., and Harold Swainson. *The Church of Sancta Sophia Constantinople: A Study of Byzantine Building*. London and New York: Kessinger Publishing, 1894, reprint 2004.

Lilla, Salvatore. 'Pseudo-Denys l'Aréopagite, Porphyre et Damascius'. In *Denys L'Aréopagite et sa postérité en orient et en occident. Actes du Colloque International Paris, 21–24 septembre 1994*, edited by Ysabel de Andia. Paris: Institut d'études augustiniennes, 1997: 117–152.

Lipinsky, Angelo. 'La crux gemmata'. *Felix Ravenna* 30 (1950): 5–62.

Loconsole, Michele. 'Il simbolo della croce tra Giudeo-Cristianesimo e tarda antichità: un elemento translatio Hierosolymae'. *Liber Annuus* 52 (2002): 217–284.

Loerke, William C. 'Observations on the representation of doxa in the mosaics of S. Maria Maggiore, Rome, and St. Catherine's, Sinai'. *Gesta* 20 (1981): 15–22.

Lossky, Vladimir. *The Mystical Theology of the Eastern Church*. Crestwood, NY: St. Vladimir's Seminary Press, 1976.

———, *In the Image and Likeness of God*. New York: St. Vladimir's Seminary Press, 1985.

Lossky, Vladimir, and Henri-Charles Puech. 'La notion des "analogies" chez Denys le

Pseudo-Aréopagite'. *Archives d'histoire doctrinale et littéraire du Moyen-Âge* 5 (1930): 279–309.
Louth, Andrew. *Maximus the Confessor*. London and New York: Routledge, 1996.
——, *Denys the Areopagite*. London and New York: Continuum, 2002.
——, 'The reception of Dionysius up to Maximus the Confessor'. In *Re-thinking Dionysius the Areopagite*, edited by Sarah Coakley and Charles M. Stang. Chichester: Wiley-Blackwell, 2009: 43–53.
MacCormack, Sabine G. *Art and Ceremony in Late Antiquity*. Berkeley: University of California Press, 1981.
MacDonald, William L. 'Some implications of later Roman construction'. *The Journal of the Society of Architectural Historians* 17 (1958): 2–8.
——, 'Roman experimental design and the Great Church'. In *The Hagia Sophia: From the Age of Justinian to the Present,* edited by Robert Mark and Ahmet S. Çakmak. Cambridge: Cambridge University Press, 1992: 3–15.
Mackie, Gillian. *Early Christian Chapels in the West: Decoration, Function, and Patronage*. Toronto: University of Toronto Press, 2003.
Macleod, Colin. 'Allegory and mysticism in Origen and Gregory of Nyssa'. *Journal of Theological Studies* 22 (1971): 362–79.
——, The preface to Gregory of Nyssa's Life of Moses'. *Journal of Theological Studies* 33 (1982): 183–91.
Macrides, Ruth, and Paul Magdalino. 'The architecture of ekphrasis: construction and context of Paul the Silentiary's poem on Hagia Sophia'. *BMGS* 12 (1988): 47–82.
Maguire, Henry. 'Truth and convention in Byzantine descriptions of works of art'. *DOP* 28 (1974): 111–40.
——, *Earth and Ocean: the Terrestrial World in Early Byzantine Art*. University Park, PA: Pennsylvania State Universtiy Press, 1987.
——, 'Magic and geometry in early Christian floor mosaics and textiles'. *JÖB* 44 (1994): 265–74.
Maguire, Joseph P. 'The differentiation of art in Plato's aesthetics'. *Harvard Studies in Classical Philology* 68 (1964): 389–410.
Mainstone, Rowland J. 'The reconstruction of the tympana of St. Sophia at Istanbul'. *DOP* 23, 24 (1969/70): 355–68.
——, *Hagia Sophia: Architecture, Structure and Liturgy of Justinian's Great Church*. London: Thames and Hudson, 1988.
Majeska, George P. 'Notes on the archaeology of St. Sophia at Constantinople: The green marble bands on the floor'. *DOP* 32 (1978): 299–308.
Mango, Cyril. *Materials for the Study of the Mosaics of St. Sophia at Istanbul*. Washington, DC: The Dumbarton Oaks Research Library and Collection, 1962.
——, 'Antique statuary and the Byzantine beholder'. *DOP* 17 (1963): 53+55–75.
——, *The Art of the Byzantine Empire 312–1453: Sources and Documents*. Toronto: University of Toronto Press, 1972, reprint 1986.
——, 'The church of Saints Sergius and Bacchus at Constantinople and the alleged tradition of octogonal palatine churches'. *JÖB* 21 (1972): 189–93.
——, 'The church of Sts. Sergius and Bacchus once again'. *Byzantinische Zeitschrift* 67 (1975): 385–92.
——, *Byzantine Architecture*. New York: H.N. Abrams, 1976.
——, 'The date of the Studius Basilica at Istanbul'. *BMGS* 4 (1978): 115–22.
——, 'Byzantine writers on the Fabric of Hagia Sophia'. In *The Hagia Sophia: From the Age of Justinian to the Present,* edited by Robert Mark and Ahmet S. Çakmak. Cambridge: Cambridge University Press, 1992: 41–56.
Mango, Cyril, and Ernest J. W. Hawkins. 'The apse mosaics of St. Sophia at Istanbul: Report on work carried out in 1964'. *DOP* 19 (1965): 115–51.

——, 'The Mosaics of St. Sophia: the church fathers in the north tympanum'. *DOP* 26 (1972): 1–41.
Mango, Cyril, and Ihor Ševčenko. 'Remains of the church of St. Polyeuktos at Constantinople'. *DOP* 15 (1961): 243–7.
Manieri, Alessandra. *L'immagine poetica nella teoria degli antichi: phantasia ed enargeia*. Pisa: Istituti editoriali e poligrafici internazionali, 1998.
Manns, James W. *Aesthetics*. New York and London: M.E. Sharpe, 1998.
Mark, Robert. *Light, Wind, and Structure: The Mystery of the Master-Builders*. Cambridge, MA and London: MIT Press, 1990.
Mark, Robert, and Ahmet S. Çakmak, eds. *Hagia Sophia from the Age of Justinian to the Present*. Cambridge: Cambridge University Press, 1992.
Markschies, Christoph. *Gibt es eine 'Theologie der gotischen Kathedrale'? Nochmals: Suger von Saint-Denis und Sankt Dionys vom Areopag*. Heidelberg: Universitätsverlag Carl Winter, 1995.
Maspero, Giulio. 'Theòria'. In *The Brill Dictionary of Gregory of Nyssa*, edited by Lucas Francisco Mateo-Seco and Giulio Maspero. Leiden and Boston: Brill, 2010: 736–738.
Mateo-Seco, Lucas Francisco. 'Imitation'. In *The Brill Dictionary of Gregory of Nyssa*, edited by Lucas Francisco Mateo-Seco and Giulio Maspero. Leiden and Boston: Brill, 2010: 502–5.
Mathew, Gervase. *Byzantine Aesthetics*. London: J. Murray, 1963.
Mathews, Thomas F. *The Early Churches of Constantinople: Architecture and Liturgy*. University Park and London: The Pennsylvania State University Press, 1971.
——, *The Clash of Gods: A Reinterpretation of Early Christian Art*. Princeton, NJ: Princeton University Press, 1995.
Mathias, Paul. *Plotin du beau: Ennéades I,6 et V, 8*. Paris: Presses Pocket, 1991.
Mazzucchi, Carlo Maria. 'Damascio, autore del Corpus Dionysiacum e il dialogo Peri Politikes Epistemes'. *Aevum: Rassegna di scienze storiche linguistiche e filologiche* 80 (2006): 299–334.
McClanan, Anne. *Representations of Early Byzantine Empresses*. New York and Houndsmills: Palgrave Macmillan, 2002.
McCrindle, John Watson, ed. *The Christian Topography of Cosmas, an Egyptian Monk*. London: Hakluyt Society, 1897.
McKenzie, Judith. *The Architecture of Alexandria and Egypt 300 BC–AD 700*. New Haven, CT and London: Yale University Press, 2007.
McVey, Kathleen E. 'The domed church as microcosm: Literary roots of an architectural symbol'. *DOP* 37 (1983): 91–121.
Meijer, Pieter A. 'Participation in Henads and Monads in Proclus' *Theologia Platonica* III, CHS. 16' In *On Proclus and his Influence in Medieval Philosophy*, edited by E.P. Bos and P.A. Meijer. Leiden, New York and Cologne: Brill, 1992: 65–87.
Meyendorff, John. 'Wisdom – Sophia: Contrasting approaches to a complex theme'. *DOP* 41 (1987): 391–401.
Michelis, Panayotis A. 'Neo-Platonic philosophy and Byzantine art'. *The Journal of Aesthetics and Art Criticism* 11 (1952): 21–45.
——, *An Aesthetic Approach to Byzantine Art*. London: Batsford, 1955.
Milner, Christine. 'The image of the rightful ruler: Anicia Juliana's Constantine mosaic in the church of Hagios Polyeuktos'. In *New Constantines: The Rhythm of Imperial Renewal in Byzantium, 4th – 13th Centuries. Papers from the Twenty-Sixth Spring Symposium of Byzantine Studies, St. Andrews, March 1992*, edited by Paul Magdalino. Aldershot: Ashgate, 1994: 73–81.
Mioni, Elpidio. 'Il Pratum Spirituale di Giovanni Mosco'. *Orientalia Christiana Periodica* 17 (1951): 61–94.

Mirti, P., A. Lepora, and L. Sagui. 'Scientific analysis of seventh-century glass fragments from the Crypta Balbi in Rome'. *Archaeometry* 42 (2000): 359–74.

Miziolek, Jerzy. 'Transfiguratio Domini in the apse of Mount Sinai and the symbolism of light'. *Journal of the Warburg and Courtauld Institutes* 53 (1990): 42–60.

Moorhead, John. 'Iconoclasms, the cross and the imperial image'. *Byzantion* 55 (1985): 165–79.

Morrisson, Cécile, and Jean-Pierre Sodini. 'The sixth-century economy'. In *The Economic History of Byzantium: From the Seventh through the Fifteenth Century*, edited by Angeliki E. Laiou. Washington, DC: The Dumbarton Oaks Research Library and Collection, 2002: 171–220.

Moutoussis, K., and Semir Zeki. 'A psychophysical dissection of the brain sites involved in color-generating comparisons'. *Proceedings of the National Academy of Science of the United States of America* 97 (2000): 806–974.

Mundell-Mango, Marlia. 'Building and architecture'. In *The Cambridge Ancient History. Late Antiquity: Empire and Successors, A.D. 425–600*, edited by Averil Cameron, Bryan Ward-Perkins and Michael Whitby. Cambridge: Cambridge University Press, 2000: 918–971.

Narbonne, Jean-Marc. 'Action, contemplation and interiority in the thinking of beauty of Plotinus'. In *Neoplatonism and Western Aesthetics*, edited by Aphrodite Alexandrakis and Nicholas J. Moutafakis. New York: State University of New York Press, 2002: 3–16.

Nelson, Robert S. 'To say and to see: Ekphrasis and vision in Byzantium'. In *Visuality Before and Beyond the Renaissance*, edited by Robert S. Nelson. Cambridge: Cambridge University Press, 2000: 143–68.

——, *Hagia Sophia, 1850–1950: Holy Wisdom Modern Monument*. Chicago, IL: University of Chicago Press, 2004.

——, 'Byzantine Art vs Western Medieval Art'. In *Byzance et le monde extérieur: contacts, relations, échanges : actes de trois séances du XXe Congrès international des études byzantines, Paris, 19–25 août 2001*, edited by Paule Pagès, Michel Balard, Elisabeth Malamut and Jean-Michel Spieser. Paris: Publications de la Sorbonne, 2005: 255–270.

——, 'Where God walked and monks pray'. In *Holy Image – Hallowed Ground: Icons from Sinai*, edited by Robert S. Nelson and Kristen M. Collins. Los Angeles: The J. Paul Getty Museum, 2006: 1–37.

Nenna, Marie-Dominique. 'Primary glass workshops in Graeco-Roman Egypt: Preliminary report on the excavations of the site of Beni Salama, Wadi Natrun (2003, 2005–2009)'. In *Glass in the Roman Empire in Honour of Jennifer Price*, edited by I.C. Freestone, J. Bailey and C. M. Jackson. Oxford: Oxbow Books, forthcoming.

Nenna, Marie-Dominique, Maurice Picon, and Michéle Vichy. 'Ateliers primaires et secondaires en Égypte à lépoque Gréco-Romaine'. In *La Route du Verre: Ateliers primaires et secondaires du millénaire av. J.-C. au Moyen Âge*, edited by M.-D. Nenna. Lyon: Maison de l'Orient Méditerranéen, 2000: 97–112.

Nesbitt, Claire. 'Space, Light and Experience in Middle Byzantine Churches'. Phd, Newcastle University, 2007.

Nicol, Donald M. 'Byzantine political thought'. In *The Cambridge History of Medieval Political Thought c. 350–c. 1450*, edited by J.H. Burns. Cambridge: Cambridge University Press, 1988: 51–79.

Nightingale, Andrea Wilson. *Spectacles of Truth in Classical Greek Philosophy: Theoria in its Cultural Context*. Cambridge and New York: Cambridge University Press, 2004.

Nijboer, Tanja C.W., Ryota Kanai, Edward H.F. de Haan, and Maarten J. van der Smagt. 'Recognising the forest, but not the trees: An effect of colour on scene perception and recognition'. *Consciousness and Cognition* 17 (2008): 741–52.

O'Meara, Dominic J. 'Textes de Plotin sur la beauté: initiation et remarques'. In *Art et vérité*, edited by I. Schüssler. Lausanne: Genos, 1996: 59–68.
Oates, Whitney J. *Plato's View of Art*. New York: Scribner, 1972.
Olcay, B. Yelda. 'Lighting methods in the Byzantine period and findings of glass lamps in Anatolia'. *JGS* 43 (2001): 77–87.
Onasch, Konrad. *Lichthöhle und Sternenhaus: Licht und Materie im spätantik-christlichen und frühbyzantinischen Sakralbau*. Dresden and Basel: Verlag der Kunst, 1993.
Onians, John. 'Abstraction and imagination in late antiquity'. *Art History* 3 (1980): 1–23.
———, *Neuroarthistory: From Aristotle and Pliny to Baxandall and Zeki*. New Haven, CT and London: Yale University Press, 2007.
Osterrieder, Markus. 'Das Land der Heiligen Sophia: das Auftauchen des Sophia-Motivs in der Kultur der Ostslaven'. *Wiener Slawistischer Almanach* 50 (2002): 5–62.
Ousterhout, Robert. 'The Temple, the Sepulchre, and the Martyrion of the Savior'. *Gesta* 29 (1990): 44–53.
Palmer, Andrew. 'Procopius and Edessa'. *AT* 8 (2000): 127–136.
Palmer, Andrew, and Lyn Rodley. 'The inauguration anthem of Hagia Sophia in Edessa: A new edition and translation with historical and architectural notes and a comparison with a contemporary Constantinopolitan kontakion'. *BMGS* 12 (1988): 117–67.
Panofsky, Erwin. *Abbot Suger on the Abbey Church of St.-Denis and Its Art Treasures*. Princeton, NJ: Princeton University Press, 1946.
———, *Gothic Architecture and Scholasticism*. LatrobePA: Archabbey Press, 1951.
Papaioannou, Stratis. 'Byzantine enargeia and theories of representation'. *Byzantinoslavica – Revue internationale des Études Byzantines* 69 (2011): 48–60.
Pearson, Birger A. 'Theurgic tendencies in Gnosticism and Iamblichus' s conception of theurgy'. In *Neoplatonism and Gnosticism*, edited by R. T. Wallis and Jay Bregman. Albany, NJ: State University of New York Press, 1992: 253–75.
Pelikan, Jaroslav. 'The Odyssey of Dionysian Spirituality'. In *Pseudo-Dionysius: The Complete Works*, edited by Colm Luibheid. New York: Paulist Press, 1987: 11–24.
Pentcheva, Bissera V. *The Sensual Icon: Space, Ritual, and the Senses in Byzantium*. University Park, PA: Pennsylvania State University Press, 2010.
———, 'Hagia Sophia and multisensory aesthetics'. *Gesta* 50 (2011): 93–111.
Perl, Eric. D. *Theophany: the Neoplatonic Philosophy of Dionysius the Areopagite*. New York: State University of New York Press, 2007.
Peterson, Erik. *Frühkirche, Judentum und Gnosis*. Rome, Freiburg and Vienna: Wissenschaftliche Buchgesellschaft, 1959.
Piaget, Jean. *Biologie et connaissance*. Paris: Gallimard, 1967.
Pickett, Raymond. *The cross in Corinth: The social significance of the death of Jesus*. Sheffield: Sheffield Academic Press, 1997.
Piotrowski, Andrzej. 'Architecture and the Iconoclastic Controversy'. In *Medieval Practices of Space*, edited by Barbara A. Hanawalt and Michal Kobialka. Minneapolis, MN: University of Minnesota Press, 2000: 101–27.
———, 'Representational function of daylight in the Katholikon of Hosios Loukas'. Paper presented at the Congress of Byzantine Studies, London, 21–24 August 2006.
Platt, Verity. 'Virtual visions: Phantasia and the perception of the divine in The Life of Apollonius of Tyana'. In *Philostratus*, edited by E. Bowie and Jaś Elsner. Cambridge: Cambridge University Press, 2009: 131–54.
———, *Facing the Gods: Epiphany and Representation in Graeco-Roman Art, Literature and Religion*. Cambridge: Cambridge University Press, 2011.
Porter, James I. *The Origins of Aesthetic Thought in Ancient Greece: Matter, Sensation, and Experience*. Cambridge: Cambridge University Press, 2010.

——, 'Is the sublime an aesthetic value?'. In *Aesthetic Value in Classical Antiquity. Mnemosyne Supplements. Monographs on Greek and Latin Language and Literature, 350*, edited by Ineke Sluiter and Ralph M. Rosen. Leiden; Boston: Brill, 2012: 47–70.

Potamianos, Iakovos. 'Light into Architecture: Evocative Aspects of Natural Light as Related to Liturgy and Byzantine Churches'. PhD, University of Michigan, 1996.

Puigarnau, Alfonso. *Estética Neoplatónica: La representación pictórica de la luz en la Antigüedad.* Barcelona: Publicaciones Promociones Universitarias, 1995.

Rahner, Hugo. *Greek Myths and Christian Mystery.* New York: Harper and Row, 1963.

Ramachandran, Vilayanur S., and William Hirstein. 'The science of art: A neurological theory of aesthetic experience'. *Journal of Consciousness Studies* 6 (1999): 15–51.

Ramelli, Ilaria. 'Good / Beauty'. In *The Brill Dictionary of Gregory of Nyssa*, edited by Lucas Francisco Mateo-Seco and Giulio Maspero. Leiden and Boston: Brill, 2010: 356–63.

Rasch, Jürgen J., and Achim Arbeiter. *Das Mausoleum der Constantina in Rome. Spätantike Zentralbauten in Rom und Latium, Vol. 4.* Mainz: Philipp von Zabern, 2007.

Remes, Paulina. *Neoplatonism.* Stocksfield: Acumen Publishing Ltd, 2008.

Restle, Marcell. 'Die Hagia Sophia Kaiser Justinians in Konstantinopel'. In *Die Hagia Sophia in Istanbul. Bilder aus sechs Jahrhunderten und Gaspare Fossatis Restaurierung der Jahre 1847–1849*, edited by V. Hoffmann. Bern: P. Lang, 1999: 17–28.

Reuterswaerd, Patrik. '"What colour is divine light?"', in Thomas B. Hess and John Ashbery (eds.), 'Light from Aten to Laser'. *Art News Annual* 35 (1969): 108–27.

——, 'The forgotten symbols of God'. *Konsthistorisk Tidskrift* 51 (1982): 103–25.

Rich, Audrey N. M. 'Plotinus and the theory of artistic imitation'. *Mnemosyne* 13 (1960): 233–9.

Riordan, William. *Divine Light: The Theology of Denys the Areopagite.* San Francisco, CA: Ignatius Press, 2008.

Rist, John. 'Plotinus and Christian philosophy'. In *The Cambridge Companion to Plotinus*, edited by Lloyd P. Gerson. Cambridge: Cambridge University Press, 1996: 386–413.

Ritter, Adolf Martin. 'Light'. In *The Brill Dictionary of Gregory of Nyssa*, edited by Lucas Francisco Mateo-Seco and Giulio Maspero. Leiden and Boston: Brill, 2010: 447–50.

Roberts, Michael. *The Jeweled Style: Poetry and Poetics in Late Antiquity.* Ithaca: Cornell University Press, 1989.

Roques, Denis. 'Les constructions de Justinien de Procope de Césarée'. *AT* 8 (2000): 31–43.

Roques, René. *L'univers dionysien: Structure hiérarchique du monde selon le Pseudo-Denys.* Paris: Aubier, 1954.

——, 'Symbolisme et théologie négative chez le Pseudo-Denys'. *Bulletin de l'Association Guillaume Budé* 4 (1957): 97–112.

Rorem, Paul, and John C. Lamoreaux. *John of Scythopolis and the Dionysian Corpus: Annotating the Areopagite.* Oxford: Oxford University Press, 1998.

Roth, Catherine P. 'Platonic and Pauline elements in the ascent of the soul in Gregory of Nyssa's dialogue on the soul and resurrection'. *Vigiliae Christianae* 46 (1992): 20–30.

Rousseau, P. 'Procopios' Buildings and Justinian's pride'. *Byzantion* 68 (1998): 121–30.

Russell, Donald Andrew. *'Longinus' on the Sublime.* Oxford: Clarendon Press, 1964.

Russo, Eugenio. *L'architettura di Ravenna paleocristiana.* Venezia: Instituto Veneto di Scienza, Lettere ed Arti Venezia, 2003.

Saffrey, Henri D. 'Le lien le plus objectif entre le Pseudo-Denys et Proclus'. In *Roma, magistra mundi. Itineraria culturae medievalis. Mélanges offerts au Père L. E. Boyle à l'occasion de son 75e anniversaire*, edited by J. Harnesse. Louvain-la-Neuve: Fédération Internationale des Instituts d'Études Médiévales, 1998: 791–810.

Sapelli, Marina. 'La Basilica di Giunio Basso'. In *Aurea Roma: dalla città pagana alla città Cristiana*, edited by Serena Ensoli and Eugenio La Rocca. Rome: L'Erma di Bretschneider, 2001: 137–9.

Sayre, Edward V., and Ray W. Smith. 'Compositional categories of ancient glass'. *Science* 133 (1961): 1824–6.

———, 'Analytical studies of ancient Egyptian glass'. In *Recent Advances in the Science and Technology of Materials, Vol. 3*, edited by A. Bishay. New York: Plenum Press, 1974: 47–70.

Schäfer, Christian. 'μονή, πρόοδος und ἐπιστροφή in der Philosophie des Proklos und des Areopagiten Dionysius'. In *Proklos Methode, Seelenlehre, Metaphysik: Akten der Konferenz in Jena am 18.–20. September 2003*, edited by Matthias Perkams and Rosa Maria Piccione. Leiden and Bosten, MA: Brill, 2006: 340–62.

Scheja, Georg. 'Hagia Sophia and Templum Salomonis'. *Istanbuler Mitteilungen* 12 (1962): 44–58.

Schibille, Nadine. 'Light in Early Byzantium: The Church of Hagia Sophia in Constantinople'. PhD, University of Sussex, 2004.

———, 'The use of light in the church of Hagia Sophia in Constantinople: The church reconsidered'. In *Current Work in Architectural History – Papers Read at the Annual Symposium of the Society of Architectural Historians of Great Britain, London, 2004*, edited by Peter Draper. London: Society of Architectural Historians of Great Britain, 2005: 43–8.

———, 'Astronomical and optical principles in the architecture of Hagia Sophia in Constantinople'. *Science in Context* 22 (2009a): 27–46.

———, 'The profession of the architect in late antique Byzantium'. *Byzantion* 79 (2009b): 360–79.

———, 'Supply routes and the consumption of glass in first millennium CE Butrint (Albania)'. *JAS* 38 (2011): 293–948.

———, 'A quest for wisdom: The sixth-century mosaics of Hagia Sophia in Constantinople and late antique aesthetics'. In *New Light on Old Glass: Recent Research on Byzantine Glass and Mosaics*, edited by C. Entwistle and L. James. London: British Museum Press, 2013: 53–9.

———, 'Light as an aesthetic constituent in the architecture of Hagia Sophia in Constantinople'. In *Manipulating Light in Pre-modern Times / Manipolare la luce in epoca premoderna*, edited by D. Mondini and V. Ivanovici. Milan: Mendrisio Academy Press / Silvana Editoriale Cinisello Balsamo, 2014.

Schibille, Nadine, Patrick Degryse, Markku Corremans, and Christian G. Specht. 'Chemical characterisation of glass mosaic tesserae from sixth-century Sagalassos (south-west Turkey): Chronology and production techniques'. *JAS* 39 (2012): 1480–92.

Schibille, Nadine, and Judith McKenzie. 'Glass tesserae from Hagios Polyeuktos, Constantinople: Their early Byzantine affiliations'. In *Neighbours and Successors of Rome: Traditions of Glass Production and Use in Europe and the Middle East in the Later First Millennium AD*, edited by D. Keller, C. M. Jackson and J. Price. Oxford: Oxbow Books, 2014: 114–27.

Schibille, Nadine, Fatma Marii, and Thilo Rehren. 'Characterization and provenance of late antique window glass from the Petra Church in Jordan'. *Archaeometry* 50 (2008): 627–42.

Schmidt, Robert F., and Gerhard Thews, eds. *Human Physiology*. Berlin and London: Springer Verlag, 1989, 2nd ed.

Schneider, A. M. 'Die Kathedrale von Edessa'. *Oriens Christianus* 3/14 (1941): 161–7.

Schöne, Wolfgang. *Über das Licht in der Malerei*. Berlin: Gebr. Mann, 1954.

Schwarzenberg, Erkinger. 'Colour, Light and Transparency in the Greek World'. In *Medieval Mosaics*, edited by Eve Borsook, Fiorella Gioffredi Superbi and Giovanni Pagliarulo. Milan: Silvana Editoriale, 2000: 15–34.

Sear, Frank. 'Roman wall and vault Mosaics'. *Mitteilungen des Deutschen Archäologischen Instituts, Römische Abteilung* 23 (1977): 13–43.

Sedlmayr, Hans. 'Das mittelalterliche Architektursystem'. *Kunstwissenschaftliche Forschungen* 2 (1933): 25–62.

Semmelroth, Otto. 'Gottes überwesentliche Einheit: Zur Gotteslehre des Ps.-Dionysius Areopagita'. *Scholastik* 25 (1950): 209–34.

——, 'Gottes ausstrahlendes Licht: Zur Schöpfungs- und Offenbahrungslehre des Ps.-Dionysius Areopagita'. *Scholastik* 28 (1953): 481–503.

Ševčenko, Ihor. 'The early period of the Sinai monastery in light of its inscriptions'. *DOP* 20 (1966): 255–64.

——, 'Levels of style in Byzantine literature'. In *Akten des XVI Internationalen Byzantinistenkongress I.1*. Vienna, 1981: 289–312.

Shahîd, Ifran. 'The church of Sts. Sergios and Bakhos at Constantinople, some new perspectives'. In *Byzantium State and Society: In Memory of Nikos Oikonomides*. Athens: Institute for Byzantine Studies, 2003: 467–80.

Shaw, Gregory. *Theurgy and the Soul: The Neoplatonism of Iamblichus*. University Park: The Pennsylvania State University Press, 1995.

Shaw, Philip. *The Sublime*. London and New York: Routledge, 2006.

Sheldon-Williams, Inglis P. 'The Ecclesiastical Hierarchy of Pseudo-Dionysius – Part I'. *The Downside Review* 82 (1964): 293–302.

——, 'The Greek Christian Platonist Tradition from the Cappadocians to Maximus and Eriugena'. In *The Cambridge History of Later Greek and Early Medieval Philosophy*, edited by A. H. Armstrong. Cambridge University Press, 1967: 425–537.

Sheppard, Anne. 'Studies on the 5th and 6th Essays of Proclus' Commentary on the Republic'. *Hypomnemata: Untersuchungen zur Antike und zu ihrem Nachleben. Heft 61* (1980).

——, 'Proclus' attitude to theurgy'. *Classical Quarterly* 32 (1982): 212–24.

——, 'Philosophy and philosophical schools'. In *The Cambridge Ancient History. Late Antiquity: Empire and Successors, A.D. 425–600*, edited by Averil Cameron, Bryan Ward-Perkins and Michael Whitby. Cambridge: Cambridge University Press, 2000: 835–54.

——, 'The role of imagination in aesthetic experience'. *Journal of Aesthetic Education* 25 (1991): 35–42.

Sillar, Bill, and Michael S. Tite. 'The challenge of 'technological choices' for materials science approaches in archaeology'. *Archaeometry* 42 (2000): 2–20.

Simson, Otto von. *The Gothic Cathedral: Origins of Gothic Architecture and the Medieval Concept of Order*. New York: Taylor and Francis, 1962, 2nd ed.

Siorvanes, Lucas. *Proclus: Neo-Platonic Philosophy and Science*. Edinburgh: Edinburgh University Press, 1996.

Siverstev, Alexei. 'The "Gospel of Thomas" and early stages in the development of the Christian wisdom literature'. *Journal of Early Christian Studies* 8 (2000): 319–40.

Sodini, Jean-Pierre. 'La contribution de l'archéologie à la connaissance du monde Byzantin (IVe-VIIe siècles)'. *DOP* 47 (1993): 139–84.

——, 'Le goût du marbre à Byzance: sa signification pour les Byzantins et les non-Byzantins'. *Études balkaniques* 1 (1994): 177–201.

Soisson, Count de. 'The aesthetic purpose of Byzantine architecture'. *Contemporary Review* 103 (1913): 92–102.

Sörbom, Göran. 'The classical concept of mimesis'. In *A Companion To Art Theory*, edited by Paul Smith and Carolyn Wilde. Oxford: Blackwell, 2002: 19–28.

Speck, Paul. 'ΓΡΑΦΑΙΣ Η ΓΛΥΦΑΙΣ. Zu dem Fragment des Hypatios von Ephesos über die Bilder mit einem Anhang zu dem Dialog mit einem Juden des Leontios von Neapolis'. *Varia* 1 (1984): 212–72.

Spieser, Jean-Michel. 'The representation of Christ in the apses of Early Christian Churches'. *Gesta* 37 (1998): 63–73.

Stanley, David J. 'New discoveries at Santa Costanza'. *DOP* 48 (1994): 257–61.

———, 'Santa Costanza: History, archaeology, function, patronage and dating'. *Arte Medievale* 3 (2004): 119–140.

Stern-Gillet, Susanne. 'Le principe du beau chez Plotin: Réflexions sur Enneads VI.7.32 et 33'. *Phronesis* 45 (2000): 38–63.

———, 'Neoplatonist aesthetics'. In *A Companion to Art Theory*, edited by Paul Smith and Carolyn Wilde. Oxford: Blackwell, 2002: 40–48.

Stichel, Rudolf H. W. In *Einblicke in den virtuellen Himmel: neue und alte Bilder vom Inneren der Hagia Sophie in Istanbul*, edited by Helge Svenshon. Tubingen: Wasmuth, 2008.

———, 'Die Hagia Sophia Justinians, ihre liturgische Einrichtung und der zeremonielle Auftritt des frühbyzantinischen Kaisers'. In *Byzanz – das Römerreich im Mittelalter, Teil 2, 1 Schauplätze*, edited by Falko Daim and Jörg Drauschke. Mainz: Römisch-Germanisches Zentralmuseum, 2010: 25–57.

Stiegemann, Christoph, ed. *Byzanz das Licht aus dem Osten: Kult und Alltag im Byzantinischen Reich vom 4. bis 15. Jahrhundert. Katalog der Ausstellung im Erzbischöflichen Diözesanmuseum Paderborn*. Mainz: Philipp von Zabern, 2001.

Stiglmayr, Josef. 'Der Neuplatoniker Proclus als Vorlage des sogenannten Dionysius Areopagita in der Lehre vom Übel' *Historisches Jahrbuch* 16 (1895): 253–73, 721–48.

Stockmeier, Peter. *Theologie und Kult des Kreuzes by Johannes Chrysostomus*. Trier: Paulinus Verlag, 1966.

Stolnitz, Jerome. '"Beauty" some stages in the history of an idea'. *Journal of the History of Ideas* 22 (1961): 185–204.

Stricevic, Giorgio. 'Iconografia dei mosaici imperiali a San Vitale'. *Felix Ravenna* 80 (1959): 5–27.

———, 'Sur le problème de l'iconographie des mosaiques imperiales de Saint-Vital'. *Felix Ravenna* 85 (1962): 80–100.

Striker, Gisela. *Essays on Hellenistic Epistemology and Ethics*. Cambridge and New York: Cambridge University Press, 1996.

Strube, Christine. *Die westliche Eingangsseite der Kirchen von Konstantinople in justinianischer Zeit*. Wiesbaden: Harrosowitz, 1973.

———, *Polyeuktoskirche und Hagia Sophia: Umbildung und Auflösung antiker Formen, Entstehung des Kämpferkapitells*. Munich: Verlag der Bayerischen Akademie der Wissenschaften, 1984.

Struck, Peter T. *Birth of the Symbol: Ancient Readers at the Limits of their Texts*. Princeton, NJ: Princeton University Press, 2004.

Suchla, Beate Regina. 'Verteidigung eines platonischen Denkmodells einer christlichen Welt. Die philosophie- und theologiegeschichtliche Bedeutung des Scholienwerks des Johannes von Skythopolis zu den areopagitischen Traktaten'. *Nachrichten der Akademie der Wissenschaften in Göttingen I. Philologisch-historische Klasse* (1995): 1–28.

Svenshon, Helge. 'Das Bauwerk als "Aistheton Soma"'. In *Byzanz – das Römerreich im Mittelalter, Teil 2, 1 Schauplätze*, edited by Falko Daim and Jörg Drauschke. Mainz: Römisch-Germanisches Zentralmuseum, 2010: 59–95.

Svenshon, Helge, and Rudolf H. W. Stichel. 'Systems of Monads' as design principle in the Hagia Sophia: Neo-Platonic mathematics in the architecture of late antiquity'. *Nexus* 6 (2006): 111–20.

Swift, Ellen. *Style and Function in Roman Decoration*. Farnham: Ashgate, 2009.

Swift, Ellen, and Anne Alwis. 'The role of late antique art in early Christian worship: A reconsideration of the iconography of the 'starry sky' in the 'Mausoleum' of Galla Placidia'. *Papers of the British School at Rome* 78 (2010): 193–217 and 352–4.

Swift, Emerson Howland. *Hagia Sophia*. New York: Columbia University Press, 1940.

Taft, Robert. 'The liturgy of the Great Church: An initial synthesis of structure and interpretation on the eve of iconoclasm'. *DOP* 34/35 (1980/81): 45–75.

Tal, Oren, Ruth E. Jackson-Tal, and Ian C. Freestone. 'New evidence of the production of raw glass at late Byzantine Apollonia-Arsuf (Israel)'. *JGS* 46 (2004): 51–66.

Tarrant, Dorothy. 'Greek metaphors of light'. *Classical Quarterly* 10 (1960): 181–87.

Tatarkiewicz, Wladyslaw. *History of Aesthetics. Vol. I. Ancient Aesthetics*, edited by J. Harrell. The Hague and Paris: PWN-Polish Scientific Publisher, 1970.

——, *History of Aesthetics. Vol. II. Medieval Aesthetics*, edited by C. Barrett. The Hague and Paris: PWN-Polish Scientific Publisher, 1970.

Taylor, Rabun. 'A literary and structural analysis of the first dome of Justinian's Hagia Sophia, Constantinople'. *The Journal of the Society of Architectural Historians* 55 (1996): 66–78.

Terezis, Christos, and Kalomoira Polychronopoulou. 'The sense of beauty (kallos) in Proclus the Neoplatonist'. In *Neoplatonism and Western Aesthetics*, edited by Aphrodite Alexandrakis and Nicholas J. Moutafakis. New York: State University of New York Press, 2002: 53–60.

Terry, Anne, and Henry Maguire. *Dynamic Splendor: The Wall Mosaics in the Cathedral of Eufrasius at Poreč* . University Park, PA: The Pennsylvania State University Press, 2007.

Teteriatnikov, Natalia B. *Mosaics of Hagia Sophia, Istanbul: The Fossati Restoration and the Work of the Byzantine Institute*. Washington, DC: The Dumbarton Oaks Research Library and Collection, 1998.

Theis, Lioba. 'Lampen, Leuchten, Licht'. In *Byzanz das Licht aus dem Osten: Kult und Alltag im Byzantinischen Reich vom 4. bis 15. Jahrhundert. Katalog der Ausstellung im Erzbischöflichen Diözesanmuseum Paderborn*, edited by C. Stiegemann. Mainz: Philipp von Zabern, 2001: 53–64.

Thiselton, Anthony C. *The First Epistle to the Corinthians: A Commentary on the Greek Text*. Grand Rapids, MI: Wm.B. Eerdmans Publishing, 2000.

Thomas, Edmund. *Monumentality and the Roman Empire: Architecture in the Antonine Age*. Oxford: Oxford University Press, 2007.

Thomas, Thelma K. 'The medium matters: Reading the remains of a late antique textile'. In *Reading Medieval Images: The Art Historian and the Object*, edited by Elizabeth Sears and Thelma K. Thomas. Ann Arbor, MI: University of Michigan Press, 2002: 38–49.

Thümmel, Hans Georg. 'Hypatios von Ephesos und Iulianos von Atramytion zur Bilderfrage'. *Byzantinoslavica – Revue internationale des Études Byzantines* 44 (1983): 161–70.

——, *Die Frühgeschichte der ostkirchlichen Bilderlehre. Texte und Untersuchungen zur Geschichte der altchristlichen Literatur*. Berlin: Academie Verlag, 1992.

Tilley, Richard. *Colour and the Optical Properties of Materials*. Chichester: John Wiley and Sons, 2000.

Tollefsen, Torstein Theodor. *Activity and Participation in Late Antique and Early Christian Thought*. Oxford: Oxford University Press, 2012.

Tougher, Shaun F. 'The wisdom of Leo VI'. In *New Constantines: The Rhythm of Imperial Renewal in Byzantium, 4th – 13th Centuries. Papers from the Twenty-Sixth Spring Symposium of Byzantine Studies, St. Andrews, March 1992*, edited by Paul Magdalino. Aldershot: Ashgate, 1994: 171–9.

Traquair, Ramsay. 'The origin of the pendentive'. *Journal of the Royal Institute of British Architects* 35 (1928): 185–7.
Trilling, James. 'Medieval art without style? Plato's loophole and a modern detour'. *Gesta* 34 (1995): 57–62.
Trout, Dennis E. *Paulinus of Nola: Life, Letters, and Poems*. Berkeley, CA: University of California Press, 1999.
Trypanis, Constantine A. 'Fourteen early Byzantine cantica'. *Wiener Byzantinische Studien* 5 (1968): 139–47.
Underwood, Paul A. 'A preliminary report on some unpublished mosaics in Hagia Sophia'. *AJA* 55 (1951): 367–70.
———, 'Notes on the work of the Byzantine Institute in Istanbul: 1954'. *DOP* 9–10 (1956): 291–4.
Underwood, Paul A., and Ernest J. W. Hawkins. 'The mosaics of Hagia Sophia at Istanbul: the portrait of the emperor Alexander, a report on work done by the Byzantine Institute in 1959 and 1960'. *DOP* 15 (1961): 187–217.
Underwood, Paul A., and Lawrence J. Majewski. 'Notes on the work of the Byzantine Institute in Istanbul: 1957–1959: the conservation of a Byzantine fresco discovered at Etyemez, Istanbul'. *DOP* 14 (1960): 205–22.
van Millingen, Alexander. *Byzantine Churches in Constantinople: Their History and Architecture*. London: Macmillan and Co. Ltd., 1912.
van Nice, Robert L. *Saint Sophia in Istanbul: An Architectural Survey*. Washington, DC: The Dumbarton Oaks Centre for Byzantine Studies, 1986.
Veh, Otto. *Prokop Bauten. Beschreibung der Hagia Sophia*. Munich: Heimeran, 1977.
Verità, M. 'Glass tesserae and gold leaf in the mosaics of Aquileia'. *Quaderni Friulani di Archeologia* 16 (2006): 7–12.
von Simson, Otto G. *Sacred Fortress: Byzantine Art and Statecraft in Ravenna*. Princeton, NJ: Princeton University Press, 1948.
Warnock, Mary. *Imagination*. Berkeley and Los Angeles, CA: University of California Press, 1976.
Watson, Gerard. *Phantasia in Classical Thought*. Galway: Galway University Press, 1988.
Webb, Ruth. 'Imagination and the arousal of the emotions in Greco-Roman rhetoric'. In *The Passions in Roman Thought and Literature*, edited by Susanna Morton Braund and Christopher Gill. Cambridge: Cambridge University Press, 1997: 112–27.
———, 'Mémoire et imagination: les limites de *l'enargeia* dans la théorie rhétorique grecque'. In *Dire l'évidence (philosophie et rhétorique antiques): actes du colloque de Créteil et de Paris (24–25 mars 1995)*, edited by Carlos Lévy and Laurent Pernot. Paris: L'Harmattan, 1997: 229–48.
———, 'The aesthetics of sacred space: Narrative, metaphor, and motion in ekphraseis of church buildings'. *DOP* 53 (1999): 59–74.
———, 'Ekphrasis ancient and modern: The invention of a genre'. *Word and Image* 15 (1999): 7–18.
———, 'Ekphrasis, amplification and persuasion in Procopius' *Buildings*'. *AT* 8 (2000): 67–71.
———, 'Accomplishing the picture: Ekphrasis, mimesis and martyrdom in Asterios of Amaseia'. In *Art and Text in Byzantine Culture*, edited by Liz James. Cambridge: Cambridge University Press, 2007: 13–32.
———, *Ekphrasis, Imagination and Persuasion in Ancient Rhetorical Theory and Practice*. Farnham: Ashgate, 2009.
Weitzmann, Kurt. 'The mosaic in St. Catherine's Monastery on Mount Sinai'. *Proceedings of the American Philosophical Society* 110 (1966): 392–405.

Westerkamp, Dirk. 'Der verklärte Körper. Kleine Ästhetik der Mandorla'. In *Drehmomente. Philosophische Reflexionen für Sybille Krämer*. Berlin, 2011. Available at: http://www.geisteswissenschaften.fu-berlin.de/v/drehmomente

Westholm, Alfred. *Cornelius Loos : teckningar från en expedition till Främre Orienten 1710–1711*. Nationalmusei skriftserie ; n.s. 6. Stockholm: Nationalmuseum, 1985.

Whitby, Mary. 'The occasion of Paul the Silentiary's ekphrasis of S. Sophia'. *Classical Quarterly* 35 (1985): 215–28.

——, 'Procopius' *Buildings*, Book I: a panegyrical perspective'. *AT* 8 (2000): 45–57.

——, 'The St. Polyeuktos Epigram (*AP* 1.10): A literary perspective'. In *Greek Literature in Late Antiquity: Dynamism, Didacticism, Classicism*, edited by Scott Fitzgerald Johnson. Aldershot: Ashgate, 2006: 159–88.

Whitby, Michael. 'Justinian's bridge over the Sangarius and the date of Procopius' de Aedificiis'. *Journal of Hellenic Studies* 105 (1985): 129–48.

Whittemore, Thomas. *The Mosaics of St. Sophia at Istanbul, Preliminary Report on the First Year's Work 1931–1932: The Mosaics of the Narthex*. Oxford: Oxford University Press, 1933.

——, *The Mosaics of St. Sophia at Istanbul, Second Preliminary Report on the Work done in 1933–1934: The Mosaics of the Southern Vestibule*. Oxford: Oxford University Press, 1936.

——, *The Mosaics of Haghia Sophia at Istanbul, Third Preliminary Report on Work done in 1935–1938: The Imperial Portraits of the South Gallery*. Oxford: Oxford University Press, 1942.

——, *The Mosaics of Haghia Sophia at Istanbul, Fourth Preliminary Report on Work done in 1934–1938: The Deesis Panel of the South Gallery*. Oxford: Oxford University Press, 1952.

——, *Notes on Light in Hagia Sophia, Istanbul, 26 January 1945, Dumbarton Oaks, Byzantine Photograph and Fieldwork Archives*. Washington, DC, unpublished.

Wöhrle, Georg. 'Ps-Aristoteles *De Coloribus* – A Theophrastean Opusculum?'. In *On the Opuscula of Theophrastus: Akten der 3. Tagung der Karl-und-Gertrud-Abel-Stiftung vom 19.-23. Juli 1999 in Trier*, edited by William W. Fortenbaugh and George Wöhrle. Stuttgart: Steiner, 2002: 91–8.

Wolf, Sophie, C.M. Kessler, W.B. Stern, and Y. Gerber. 'The composition and manufacture of early medieval coloured window glass from Sion (Valais, Switzerland) – a Roman glass-making tradition or innovative craftsmanship?'. *Archaeometry* 47 (2005): 361–80.

Woods, David. '"Constantius", and a church-inscription from Antioch'. *Vigiliae Christianae* 59 (2005): 54–62.

Zaloziecky, Wladimir R. *Die Sophienkirche in Konstantinopel und ihre Stellung in der Geschichte der abendländischen Architektur* (Studie di Antichita Cristiana 12). Rome and Freiburg: Pontificio istituto di archeologia cristiana, 1936.

Zanker, G. 'Enargeia in the ancient criticism of poetry'. *Rheinisches Museum für Philologie* 124 (1981): 297–311.

Zányi, Eva, Carla Schroer, Mark Mudge, and Alan Chalmers. 'Lighting and Byzantine glass tesserae'. *EVA London Conference 11–13 July 2007* (2007): 22.12–2.8.

Zeki, Semir. *Inner Vision: An Exploration of Art and the Brain*. Oxford: Oxford University Press, 1999.

——, 'Essays on science and society: Artistic creativity and the brain'. *Science* 293 (2001): 51–2.

Zeki, Semir, and Ludovica Marini. 'Three cortical stages of colour processing in the human brain'. *Brain* 121 (1998): 1669–85.

Index